Titles in *Counseling and Professional Identity series*

CACREP Standards	*Sangganjanavanich, Introduction to Professional Counseling*	*Watson, Counseling Assessment and Evaluation*	*Conyne, Group Work Leadership*	*Parsons, Becoming a Skilled Counselor*	*Parsons, Counseling Theory*	*Wong, Counseling Individuals Through the Life Span*	*Duan, Becoming a Multiculturally Competent Counselor*	*Wright, Research Methods for Counseling*	*Tang, Career Development and Counseling*	*Scott, Counselor as Consultant*	*Zhang, Field Experience*
1. PROFESSIONAL ORIENTATION AND ETHICAL PRACTICE	1a 1b 1d 1e 1f 1g 1h 1i 1j	1j	1b 1j	1b 1d 1e 1j	1j	1j	1j	1j	1b 1j	1b 1j	1b 1c 1d 1e 1f 1g 1h 1i 1j
2. SOCIAL AND CULTURAL DIVERSITY	2c 2f 2g	2g	2d 2e 2g	2b 2c 2g	2c 2e 2g	2a 2b 2c 2d 2e 2g	2c 2e 2f 2g	2g	2g	2d 2g	2d
3. HUMAN GROWTH AND DEVELOPMENT			3f		3b	3a 3b 3c 3d 3e 3f 3g	3d 3e		3e		
4. CAREER DEVELOPMENT		4f							4a 4b 4c 4d 4e 4f 4g	4c	4b 4c 4e 4g
5. HELPING RELATIONSHIPS	5a 5b 5c 5f 5g 5h		5b 5c 5d 5e	5a 5b 5c 5d	5b 5c 5d 5e 5g	5b	5b 5e		5b 5c	5b 5c 5f 5g 5h	5c 5d 5e 5f 5g
6. GROUP WORK			6a 6b 6c 6d 6e								6d 6e
7. ASSESSMENT		7a 7b 7c 7d 7e 7f 7g	7b	7b		7f		7c 7d 7e			7g
8. RESEARCH AND PROGRAM EVALUATION								8a 8b 8c 8d 8e			8d 8e 8f

Counseling and Professional Identity

Series Editors: Richard D. Parsons, PhD, and Naijian Zhang, PhD

Becoming a Skilled Counselor—Richard D. Parsons and Naijian Zhang

Research Methods for Counseling: An Introduction—Robert J. Wright

Group Work Leadership: An Introduction for Helpers—Robert K. Conyne

Introduction to Professional Counseling—Varunee Faii Sangganjanavanich and Cynthia Reynolds

Counseling Theory: Guiding Reflective Practice—Richard D. Parsons and Naijian Zhang

Counselor as Consultant—David A. Scott, Chadwick W. Royal, and Daniel B. Kissinger

Counseling Assessment and Evaluation: Fundamentals of Applied Practice—Joshua C. Watson and Brandé Flamez

Counseling Individuals Through the Lifespan—Daniel W. Wong, Kimberly R. Hall, Cheryl A. Justice, and Lucy Wong Hernandez

Becoming a Multiculturally Competent Counselor—Changming Duan and Chris Brown

Ethical Decision Making for the 21st Century Counselor—Donna S. Sheperis, Michael Kocet, and Stacy Henning

Career Development and Counseling: Theory and Practice in a Multicultural World—Mei Tang and Jane Goodman

Field Experience: Transitioning From Student to Professional—Naijian Zhang and Richard D. Parsons

Field Experience

Transitioning From Student to Professional

Los Angeles | London | New Delhi
Singapore | Washington DC | Boston

FOR INFORMATION:

SAGE Publications, Inc.
2455 Teller Road
Thousand Oaks, California 91320
E-mail: order@sagepub.com

SAGE Publications Ltd.
1 Oliver's Yard
55 City Road
London EC1Y 1SP
United Kingdom

SAGE Publications India Pvt. Ltd.
B 1/I 1 Mohan Cooperative Industrial Area
Mathura Road, New Delhi 110 044
India

SAGE Publications Asia-Pacific Pte. Ltd.
3 Church Street
#10-04 Samsung Hub
Singapore 049483

Copyright © 2016 by SAGE Publications, Inc.

Printed in the United States of America

Cataloging-in-Publication Data is available for this title from the Library of Congress.

ISBN 978-1-4833-4453-9

This book is printed on acid-free paper.

Acquisitions Editor: Kassie Graves
Editorial Assistant Carrie Montoya
Production Editor: Kelly DeRosa
Copy Editor: Brenda Weight
Typesetter: C&M Digitals (P) Ltd.
Proofreader: Dennis W. Webb
Indexer: Scott Smiley
Cover Designer: Candice Harman
Marketing Manager: Shari Countryman

15 16 17 18 19 10 9 8 7 6 5 4 3 2 1

Field Experience

Transitioning From Student to Professional

Naijian Zhang
West Chester University of Pennsylvania

Richard D. Parsons
West Chester University of Pennsylvania

SAGE

Los Angeles | London | New Delhi
Singapore | Washington DC | Boston

Brief Contents

Editors' Preface: Introduction to the Series		xvi
Authors' Preface		xix
Acknowledgments		xxii
Chapter 1	Field Experience as Formative to Professional Identity	1
Chapter 2	Matching Self to Site	24
Chapter 3	From the Ideal to the Real	58
Chapter 4	The Ethics of Practice: More Than Knowing, Being	82
Chapter 5	Reflecting on Practice	107
Chapter 6	Growing Through Supervision	134
Chapter 7	Multicultural Counseling in Practice	163
Chapter 8	Crisis Prevention and Intervention: Suicide and Homicide	191
Chapter 9	Reducing Risk	214
Chapter 10	Documentation and Record Keeping	233
Chapter 11	Termination and Closure	258
Chapter 12	Self-Care and Self-Protection—Necessary for All Counselors	282
Chapter 13	Transition From Practice to Career	315
Chapter 14	Transitions: Self as Counselor	342
Index		363
About the Authors		374

Detailed Contents

Editors' Preface: Introduction to the Series xvi

Authors' Preface xix

Acknowledgments xxii

Chapter 1 Field Experience as Formative to Professional Identity 1

Field Experience: A Unique Learning Experience 2
Shift in Focus: From "Knowing" to "Doing" 2
Shift from Other- to Self-Taught 3
Increased Independence and Self-Direction 3
Focus on Outcomes Versus Grades 5
Seeking Evaluation and Soliciting Corrective Feedback 6
Shift From Ideal to Real 7
Shifting Identity Focus: From Self-as-Student to Self-as-Emerging-Professional 9
Field Work: Fostering an Emerging Professional Identity 9
Counselors: A Collective Identity 10
Shared Values and Perspectives 10
Developmental Perspective 11
Wellness Perspective 12
Prevention 14
Primary Prevention 14
Secondary Prevention 14
Tertiary Prevention 15
Empowerment and Advocacy 16
Nurturing Your Professional Identity 19
Postscript 20
Keystones 22
Additional Resources 22
References 22

Chapter 2 Matching Self to Site 24

It Starts With Self-Appraisal 25
Core Knowledge and Skills 25
Professional Orientation 25

Human Growth and Development 26
Social and Cultural Foundations 26
Helping Relationship 27
Groups 27
Lifestyle and Career Development 27
Appraisal and Assessment 28
Research and Evaluation 28
Beyond the Core: Specialty Knowledge and Skills 36
Credentialing Specialties 37
Assessing Field Placement Options 45
Site Characteristics: Specifics to Consider 46
Accreditation 46
Mission 47
Population Served 49
Services Provided 50
Models and Theories 50
Issues Addressed 50
What to Expect 51
Level of Responsibility 51
Site Supervisor 52
Theoretical Orientation 52
Training and Experience 53
Comfort and Compatibility 53
Matching Self to Site: Targeting Professional Development 54
Keystones 55
Additional Resources 56
Web Based 56
Print Based 56
References 56

Chapter 3 From the Ideal to the Real 58

Knowing the Ideal 59
Ideal: Defined by the Profession 59
Ideal: Roles and Function in Line With Mission 64
Performance Assessment: Suggesting Priorities 64
Role and Function in Service of the Mission 65
The Real Is Often Less Than Ideal 69
Even Interns Can Effect Change and Define Roles 74
Expert Power 75
Informational Power 76
To Get Much . . . Much Is Expected 79

Keystones 80
Additional Resources 81
References 81

Chapter 4 The Ethics of Practice: More Than Knowing, Being 82

The Need and Value of Professional Ethics 83
The What: In Principle 91
Autonomy 91
Confidentiality 93
Right to Terminate 93
Nonmaleficence 95
Beneficence 97
Justice 100
Fidelity 102
From the Ideal to the Real 104
Keystones 104
Additional Resources 105
Web Based 105
Print Based 105
References 106

Chapter 5 Reflecting on Practice 107

Reflecting *on* Practice: Case Conceptualization 108
Reflecting *in* Practice: Guiding Moment-to-Moment Decisions 118
Reflective Practice: Supporting Efficacy and Accountability 122
Reflection: For Professional Development 124
Assessment 125
From Assessment to Development 128
Step 1: Self-Assessment 128
Step 2: Identification of Goals 128
Step 3: Identification of Resources 129
Action Steps 130
Keystones 132
Additional Resources 132
Web Based 132
Print Based 133
References 133

Chapter 6 Growing Through Supervision 134

Counseling Supervision 135
What Is Counseling Supervision? 135
Why Is Counseling Supervision Necessary and Required? 136
When and How Often Is Counseling Supervision Conducted? 137

Expectations of Counseling Supervision 138
Forms of Counseling Supervision 144
Classroom Versus On-Site Supervision 144
Individual Versus Group Supervision 144
Process and Content of Supervision 145
Audio- and Videotape and Case Presentation 145
Case Conceptualization 147
Role-Play 147
Feedback and Evaluation 150
Counseling Supervision Models 151
Issues and Dilemmas in Supervision 152
Conflicts in Supervisory Relationships 152
Resolving Conflicts in Supervisory Relationships 155
Boundaries: Supervision Versus Therapy 156
Transference and Countertransference 156
Supervision and Multiculturalism 158
Transitioning From Student to Professional Counselor in Supervision 159
Keystones 160
Additional Resources 160
Web Based 160
Print Based 160
References 160

Chapter 7 Multicultural Counseling in Practice 163

Multiculturalism in Counseling 164
Issues in Multicultural Counseling 166
Ethics and Working With Multicultural Clients 167
Multicultural Counseling Competence 171
Counseling Competence Versus Multicultural Counseling Competence 172
A Model Guiding the Development of Competency 173
Developing Multicultural Counseling Competence 174
Counselor Awareness of Own Cultural Values and Biases 174
Counselor Awareness of Client's Worldview 178
Culturally Appropriate Intervention Strategies 182
Multicultural Counseling Competence and Professional Identity 185
Keystones 187
Additional Resources 187
Web Based 187
Audio-Visual Materials 187
Print Based 188
References 188

Chapter 8 Crisis Prevention and Intervention: Suicide and Homicide **191**
The Nature of Crisis and Crisis Intervention 192
Phases of Crisis and Counselor Response 193
Acute Phase 193
Outward Adjustment Phase 193
Integration Phase 194
Suicide 195
Myths About Suicide 195
Identifying Risk: Common Characteristics of Suicide 196
Assessment: The First Step in Intervention 199
Document 205
When Harm Is Other Directed 205
Prevalence and Potential for Violence 205
Predictors of Violent Behavior 206
Assessment: The First Step 206
Step Two: Intervention 206
Step Three: Following Up 208
AIDS: A Special Challenge 208
Site Policy on Crisis Procedures 210
Keystones 211
Additional Resources 211
Web Based 211
Print Based 212
References 212

Chapter 9 Reducing Risk **214**
The Risk of Physical Harm 215
Reducing the Risk 215
Indicators of Potential Violence 215
Preventive Measures 218
De-escalation 218
Reducing Legal Risks 219
Confidentiality 220
Identify the Client 222
Respect Client's Autonomy 223
Professional Boundaries 224
Boundary Crossing 225
Boundary Violations 226
Practice Within Competence 227
Document, Document, and Then Document 228
Postscript 229
Keystones 231

Additional Resources 231
Web Based 231
Print Based 231
References 232

Chapter 10 Documentation and Record Keeping **233**

Purpose of Documentation and Record Keeping 234
Standard of Care 234
Communication 234
Desirable Defense Against Litigation 235
Ethical and Legal Ramifications 235
The "What" of Case Documentation 237
Treatment Plans 238
Progress Notes: A Fundamental and Practical Form of Recording 239
Recommendations for Case Notes Writing and Record Keeping 241
The "How," or Format, of Case Documentation 243
SOAP Notes 244
Subjective 244
Objective 244
Assessment 245
Plan 245
Individual Psychotherapy Session Note (IPSN) 248
Date, Assessment, and Plan (DAP) 251
Data (Description) 252
Assessment (Analysis) 252
Plan 252
Description, Assessment, Response, and Treatment Plan (DART) 253
Description 253
Assessment 254
Response 254
Treatment Plan 254
Concluding Thoughts 255
Keystones 256
Additional Resources 256
Web Based 256
Print Based 256
References 257

Chapter 11 Termination and Closure **258**

Terminating the Counseling Relationship 259
Counseling Termination Defined 259
An End That Starts at the Beginning 259
The Ethics of Termination 260

Competence 261
Values 262
Appropriateness 263
Process 263
Factors Involved in Appropriate Termination 264
Challenges to Effective and Ethical Termination 267
Termination Due to Lack of Progress 268
Termination Due to Being Out of Area of Competence 268
Termination Due to Fee Issue 269
Termination Due to Counselor's or Client's Life Circumstances 271
Transferring Clients to Another Counselor: A Special Form of Termination 274
Steps Toward Effective and Ethical Termination 275
Terminating Other Relationships at Internship 277
Terminating Your Supervisory Relationship 278
Keystones 279
Additional Resources 280
Web Based 280
Print Based 280
References 280

Chapter 12 Self-Care and Self-Protection—Necessary for All Counselors 282

Counseling: Challenging the Well-Being of the Counselor 283
Burnout 285
Counselors at Risk 286
The Unfolding of Burnout 287
Preventing Burnout 288
Increase Self-Awareness 288
Engage in Healthy Life Habits 289
Nutrition 290
Exercise 290
Social Engagement 290
Nurturing an Inner Life 291
Play and Be Playful 291
Work Management 291
Recharge 291
Compassion Fatigue 292
Symptoms 293
Risk Factors 295
Assessing the Risk 296
Reducing the Risk 303
Work Setting 303
Lifestyle Adjustments 304

Intervening When Necessary 305
Intentionality, Recognition, and Acceptance 305
Connection 305
Anxiety Management/Self-Soothing 306
Self-Care 306
What Next? 306
Keystones 310
Additional Resources 311
Web Based 311
Print Based 311
References 312

Chapter 13 Transition From Practice to Career 315

Connection Between Internship and Career 316
Apprenticeship: Stepping Into the World of the Professional 316
Preparation for Employment 317
Self-Evaluation 317
Résumé 320
Cover Letter 325
Letters of Recommendation 326
Job Interviews 328
Phone/Online Video Interview 331
On-Site Interview 332
Job Interview Questions 334
Employment for International Students: Special Opportunity/Special Challenge 336
Job Offers and Your Decision 336
Placement Resources 337
Networking 337
Advanced Education 337
Doctoral Programs 337
Letters of Recommendation 338
Official Transcript 339
Personal Statement 339
Financial Support 340
Postscript 340
Keystones 340
Additional Resources 341
Web Based 341
Print Based 341
References 341

Chapter 14 Transitions: Self as Counselor **342**
Identity 343
To Be a Counselor 345
A Closer Look at Defining Characteristics 347
A Development Perspective 347
A Wellness Perspective 348
A Prevention Perspective 350
An Empowerment Perspective 351
Professional Identity: Both Common and Unique 353
Responding to the Calling 354
Through the Lens of a Counselor 354
Professional Ethics: From Knowing to Valuing 355
Contributing to the Professional Community 357
With Pride 358
Keystones 360
Additional Resources 361
Web Based 361
Print Based 361
References 361

Index **363**

About the Authors **374**

Editors' Preface: Introduction to the Series

Counseling and Professional Identity in the 21st Century

The primary purpose of field experience is to assist counseling students in learning how to apply the principles, knowledge, and skills they have learned from books and in classrooms to real work situations. In this integration process, counseling students are prepared to achieve their lifelong career goals. For this reason, field experience in counseling is considered by counseling professionals and students as the most critical component of counselor training. In this training process, counseling students will not only enhance their personal and professional development in guided and controlled experiences with counseling professionals in the real world, but also prepare themselves for their employment and career. The book *Field Experience: Transitioning From Student to Professional* is a vehicle that will help you move from where you are now as a counseling student to where you want to be as an emerging counseling professional.

Field Experience: Transitioning From Student to Professional is a road map of this transitional process and the valuable role played by one's field experience. This book discusses the ideal, as presented within the classroom, and the real, experienced in practice. It depicts how a counseling student becomes an emerging professional in his or her field experience and helps the reader conceptualize the occurrence of such transitioning. Most important, the book provides a unique perspective for counseling students to see where they were, where they are, and where they will be as a result of the process of their field experience.

Field Experience: Transitioning From Student to Professional helps counseling students identify those areas of professional competency needing development and thus serving as targets for professional growth to be achieved during their field experience. These areas include but are not limited to clinical supervision, multiculturalism, ethics in practice, crisis intervention, reducing risk for self, documentation and record keeping, self-care, and termination. The book also outlines the challenges and obstacles counseling students may face while they are developing their professional competence at the final stage of their training.

Finally, *Field Experience: Transitioning From Student to Professional* is the book that assists counseling students in developing their professional identity while they are doing their field study. The text clearly defines the nature of professional identity, its value to the profession and the professional, and ways to further develop one's professional identity during field experience.

Although we are proud of the depth and breadth of the topics covered within this text, we are more than aware that one text, one learning experience, will not be sufficient for the development of a counselor's professional competency. The formation of both one's professional identity and practice will be a lifelong process. It is a process that we hope to facilitate through the presentation of this text and the creation of our series *Counseling and Professional Identity in the 21st Century.*

Counseling and Professional Identity in the 21st Century is a new, fresh, pedagogically sound series of texts targeting counselors in training. This series is *not* simply a compilation of isolated books matching that which are already in the market. Rather, each book, with its targeted knowledge and skills, will be presented as but a part of a larger whole. The focus and content of each text serves as a single lens through which a counselor can view his or her clients, engage in his or her practice, and articulate his or her own professional identity.

Counseling and Professional Identity in the 21st Century is unique not only in the fact that it "packages" a series of traditional texts, but because it provides an *integrated* curriculum targeting the formation of the reader's professional identity and efficient, ethical practice. Each book within the series is structured to facilitate the ongoing professional formation of the reader. The materials found within each text are organized in order to move the readers to higher levels of cognitive, affective, and psychomotor functioning, resulting in their assimilation of the materials presented into both their professional identity and their approach to professional practice. Although each text targets a specific set of core competencies (cognates and skills), competencies identified by the Council for Accreditation of Counseling & Related Educational Programs (CACREP) as essential to the practice of counseling (see Table P.1), each book in the series will emphasize each of the following:

- the assimilation of concepts and constructs provided across the text found within the series, thus fostering the reader's ongoing development as a competent professional;
- the blending of contemporary theory with current research and empirical support;
- a focus on the development of procedural knowledge, with each text employing case illustrations and guided practice exercises to facilitate the reader's ability to translate the theory and research discussed into professional decision making and application;
- the emphasis on the need for and means of demonstrating accountability; and
- the fostering of the reader's professional identity and, with it, the assimilation of the ethics and standards of practice guiding the counseling profession.

Table P.1 Books and Corresponding CACREP (Council for the Accreditation of Counseling and Related Educational Programs) Competencies

Counseling and Professional Identity	
Books in the Series	Typical Courses Served by the Text
Introduction to Professional Counseling Varunee Faii Sangganjanavanich and Cynthia A. Reynolds	Introductory
Becoming a Skilled Counselor Richard D. Parsons and Naijian Zhang	Basic skills
Becoming a Multiculturally Competent Counselor Changming Duan and Chris Brown	Multicultural and diversity
Counseling Individuals Through the Lifespan Daniel Wai Chung Wong, Kim Hall, Cheryl Justice, and Lucy Wong Hernandez	Human development
Counseling Assessment and Evaluation: Fundamentals of Applied Practice Joshua C. Watson and Brandé Flamez	Assessment
Research Methods for Counseling Robert Wright	Fundamental research
Counseling Theory: Guiding Reflective Practice Richard D. Parsons and Naijian Zhang (Eds.)	Theories
Career Development and Counseling: Theory and Practice in a Multicultural World Mei Tang and Jane Goodman	Career counseling
Counselor as Consultant David Scott, Chadwick Royal, and Daniel Kissinger	Consultation and coordination
Group Work: An Introduction for Helping Professionals Robert Conyne	Group dynamics, group counseling
Field Experience Naijian Zhang and Richard D. Parsons	Professional practice

We are proud to have served as coeditors of this series, feeling sure that all of the text included, just like *Field Experience: Transitioning From Student to Professional,* will serve as a significant resource to you and your development as a professional counselor.

Richard Parsons, PhD
Naijian Zhang, PhD

Authors' Preface

This field experience book was originally started as a result of a discussion between the two of us about the issue of the value of a text for those engaged in field experience. This was not ours alone to ponder; many of our colleagues who teach practicum and internship classes and students who take field experience courses shared our concern. The question, while targeting the need for a text, really was challenging us to consider the value of field experience to the overall professional development of our students. As a result, other questions began to emerge. "What do we teach our students in the field experience courses and how do our students learn while they are studying in the field?" "How do our counseling students transition from students to professionals and how might the experience in the field facilitate this transition?" And finally, "How might one's professional identity be given shape by the uniqueness of one's field experience?"

It is clear that field experience plays a pivotal role in the professional formation and development of counselors. As such, we turned to existing research, anecdotal reports from those who teach and supervise field experience, and input from students who successfully navigated their field experiences, to identify those elements deemed essential to successful field experience and, with it, meaningful growth and professional development. The results of our reflections and data gathering are the creation of this text, *Field Experience: Transitioning From Student to Professional.*

The book *Field Experience: Transitioning From Student to Professional* includes 14 chapters, with each focusing on a special area of counseling trainees' entire field experience.

We began with a big picture of what field experience is and how it happens by discussing the specifics of this unique learning experience, such as "shift in focus: from knowing to doing," "from other- to self-taught," "from ideal to real," and "from self as student to self as emerging professional." The most important piece in this picture is how counseling trainees form their professional identity from developmental, wellness, prevention, and empowerment and advocacy perspectives. Chapter 2 is about how to match self to site. We are aware that at the time of reading this book, the counseling trainee has most likely completed at least his or her first field experience placement. We don't believe this is a belated topic or effort because the majority of the counseling or counseling psychology programs have one practicum class and two internship classes. In addition, thoroughly assessing self and the site is very useful even when the counseling trainee has been placed on a practicum or internship site. Chapter 3 discusses how counseling trainees transition from the ideal to the real. The chapter particularly focuses on what is the ideal and the real, why the ideal is always less than the real, and how counseling trainees effect change in this transitioning process. Chapter 4 continues the theme of moving from the ideal to the real by providing the topic of the ethics of practice in the real world. In terms of ethics, the question of why *being* is more than knowing in the process of transitioning from a student to a counseling professional is specifically answered. Chapter 5 intends to assist counseling trainees in discovering what the essentials are in the process of reflection on counseling practice and professional development. Specifically, it describes the moment-to-moment decisions made by counseling trainees and their intentionality behind what they are doing to increase the efficacy of their decisions and effectiveness as emerging counseling professionals.

Although we did not divide the book into sections, it has a clear line in that the first five chapters focus on the overall picture of counseling field experience and the later chapters target the specifics that counseling trainees need to learn in the process of their field experience. Chapter 6 focuses on the essentials of counseling supervision and how counseling trainees can emerge as professionals with their supervision experience. This chapter not only emphasizes what counseling supervision is and why counseling supervision is important, but also centers on the preparation of counseling trainees for a variety of issues they may encounter in their counseling supervision. With the feedback from the book reviewers, we have placed the chapter "Growing Through Supervision" before all the chapters that contain the basics of field experience because we believe both the site supervisor and the faculty supervisor are the backbone of counseling trainees. In other words, they are the first-line supporters for consulting whenever the counseling trainees encounter difficulty. Chapter 7 affirms the important aspect of multicultural counseling in the field experience. This chapter targets the counseling trainees' multicultural counseling competence in the real world, and attention is specifically given to counseling trainees' multicultural awareness and sensitivity when applying traditional counseling theories, skills, and techniques to multiculturally diverse clients in their practice. To help counseling trainees grow as emerging counseling professionals, Chapter 8 targets the strategies and skills of crisis intervention. The what, how, why, and when questions concerning crisis intervention are all answered for counseling trainees in this chapter. Violence and aggression to counselors have become a reality nowadays in the counseling field, and this issue is oftentimes not adequately emphasized in counseling practicum and internship. So, Chapter 9 is devoted to the skills and techniques important to reducing risk for counseling trainees themselves in the practice. The uniqueness of Chapter 10 is that this chapter logically depicts the key elements of documentation and record keeping through thoroughly discussing ethical/legal requirements and issues involved in documentation and record keeping. It then offers strategies for appropriate documentation and record keeping and a variety of progress-note-taking formats for counseling trainees to choose from based on their needs. We believe the most important person in the helping process is the counselor himself or herself. Taking care of self and making the counselor-self remain sound physically and mentally is the fundamental for counseling effectiveness. Chapter 11 covers self-care and self-protection. This chapter helps counseling trainees both to become aware of what burnout and compassion fatigue are and to learn how to prevent them. Chapter 12 affirms the importance of achieving a successful field experience termination and closure with clients, supervisors, and other counseling staff. Common issues and essentials involved in termination and closure at the internship site are thoroughly discussed, and specific steps to achieve the success of termination are offered. For counseling trainees, career is very important in their lives. Chapter 13 contains the practicalities for counseling trainees to transition from practice to career. This chapter not only helps counseling trainees understand the connection between their internship and career but also offers strategies and skills for them to walk into the field. The final chapter, Chapter 14, invites counseling trainees to use all they have learned to craft their professional identity in the process of transitioning to self as counselor.

We strongly believe *Field Experience: Transitioning From Student to Professional* provides not only the nuts and bolts but also a road map that counseling trainees can use to guide their transition from being a student to becoming an emerging professional in the process of their field experience.

NZ/RP

Acknowledgments

While we, the authors of this text, are given credit for its creation, the truth is that the formation of the ideas contained, as well as the crafting of the presentation, required the contribution of many others. These individuals include those who have made contributions to the existing literature on the topic of the book and those who have offered ideas and insights. We wish to express our appreciation to them for their contributions.

First, we want to thank our colleagues and those who shared their ideas, insights, and experiences of teaching field experience courses. Their wisdom helped us in the process of developing the book proposal.

We want to thank the reviewers who have encouraged us after they reviewed our initial proposal. We also appreciate their candid feedback on how we should make changes and improve the text. These individuals, not including those who chose to be anonymous, are Ronica Arnold Branson, Jackson State University; Britney G. Brinkman, Chatham University; Kathy DeOrnellas, Texas Woman's University; Laura L. Lansing, Mount Aloysius College; Catherine M. Pittman, Saint Mary's College; Chuck Reid, The University of Texas-Pan American; Elizabeth Ruiz, Governors State University; and Gina Zanardelli, Chatham University.

We also want to sincerely thank the reviewers who spent enormous time reading our draft manuscript and wrote long, detailed, and helpful feedback and suggestions. We have made changes based on their feedback and suggestions. Their time and expertise are greatly appreciated. These individuals, not including four people who chose to be anonymous, are Mary Olufunmilayo Adekson, St. Bonaventure University; Josue Gonzalez, The University of Texas at San Antonio; Danielle M. Kohlo, University of Northern Colorado; Ann Leonard-Zabel, Curry College; Chuck Reid, The University of Texas-Pan American; and Gina Zanardelli, Curry College.

Finally, we would like to acknowledge the support and encouragement from the editorial team at SAGE. Especially, our thanks go to Carrie Montoya, Assistant to the Editor; Abbie Rickard, Associate Editor; Brenda Weight, Copy Editor; Kelly DeRosa, Production Editor; Candice Harman, Cover Designer from the Production Department; and our friend Kassie Graves, the Editor.

NZ/RP

1

Field Experience as Formative to Professional Identity

Learning is pleasurable but doing is the height of enjoyment.

Novalis

The quote from this 19th-century German poet may not completely ring true to those experiencing initial anxieties as they venture out of the confines of a classroom to begin the application of their knowledge in the world of the professional. Although there are anxieties tied to engaging in field work, there are also many opportunities for growth as a professional and for facilitating the unfolding of one's professional identity. Field experience—be it called practicum, internship, apprenticeship, or field study—is a pivotal and invaluable contributor to the transitioning from student to professional.

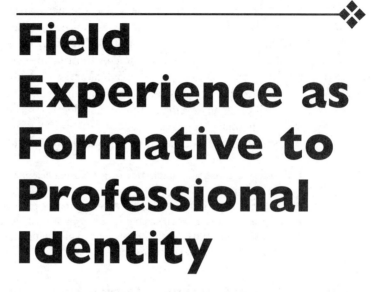

The transition from student to professional brings with it a desire to use the knowledge and skills acquired in the classroom in the service of one's professional role and function. The transition from student to professional is one in which the self-concerns of student are replaced by the heartfelt concerns for another. The transition from student to professional is one in which concerns over grades and external demands for performance are replaced by an internal desire for effectiveness. The transition from student to professional is accompanied by the increased awareness that being a professional helper is not only an awesome responsibility . . . but an awesome gift to be respected and valued.

The experience of serving in the role and function as a counselor within the field invites a student to experience not only the tasks of counseling but the values and philosophical assumptions that guide the performance of those tasks. Interacting within the role of counselor and engaging with other professionals within the field provides the student the opportunity to more fully integrate his or her self-concept and identity with that commonly shared by those laying claim to the label of counselor. The transition from student to professional and with it the development of one's professional identity as a counselor takes flight during one's field experience. It is this process of transitioning to develop a professional identity as a counselor that serves as the focus for this chapter.

Specifically, at the end of this chapter readers will be able to

- describe those characteristics of a field experience that makes it a unique learning environment;
- describe those factors that can reduce or enhance professional growth via field experience;
- explain what is meant by a counselor's "professional identity"; and
- describe the values, assumptions, and philosophical perspective that shape the unique professional identity of counselors.

Field Experience: A Unique Learning Experience

Field experience—be it called practicum, internship, or simply field experience—is an integral part of the curriculum of most, if not all, counselor education programs. It may appear in a catalog and be listed on registration materials similarly to all the other required courses. However, to assume that field experience is just another course, another group of credits to be acquired, similarly to all other courses within a program, would be a mistake.

What distinguishes field experience from other parts of the curriculum is not merely its content. Field experience is a unique learning experience, and it is this uniqueness that not only provides a special opportunity for professional development but also presents a number of challenges to one accustomed to the "safety" of a classroom.

Contrasted to most classroom experiences, field experience occurs, by definition, in a unique, nonclassroom learning environment; employs unique performance requirements targeting application rather than acquisition of knowledge and skills; and presents unique challenges to and opportunities for professional growth and development of one's professional identity.

Shift in Focus: From "Knowing" to "Doing"

Field experience plays an irreplaceable role in one's professional development. During field experiences, one is provided hands-on learning opportunities where the connection of theoretical and conceptual information acquired in the classroom is extended to the professional world of practice. During field experience, there is a shift in focus from knowing and understanding to doing and applying. It is no longer one's ability to describe, explain, or discuss a theoretical construct or research finding that is called for but rather the ability to translate these concepts and constructs into actions which ultimately will best serve the clients.

Shifting From Other- to Self-Taught

In most counselor education graduate programs, field experience follows upon the completion of a number of classroom courses focusing on fundamental knowledge and skills. In these classroom experiences, there was most likely a teacher whose role was to structure the learning experiences, direct or guide the sharing of information, and provide measures of achievement. This role was contrasted to that of student.

The student in this learning environment was given the charge to attend, to participate, to acquire designated knowledge and skills, and to perform successfully on the measures of achievement. This formula, of a teacher-designed and -directed learning experience, was, with minor variations, one students most likely had encountered previously throughout their years of education. This familiarity with the roles assigned made these learning encounters somewhat comfortable, even safe and predictable.

The field as a learning environment, however, challenges the familiar roles and structure of education. Upon entering one's field placement, it becomes quite obvious that this is quite a unique learning environment. Perhaps it's the absence of neatly arranged desks or instructor with a PowerPoint presentation, or perhaps it is the lack of a class scheduled in line with the tightly developed sequential curriculum, but the absence of that with which students are accustomed grabs their attention and announces that this is a unique learning environment.

Much of what is listed above is obvious—but these are only the superficial differences to be experienced within this learning environment. The more substantive differences between the field and classroom experiences rests in the unique demands placed on students as they attempt to maximize the learning opportunities presented in the field. It is a demand to step into the role of self-as-teacher and is marked by an increased call for independent, self-directed learning; a shift in focus from grades to outcomes; and a pursuit of, rather than a retreat from, evaluation and corrective feedback. Students who are able to embrace these new demands will be the ones who maximize their learning experiences in their field placement.

Increased Independence and Self-Direction

There is a comfort in knowing what is expected of us, when it is due, and the rubric employed for assessment. A good classroom teacher develops syllabi and lesson plans that provides this structure. While those entering their field experience may receive syllabi with objectives, tasks and timelines, these most often reflect the "classroom component" and not the objectives, tasks, and timelines encountered in the field.

From the first moments of their field experience, the reality is that to some degree what students do, or pursue, may be the result of self-direction rather than other direction. This is not to suggest that students in the field have carte blanche to do whatever they desire, but rather that the field is an environment that is fluid—presenting crises, demands, challenges, and opportunities that do not lend themselves neatly to a schedule or fixed plan. Students who will maximize the benefit of the field experience are those who initiate their own learning, who are not only open to but seek out opportunities to observe, participate, and do. Students who benefit most from the field experience will be the ones who embrace the increased independence and potential for student-directed learning rather than passively await moment-to-moment direction from their supervisor.

As noted, this is not to suggest that students in the field should go off and simply do their "own thing," but rather that they may need to look for experiences that they feel will prove growth filled and invite the supervisor to consider sanctioning these experiences. Exercise 1.1 is provided to stimulate your reflections about those types of experiences you feel would be most beneficial to your professional development.

EXERCISE 1.1

Seeking Growth

Directions: There may be a temptation to engage in activities with which you feel you have basic competence and could demonstrate to a supervisor your capabilities to perform successfully. This is understandable, because no one really enjoys struggling or exhibiting inadequacy. But for growth to occur, you need to venture beyond your current level of success and experience things that stretch your capabilities. As you engage in your field experience, it would be helpful to reflect on your knowledge and skill and identify areas where growth is desired. Complete the following table and consider sharing it with your own site supervisor so that collaboratively you can develop a plan for growth and development.

Area of Focus	**Assessment (Scale: 3 = mastery, 2 = basic competency, 1 = minimum to absent)**	**Plan for Professional Development (including specific tasks, activities, experiences)**
Establishing a Therapeutic Alliance		
Case Conceptualization and Treatment Planning		
Preventive Programming		

Area of Focus	Assessment (Scale: 3 = mastery, 2 = basic competency, 1 = minimum to absent)	Plan for Professional Development (including specific tasks, activities, experiences)
Therapeutic Group Work		
Task Group Facilitation		
Empirically Supported Treatments (Knowledge and Application)		
Systems Intervention		
Documentation		
Ethical and Legal Practice		
Assessment: Client		
Assessment: Counseling Process (Formative and Summative)		
Consultation		
(OTHER)		
(OTHER)		
(OTHER)		

Focus on Outcomes Versus Grades

Ours is still a grade-conscious culture, and even those stepping out of the classroom and into the field have legitimate interest in and concerns about their academic performance and grades. But as you move from the culture of the classroom to that of the field, you will soon begin to appreciate the need and value of shifting your focus from grades to outcomes.

Yes, grades on assignments will certainly retain a position of importance in directing your energies and focus. However, you will soon realize that it is your effectiveness, the outcomes you achieve, and the impact your work has on those you serve that will take primary importance in directing all that you do.

This is not an immediate transition. Initially, those entering the field may still be concerned about knowing "the number of pages required," the specific chapters that must be read or the specific number of hours that must be contributed, but these markers will slowly be replaced by a desire to do whatever is necessary to prove effective in their role as counselor-in-training, effective not just in the supervisor's eyes, but in their own and those of their clients.

Students who find the field experience to be growth filled will soon realize that they are engaged in more hours than those required; seek out readings, research, and information that goes beyond the "requirement"; and use client progress—not a teacher-developed rubric—as the marker that guides their focus and engagement.

Seeking Evaluation and Soliciting Corrective Feedback

Perhaps you, like us, have been amazed by the fact that students of all ages—when engaged in private instructions on a musical instrument or in an athletic endeavor—will gladly seek feedback, evaluation, and direction in regards to their performance, in hopes of finding ways to improve. Yet these same students will often find ways to "hide" in the classroom for fear of demonstrating areas of confusion or lack of skill and sadly, as a result, miss opportunities to receive the feedback that could facilitate growth. Perhaps this hiding is a response to focusing on grade achievement versus personal development. In any case, for the field experience to be maximally beneficial, the desire to hide needs to be replaced by the desire to elicit corrective feedback. Your supervisor is a source of knowledge and experience and has navigated many of the challenges you now encounter. To fail to tap this resource would certainly be a missed opportunity, but to do so requires you to be vulnerable and open to having both your strengths and your limitations identified.

This will not be an easy process because many of us have been enculturated or, perhaps more accurately, "schoolized" to see evaluation and grading as often punitive, focusing on our weaknesses or failures without prescription for improvement. Knowing what I got wrong on the test does not automatically help me grow. It is when I understand that I have fallen short of a goal and am given the opportunity to understand the why of that "failure" and the how of improving, that growth and development are fostered. This is the potential gift to be found in field experience and the supervision provided.

To maximize the potential for growth, students in the field need to place their egos aside and embrace the truth that no one is perfect and that all counselors, including those just starting out as well as seasoned professionals, remain students in a process of continual development. From this perspective, the student will be able to replace a desire to hide or defend with a willingness to be vulnerable. Perhaps you can remember the first time you had a practice session taped and reviewed by a professor. For some students this experience is terrifying. They sit on the edge of their seat, attempting to explain why they forgot to do, or failed to do, or inappropriately did this or that. They seem more interested in finding excuses or justifications for falling short of the desired goals rather than on an open exchange about the how, the why, and the what to do about these shortcomings. For these students, their anxiety and self-defending often block their reception and assimilation of the teacher's corrective feedback. For maximum benefit in the field, this performance anxiety and self-defending behaviors need to be replaced by an openness and willingness to be vulnerable in service of professional development. This issue of maximizing growth through supervision will be addressed in more detail in Chapter 6. The point to be made here is that field experience calls for a shift in the way we "value" evaluation.

Shift From Ideal to Real

The ability to employ and apply what has been learned in the classroom to the lived experience in the field is not easy. Within the classroom, students have been presented with pure theory and illustrations of application within ideal conditions. Although perfection is not achievable, models are often presented as in the ideal form. The skills practiced on campus are often done under the conditions of simulation, where the environment can be controlled to allow for micro-skill practice and corrective feedback and adjustment at the moment.

While a counselor-in-training's first encounter with a peer-volunteer in a simulated intake interview may be anxiety provoking, typically the focus of the anxiety is on his or her performance and the implications this will have for evaluation. Having read and perhaps seen what is supposed to be done, most students who enter this training experience find themselves absorbed in self-critical observations and internal commentary. The mental tape recording is operating, with the voice of the professor noting the importance of attending skills, open questions, and so forth drowning out the disclosures being shared by the client. It is not unusual for counselors-in-training to turn their attention away from the client and focus on concerns as to how they may look to their peers and professor. And although these training sessions may be anxiety provoking, there is a degree of safety and comfort in knowing that the event is occurring within the confines of a campus lab or university clinic and the "volunteer" client is to a varying degree simply role-playing. There is comfort in knowing that one has a full 50 minutes, if not more, to get to some point of conclusion. And there is a comfort in knowing that the student is not really responsible to facilitate or effect change for this client. Stepping off campus and entering the field of practice removes these areas of comfort.

The field is an arena where the ideal of practice in the classroom meets the reality of day-to-day professional practice. Although this shift may be obvious, the demands on the student entering the field and being expected to function may not be as obvious. A primary challenge for students entering a field experience is their ability to integrate the theory and research presented in the classroom with the demands and roadblocks encountered in the world of practice. Consider, for example, the experience of a student whose field experience is to take place in a middle school setting. During one class, where the focus was on the development of fundamental communication and counseling skills, the assigned "client" contact was structured so as to allow her the luxury of spending a couple of initial sessions practicing her fundamental communication skills and building rapport and a working alliance with her volunteer client. This simulated counseling contract was set for six sessions and the goal was relatively simple, "to develop a working alliance along with an initial case conceptualization and treatment plan." This formula of a number of specified sessions for a given amount of time, all focusing on modest goals, is a pretty typical assignment for many of these early skill training courses. Now contrast this with the reality experienced within the field.

From day one in her field placement, our student became more than aware that she was no longer in the safety of a campus clinic. No longer was it a classmate, serving as a volunteer client, who sat across from her in the counseling office. Nor was there the luxury of multiple sessions and extended time during each session to be able to develop a working alliance. No—our illustrative student-in-praxis has found herself confronted with an angry seventh grader, protesting his presence in the counselor's office and presenting a teacher referral reading, *"Thomas is unbearable, I don't want him back until he learns to follow class rules."*

Given the teacher's sense of urgency and the reality that Thomas cannot be excluded from his education, along with the fact that the counselor has a meeting in 10 minutes, a parent who desires a call back, and a 5th-grade student sitting outside her office upset about losing her backpack, the luxury of building rapport over two sessions is replaced by the very practical need to develop a trusting, working relationship, AND developing at least the initial plans for intervention—within the next 10 minutes.

Yes, the ideal presented in class finds challenges and need for adaptation once one is operating in the trenches. Exercise 1.2 is provided to help further highlight this need for adaptation as a practicing counselor.

EXERCISE 1.2

Adapting the Ideal to the Real

Directions: As noted in the text, once a counselor-in-training enters the world of practice, the various and often competing requirements require the counselor to adapt the skills honed in the classroom to the constraints of his or her reality. In this exercise, you are directed to "interview" your site supervisor (or another practicing counselor at your site) using the following questions. It would be helpful to share your findings with your classmates in order to identify points of commonality to the lived experience of the professional counselor.

1. How would you compare or contrast what you learned about the role of counselor and the process of counseling while you were a graduate student to what you experience day to day, here at work?
2. What external factors or nonclient factors—such as insurance requirements, organizational policies, procedures, organizational culture, or even caseload—affect the way you approach your counseling? How have you adapted to these forces while serving your clients?
3. In graduate school, we learn about theories of counseling and the concept of empirically supported treatments (EST). Given the reality of your work, what place, if any, does theory and/or EST have in your practice decisions?

Shifting Identity Focus: From Self-as-Student to Self-as-Emerging-Professional

The transition from a sense of self as a student to experiencing oneself as a professional is not an all-or-none event. Counselors—even those with extensive experience and professionalism—remain students. Ours is a developing profession. New research provides new insights into the human condition and those factors that can facilitate (and hinder) adaptive functioning and health. As such, regardless of terminal degrees, the ethical, effective counselor remains a student of counseling and will continue to pursue knowledge of the profession as well as knowledge of self-as-professional.

Along a similar line, each student, regardless of the number of credits earned or the types of courses and experiences encountered, has begun the process of transitioning to a sense of self as professional. Students who have entered their graduate training not merely in hopes of attaining a job or even starting a career but in response to a felt calling are beginning to experience what it is to be a counselor. Being called to a service, or a function, is a hallmark of a professional. Similarly, students who, even in the earliest stages of their formation, find they are motivated by an intrinsic curiosity about the human condition and those factors influencing one's adaptive functioning and overall well-being, also reflect that which is characteristic of the professional counselor. Finally, the student who has a desire to go beyond simply understanding to being able to apply or employ that understanding in service of those seeking assistance, is again tapping into the identity of professional counselor. This desire to facilitate development and assist another serves as the beacon calling professional counselors to continuing development.

Thus, it is apparent that the transition of one's concept of self-as-student to concept of self-as-counselor is a transition that begins with the first experience in one's counselor education. However, it is during the field experience that one begins to tip the scale from student-counselor to counselor-as-student. Functioning in the world of the profession will prove significant for the student's professional socialization and development of professional identity.

Field Work: Fostering an Emerging Professional Identity

Counselors can be defined by the role they assume and enact. Counselors can be defined by membership within a specific organization (e.g., member of ACA). Counselors can be defined by state law, as would be the case for defining a professional licensed counselor. But perhaps the most important definition of counselor comes from the self-perception of the one identified as counselor. Being able to articulate, value, and operate from a knowledge base, skill set, and philosophical perspective that distinguishes you from other helping professionals, while aligning you with those self-identified as counselors is the core of your professional identity.

The questions "what is counseling" and "what does it mean to be a counselor" may not be new to you. Perhaps it is a question you pondered and researched prior to selecting a graduate program or maybe it is one posed to you at a party, at a family gathering, or within your current place of work. And while your own reflections, research, and readings may have helped you begin to formulate and answer these questions, it is during your field experience that the answers will become more personal and more integral to your professional practice.

Counselors: A Collective Identity

What it means to be a counselor is at one level a very personal experience, reflecting your own sense of calling and purpose as well as your personal perspective on this particular helping profession. However, what it means to be a counselor is also grounded in an extensive history of the profession and reflects a collective identity stemming from shared goals, resources, and aspirations for the profession (Daniels, 2002).

As you settle into your field placement, you will most likely begin to experience the unique roles and functions served by those identified as counselors. This may be even more obvious if your site engages the services of those from other helping professions such as social work, psychology, and/or psychiatry. As you observe and discuss the what and why of a counselor's job, you may find the uniqueness rests not just in job title or assigned duty but in the unique knowledge base and skill set employed by counselors to perform these duties. Or . . . perhaps you will not. Perhaps it is difficult to differentiate that knowledge base and skill set and thus you may question the uniqueness of the counseling profession. While a counselor's skill set and knowledge base may position him or her to engage in some activities and not others and thus be used as criteria for differentiating professional identities, these are not the primary criteria for the identification of a counselor's unique professional identity. It is not just what we do or the skills we employ to do it that defines our uniqueness. Rather, it is the underlying set of professional values, beliefs, and assumptions that serve as the underpinning of what we do and how we do it that distinguishes our profession. A counselor's professional identity reflects the personal assimilation of "a core set of values, beliefs, and assumptions about the unique characteristics of one's selected profession that differentiates it from other professions" (Weinrach, Thomas, & Chan, 2001, p. 168).

Shared Values and Perspectives

The values and assumptions that serve as the common foundation for all counselors' professional identities are best understood by simply reviewing the definition of counseling as proposed by the American Counseling Association: "Counseling is a professional relationship that empowers diverse individuals, families, and groups to accomplish mental health, wellness, education, and career goals" (ACA, 2010).

Embedded within this definition are the pillars of the collective identity held by counselors, an identity that distinguishes counselors from other helping professionals.

Counselors are unique in that we approach our roles and functions guided by four fundamental perspectives: (a) developmental perspective (Myers, Sweeney, & Witmer, 2001; Remley & Herlihy, 2007), (b) a wellness perspective (Myers, et al., 2001; Remley & Herlihy, 2007), (c) a prevention perspective, and (d) an empowerment perspective (Remley & Herlihy, 2007). With the preceding being integral to all that we do, it can be assumed that counseling is a profession that serves normal functioning populations as well as those with severe emotional and psychological difficulties and does so in ways that move beyond mere remediation and resolution of presenting concerns to the promotion of wellness, personal growth, education, and career development (ACA, 2014).

As you approach your field work, it will be essential for you to integrate these elements into all that you do as a professional. It is approaching one's role and function from these perspectives that serves as the hallmark of the professional counselor. Given their importance in the formation of one's professional identity as a counselor, each will be discussed in some detail.

Developmental Perspective

Counselors have a "distinctive educational-developmental view of the helping process" (AMHCA, 2010, p. 22). Counselors assume that life tasks and challenges are part of the normal experience of living. Further, counselors believe that to a great extent, our psychological well-being is determined by how well we adjust to the inevitable life changes that confront us across the life cycle. Therefore, counselors focus on assisting those having difficulty in navigating these normative challenges. This can be contrasted to helping professions that focus on pathology and remediation of psychopathological disorders.

While professional counselors do not deny the existence of psychopathology, and many engage in the treatment of those with severe pathology, they generally see such pathology as a unique and extreme end result of prolonged dysfunction rather than a common occurrence. The developmental lens that colors a counselor's perspective on a client's presenting complaint directs the counselor to first consider the normative characteristics of the presenting challenge, rather than to immediately label as pathological. From their developmental perspective, counselors will often engage in activities and strategies that help clients build competence in dealing with normative life changes. Exercise 1.3 is provided in hopes of further clarifying this unique perspective.

EXERCISE 1.3

Developmental Challenge or Pathology

Directions: Below you will find a listing of a number of common concerns that may be brought to a counselor's office. Your task is to discuss each with your instructor, supervisor, and/or colleagues in an attempt to identity which and when these are normative developmental challenges and which and when they could reflect severe psychopathology.

(Continued)

(Continued)

Presenting Concern	Conditions Defining as Normative Challenge	Conditions Indicating Psychopathology
Grieving following the death of a loved one		
Underage alcohol consumption		
Engaging in physical aggression		
Performance anxiety		
Sadness and loss of energy and interest following the loss of a job		
Social isolation and withdrawal from peers		
Difficulty attending and remaining task focused		
Inability to socially assert self		
Somatic complaints in response to current high levels of stress		
Relational conflict and difficulties		
Manifesting checking and rechecking behaviors		
Fear and avoidance of insects—specifically spiders		
Night terrors that disturb sleep		
Food refusal and calorie restriction		

Wellness Perspective

As an extension of the developmental perspective, counselors value the promotion of positive mental health and therefore are proactive in promoting wellness. From a counseling perspective, this wellness can be defined as

> a way of life oriented toward optimal health and well-being, in which body, mind, and spirit are integrated by the individual to live life more fully within the human and natural community. Ideally, it is the optimum state of health and well-being that each individual is capable of achieving. (Myers, Sweeney, & Witmer, 2000, p. 252)

This wellness perspective or paradigm directs counselors to facilitate the client's conscious integration of the mind, body, and spirit in ways that promote holistic well-being (Myers & Sweeney, 2008). With this perspective as a pillar to a counselor's professional identity, a counselor's focus expands beyond just engaging in problem-solving activities and services to engaging in activities and services that facilitate client development across and within all domains: behavioral, spiritual, systemic, and cultural, as well as psychosocial.

Thus, even though counselors function in service of those experiencing life challenges, they also engage in activities and services for those seeking growth and development. Further, even when engaged with clients who are expressing difficulties within one domain or aspect of life, counselors attempt to not only assist in these difficult situations but do so with an eye to facilitating the client's abilities to move beyond simple remediation to reach optimal levels of well-being (Witmer & Granello, 2005). Consider Case Illustration 1.1 as reflecting the subtle influence of a wellness perspective on the decisions made by this counselor.

CASE ILLUSTRATION 1.1

More Than One Person

As a counselor working within a faith-based counseling center, it was not unusual for Lisa to encounter young couples struggling during their early days of marriage. While the specifics varied and included concerns such as money decisions, intimacy, navigating in-laws, and so forth, she noted that most had two things in common. First, the couples presenting in her office most often failed to understand and thus appreciate the developmental stages normatively encountered in a relationship, including those enveloped in conflict. Second, most of these couples demonstrated a need for the development of specific communication skills—especially those called for in times of conflict and conflict resolution. With the focus on interpersonal conflict, the interventions took on a relatively standard format, including training in active listening and disclosure skills, development of win-win conflict resolution skills, and training in assertiveness.

Perhaps it was a function of working in a faith-based counseling center or a reflection of her own personal assimilation of a wellness perspective, but in either case, Lisa's approach to working with these couples did not focus only on interpersonal skill development. She would encourage the couples to identify activities that promoted individual and dyadic well-being. For some, this included engaging in physical activities; for others it took the form of identifying social interests and concerns and engaging in service to others. With a concern for the wellness of the individual as well as the couple and, again, given the faith-based nature of the service, the discussions would often point to faith-based concerns and the prescription would include directions for further engagement in a personal faith journey. Lisa found that helping the individual pursue strategies for his

(Continued)

(Continued)

or her physical, emotional, and spiritual well-being positioned him or her in ways that facilitated the ongoing healthy development of the couple's relationship.

For clients approaching counseling in this center, with this wellness-focused counselor, what began as one targeted complaint—he doesn't listen, we never have sex, she's spending too much money—often resulted in a refocusing on perspectives that would not only improve the relationship but position each member of that relationship on a path to personal wellness.

Prevention

Because counselors value a developmental and wellness perspective, their energies are expended not merely in assisting those encountering blocks to wellness but also in investing in programs, activities, and services that facilitate prevention. A third pillar to the unique identity of the professional counselor is the valuing of and engaging in measures of preventive care (Remley & Herlihy, 2007). Often this valuing takes form in services that could be characterized as offering primary, secondary, and tertiary prevention.

Primary Prevention

Primary prevention refers to programs, activities, and services that are provided to a group of individuals prior to any evidence of their experiencing a specific mental health problem. The goal of primary prevention is to prevent a problem from developing in the first place. Examples of primary prevention programs include education programs, such as offering parent effectiveness training (Gordon, 2000) for couples expecting their first child, or providing elementary-grade students training in self-protection strategies.

Secondary Prevention

Secondary prevention strategies target specific at-risk populations where there are early indicators or evidence of the developing difficulty. The intent of the services offered is to reduce the likelihood that what is identified at an early stage or demonstrated to be an at-risk condition can be prevented from developing into a full-blown mental health issue. One frequently used example of secondary prevention is Head Start. The Head Start programs are typically focused on an economically disadvantaged group who may not have the early childhood stimulation and learning opportunities that are necessary for success in the first few years of school. Recognizing that if not addressed, these children could develop learning problems, Head Start attempts to prevent that condition from becoming developed by providing the structured stimulation and early education needed to position the children for success in school. Another example of a secondary prevention program is the structured debriefing that may be provided to military personnel returning from major battle or combatant incidents. The goal for such debriefing is to minimize or prevent the development of posttraumatic stress disorder among those engaged in the episode. Case Illustration 1.2 provides an example of a secondary prevention program that sprang from one client interaction in a university counseling center.

CASE ILLUSTRATION 1.2

Beyond Remediation to Prevention

As a counselor working in the university counseling center, Dr. Paulson had occasion to work with a number of the student-athletes. Jason, a freshman wrestler, was one of those students.

Jason's issues were not atypical for a freshman coming to the counseling center. He presented as one experiencing some difficulty adjusting to college life and manifesting a number of stress-related symptoms. He complained about having difficulty sleeping as well as experiencing a number of physical complaints such as headaches, stomach upset, and loose bowels. Over three sessions, Dr. Paulson was able to help Jason identify the sources of his stress and employ a number of behavioral and cognitive strategies to help him reduce the stress he was experiencing.

One of the targets for behavioral intervention was Jason's eating regimen. By his own admission, fast foods and soda had served as his primary food group and he was spending more time at the desserts counter than at the fruits and vegetables counter. Among a number of behavioral interventions introduced, including learning and employing deep muscle relaxation techniques and time management strategies as a way of gaining control over schoolwork, they developed a plan to modify Jason's eating regimen to include more regularly scheduled eating and a reduction in his intake of caffeine and sugar. It was during that planning that Jason shared that his diet "was not the best" because he was "splurging" prior to training for wrestling season. It was that discussion that spurred Dr. Paulson to reflect on the training many student-wrestlers engaged in and the possibility that some may engage in extreme calorie-restricted diets that could be detrimental to their health. Consequently, he developed a secondary prevention program—an eating disorders awareness program—that he provided the wrestling team.

Tertiary Prevention

Tertiary prevention programs and services target those who are presenting with mental health problems. Since the problems have already manifested, they cannot be prevented; however, what can be prevented is the "normal" course for these disorders.

Under these conditions, counselors will employ processes that not only help remediate the current situation but do so in a way that positions the client to be more prepared to cope with these and other life challenges in the future.

Counselors engaging in tertiary intervention will employ strategies that focus on decreasing the duration (including preventing relapse) but also severity and negative consequences of the condition. An example of tertiary prevention programming would include the development of self-help groups for those with addictions and compulsions where ongoing support is provided as assistance to continued sobriety. Also, counselors working in the legal system who provide support for those who have experienced sexual assault by helping them with the trauma-based symptoms as well as the stress they will encounter as they move through the legal system, are providing tertiary prevention services.

Empowerment and Advocacy

While the previous perspectives help to distinguish counseling as a profession and serve as the pillars of a counselor's professional identity, the one element that could be identified as a singular beacon highlighting the uniqueness of counseling is the profession's emphasis on and valuing of the empowerment of others. From a perspective of empowerment, a counselor avoids deficit and pathological models of counseling and "considers wellness versus illness, and competence versus deficiency" (Zimmerman & Warchausky, 1998, p. 5).

Empowerment and encouragement are integral goals associated with the counseling relationship. Counselors with this focus approach the counseling relationship as a partnership, one formed to achieve the empowerment of the client (Zimmerman & Warschausky, 1998). Counseling is seen as an egalitarian encounter, where dialogue and mutuality are valued and expert prescriptions and focus on deficits are rejected. With empowerment serving as a goal, counselors engage with their clients in ways that demonstrate their value for and desire to promote client independence and self-directedness. Counselors often implement this process of empowerment through an emphasis on a client's personal strengths and expanding on previous successes in life—pulling those abilities forward to assist in the current situation. Consider Case Illustration 1.3, the case of Kabira, as an example of one counselor's strength-based approach to empowerment.

CASE ILLUSTRATION 1.3

Kabira

While navigating in a new high school can be a challenge for any transfer student, that challenge was compounded for one student, Kabira Ngugi. Kabira was a recent arrival not just to W. B. Birdsong High School but to the United States. Kabira moved with her family from Kenya following her father's work transfer.

The first month of school was particularly difficult for Kabira. Academically, she excelled. She was, according to her teachers, a "delightful" student–one who quickly grasped concepts and showed an enthusiasm for learning. These same teachers, however, remarked that she appeared to be "constrained" in the classroom. They noted that she did not volunteer answers or ask questions readily but would respond when called on. One teacher stated that "Kabira appeared to want to be invisible in class, blending into the background as much as possible."

In meeting with Kabira, the counselor discovered that she was feeling socially out of place. Being unfamiliar with most of the video games, television shows, music, and musical groups discussed by her peers, she felt isolated and alone. She shared that a number of students made fun of her accent, her name, and even her manner of dress. All of which made her feel out of step and longing to return to Kenya.

Over the course of a couple of meetings, the counselor discovered two things. First, Kabira is an African name meaning "powerful," and second, this Kabira, whose father was a Kenyan Olympic long distance runner, was not only a talented cross country runner herself, but a talented dancer. Helping Kabira see her "power," as illustrated in her academic success and her previous success in dance and athletics, the counselor was able to encourage her to join the cross country and track teams, and sign up for the fall student talent event. Building on her strengths empowered her to engage socially with other students and eventually build the social support network that allowed her to feel a part of the high school community.

For some counselors, this focus on empowerment moves beyond the single client or the nature of their counseling relationships. Some counselors see empowerment in a broader light, as a process of effecting change for families, groups, and society as a whole. As such, counselors can be seen as proactively taking steps to advocate for those marginalized and disempowered, the communities served by professional counselors and the counseling profession itself (Myers, Sweeney, & White, 2002). Counselors will engage in activities that result in the procurement of resources and services for a client, while at the same time lobbying and advocating in support of the counseling profession. These are all illustrations of the advocacy value that pervades the profession and one's professional identity.

As a counselor-in-training, one way to embrace this empowerment perspective and engage in advocacy in support of the counseling profession is to become engaged with your local, state, regional, and national counseling organizations. Table 1.1 provides contact information for a number of those professional organizations advocating for counselors and counseling.

Although you may feel that joining a professional organization at this point in your education is a bit premature, it is not. Most of these organizations have student divisions and invite student involvement. You do not need to wait to be degreed to benefit from and be a benefit to these organizations. There are opportunities for you to give voice to the future of the counseling profession by engaging, for example, with the American Counseling Association (http://www.counseling.org/Students/RoleInACA/TP/Home/CT2.aspx) and/or the American School Counseling

Table 1.1 A Sampling of Professional Associations

Organization	*Mission*	*Website*	*Contact Information*
American Counseling Association	The mission of the American Counseling Association is to enhance the quality of life in society by promoting the development of professional counselors, advancing the counseling profession, and using the profession and practice of counseling to promote respect for human dignity and diversity. See more at http://www.counseling.org/about-us/about-aca/our-mission#sthash.NholLTUb.dpuf	http://www.counseling.org/	American Counseling Association 5999 Stevenson Ave. Alexandria, VA 22304 ACA Fax Number: (703) 823-0252 ACA Toll-Free Numbers: ACA: (800) 347-6647 FAX: (800) 473-2329
American College Counseling Association	ACCA is an association for those in higher education to include colleges, universities, community, and technical college settings, whose professional identity is counseling and whose purpose is fostering students' development.	http://www.collegecounseling.org/	Through website at http://www.collegecounseling.org/contact-acca
American School Counselor Association	The American School Counselor Association (ASCA) supports school counselors' efforts to help students focus on academic, personal/social, and career development so they achieve success in school and are prepared to lead fulfilling lives as responsible members of society.	http://www.schoolcounselor.org/	American School Counselor Association 1101 King St., Suite 625 Alexandria, VA 22314 (703) 683-ASCA Toll-free: (800) 306-4722 (703) 683-1619, fax
American Mental Health Counselors Associations	Its mission is to enhance the profession of clinical mental health counseling through licensing, advocacy, education, and professional development.	http://www.amhca.org/	American Mental Health Counselors Association 801 N. Fairfax Street, Suite 304 Alexandria, VA 22314 800-326-2642 or 703-548-6002
American Association of Pastoral Counselors	The mission of the American Association of Pastoral Counselors is to bring healing, hope, and wholeness to individuals, families,	http://www.aapc.org	9504A Lee Highway Fairfax, VA 22031-2303 info@aapc.org 703-385-6967 Fax: 703-352-7725

Organization	*Mission*	*Website*	*Contact Information*
	and communities by expanding and equipping spiritually grounded and psychologically informed care, counseling, and psychotherapy.		
American Rehabilitation Counseling Association	Its mission is to enhance the development of people with disabilities throughout their life span and to promote excellence in the rehabilitation counseling profession.	http://www.arcaweb.org/	President-Elect: Joseph Keferl, RhD, CRC Department of Human Services M052 Creative Arts Center 3640 Colonel Glenn Highway Dayton, OH 45435-0001 Office: (937) 775-2076 Office: (937) 775-2075 (general office) Fax: (937) 775-2042 Web: www.cehs.wright.edu/rehab/ E-mail: joseph.keferl@wright.edu
Additional national associations can be found at research website		http://research.udmercy.edu/find/by_subject/career.php?discipline_id=16&page_id=2&list_id=24	

Association (www.schoolcounselor.org) and the American Mental Health Counselors Association (http://www.amhca.org/become/student.aspx).

It is through participation in your profession and with other counseling professionals that your own professional identity as a counselor will take shape.

Nurturing Your Professional Identity

A counselor's professional identity is the emerging sense of self as a professional along with competency to perform within that professional role (Parsons & Zhang, 2014). It is the result of integrating professional training with personal attributes in the context of a professional community (Nugent & Jones, 2009), and it serves as a cognitive frame of reference for determining one's counseling role and responsibility. A counselor's evolving professional identity enables the counselor to articulate his or her role, philosophy, and approach to others within and outside of his or her chosen field.

While each counselor will develop his or her own unique professional identity by identifying his or her own operative theory or model and preferred strategies, these will need to be integrated with those values and assumptions that bind all counselors to the profession. This will be true for you. As you expand your knowledge and skill set through your field experience, it is equally important that you continue to embrace, assimilate, and embody the core set of values, beliefs, and assumptions that reflect the uniqueness of counseling as a profession. Exercise 1.4 invites you to begin this process of embodying the core perspectives of counseling in your field work.

EXERCISE 1.4

Engaging the Four Perspectives of Counseling

Directions: As you begin to identify the specific tasks, roles, and functions that define a counselor and counseling in your field placement, it is helpful to identify how the performance of these is colored by the unique values and perspectives shared by counselors.

Through observation and discussion with your site supervisor, identify five tasks, activities, and/or functions served by counselors at your site (e.g., individual counseling, group work, educational programming, political advocacy, etc.) and identify the ways the performance of these tasks do or could reflect the uniqueness that is counseling.

Tasks Performed	Developmental Component	Wellness Quality	Prevention Focus	Empowerment Engagement

Postscript

This chapter has highlighted some of the opportunities and challenges to be experienced during your field experience. It has described what is meant by professional identity and has identified the core elements to a counselor identity. Although the tasks outlined may seem daunting—with the implied demands for expansive knowledge and skill set, as well as the awesome responsibility of serving and assisting others—the one thing that may be lost in the discussion is that being a counselor is a gift. As counselors, being entrusted with the personal story of others and their invitation to journey with them through what might be a difficult time is not only a daunting responsibility but also a wonderful gift. It is important not to get lost in the paperwork, the assignments, the deadlines, and the noise of your field setting, such that you lose this sense of gift. And although it was not one of the pillars that we discussed as core to a counselor's professional identity, a sense of pride both in what you are doing and the profession within which you are identifying needs to be added to the formula of your professional identity.

It should be obvious that one's professional identity is evolving. This evolution is not only a reflection of each counselor's individual experience and unfolding perspectives on the profession but also the actual evolution of the profession itself. This development begins with the counselor's first experience in training and will continue throughout his or her professional career (Brott, 2006; Remley & Herlihy, 2007). Thus, while your own sense of self as professional may begin to truly emerge during your field experience, it is by far neither the only nor final version to be developed. Exercise 1.5 invites you to take a snapshot of your professional identity as you enter your field experience. It will be useful to revisit this snapshot and see how it evolves with your own expanding knowledge, competence, and experience as a counselor.

EXERCISE 1.5

An Evolving Professional Identity

Directions: As noted within the chapter, a counselor's professional identity will continue to evolve, adjust, and develop throughout his or her career. It is useful to note the direction of the evolution. As such, it is suggested that you complete the following and throughout the remainder of your academic career revisit your responses, adjusting where appropriate.

1. How would you respond to a family member or friend who asked the following: "What is the difference between a counselor and a psychologist?"
2. What models, theories, or operating assumptions do you currently employ when working with your clients?
3. For each of the following, describe the degree to which you personally value each as essential to your counseling practice and provide an example of where or how you have incorporated it within your practice.

   Developmental perspective:

   Wellness perspective:

   Prevention perspective:

   Empowerment perspective:
4. Over the course of the past 12 months, what, if any, engagement have you had with your local, state, regional, or national counseling organization(s)?
5. What one new insight have you acquired that has changed your view of counseling as a process and/or a profession?

KEYSTONES

- Contrasted to most classroom experiences, field experience occurs, by definition, in a unique, nonclassroom learning environment; employs unique performance requirements targeting application rather than acquisition of knowledge and skills; and presents unique challenges to and opportunities for professional growth and development and the formation of one's professional identity.
- During field experience, there is a shift in focus from knowing and understanding to doing and applying.
- The field as a learning environment is one in which the role of self-as-teacher emerges and is marked by an increased call for independent, self-directed learning; a shift in focus from grades to outcomes; and a pursuit of, rather than a retreat from, evaluation and corrective feedback.
- The "field" is an arena where the ideal of practice in the classroom meets the reality of day-to-day professional practice.
- Counselors can be defined by many measures, including credentials, roles assigned, and membership in various organizations. The most important definition of counselor comes from the self-perception of the one identified as counselor. Being able to articulate, value, and operate from a knowledge base, skill set, and philosophical perspective that distinguishes you from other helping professionals, while aligning you with those self-identified as counselors, is the core to one's professional identity.
- A counselor's professional identity reflects the personal assimilation of "a core set of values, beliefs, and assumptions about the unique characteristics of one's selected profession that differentiates it from other professions" (Weinrach, Thomas, & Chan, 2001, p. 168).
- Counselors are unique in that we approach our roles and functions guided by four fundamental perspectives: (a) a developmental perspective, (b) a wellness perspective, (c) a prevention perspective, and (d) an empowerment perspective.

ADDITIONAL RESOURCES

Calley, N. G., & Hawley, L. D. (2008). The professional identity of counselor educators. *The Clinical Supervisor, 27,* 3–16.

Granello, D., & Young, M. E. (2012). *Counseling today: Foundations of professional identity* [MyHelpingLab Series]. Columbus, OH: Merrill.

Nassar-McMillan, S., & Niles, S. C. (2010). *Developing your identity as a professional counselor: Standards, settings, and specialties*. Belmont, CA: Brooks-Cole.

REFERENCES

American Counseling Association. (2010). 20/20: Consensus definition of counseling. Retrieved from http://www.counseling.org/knowledge-center/20-20-a-vision-for-the-future-of-counseling/consensus-definition-of-counseling

American Counseling Association. (2014). *ACA code of ethics.* Retrieved from http://www.counseling.org/docs/ethics/2014-aca-code-of-ethics.pdf?sfvrsn=4

American Mental Health Counselors Association. (2010). Retrieved from https://www.amhca.org/assets/news/AMHCA_Code_of_Ethics_2010_w_pagination_cxd_51110.pdf

American School Counselor Association. (2010). *Ethical Principles for School Counselors.* Retrieved from http://www.schoolcounselor.org/files/EthicalStandards2010.pdf

Brott, P. (2006). Counselor education accountability: Training the effective professional school counselor. *Professional School Counseling, 10,* 179–188.

Daniels, L. G. (2002). The relationship between counselor licensure and aspects of empowerment. *Journal of Mental Health Counseling, 24*(3), 213–223.

Gordon, T. (2000). *Parent effectiveness training.* New York, NY: Three Rivers Press.

Myers, J. E., & Sweeney, T. J. (2004). Advocacy for the counseling profession: Results of a national survey. *Journal of Counseling and Development, 82,* 466–471.

Myers, J. E., & Sweeney, T. J. (2008). Wellness counseling: The evidence base for practice. *Journal of Counseling & Development, 86*(4), 482–493.

Myers, J. E., Sweeney, T. J., & White, V. E. (2002). Advocacy for counseling and counselors: A professional imperative. *Journal of Counseling and Development, 80,* 394–402.

Myers, J. E., Sweeney, T. J., & Witmer, J. M. (2000). The wheel of wellness counseling for wellness: A holistic model for treatment planning. *Journal of Counseling and Development, 78*(3), 251–266.

Myers, J. E., Sweeney, T. J., & Witmer, J. M. (2001). Optimization of behavior: Promotion of wellness. In D. C. Locke, J. E. Myers, & E. L. Herr (Eds.), *The handbook of counseling* (pp. 641–652). Thousand Oaks, CA: Sage.

Nugent, F. A., & Jones, K. D. (2009). *Introduction to the profession of counseling* (5th ed.). Upper Saddle River, NJ: Pearson.

Parsons, R. D., & Zhang, N. (2014). *Becoming a skilled counselor.* Thousand Oaks, CA: Sage.

Remley, T. P., & Herlihy, B. (2007). *Ethical, legal, and professional issues in counseling* (Updated 2nd ed.). Upper Saddle River, NJ: Pearson Merrill Prentice Hall.

Weinrach, S. G., Thomas, K. R., & Chan, F. (2001). The professional identity of contributors to the *Journal of Counseling & Development:* Does it matter? *Journal of Counseling and Development, 79,* 166–170.

Witmer, J. M., & Granello, P. F. (Eds.). (2005). *Counseling for wellness: Theory, research, and practice* (pp. 261–271). Alexandria, VA, US: American Counseling Association, 2005.

Zimmerman, M. A., & Warchausky, S. (1998). Empowerment theory for rehabilitation research: Conceptual methodological issues. *Rehabilitation Psychology, 43,* 3–16.

2

Matching Self to Site

Experience: the most brutal of teachers. But you learn, my God do you learn.

C. S. Lewis

The reflection by C. S. Lewis may not be something you want to read as you prepare to engage or reengage in field work. Experience can be a vehicle for learning—and yes, at times it can feel "brutal." But thoughtful selection and engagement in one's field experience can help to reduce the "brutality" and increase the learning and professional development provided.

For most students, their field experience will be their introduction to the world of the professional counselor and their real engagement with clients seeking counseling support. It is a time when that which has been learned and demonstrated in the confines of the classroom or university-based clinic will now be tested in the "real world."

Experience in the field will certainly test a student's knowledge and skill. But it is not about the testing of the student. Rather, the field is where one can develop the knowledge and hone the skills necessary for entrance into the profession. Thus, the selection of one's field experience needs to be done with a critical eye and thoughtful reflection. When approached reflectively, field experiences can be and need to be selected and tailored in a way that provides maximum growth.

It is incumbent upon students to reflect on their learning needs and to match those needs, that sense of their developing professional self, to the opportunities offered by any one site. Matching one's self to a field site is the focus of the current chapter. The material provided within this chapter will facilitate the reader's self-evaluation as a counselor-in-training and provide the tools for identifying sites that will offer maximum opportunity for development as a professional counselor.

Specifically, upon completion of this chapter, readers will be able to

- describe the areas of core knowledge and skill in which they would like to grow and develop as a result of their field experience;

- identify specific areas of knowledge and skill that they feel are fundamental to the professional engagement in their area of counseling specialization and in which they would like to have the opportunity to develop;
- apply specific criteria for the assessment of placement site possibilities; and
- identify placement sites that offer the greatest opportunity for their own professional growth and development.

It Starts With Self-Appraisal

Moving from the classroom to the field provides you with a wide variety of learning experiences and opportunities, but as noted above, to employ these experiences in a way that maximizes your professional growth requires an awareness of both your areas of professional strength and those areas where professional growth is needed. This awareness starts with an honest, valid self-appraisal.

As with all assessments or appraisals, a standard or criteria against which to judge current conditions is needed. The question to be answered prior to engaging in a self-appraisal is, "What level of knowledge and skills are fundamental to entry-level professional practice?" Whereas this question could be answered using a number of reference points, we have elected to employ standards articulated by the Council for Accreditation of Counseling and Related Educational Programs (CACREP, 2009) as well as those found in Draft #2 of the 2016 CACREP Standards (2014). The CACREP Standards were developed and promoted in an attempt "to ensure that students develop a professional counselor identity and master the knowledge and skills to practice effectively" (CACREP, 2009, p. 2) and, as such, appear useful as a measure against which to assess one's own current level of professional knowledge and skill. This is not to suggest that these are the only standards that could be employed as a reference for self-evaluation. However, it is our opinion that they present a comprehensive set of standards, and they are used by many training programs in the development of their curriculum. The CACREP standards provide a detailing of what can be considered as core knowledge and skills fundamental to effective practice as well as additional competencies demanded of those entering specific counseling specialties.

Core Knowledge and Skills

What follows is a brief description of the core or common areas of knowledge and skills identified by CACREP (2009, 2014) as fundamental for effective practice by all in the counseling profession. Following the brief descriptions of these eight core areas, you will find an exercise (Exercise 2.1) that will help you coordinate your self-evaluation across these core areas.

Professional Orientation

As a member of a profession, it is essential that one understands the diverse roles and functions served by those within that profession. It is also important that members of that profession understand and value those characteristics that help define their profession as unique. This is certainly true for all of us in counseling. Being able to define that which makes counseling as a profession and a practice unique from other forms of human helping service is evidence of one's competency in the area of professional orientation.

Specifically, those meeting this criterion can demonstrate knowledge of the history of counseling, its fundamental philosophical pillars (see Chapter 1), and the unique roles and functions served by the professional counselor. The counselor who meets the minimal competence in this area of professional orientation understands the availability and requirements for professional credentialing (e.g., certification and licensure); the nature and value of counseling supervision; the value of membership in professional organizations; the what, why, and how of advocating for the profession; and ways to manage self-care. One who can demonstrate competency in this area can demonstrate knowledge of the ethical code and legal considerations that guide practice decisions. Finally—and somewhat simplistically—one who can demonstrate competence in this area of professional orientation can answer the following questions: "What is counseling? "What is the difference between a counselor and a psychologist, psychiatrist, or social worker?" and "What makes counseling a profession?"

Human Growth and Development

Fundamental to effective practice as a counselor is an understanding of the nature and needs experienced by each of us at the various points in our human development. It is also essential for us to understand those factors that affect the development of normal and abnormal human behavior. Therefore, it is important for the professional counselor to understand theories describing and explaining transitions across the life span, as well as those explaining the process of learning and personality development. In addition to understanding the factors and processes involved in normal development, the competent counselor is knowledgeable of the factors contributing to the development of abnormal behavior, including the effects that trauma and crises can have on normal development. The counselor demonstrating competence in this core area understands not only the challenges to healthy human development and functioning but also theories and approaches for promoting optimal development and wellness.

Social and Cultural Foundations

Ours is a diverse and pluralistic society, and those seeking our service will reflect that diversity. The competent professional counselor understands and values the diversity of our culture and clientele and approaches professional practice with the knowledge of multicultural and pluralistic trends, theories of multicultural counseling, and strategies for working with and advocating for diverse populations. In addition to this understanding of diversity, the competent professional is also aware of his or her own attitudes, beliefs, and acculturative experiences as these differ from those of culturally diverse backgrounds.

Helping Relationship

Core to the counseling profession is the ability to help or assist another. This helping most often occurs in the context of a relationship, the helping relationship. This helping relationship is the foundation for the change of clients and consultees to occur, and it must be positive, productive, therapeutic, and treatment-outcome enhancing. Therefore, to be competent as a professional counselor requires one to be knowledgeable of the theories guiding practice as well as possess and employ those skills necessary for effectively facilitating client and consultee change. Specifically, an effective professional counselor will employ theory and research to guide his or her case conceptualization and treatment planning and engage those characteristics and skills that facilitate the creation and maintenance of the helping dynamic and process.

The effective counselor is knowledgeable and skilled in providing direct and consultative services with individuals, families, and various systems. He or she is skilled in psychological first aid strategies such as crisis intervention and suicide prevention, as well as programming for wellness and optimal growth and development.

Groups

A professional counselor will not only understand group development and dynamics but also possess the skills necessary for the facilitation of group functioning. Specifically, the professional counselor will understand the nature of group formation and functioning and employ group leadership and facilitation skills. The competent, effective professional counselor will be able to engage in group counseling methods when such methods are demonstrated to be effective modes of service.

Lifestyle and Career Development

Counseling, as a unique discipline and profession within the helping professions, has a rich history in the area of lifestyle and career development. Therefore, the competent professional counselor will have knowledge of career development theories; occupational and educational information sources and systems; career and leisure counseling theories and models; guidance and education paradigms; lifestyle and career decision-making processes and strategies; and career development program planning, resources, and evaluation.

Appraisal and Assessment

Knowledge and skills in the use of individual, group, and program assessment are essential to effective practice. Professional counselors will have the knowledge of and skills in psychometric theories and approaches to appraisal, data and information-gathering methods, issues of validity and reliability, psychometric statistics, factors influencing appraisals, and the use of appraisal results in helping processes.

Research and Evaluation

As a "young" profession, the knowledge/research base for our practice is continually evolving. The professional counselor needs to be able to be not only an informed consumer of that research but a valuable contributor to it. Specifically, a professional counselor needs to understand and value the importance of research in advancing the counseling profession. Further, the competent professional counselor is familiar with a variety of research methods, including qualitative, quantitative, single-case designs, action research, outcome-based research, and the various statistical methods used in conducting research and program evaluation.

As previously noted, these standards of core counseling competencies are those identified by one accrediting organization, CACREP (2009, 2014). These are not the only measure of one's professional competence or the only standard that could be used or developed. It is our belief, however, that they are intuitively appealing and quite inclusive. They appear widely accepted and many if not most universities cover these areas within their counselor training programs. It is for these reasons that we have selected to employ them as useful standards against which to invite you, the reader, to assess your own current state of competency.

Exercise 2.1 is provided as a tool to guide your self-assessment. It is recommended that you complete Exercise 2.1 as a way of identifying areas in which development is needed and desired. Knowing the specific areas of desired professional development can serve as a guide to your selection of a field experience. The field experience that will hold the highest value will be the one that offers you the greatest opportunity to not only employ the knowledge and skills that you have identified as strengths but also receive the corrective feedback and supervision essential to growth in those areas identified as targets for growth. Beyond this initial assessment, Exercise 2.1 may prove helpful throughout your professional career. Periodically returning to the checklist and engaging in an honest self-assessment will help you identify target areas for your ongoing professional development.

EXERCISE 2.1

Self-Assessment

Directions: Below you will find a listing of core competencies presented in the CACREP 2009 Standards. Your task is to assess your degree of mastery and identify areas that you would like to target for development during your field experience.

Area	**Specific Competency: Ability to . . .**	**Degree of Mastery: 5 = mastery, 0 = knowledge and skill absent**	**Targets for Professional Development Throughout Field Experience**
Professional Orientation	Identify professional roles and functions, including similarities and differences with other types of professionals.		
	Evaluate professional organizations, including membership benefits, activities, services to members, and current emphases.		
	Relate the history of the helping professions, including significant factors and events.		
	Demonstrate an understanding of ethical and legal standards; their evolution, methods, or change; and applications to various professional activities.		
	Compare professional preparation standards, their evolution, and current applications.		
	Value professional credentialing including certification and licensure, and accreditation including practices and standards.		
Human Growth and Development	Apply life-span theories of human development.		
	Demonstrate working knowledge of major theories of personality development and historical influencing factors.		

(Continued)

(Continued)

Area	Specific Competency: Ability to . . .	Degree of Mastery: 5 = mastery, 0 = knowledge and skill absent	Targets for Professional Development Throughout Field Experience
	Recognize and differentiate between normal and abnormal human behavior as well as identify the influence of psychological and sociological factors.		
	Apply major learning theories and recognize historical influencing factors.		
	Demonstrate working knowledge of cognitive-structural developmental theories concerned with moral, intellectual, and ethical development.		
Social and Cultural Foundations	Identify and define socioeconomic trends and changes in society, including sources of conflict, methods of conflict resolution, and responses to change.		
	Recognize and understand trends and changes in human roles, including traditional and nontraditional male and female roles and identify factors influencing role development and change.		
	Maintain ongoing familiarity with and sensitivity to multicultural and pluralistic trends, including characteristics and concerns of subgroups,		

Area	Specific Competency: Ability to . . .	Degree of Mastery: 5 = mastery, 0 = knowledge and skill absent	Targets for Professional Development Throughout Field Experience
	subgroup and societal interaction patterns, and methods of conflict resolution.		
	Identify major societal concerns, including stress; person abuse; substance abuse; discrimination on the basis of human characteristics such as age, race, religious preference, physical condition, sexual preference, ethnicity, or gender; and methods for alleviating these concerns.		
Helping Relationship	Demonstrate counselor or consultant characteristics and behaviors that influence helping processes, including gender and ethnic differences; verbal and nonverbal behaviors; and personal characteristics, orientations, and skills.		
	Demonstrate an understanding of client or consultee characteristics and behaviors that influence helping processes, including gender and ethnic differences, verbal and nonverbal behaviors and personal characteristics, traits, capabilities, and life circumstances.		
	Apply knowledge of those factors, other than participation, that influence		

(Continued)

(Continued)

Area	Specific Competency: Ability to . . .	Degree of Mastery: 5 = mastery, 0 = knowledge and skill absent	Targets for Professional Development Throughout Field Experience
	helping processes, including environmental and societal factors, relationships external to the helping process, and commitment to change.		
	Explain major counseling and consultation theories, including research and factors considered in application.		
	Explain major counseling and consultation theories, including research and factors considered in application.		
Groups	Demonstrate an understanding of principles of group dynamics, including group process components, developmental stage theories, and group members' roles and behaviors.		
	Differentiate group leadership styles and approaches, including characteristics of various types of group leaders and leadership styles.		
	Explain and assess theories of group counseling, including commonalities, distinguishing characteristics, and pertinent research and literature.		
	Demonstrate an understanding of group counseling methods, including group counselor orientations and behaviors,		

Area	Specific Competency: Ability to . . .	Degree of Mastery: 5 = mastery, 0 = knowledge and skill absent	Targets for Professional Development Throughout Field Experience
	ethical considerations, appropriate selection criteria and methods, and methods of evaluation of effectiveness.		
	Identify and assess other types of small-group approaches, theories, and methods.		
Lifestyle and Career Development	Explain major career and lifestyle development theories.		
	Identify career, avocational, and educational information systems, including local and national sources, print media, computer-assisted career guidance, and computer-based career information.		
	Integrate major career and lifestyle counseling, guidance and education theories, and implementation models.		
	Demonstrate an understanding of life-span career development and career counseling program planning.		
	Demonstrate an understanding of changing roles of women and men as related to career development and career counseling.		
	Evaluate interrelationships among work, family, and leisure.		

(Continued)

(Continued)

Area	Specific Competency: Ability to . . .	Degree of Mastery: 5 = mastery, 0 = knowledge and skill absent	Targets for Professional Development Throughout Field Experience
	Identify career development and lifestyle needs and career counseling resources and techniques applicable to special populations.		
	Manage career and educational placement, follow-up, and evaluation.		
	Integrate career and education decision-making theory.		
	Select assessment instruments relevant to career planning and decision making.		
Appraisal	Differentiate types of educational and psychological appraisal.		
	Integrate theoretical bases for appraisal techniques and methods of interpretation of appraisal data and information.		
	Demonstrate an understanding of validity, including methods of establishing content, construct, and empirical validity.		
	Demonstrate an understanding of reliability, including theory of measurement error, models of reliability, and the use of reliability information.		
	Use major appraisal methods, including environmental assessment, individual test		

Area	Specific Competency: Ability to . . .	Degree of Mastery: 5 = mastery, 0 = knowledge and skill absent	Targets for Professional Development Throughout Field Experience
	and inventory methods, behavioral observations, and computer-managed and computer-assisted methods.		
	Apply psychometric statistics, including types of test scores, measures of central tendency, indices of variability, standard errors, and correlations.		
	Integrate principles of appraisal data and information interpretations in helping processes.		
	Apply ethical and legal considerations in the use of appraisal data and information in helping processes.		
Research and Evaluation	Compare and contrast basic types of research.		
	Demonstrate an understanding of basic statistics.		
	Demonstrate principles of research proposal and report development and evaluation.		
	Integrate principles of needs assessment.		
	Integrate principles of program evaluation.		
	Demonstrate an understanding of ethical and legal considerations in research.		
	Identify uses of computers for data management and analysis.		

Beyond the Core: Specialty Knowledge and Skills

The American Counseling Association lists 20 divisions, which are organized around specific interest and practice areas (see http://www.counseling.org/about-us/divisions-regions-and-branches/divisions). This listing demonstrates the profession's interest in and ability to address the diverse needs of the counseling community. Whereas some of these divisions call together those sharing interests, a number reflect a group of professionals with unique training and credentialing. In 1995, the American Counseling Association's policies and procedures manual (American Counseling Association, 1995, p. 70), defined a specialty as officially recognized when it achieves either a specialty accreditation through the Council for Accreditation of Counseling and Related Educational Programs (CACREP) or the Council on Rehabilitation Education (CORE), or a certification through the National Board for Certified Counselors (NBCC) or the Commission on Rehabilitation Certification (CRCC). At that time, seven had been recognized by ACA. With the addition of addictions counseling, we can identify eight recognized specialties: addictions counseling, career counseling, college counseling, gerontological counseling, marriage and family counseling, mental health counseling, rehabilitation counseling, and school counseling.

The acquisition of certification in an area of specialization indicates that this counselor has experienced specialized training and experience in a particular area of professional counseling. Thus, in addition to general core competency, professional counselors who seek to specialize will need to meet additional training and experience standards. Table 2.1 provides links to credentialing bodies that list requirements needed for certification.

Table 2.1 Credentialing Bodies and Requirements:Specializations in Counseling

Specialization	*Credentialing Body*	*Link*
Addictions Counselor	The Association for Addiction Specialist	http://naadac.org/certification
Marriage and Family Counseling	American Association for Marriage and Family Counselors (AAMFT)	http://www.aamft.org/iMIS15/AAMFT/Content/About_AAMFT/Qualifications.aspx
Mental Health Counselor	American Mental Health Counselors Association	http://www.amhca.org/about/related.aspx
Nationally Certified Counselor	National Board of Certified Counselors	http://www.nbcc.org/certification
School Counselor Certification	General requirements listed by American School Counselor Association but state specific requirements can be acquired at the licensing board website for the state in which one is employed	http://www.schoolcounselor.org/school-counselors-members/careers-roles/state-certification-requirements
Rehabilitation Counselor	Commission on Rehabilitation Counselor Certification	http://www.crccertification.com/pages/rehabilitation_counseling/30.php

Credentialing Specialties

Whereas the actual credentialing of these specialties is most often controlled by the professional organizations representing that specialty and typically focus on post-master's supervised experience, the fundamental knowledge and skills required prior to that post-master's experience has been articulated by organizations such as CACREP, who set the standards for the following specialty areas: addictions counseling, career counseling, school counseling, and clinical mental health counseling. Exercise 2.2 provides a sampling of the skills identified by CACREP (2009, 2014) as fundamental for each of these specialty areas. The exercise invites you to assess your current level of proficiency in skills identified as fundamental to your specialization. The insight gained by completing Exercise 2.2 in combination with the awareness you gained by completing Exercise 2.1 will help direct you to field placement experiences that will meet your needs for professional development.

EXERCISE 2.2

Self-Assessment: Specialty Area

Directions: The following reflects modification of a small sampling of the skills identified by CACREP (2009) as fundamental to each of the specialty areas listed. A full listing of both the knowledge and skills identified as fundamental to each of the specialty areas can be downloaded at http://www.cacrep.org, under the section called "resources."

Your task is to identify your specialty area and assess your degree of mastery for the skills listed. This self-assessment, along with the assessment of your core competencies, can help highlight those areas that you would like to target for development during your field experience.

Specialty Area	**Specific Competency: Ability to . . .**	**Degree of Mastery 5 = mastery, 0 = knowledge and skill absent**	**Targets for Professional Development Throughout Field Experience**
Addictions			
	Is capable of individualizing helping strategies and treatment modalities to each client's stage of dependence, change, or recovery.		
	Can provide appropriate counseling strategies when working with clients with addiction and co-occurring disorders.		
	Has the ability to use procedures for assessing and managing suicide risk.		

(Continued)

(Continued)

Specialty Area	Specific Competency: Ability to . . .	Degree of Mastery 5 = mastery, 0 = knowledge and skill absent	Targets for Professional Development Throughout Field Experience
	Can provide counseling and education about addictive disorders to families and others who are affected by clients with addictions.		
	Is able to provide referral to self-help and other support groups when appropriate.		
	Can provide culturally relevant education programs that raise awareness and support addiction and substance abuse prevention and the recovery process.		
	Can adjust counseling systems, theories, techniques, and interventions to make them culturally appropriate for diverse populations of addiction clients.		
	Has the skill necessary for conducting an intake interview, a mental status evaluation, a biopsychosocial history, a mental health history, and a psychological assessment for treatment planning and case management.		
	Is capable of employing diagnostic tools, including the current edition of the DSM, to describe the symptoms and clinical presentation of clients with addictive disorders and mental and emotional impairments.		
	Is able to conceptualize an accurate diagnosis of disorders presented by clients and communicate the differential diagnosis with collaborating professionals.		

Career Counseling			
	Has the ability to identify and understand clients' personal, family, and cultural characteristics related to their career development.		
	Is able to assist clients in the acquisition of a set of employability and job search skills.		
	Can establish and maintain a consulting relationship with persons who can influence a client's career.		
	Has the ability to make accommodations for career needs unique to multicultural and diverse populations.		
	Can explain, articulate, and advocate for the importance of career counseling, career development, life-work planning, and workforce planning to legislators, other policymakers, and/or the general public.		
	Is able to administer, score, and appropriately report findings from career assessment instruments involving issues such as leisure interests, learning style, life roles, self-concept, career maturity, vocational identity, career indecision, work environment preference (e.g., work satisfaction), and other related life-career development issues.		
	Can analyze and utilize data to increase the effectiveness of career counseling programs and interventions.		
	Is capable of implementing career development programs in collaboration with others.		
	Knows the community/professional resources available to assist clients in career planning, including job search.		
	Can initiate and implement a marketing and public relations campaign on behalf of career development activities and services.		

(Continued)

(Continued)

Clinical Mental Health Counseling			
	Is capable of applying knowledge of public mental health policy, financing, and regulatory processes to improve service delivery opportunities in clinical mental health counseling.		
	Can apply multicultural competencies to clinical mental health counseling involving case conceptualization, diagnosis, treatment, referral, and prevention of mental and emotional disorders.		
	Is able to apply effective strategies to promote client understanding of and access to a variety of community resources.		
	Can use culturally responsive individual, couple, family, group, and systems modalities for initiating, maintaining, and terminating counseling.		
	Is capable of providing appropriate counseling strategies when working with clients with addiction and co-occurring disorders.		
	Can modify counseling systems, theories, techniques, and interventions to make them culturally appropriate for diverse populations.		
	Can identify and employ standard screening and assessment instruments for substance use disorders and process addictions.		
	Is able to select appropriate comprehensive assessment interventions to assist in diagnosis and treatment planning, with an awareness of cultural bias in the implementation and interpretation of assessment protocols.		

Clinical Mental Health Counseling			
	Can employ skills of conducting an intake interview, a mental status evaluation, a biopsychosocial history, a mental health history, and a psychological assessment for treatment planning and caseload management.		
	Is able to conceptualize an accurate diagnosis of disorders presented by a client and discuss the differential diagnosis with collaborating professionals.		

Marriage, Couple, and Family Counseling			
	Has the ability to select models or techniques appropriate to couples' or families' presenting problems.		
	Is able to use preventive, developmental, and wellness approaches in working with individuals, couples, families, and other systems, such as premarital counseling, parenting skills training, and relationship enhancement.		
	Can use systems theory to conceptualize issues in marriage, couple, and family counseling.		
	Is able to use systems theories to implement treatment, planning, and intervention strategies.		
	Can provide effective services to clients in a multicultural society.		
	Has the ability to modify counseling systems, theories, techniques, and interventions to make them culturally appropriate for diverse couples and families.		

(Continued)

(Continued)

Marriage, Couple, and Family Counseling			
	Can employ systems assessment models and procedures to evaluate family functioning.		
	Has the ability to determine which members of a family system need to be involved in treatment.		
	Can analyze and use data to increase the effectiveness of marriage, couple, and family counseling interventions and programs.		

School Counseling			
	Can provide individual and group counseling and classroom guidance to promote the academic, career, and personal/social development of students.		
	Is capable of designing and implementing prevention and intervention plans related to the effects of (a) atypical growth and development, (b) health and wellness, (c) language, (d) ability level, (e) multicultural issues, and (f) factors of resiliency on student learning and development.		
	Possesses multicultural competencies in relation to diversity, equity, and opportunity in student learning and development.		
	Can engage parents, guardians, and families to promote the academic, career, and personal/social development of students.		
	Is capable of advocating for school policies, programs, and services that enhance a positive school climate and are equitable and responsive to multicultural student populations.		

School Counseling			
	Can plan and present school-counseling-related educational programs for use with parents and teachers (e.g., parent education programs, materials used in classroom guidance, and advisor/advisee programs for teachers).		
	Is able to analyze assessment information in a manner that produces valid inferences when evaluating the needs of individual students and assessing the effectiveness of educational programs.		
	Is able to implement strategies and activities to prepare students for a full range of postsecondary options and opportunities.		
	Can consult with teachers, staff, and community-based organizations to promote student academic, career, and personal/social development.		
	Is able to engage in the design, implementation, management, and evaluation of a comprehensive developmental school counseling program.		

Student Affairs and College Counseling			
	Is able to apply knowledge of issues that affect student affairs practice (e.g., public policy, finance, governance, cultural contexts, international education, and global understanding).		
	Is capable of participating in the design, implementation, management, and evaluation of student affairs programs,		

(Continued)

(Continued)

Student Affairs and College Counseling			
	and is aware of various systems and environmental contexts that affect participants.		
	Can apply multicultural competencies to the practice of student affairs and college counseling.		
	Possesses the skills necessary for postsecondary students coping with personal and interpersonal problems, as well as skills in crisis intervention in response to personal, educational, and community crises.		
	Is capable of participating in the design, implementation, and evaluation of programs that promote wellness, as well as prevention and intervention services for students in postsecondary education.		
	Can address multicultural counseling issues as they relate to student development and progress in postsecondary education (e.g., discrimination, power, privilege, oppression, and values).		
	Is able to analyze and employ multiple data sources, including institutional data, to make decisions about improving differentiated student programs.		
	Has the ability to prepare a research proposal for a human subjects/ institutional review board review.		
	Can analyze and use data to enhance student affairs and college counseling programs.		
	Is able to apply relevant research findings to inform the practice of student affairs and college counseling.		

Assessing Field Placement Options

Field experiences will vary as a function of the site, the population served, the mission, the policies and procedures employed, and of course the parties involved (student and supervisor). However, even with this as a caveat, it is safe to say that there are a couple of bare-bones elements to a field experience that need to be in place in order for that experience to be educational and formative in nature.

At its core, an effective field experience is one that consists of properly administered, planned, structured, sequential, and professionally supervised training experiences. Students serving in a field experience are not simply cheap labor or administrative assistants. They are students and have the right to engage in activities that are truly educative and formative in nature. As you investigate field placement possibilities and start your practicum or internship, this opportunity for educational and professional formational experience needs to be considered. Beyond providing generic educational experiences, a formative field experience would be characterized by a depth, breadth, duration, frequency, and intensity of experience tailored to the individual needs of the student in order to allow for the maximum development of the student and his or her integration of academic knowledge, professional attitudes, and professional skills.

The search for a proper placement can be daunting. Anxiety to secure a spot may direct one to simply jump at the first opportunity presented. It is essential, however, that the student remembers that field experience is not simply a thing to do or a check-off on the list of degree requirements. Field experience provides an abbreviated immersion into the world of professional practice. It is an opportunity to experience the tasks, functions, demands, and challenges encountered by the professional counselor. As such, the field experience is core to one's preparation for the profession. The effective field experience is one that will foster counselor development, as professional (Pate, 2010). Approaching the selection of one's field placement with a realization of its value as a pivotal element to one's professional formation will direct the searcher to take the time to gather the data needed to assess the options available and select one that best services his or her professional needs. Whereas there are specific elements to consider in selecting a field placement site, elements to be discussed later within this chapter, it is important to remember that the effective placement will

1. promote the integration of academic knowledge with practical experience by challenging the student to apply and extend the knowledge, skills, and attitudes learned in the program's didactic and classroom-based experiential components to produce increasingly sophisticated levels of understanding and skill (Hatcher & Lassiter, 2007);

2. facilitate the student's development of professional competencies that would be necessary for entry-level practice; and as noted in Chapter 1,

3. serve as the springboard for the development of the student's professional identity as a counselor by immersing the student in the counseling culture, putting him or her into the role and function of a counselor as enacted within that site, and providing interaction with other counselors, as well as other mental health professionals (Harper & Ritchie, 2009).

Thus, when searching for the "ideal" site, you will want to seek that placement that will provide opportunity to both demonstrate and expand on professional strengths while at the same time increasing competency in areas of professional challenge. It would be comfortable and relatively stress free to find an experience that allows you to stay within your comfort zone, performing only tasks and functions for which you feel fully qualified. However, without some testing of your limits and stretching of your capabilities, within the context of qualified supervision, growth will not be possible.

Site Characteristics: Specifics to Consider

The options for placement can be wide and vast depending on your location and your university's policies. Counselors can be found functioning within settings as varied as schools, mental health clinics, substance abuse treatment centers, hospitals, university student centers, and women's shelters, to identify but a few. The specific setting—with its unique characteristics—will affect the client population to be served, the types of presenting issues typically experienced, and the nature of services provided (Ponton, 2009). As such, setting characteristics need to be considered when selecting a site for one's field experience.

Although it is impossible to know exactly what to expect prior to engaging within a field placement site, there are certain factors that can and need to be identified as a way of developing a site profile and an expectation of what the site may have to offer as a learning experience. To develop a meaningful profile, it is helpful to gather information on each of the following.

Accreditation

As is true for graduate training programs, some field placement sites have sought out and received accreditation by a national or international organization as a way of demonstrating their commitment to quality and their upholding of articulated standards. Working in an accredited field site may increase the possibility that the student will have a valuable training experience and may, by the fact that the site was accredited, add value to one's résumé. This is not to suggest that sites that are not certified or accredited by national or international agencies should be avoided, or are to be assumed to provide inferior training opportunities. It is possible that those sites have chosen, for a variety of non-clinical and non-educational reasons, not to apply for accreditation, or they may simply not have an accrediting body available to sanction such approval. The following is a sample of the types of accreditation that a setting may seek.

For those seeking placement in a school setting (elementary, middle, or high school), it may be desirable to investigate schools that employ the ASCA model (http://www.ascanationalmodel.org/) and have achieved the Recognized ASCA Model Program (RAMP) designation from the American School Counselor Association. For those working in health care settings, it would be desirable to be sure that the setting has received accreditation by the Joint Commission (www.jointcommission.org), which is an agency that provides accreditation status to health-care organizations that comply with their standards of patient care. For those engaged in addiction and substance abuse work or rehabilitation counseling, the Commission of Accreditation of Rehabilitation Facilities (www.carf.org) is the organization that would provide the accreditation for settings seeking accreditation in these areas of specialization. Finally, students seeking placement in a college or university counseling center may investigate whether those centers have received accreditation through the International Association of Counseling Services (www.iacsinc.org).

Mission

Although it may seem obvious, knowing why the site exits and what drives its service is essential to selecting a valuable educational placement. The reason for a system's existence is often articulated in that organization's mission statement. Through a review of an organization's mission statement, one can gain insight into (a) the uniqueness of the organization, (b) the services provided, and (c) the specific population or "market" served. An organization's mission statement provides a brief overview into that which distinguishes this organization, this system, this agency from others of a similar nature. What is important for those thinking about a specific placement is that the role and function of a counselor, or, for that matter, anyone who works in that setting, would have been crafted to meet the needs, goals, and uniqueness of that organization's mission. For example, counselors who are working in a setting that espouses the promotion of wellness within a specific population can be assured that they will be engaged in tasks and services of a preventive, developmental, and wellness nature. This could be contrasted to counselors who are working in a setting where the mission is to provide short-term crises interventions. In this setting, the counselor's role and duties may be focused on crises intervention and triage work with limited opportunity for the provision of developmental services or activities.

It is not only the counselor's role and function that will be colored by the agency's mission. Just as a counselor's role and function will have been defined as it services the organization's mission, so will the policies and procedures unique to that setting be mission focused. Thus, when seeking a setting for maximum growth, a review of the organization's mission statement will provide a quick, initial data point from which to glean the type of professional experience to be encountered while engaging in field work at that setting. Exercise 2.3 invites you to analyze the possible role and functions of counselors working in two different settings.

EXERCISE 2.3

Analyzing a Mission Statement

Directions: As you begin to search for field placement sites that have the highest potential for fostering your professional development, it is important to understand the unique purpose for which a particular site exists. A mission statement can provide insight into the reason for a site's existence, the population it hopes to serve, and even the values that direct the services provided.

(Continued)

(Continued)

Sample Mission (to be used as a model throughout the exercise)
XYZ counseling center develops and provides quality, outcome-based services that enhance the emotional strength and well-being of Happyville residents throughout their lives by

- providing counseling, prevention, and education to resolve personal and interpersonal issues through traditional and specialty services;
- identifying, evaluating, and responding to community needs through innovative services;
- encouraging community collaboration and partnerships through leadership and advocacy; and
- promoting quality of care and best practices in our community by providing consultation, education, and training.

Using the example as a model, your task is the following:

a. Identify the general area in which you are seeking placement (i.e. school, mental health, addictions, student services, etc.). (*Sample: Community Counseling Centers*)

b. Select two possible placement sites within your area of specialization and acquire their mission statements. *(Sample: XYZ Counseling Center)*

c. For each mission statement, extract the answers to the following questions:

   1. Population(s) served (consider implications of demographics, diversity etc.)

      (Sample: residents of Happyville, upper middle and highly mobile community, 97% Caucasian, 3% African American)

   2. Goals (reflects the consumer needs being addressed)

      (Sample: to enhance the emotional strength and well-being– valuing prevention and growth)

   3. Services (suggest role and function to be served by counselor)

      (Sample: intervention, prevention, educative, and advocacy)

   4. Value indicators (what does the organization value or hold as valued?)

      (Sample: outcome-based services–valuing effectiveness and accountability)

d. Develop hypotheses regarding the role and function of counselors in the settings as well as possible limitations to role and function.

   (Sample: Function in both remedial/intervention and preventive services; question possibility of engaging in long-term, dynamic forms of therapy?)

e. Interview a counselor or administrator at each site to test your hypotheses regarding role and function focus and limitations.

f. Use these data to identify the site most likely to provide the opportunity for you to develop your knowledge and skills as a school counselor.

Population Served

In addition to understanding the organization's mission and its basic reason for existence, it is important to know for whom it exits or what population it services. Having an understanding of the typical clientele served by a field placement site is also critical to the selection of an "ideal" site.

On first reflection, the issue of population served may seem obvious and easily compartmentalized. For example, a counselor who is interested in working in the school not only understands that the clientele will consist primarily of school-aged children, but may even discern further the services he or she offers as being geared to students at the elementary school, middle school, or senior high levels. But this identification of the population to be served needs to move beyond the obvious and drill down beyond gross levels of distinction. For example, within the broad groupings of school-aged children (e.g. elementary, middle, or secondary schools), one can find further client characterizations such as students "at risk"; students with exceptionalities; students presenting with normative, developmental issues; students seeking career and post–high school guidance; or perhaps students manifesting more serious psychoemotional difficulties. This same process of discernment is needed for those engaging in field placement in mental health, rehabilitation, addiction, and marriage/family counseling. Questions to be answered include the following: Is the setting one servicing inpatient, outpatient, or both populations? Is the setting targeting a specific age group or groups? Is the setting working with broad-based presenting issues (e.g., mental health, relationship issues, etc.) or more narrow and specific forms of presenting complaint (e.g., mood disorder, anger issues, etc.)? Is the agency a private, fee-for-service setting, or a public, community agency? Knowing the nature of the typical caseloads serviced by the counselors at any one possible site will be helpful in the identification and selection of a site that will afford the learning experience desired.

In addition to gathering data about the number of clients served and the types and frequency of issues presented, a review of a potential field placement site needs to include information regarding the level of diversity reflected within the agency and among those served. The presence of and experience with diverse populations is essential for the development of your multicultural competencies. Considering client socioeconomic status, religion, culture, race, ethnicity, and sexual orientation—especially as these differ from your own—will allow you to consider your current levels of knowledge and skill as they reflect your ability to be of service to the clients served by that agency. Further, these data will also help you identify opportunities to expand your knowledge and skill by working with a diverse population under the auspices of a qualified supervisor.

The issue of population served targets not only the demographic information such as age, gender, socioeconomic status, and diversity but also the configuration of the population served, including individuals, couples, families, groups, organizations, and even communities. Many students seeking professional development may feel that their preparation in working with families is lacking and needs assistance; or perhaps their calling is toward community advocacy and they wish to engage in processes that facilitate change in groups, organizations, or communities. Understanding the population to be served within any one field placement site, even when viewed in the broadest sense of that term, will help you identify sites that will maximize your development.

Services Provided

Throughout your course work, you may have studied a number of services that are provided by professional counselors. Counselors engage in a wide variety of service in support of their clients. These services include such things as assessment, treatment (individual, family, and group), consultation, management, coaching, administration, supervision, education, advocacy, program development, and evaluation. While all of these services fall within the professional realm of a counselor, not all counselors—at all sites—provide all of these services. Thus, knowing which services are provided at any one site serves as an additional data point for guiding your selection of the "ideal" site.

Models and Theories

In addition to knowing the types of services offered, understanding the preferred model or theory of service delivery is needed when selecting a potential field placement site. Do counselors within the setting operate from multiple models and theories or is there a preferred, even prescribed approach? Perhaps you feel an alignment with a particular theory of counseling (e.g. behavioral, dynamic, humanistic, cognitive, relational, family/systems, etc.) or a specific modality of service delivery (individual, group, consultative, preventive, etc.). Knowing the model, theory, and modality employed within a particular setting will again prove beneficial to your selection of an ideal site.

Issues Addressed

As an extension of the analyses of the characteristics of the population served, it is important to know if the counselors within any one setting are generalists, addressing various life issues confronting their clients, or if they are specialized and narrow in issues addressed. There is a difference between the professional experience of those working in hospital settings targeting clients with eating disorders and those at psychiatric centers, where the clientele generally present with major mood and anxiety disorders, as well as those working in community centers, where adjusting to life challenges of work, family, and health take center stage. For students seeking to develop the knowledge and skills necessary to assist those in career transition, placement in an addictions center or hospital setting, while certainly educative, would most likely not provide the experience necessary to foster the development desired. Thus, identifying the typical issues addressed and services provided is pivotal to your selection process.

The identification of an ideal site requires research and reflection. There is quite a bit of information about a potential field site that needs to be gathered and considered in the discernment process. Exercise 2.4 is offered as a way of helping you begin this process of site profiling.

EXERCISE 2.4

Site Profile

Directions: As you begin to research possible sites for your field experience, it would be useful to gather the following specific information for quick comparing and contrasting. Your task is to gather the data necessary to complete the following table.

Name of Site	Essential Mission Elements	Population(s) Served	Services Provided	Theories and Modalities Guiding Service	Issues Typically Presented

What to Expect

Although it is important to profile the characteristics of the site in terms of purpose, goals, services, and culture, it is just as important to profile the experience you can anticipate as a student functioning within that setting. In addition to gathering information about the opportunities you will be afforded as a counselor-in-training, as well as the support and supervision you can anticipate, it is important to assess the degree to which you will be comfortable with those with whom you will be working. Thus, the analyses of potential field placement sites need to include data collection on each of the following: level of responsibility/autonomy required, quality of supervision provided, and level of work, cultural, and personal compatibility.

Level of Responsibility

While your goal and that of your university and site supervisors is to foster your development of professional competencies, this is done with primary concern given to the well-being of the clients you serve. Consequently, it is to be expected that you will initially engage with clients under restricted and closely supervised conditions. This may initially feel somewhat constraining and frustrating. It is important for you to remember that this is the real world, with real clients, who need and expect assistance and, as such, your supervisors are ethically bound to provide for their safety and well-being.

With your development and demonstration of increasing knowledge and skill, you will experience increasing autonomy in role enactment. Settings that either fail to support this increasing autonomy or that initially provide too much independence are not fertile grounds for professional development and should not be considered among the list of ideal sites to be considered.

Site Supervisor

The site supervisor plays an essential role in making the field experience beneficial and growth filled. The supervisor's insightful comments and corrective feedback are invaluable in the promotion of a student's professional development (see Chapter 6: Counseling Supervision).But, it is not only the supervisory feedback that is essential for a student's development. The site supervisor is truly a model and a mentor. He or she stands as the tangible representative of counseling and "the counselor" in that field placement site. He or she is the teacher at the moment and the student will learn much through simple observation. Therefore, it is important to have a supervisor who is not only competent but also clearly available and approachable.

Those who serve as site supervisors, regardless of whether this activity is part of their formal role and function or truly an addition to that job and function, are generously sharing their workday. The presence of a field student, especially during the initial stages of his or her field experience, adds to rather than diminishes the workload for supervisors. Thus, while respecting their contribution to your development, it is important to know that they have the time, the energy, the interest, and the opportunity to make themselves available to you in light of all that they do. It is important that the supervisor not only allows the student to observe what he or she does and provide corrective feedback on what the student does, but also has given time and energy to the structuring of experiences uniquely crafted to foster that student's knowledge and skill, thus leading to increased autonomy of function. Information regarding the skills and availability of a particular supervisor may be acquired by talking to your campus advisor, field placement coordinator, or even your peers/colleagues who have worked within a particular setting.

In addition to considering issues of supervisor availability, approachability and planning, it is helpful to consider each of the following when considering a site and a supervisor for your field placement experience.

Theoretical Orientation

A counselor's theoretical orientation colors the way that counselor conceptualizes a case and proceeds with treatment planning and implementation. Observing a counselor at work is, by definition, observing that counselor's enactment of his or her theoretical model or operating framework. Consequently, it is important to know the supervisor's theoretical orientation. This knowledge will allow you to select that supervisor whose approach is the one you wish to develop or at minimum whose approach will provide you with the framework for understanding the supervisor's professional actions and decisions.

Training and Experience

Being a competent practitioner does not automatically translate into being an effective supervisor. While there are a variety of standards that could be employed in assessing the competency of one to do supervision, a relatively simple list of minimal credentials has been identified by the Council for Accreditation of Counseling and Related Education Programs (2009, 2014). Gathering information about the training and experience of your potential supervisor and contrasting it to the standards described by CACREP (2009, p. 15) may prove beneficial to your decision regarding a particular site:

1. A minimum of a master's degree in counseling or a related profession with equivalent qualifications, including appropriate certifications and/or licenses.
2. A minimum of 2 years of pertinent professional experience in the program area in which the student is enrolled.
3. Knowledge of the program's expectations, requirements, and evaluation procedures for students.
4. Relevant training in counseling supervision.

Comfort and Compatibility

One's relationship with a site supervisor often parallels that of client to counselor, and characteristics of a supervisor found to promote working alliances with supervisees are similar to those identified as facilitating a working alliance in a counseling relationship, a point to be developed in Chapter 6. It appears, however, that supervisors who are identified as nonjudgmental, providing validation, supporting exploration, imparting an empathic attitude, and normalizing anxiety and tension, are more effective in strengthening a working alliance than those described as rigid, overly critical, lacking respect and openness, and lacking encouragement and praise (Nelson & Friedlander, 2001; Ramos-Sánchez et al., 2002). As with counselors, supervisors who convey a sense of being trustworthy, affirming, flexible, interested, alert, relaxed, confident, respectful, and clear communicators encourage the development of a positive alliance (Ackerman & Hilsenroth, 2003) and invite a supervisee's willingness to risk vulnerability in hopes of experiencing growth. Assessing a potential supervisor along these dimensions will not be easy. Impressions drawn at the time of initial inquiry or interview are not always indicative or valid. Perhaps a better source of information would be peer and collegial feedback.

Matching Self to Site: Targeting Professional Development

Knowing what a site offers is but one step in the process of selecting an ideal field placement site. Implied throughout the previous section is that it is important to know not only the unique profile of the agency that is needed but also how that profile blends with your own professional developmental needs.

We are not naïve. We understand that there are many demands, many drains, and many tugs on your time and energies. It could be easy and attractive to simply take the first placement offered, or to choose a site based on ease of location or history of placing low demands on interns. What needs to be highlighted is that the value of one's field placement for fostering professional development cannot be overemphasized.

Your field experience not only provides you with the opportunity to serve in a professional role and develop that knowledge and hone those skills that are the hallmarks of a professional counselor but also is your initiation as a member of our profession. Matching your needs, your professional goals and your emerging professional identity to the unique learning and developmental opportunities to be found within your ideal setting takes work. But it is work that is well worthwhile and offering an invaluable payoff. Don't cheat yourself. Don't take a shortcut or the easy route. Do your research. Do your reflections. Engage with those offering their support to you and your decision. You will be glad you did.

As we finish this chapter, we offer you one more exercise (Exercise 2.5). It is time to roll up your sleeves and get to work! So let's begin.

EXERCISE 2.5

Securing a Site

Directions: The following is offered as a checklist to guide your process of securing the ideal field placement. It is suggested that you establish timelines and maintain notes on outcomes for each stage.

Focus	Timeline to Complete	Notes
Start yesterday: With an eye to the developmental value of your field experience, it is important for you to begin to consider the nature of the services, the population served, the organizational mission and structure, and the types of supervision available, starting with your first graduate course. As you proceed through the prerequisite experience, you may want to note areas of strength you can expand upon, as well as areas of your knowledge and skill base that you know need further development. These can serve as goals for your field experience and guide your selection.		

Research: a. Departmental sites: Often your department will have a listing of previously approved sites.		
b. Colleagues as resources: Talk to those in the field. Get the lived experience from them. Consider dialoguing with those in other training programs.		
c. Complete site profiles (see Exercise 2.1).		
d. Connection and networking: 1. Identify contacts and call or e-mail a cover letter of interest and your résumé and then follow up. 2. Visit sites.		
Prepare to be interviewed and to interview: a. Create a resume and statement of professional identity. b. Develop your own list of questions, including the practical (e.g., hours, days, and task), resources available (e.g., video/audio equipment, inservices, and training), guidance (e.g., supervision and opportunities to observe), and practice (e.g., number and types of clients and client services you will be able to engage).		

KEYSTONES

- One's field experiences can be and need to be selected and tailored in a way that provides maximum growth.
- Selecting one's field site should be guided by a self-assessment of one's level of knowledge and skill in each of the following core areas: professional orientation, human growth and development, social and cultural foundation, helping relationship, groups, lifestyle and career development, appraisal and assessment, and research and evaluation.
- In addition to assessing one's level of competency in the core areas, it is important to assess strengths and areas for development in the knowledge and skill required by one's specialization area.
- In considering a site for a possible field placement, one needs to consider the degree that the experience to be gained at the site will help

  a. promote the integration of academic knowledge with practical experience by challenging the student to apply and extend the knowledge, skills, and attitudes learned in the program's didactic and classroom-based experiential components to produce increasingly sophisticated levels of understanding and skill (Hatcher & Lassiter, 2007);

  b. facilitate the student's development of professional competencies that would be necessary for entry-level practice; and as noted in Chapter 1,

   c. serve as the springboard for the development of the student's professional identity as a counselor by immersing the student in the counseling culture, stepping into the role and function of a counselor as enacted within that site, and also interacting with other counselors, as well as other mental health professionals (Harper & Ritchie, 2009).

- Factors to be considered when assessing the potential value of a particular site include specific mission, population served, service provided, models and approaches employed, typical issues presented by clients, and any accreditation awarded the site.
- In addition to assessing the site profile, it is important to gather information regarding the resources that will be made available to the student, including levels of responsibility and autonomy, the nature and quality of supervision, and the overall compatibility and comfort level of student to site.

ADDITIONAL RESOURCES

Web Based

Association of Multicultural Counseling and Development: http://www.multiculturalcounseling.org/
Commission of Accreditation of Rehabilitation Facilities: http://www.carf.org
Commission on Rehabilitation Certification (CRCC): http://www.crccertification.com/
Council on Rehabilitation Education (CORE): http://www.core-rehab.org/
International Association of Counseling Services: www.iacsinc.org
Joint Commission: www.jointcommission.org
National Board for Certified Counselors (NBCC): http://www.nbcc.org/

Print Based

Baird, B. B. (2014). *Internship, practicum, and field placement handbook* (7th ed.). Upper Saddle River, NJ: Pearson.

Brandt, M. A., & Porteus A. J. (2009). Maximizing continuity of pedagogy in exemplary school-based practicum. In R. L. Astramovich (Ed.), *ACES Spectrum, 69*(3), 35–39.

Carlozzi, A. F., Romans, J. S. C., Boswell, D. L., Ferguson, D. B., & Whisenhunt, B. J. (1997). Training and supervision practices in counseling and marriage and family therapy programs. *Clinical Supervisor, 15*(1), 51–60.

Jordan, K., & Kelly, W. E. (2004). Beginning practicum students' worries: A qualitative investigation. *Counseling and Clinical Psychology Journal, 1*(4), 100–105.

Tryon, G. S. (1996). Supervisee development during the practicum year. *Counselor Education and Supervision, 35*(4), 287–294.

Walter, S. M., & Lambie, G. W. (2009). The counseling internship: Supervision experience, developmental levels, and occupational stress of site supervisors and interns. *ACES Spectrum, 69*(3), 44–48.

REFERENCES

Ackerman, S. J., & Hilsenroth, M. J. (2003). A review of therapist characteristics and techniques positively impacting the therapeutic alliance. *Clinical Psychology Review, 23*, 1–33.

American Counseling Association. (1995). *Policies and procedures manual of the American Counseling Association.* Alexandria, VA: Author.

American School Counseling Association. (2012). *The ASCA national model: A framework for school counseling programs* (3rd ed.). Alexandria, VA: Author.

Council for Accreditation of Counseling and Related Educational Programs. (2009). *CACREP 2009 accreditation standards.* Alexandria, VA: Author.

Council for Accreditation of Counseling and Related Educational Programs. (2014). *Draft #2 of the 2016 CACREP standards.* Retrieved from http://www.cacrep.org/wp-content/uploads/2012/07/2016-Standars-Draft-2.pdf

Harper, H. L., & Ritchie, M. (2009). Advantages and disadvantages of field-based supervision in counseling practicum. *ACES Spectrum, 69*(3), 21–23.

Hatcher, R. L., & Lassiter, K. D. (2007). Initial training in professional psychology: The practicum competencies outline. *Training and Education in Professional Psychology, 1,* 49–63.

Nelson, M. L., & Friedlander, M. L. (2001). A close look at conflictual supervisory relationships: The trainee's perspective. *Journal of Counseling Psychology, 48,* 384–395.

Pate, R. H., Jr. (2010). Ethical dilemmas and counselor education clinics: Still more questions than answers. In J. E. Myers (Ed.), *Developing and maintaining counselor education laboratories* (pp. 83–90, 200, xviii). Alexandria, VA: American Counseling Association.

Ponton, R. F. (2009). Promoting positive counselor identity through counseling field placements. *ACES Spectrum, 69*(3), 7–13.

Ramos-Sánchez, L., Esnil, E., Goodwin, A., Riggs, S., Touster, L. O., Wright, L. K., Ratanasiripong, P., & Rodolfa, E. (2002). Negative supervisory events: Effects on supervision satisfaction and supervisory alliance. *Professional Psychology: Research and Practice, 33,* 197–202.

3

From the Ideal to the Real

The true ideal is not opposed to the real but lies in it . . .

James Russell Lowell

In Chapter 2, we outlined a number of qualities and characteristics that we posited may need to be present in an "ideal" field placement setting. These elements have been gleaned from general theory, standards articulated by accrediting bodies, and simply our personal perspective on what would constitute an ideal field placement setting. As you research potential sites, there is a good chance that you will find that they fall short of this ideal and lack some of the characteristics listed as desirable.

As should be obvious, the ideal is a vision of that toward which one may want to strive and, as such, invites continual improvement. These ideals should not be embraced as a black-and-white standard from which one rejects all sites failing to reach that criterion. To do so would result in a failure to find any site that would be acceptable.

As you engage in the process of assessing potential field placement sites, you will discover much similarity across sites and yet much that is unique to that site. The uniqueness of a setting, including its location, resources, special challenges encountered as a result of working with a unique population of clients, and day-to-day realities experienced by the professionals working within that setting gives uniqueness to the shape of the job duties, responsibilities, and opportunities encountered by the professional counselor in any one setting. These forces will clearly shape the nature of the role and function served by a counselor and will similarly be those that give shape to your actual field experience.

The ideal presented in the ivory tower of academics will bend and give way to the reality of day-to-day experience of a counselor's professional life. The fact that the ideal may only exist in the literature or classroom is not something that should elicit a sense of despair or resignation. No, the quote by James Russell Lowell can serve as our beacon. The ideal can be found within the real, and with the right skills one can move the lived experience found within a field placement site closer to the ideal desired. This will be the point of discussion within the current chapter.

Specifically, after completing this chapter readers will be able to

- describe criteria that can be employed to assess a counselor's role and function as contrasted to that presented within the profession as ideal,
- explain the relationship between an organization's mission and the role and function of the counselor working there,
- describe what is meant by formal and informal systems, and
- describe strategies for increasing one's expert and informational social power as a method for redefining role and function.

Knowing the Ideal

In Chapter 2, we identified what we felt were meaningful characteristics of a field setting, characteristics that would ensure that a student's experience would truly be formational. As we attempt to develop a profile of a valuable field setting, it would be helpful if in fact we could point to a template or a model that would detail what would constitute the ideal placement and the desired role and function enacted by the professional counselor. Sadly, a universal template does not exist, nor could it be meaningfully developed to apply to all counseling specialties and settings.

Although no one ideal set of standards exits that could be used as a measure against which to assess assigned roles and functions for a counselor in a particular site, there are ways to identify the roles and functions served by a counselor and the degree to which these reflect a professional standard of practice.

Ideal: Defined by the Profession

A number of professional organizations (e.g., CACREP, CORE, etc.) have identified minimum standards regarding the levels of knowledge and skill necessary to function as a professional counselor. These standards are typically directed to those training future counselors and focus on the unique knowledge and skills acquired by the students within those programs. The standards, while useful for such counselor educators, do not address the specifics of the roles and functions for which these students were being prepared. Very few national organizations have provided standards for defining the specific roles and functions to be served by a professional counselor in any one site. So, as one seeking to begin practice within a field, the question becomes what role and function are reasonable and desirable, and what should be expected of one serving in such a professional capacity.

While there are few clearly articulated presentations of a professional counselor's role and function, the one notable exception is in the area of school counseling. The American School Counseling Association is one professional body that has not only attempted to define the expected role and function of a counselor, but also specified general parameters for how the counselor wants to allocate his or her time to specific functions. ASCA (2012) holds that school counselors are supposed to spend most of their time in direct service to and contact with students. While recognizing that some time is allocated to system support, ASCA contends that school counselors need to focus at least 80% of their professional energies to the delivery of guidance curriculum, individual student planning, and responsive services of both a remedial and preventive nature (Gysbers & Henderson, 2012). In articulating a national model for school counseling programs (ASCA, 2012), the American School Counseling Association has identified the types of functions to be provided by a professional school counselor and those that are deemed inappropriate. Such a presentation can prove invaluable not only to those professionals attempting to craft their role and function but to potential students assessing the opportunities to be experienced within any one potential school-placement site. A listing of these do's and don'ts can be found in Table 3.1.

Table 3.1 ASCA's Listing of School Counselor Activities

Appropriate Activities for School Counselors	*Inappropriate Activities for School Counselors*
• individual student academic program • planning • interpreting cognitive, aptitude, and achievement tests • providing counseling to students who are tardy or absent • providing counseling to students who have disciplinary problems • providing counseling to students as to appropriate school dress • collaborating with teachers to present school counseling core curriculum lessons • analyzing grade-point averages in relationship to achievement • interpreting student records • providing teachers with suggestions for effective classroom management • ensuring student records are maintained as per state and federal regulations • helping the school principal identify and resolve student issues, needs, and problems • providing individual and small-group counseling services to students	• coordinating paperwork and data entry of all new students • coordinating cognitive, aptitude, and achievement testing programs • signing excuses for students who are tardy or absent • performing disciplinary actions or assigning discipline consequences • sending students home who are not appropriately dressed • teaching classes when teachers are absent • computing grade-point averages • maintaining student records • supervising classrooms or common areas • keeping clerical records • assisting with duties in the principal's office • providing therapy or long-term counseling in schools to address psychological disorders • coordinating schoolwide individual education plans, student study teams, and school attendance review boards • serving as a data entry clerk

Appropriate Activities for School Counselors	Inappropriate Activities for School Counselors
• advocating for students at individual education plan meetings, student study teams, and school attendance review boards analyzing disaggregated data	

Source: ASCA National Model: Appropriate and Inappropriate Activities for School Counselors.

Note: Reprinted from "Appropriate Activities of School Counselors" by American School Counselors Association, 2005. Retrieved from http://www.schoolcounselor.org/asca/media/asca/home/appropriate-activities-of-school-counselors.pdf.

This ASCA National Model is not mandated and thus not necessarily followed by all counselors working within a school setting. It is one organization's attempt to articulate those elements, characteristics, and processes that it felt maximized the professional role and function of those serving in a particular counseling role, which in this case is that of school counselor. And as a single organization's position, it should not be assumed that any setting that did not completely adhere to these standards would be of little to no value as a placement site. The standards are merely a potentially useful reference point for better understanding what roles and functions may be performed by one serving in the role of school counselor.

For those seeking some clarification of the desirable roles and functions of a counselor working in other specialty areas, such clear articulation and presentation of national standards are not as readily available. In the area of substance abuse, the role and function of the counselors will truly be unique to any one setting, having been affected by the uniqueness of the setting, the population served, and the rules of funding and licensing bodies. Even with this as a caveat, some insight into a general standard of expected role and function may be gained by reviewing the report developed by the Department of Health and Human Services, Office of Applied Studies, titled "The National Substance Abuse Treatment System: Facilities, Clients, Services and Staffing" (2003). Although this report does not provide an explicit set of standards or a listing of do's and don'ts similar to that found within the ASCA model, it does provide insight into the types of services and staffing resources of addictions counseling services and facilities. This document identifies the scope of practice desired, the extent and type of work experience encountered by counselors engaged in substance abuse and addictions counseling, and the training hours required. These descriptions of services and staffing requirements deemed as desirable for addiction counseling provide a reference point against which to review those same characteristics of a site you may be investigating. Beyond this somewhat general outline of role and function, a more detailed listing has been described by Herdman (2013). This listing of twelve core functions of addictions counseling has been generally embraced by those offering counseling services, as well as those educating and credentialing addictions counselors. While lacking the specificity of ASCA's listing of counselor functions, these twelve core functions (see Table 3.2) can still be used as a reference point against which to assess the potential experience being offered by a particular addictions field placement site.

Table 3.2 Twelve Core Functions of the Addictions Counselor

I. Screening: This is the initial evaluation stage, during which a potential patient's physiological, psychological, and social symptoms of substance abuse are evaluated. The client's need and eligibility for treatment is assessed, and based on these and other factors, a counselor will decide whether or not to admit the patient for treatment.

II. Intake: For all intents and purposes, this can be seen as an extension of the screening stage. During this process, the decision to admit the patient is documented extensively and made official. The intake will include completing admission, assessment, and other program forms; obtaining releases of information; and assigning a primary counselor to the client.

III. Orientation: The main goal of orientation is to familiarize the client with the goals of the counseling, the general rules of conduct and infractions that can lead to disciplinary action or discharge, and what the client can and should expect over the course of treatment.

IV. Assessment: The counselor works with the patient to gather his or her history, relating but not limited to any problems with substance abuse. This information gathering can take the form of interviews, testing, and review of patient records. The counselor identifies and evaluates an individual's strengths, weaknesses, problems, and needs in order to develop a treatment plan. This usually results from a combination of focused interviews, testing, and/or record reviews.

V. Treatment Planning: Together with the client, the counselor begins identifying and ranking problems needing resolution; establishing agreed-upon immediate and long-term goals; and deciding on a treatment process and the resources to be utilized. A written treatment contract (or recovery plan) is based on the assessment and is a product of a negotiation between the client and the counselor to ensure that the plan is tailored to the individual's needs.

VI. Counseling: Basically, this is the relationship in which the counselor helps the client mobilize resources to resolve his or her problem and/or modify attitudes and values.

VII. Case Management: This is knowing how to bring outside services, agencies, and resources to assist the client to recovery and attain other goals of the treatment plan. It is a core function of the counselor to bring the various parties and resources together for the purpose of coordinating services for the client.

VIII. Crisis Intervention: Of the 12 core functions of a substance abuse counselor, this one may be the most intermittent. It involves taking immediate action in response to any serious or crucial crises that come up during the course of treatment. The counselor will engage in those activities necessary to assist the client's needs during acute emotional and/or physical distress that threatens to compromise or destroy the rehabilitation effort.

IX. Client Education: Counselors will engage in activities that educate the client in ways that support recovery from alcohol and drug addiction. This education can be provided in a variety of ways; a sequence of formal classes may be conducted or outside educational resources may be used. Beyond the education of a client, the addictions counselor will engage in activities that provide resources and information to other groups and individuals who may also have issues with substance abuse. These resources should be aimed at informing and educating the general public, and letting them know what resources and services are available.

X. Referral: Counselors will identify the needs of a client that cannot be met by the counselor or agency (mission) as well as assist the client to access the support systems and community resources available.

XI. Report and Record Keeping: Addictions counselors document the administration and results of assessments and treatment. Counselors are responsible for taking notes, writing reports, and keeping track of other data relating to each patient. Charting the results of treatment; writing reports, progress notes, discharge summaries, and other client-related data are all functions of an addictions counselor.

XII. Consultation: Counselors will consult with in-house staff or outside professionals to ensure comprehensive, quality care for the client. This involves meetings for discussion, decision making, and planning.

Source: John Herdman's, (2013). Global Criteria: The 12 Core Functions of the Substance Abuse Counselor (6th Edition).

For those entering other areas of specialization, finding a template or standard for defining a role and function is even more challenging. For example, for those specializing in the area of career counseling, some direction may be found by reviewing the National Career Development Guidelines (http://ncda.org/aws/NCDA/asset_manager/get_file/3384?ver=47393). These guidelines were created to help states, schools, colleges, and human services agencies develop and provide comprehensive, competency-based career, guidance, and education programs. Although the descriptions are not specific to the details of role and function served by a career counselor, they do provide descriptions of the types of outcomes a counselor working in career counseling seeks to achieve. For the reflective and insightful student/supervisee attempting to assess the potential value of the role and function served by those within a particular setting, these outcomes can be analyzed as they reflect the types of roles, functions, and processes those counselors would employ to achieve these outcomes. An alternative source of information, for those moving into the realm of career counseling and seeking guidance as to standards for assessing the formational value of a particular setting, is the work of the Network for Innovation in Career Guidance and Counseling in Europe (NICE, http://www.nicec.org/). This group of 45 European institutions of higher education in the field of career counseling has identified five roles deemed as core to the role and function of career counselors (Schiersmann et al., 2012). With the caveat that generalizing the tasks identified by this European body to the role as delivered in the United States should be done with caution, we believe the listing (see Table 3.3) may serve as a point of initial discussion and evaluation of the opportunities offered by any one field placement site.

Other specializations fail to provide clear lists of roles and functions or details of tasks to be performed by those operating within those areas of specialization. In these situations, the student would do well to review the standards set by accrediting bodies for those training or educational bodies seeking certification and accreditation within that specialty area of counseling. Although these standards are directed to sites seeking accreditation and are not intended as standards for identifying the role and function of

Table 3.3 Core Roles and Functions of Career Counselors

- Career counselors support people in developing their own career management competences.
- Career counselors assess client personal characteristics and needs, matching these with educational systems and opportunities reflected in the labor market.
- Career counselors work with clients in assisting them in their understanding of their situations, to work through issues toward solutions.
- Career counselors ensure the quality and delivery of career guidance services.
- Career counselors support clients in crises.

Source: Adapted from "Core Competences for Career Guidance and Counselling Professionals" in *NICE Handbook for the Academic Training of Career Guidance and Counselling Professionals* (pp. 41–60), by C. Schiersmann, B.-J. Ertelt, J. Katsarov, R. Mulvey, H. Reid, & P. Weber (Eds.), 2012, Heidelberg: Heidelberg University, Institute of Educational Science. Copyright 2012 by University Institute of Education Science. Adapted with permission.

one practicing in the specialization, they provide some insight into knowledge and skills possessed by those serving in those settings and, with creative extrapolation, may allow one to assume the types of roles and functions performed.

Ideal: Roles and Function in Line With Mission

Whereas the previous discussion has directed our attention to finding or extrapolating descriptions of the ideal role and functions served by those within various counseling specialties by seeking out national standards, such as that offered by ASCA (2012), the use of national standards as the definition for ideal role and function is not the only approach to such a task. A student/supervisee attempting to assess the opportunities to be provided by a potential site would do well to not only review the formal job description and method of performance evaluation presented for a counselor working within a site under consideration, but also learn to assess these against the stated mission of the institution.

A counselor's job description prescribes the what, and even the how, of a counselor's professional practice and serves as a public statement of the focus and boundaries defining that role. Obviously, knowing what is publicly expected serves as a good starting point for anticipating what an intern may observe being done and what he or she may be asked to do. But the formal job description may not be the most accurate picture of what may be expected.

Performance Assessment: Suggesting Priorities

Whereas the job description should provide a formal, public disclosure of the nature of the role and function of the position of counselor within that setting, the actual mechanism and criteria employed for assessing the performance of one's job provides insight into what the organization actually values or holds as a priority for that role and function. Consider the following example. Community mental health clinic XYZ describes the role of the mental health counselor as "providing psychotherapy services for those struggling with depression, anxiety, and other major psychiatric mental and psychological disorders." It is possible that one reading this brief description could assume that a counselor working within this setting would engage in intense, longer term methods of psychotherapy to assist individuals presenting with major psychiatric disorders. However, this conclusion regarding role and function may be altered once one reviews the 10-item scale used to assess counselor job performance. Out of these 10 items, three address administrative functions (i.e., timely completion of reports, maintenance of accurate client files, and monitoring of insurance billing), two target community education (i.e., providing community education programs, educating community-to-clinic services), and three items focus on client turnaround (i.e., developing meaningful short-term client objectives, engaging in effective short-term intervention strategies, serving in a support and consultative role for clients needing long-term treatment). Thus, while one may have concluded that a counselor working in that setting would be primarily engaged in providing longer term psychotherapy to individuals experiencing major psychiatric disorders, the assessment tool doesn't appear to support that function as a priority. Only two items on the scale of 10 address this role as longer term psychotherapist (i.e., develop case conceptualizations that include intervention and prevention outcomes and employ empirically supported treatments).

Role and Function in Service of the Mission

A review of the formal job definition in light of the method of job performance evaluation provides insight into what is done and what is valued. However, seeking to identify the degree to which what is done and valued reflects some form of ideal role and function requires that we assess the degree to which this role and function serves the agency in fulfillment of its mission. As with all positions within an organization, a counselor's role was, or should have been, developed to be of service to the specific mission of that organization. All organizations, agencies, or systems come into existence in response to a recognized need. As such, while each system will craft a mission that reflects its uniqueness, the generic goal of all missions is to meet the identified consumer needs. To do this, systems develop policies and procedures and establish a variety of roles and functions in order to deliver programs, products, and services that will satisfy the identified need. Thus, when viewing the role and function of a counselor within any one setting, this ideal from a systems perspective would be one that has been developed in response to clearly identified consumer needs and has been formulated to ensure the satisfaction of those needs. As such, a counselor's role at one agency, while sharing similarities with a counselor's role in another agency, will have a number of characteristics that are unique as determined by the specific nature of the mission of each institution. Thus, from a systems perspective, the desirable role and function are one that is truly in service of that system's mission. Consider Case Illustration 3.1, Breaking Free.

CASE ILLUSTRATION 3.1

Breaking Free

After legislatures passed laws permitting legalized gambling, the city saw an explosion in the development of casinos. A number of social challenges, including the presence of trafficking of illegal drugs and the increase in reported crimes and incidence of violence, appeared to accompany the influx of casinos. However, one particular issue appeared to be falling through the cracks with no existing agency or service addressing it. The presence of the casinos and the freely available vehicles for gambling that were spread throughout the city (e.g., slot machines) resulted in the emergence of a population meeting criteria for gambling addiction. Those responsible for the creation of Breaking Free, a for-profit counseling center specializing in the treatment of gambling addictions, identified this need and created a physical center, staffed by qualified counselors, and established policies and procedures for marketing, evaluating, and billing for services. The center was structured to provide individual counseling offices as well as space for group meetings and a larger center for an open Gamblers Anonymous weekly meeting. In addition to developing a physical space that would support its unique services, Breaking Free created policies and standards for hiring, developing, assessing, and promoting staff and services providers. These are but a few of the policies and procedures developed, and all were unique to the consumer served and the nature of that consumer's need.

From the information provided in Case Illustration 3.1, it becomes clear that both the criteria for employment and the listing of formal duties reflect the nature of this clinic's mission. If evidence suggests that the counselors employed are able to successfully carry out these tasks and meet the needs of their clientele, we can assume that such role and function are "ideal" for that particular agency and its unique mission. It is this connection of formal role and function to the embodiment and fulfillment of the mission that serves as a functional standard for assessing a formal role and job description. Exercise 3.1 will help clarify this point.

EXERCISE 3.1

The Tale of Two School Counselors

Directions: Below you will find a list of *primary* functions often performed by a counselor working within a secondary school. Your task is to match the task listed to the specific counselor as an indication that this task would be a primary function for that counselor. Information regarding each counselor's place of employment is provided to help you in the matching process. It may be helpful to discuss your responses with a colleague or classmate.

Counselor A: This counselor works at Westin Vocational Tech School. The school is a regional high school serving students from five neighboring districts. The mission of the school is to help students master the fundamental knowledge and skills necessary to achieve their employment goals.

Counselor B: This counselor works at Wistar School, whose mission reads as follows: Wistar is dedicated to the pursuit of truth through academic excellence and the growth of each of its students, so that he or she is prepared fully for college and for a life of integrity and courageous leadership.

	Counselor A	**Counselor B**	**Both Counselors**
Example: Develop helping alliance with students			x
Complete college applications			
Employ vocational interest tests			
Provide family information nights			
Oversee academic planning and course selection			
Provide guidance on job application processes			
Provide individual counseling with students exhibiting test anxiety			
Administer college entrance testing			
Employ aptitude tests			
Complete letters of recommendation			
Teach and practice job skills, such as résumé writing, interviewing, and networking			
Teach time-management skills			
Provide developmental guidance about issues of separation from home			

There is no right or wrong when identifying the roles and functions of our two illustrative school counselors. And, as you review the roles and functions of the two counselors depicted in Exercise 3.1, you may find yourself assessing some task as one that you enjoy and even conclude that the counselor engaged in those tasks is occupying a more ideal role.

Although it is important to be engaging in tasks you enjoy, from a functional, systemic point of view, the most desirable role or function, the one most approaching a functional ideal, would be the one that most clearly aligns with and helps fulfill the mission of the institution (Parsons & Kahn, 2005). Exercise 3.2 is provided as a way of gathering more data about sites you may be considering as possible field placement opportunities. The exercise invites you to assess the degree to which a counselor's role and function reflects and is in service of the organization's mission.

EXERCISE 3.2

In Service of the Mission

Directions: When attempting to identify an ideal field placement site, it is important to gather information reflecting the degree to which that site has the policies, procedures, resources, roles, and function that ensure mission fulfillment. It may not be possible to gather all the information needed to assess the degree to which any one site is meeting its goals and its objectives and thus meeting its mission, but the following will help provide the essentials for a comparison.

1. What are the demographic characteristics of the consumers of the site's services?
2. Have needs assessments been done within the last 5 years on their consumers?
3. What are the specific goals and objectives outlined for the agency/service?
4. What specific programs, services, and activities (i.e., processes) are provided?
5. How are the specific programs, services, and activities assessed for effectiveness?

Data Analysis: With a colleague, review the data you collected. Consider each of the following as they reflect some of the characteristics of a mission-effective organization.

1. Can you see the linkage between consumer need and outcome goals?
2. Do the specific programs, services, and activities appear to be logically or intuitively in line with consumer need? Articulated goals?
3. Are there data reflecting goals and outcomes achievement? Are these data used to improve services?
4. Does it appear there are sufficient resources (materials, space, personnel, etc.) to effectively provide programs, services, and activities?

What has been presented here is the proposition that when national standards defining the ideal role and function of a professional counselor exist, these should be used to assess that being offered by any one potential field placement site. However, recognizing both the narrow pool of such national standards as well as appreciating that the ideal needs to be configured to the unique demands and services of any one agency and the counselor serving that agency, we suggest that your assessment of a potential field site may need to go beyond comparison to these standards. In assessing the potential experience to be found in a field placement site, insight can be gained by (a) identifying the formal role and function describing what is to be expected of a counselor within that site, (b) assessing the criteria for job performance evaluations as a reflection of the priorities and values given to specific job functions, and (c) noting the degree to which these job functions fulfill that site's mission.

The Real Is Often Less Than Ideal

The sites that you may be considering for field placement will have formal statements of roles of not just counselors but all personnel working within that organization. There will be charts that depict the hierarchy of authority. There will be statements of procedures and policies that describe the way things are to be done. Collectively, this information comprises what is often called the formal structure of an organization. While this information, in general, and the counselor's formal job description and performance evaluation criteria, in particular, provide a profile of what can be expected of one occupying the role and function at any one setting, this is not the whole story. These formal statements depicting the organizational structure and processes present a picture of the way things are supposed to be done. Such a picture may be a less-than-accurate depiction of how things are actually done.

As organizations develop and respond to the various internal and external challenges to getting things done, these formal structures and processes become adapted by those within the system, often in service of their own subjective interests. The realities encountered by those working within an organization often stimulate the development of shortcuts and creative approaches to the delivery of services. It is not unusual for the formal boundaries separating tasks and roles and functions to become blurred or permeable, with the result being that one may take on roles not officially assigned to the formal job description or omit some that are. These adaptations of the formal role and responsibilities and the adjustment to the way things are supposed to be done constitute an *informal* operational system.

Most of us working within any organization have experienced this disparity between the formal system and its explication of how things are supposed to be done and the informal system, denoting how things "really" get done. For example, in your own graduate program, there are rules and policies governing such as things as scheduling, course assignments, and field placements. Perhaps there are rules about deadlines or the need to gain advisor approvals on this or that. If your program is like most, while these formal rules and policies are known and typically followed, there are alternative and perhaps less cumbersome ways to schedule, or gain access to, a course or a specific field placement. Perhaps the department secretary or a particular professor is known to help students take shortcuts, not as an ethical or legal violation but as a functional modification of what may be perceived as a cumbersome element to the formal system. Again, if such shortcuts can be found, they represent the informal system.

Just as the actual day-to-day functioning of the counselor may reflect an adaptation of the formal job description, so too will the role and function of an intern operating within that setting be a reflection of the adapted, rather than formal, job description. As such, it is important, when considering a potential field placement site, to include the data that reveal the existence of an informal system as it colors the actual day-to-day life of a professional counselor.

The difficulty with attempting to incorporate the elements of an informal system into your appraisal of a field placement site is that the elements of an informal system are not publicly listed or found in written form. As part of the culture, the specifics of this informal system may operate below a level of awareness even for those who are engaging with them. For example, while the ASCA model (2005) and the formal job description for the M. L. King High School counselor did not include serving as a lunchroom monitor, counselor Ms. Jackson has found over the years that working in that role has helped her strengthen her relationships with faculty, having served in the "trenches" as they do, and provides her with a unique opportunity to converse with the children in this more comfortable and natural environment.

Given the difficulty of identifying these informal adaptations, the question becomes how could one assess them prior to engaging with them? One strategy may be to "shadow" a potential supervisor as he or she performs his or her duties throughout a typical day. If you could gain a counselor's permission to shadow him or her for a day, you could perform a modified time study of his or her job performance. The process would require you to list all the specific tasks performed by the counselor throughout the day, identifying the actual or an estimated amount of time spent on each task. Case Illustration 3.2 outlines the time study performed on Dr. Zach, a school counselor, and could be used as a template for your own time study of a potential site supervisor's job functioning.

CASE ILLUSTRATION 3.2

Dr. Zach's Time Study

Andre Zach has been a secondary counselor at Williams High School for over 22 years. He has invited a small group of potential interns to shadow him throughout his day as a way of allowing them to experience "a day in the life of Dr. Z." Data were recorded by one of the interns and are presented below.

Time of Day	Task	Time on Task (estimated)	Dr. Zach's Response to Time Study
7:30 (start of day)	Read and responded to e-mails—from teachers, administrators, parents, and professional colleagues	15 min	

Time of Day	Task	Time on Task (estimated)	Dr. Zach's Response to Time Study
	Responded to student who lost her cell phone	20 min	He feels that he spends a lot of time addressing adolescent "crises."
	Returned to e-mails	10 min	
	Responded to phone call from parent	10 min	
8:30	Returned to e-mail	5 min	He complained about all the e-mails he receives.
	Met with principal regarding district bullying policy	40 min	He appreciates that he is called upon as a primary resource and consultant to the principal even though that was not on his formal job description.
	Bathroom	5 min	
9:30	Faculty lounge–coffee and informal discussion with teacher about upcoming football game	10 min	
	Responded to student in hall who was late for class and asking for an excuse note–which he denied	10 min	
	Went to supervise study hall–an assigned duty	50 min	He feels that this takes him away from student service. It is not in his job description nor is it approved by the American Counseling Association.
10:30	Met with student–college planning	25 min	

(Continued)

(Continued)

Time of Day	Task	Time on Task (estimated)	Dr. Zach's Response to Time Study
	Assisted three students working on a self-directed career search	20 min	
	Met with a teacher regarding a child with special needs	15 min	
11:30	Lunch in faculty lounge (discussed district bullying policy and program that is to be implemented)	30 min (10 min of the lunch spent discussing district policy)	
12:00	Returned parent phone call—question regarding financial aid forms	20 min	
	Handled student drop-in visit—handled upset about the ending of a romantic relationship	30 min	
	Had phone discussion with college admissions officer who was requesting to visit	10 min	He feels it is important to maintain personal relationships with the admission people—but sometimes feels the phone calls and e-mails take up too much of his time.
1:00	Met with principal and dean of discipline (assistant principal) regarding a student discipline issue	20 min	
	Called parents of the student who was the focus of the discussion with principal and vice principal	20 min	He feels that this was more appropriately the role of the principal or the assistant principal/dean of discipline.

Time of Day	Task	Time on Task (estimated)	Dr. Zach's Response to Time Study
	Met with principal	10 min	
2:00	Bathroom and coffee break	15 min	
	Filed standardized test results	25 min	He feels there is a lot of paperwork—and the department does not have an assigned secretary.
	Met with a small group of students (five) who served as new student ambassadors	20 min	
3:00	Stood in hallway—informally connecting with students as they exited	20 min	
	Met with one student reviewing college application	20 min	
	Relieved teacher who was supervising in-house suspension	20 min	He finds that he is sometimes asked to substitute on these types of duties when a teacher is absent or in this case had to leave early. Not part of the original job description and not approved by ASCA.
4:00	Reviewed e-mails	20 min	
	Returned parent phone call—and provided parent with list of district-approved tutors	10 min	
	Watched football team practice—interacted with coaches	20 min	
	Closed office and left for the day		

The result of Dr. Zach's time study revealed that he often engages in activities that were not on his original job description and that a couple that have become part of his responsibilities would not be the type approved by the American School Counseling Association. Dr. Zach was also surprised to find the amount of time he spent on other-than-direct student contact. The purpose of the time study is simply to provide information and raise awareness. Upon review, Dr. Zach may decide that the unofficial, informal duties he has embraced are things he wishes to continue or maintain, or he may decide that these activities are taking him away from those formal duties and responsibilities that he and the organization truly value. In either case, the data, as information, provide him the base from which to decide how to proceed.

For a student/supervisee considering Dr. Zach as a potential supervisor and this setting as a potential field site, these data, reflecting the existence of an informal system, will prove valuable in guiding that student's decisions. Including these data along with that depicted in the formal job description provides the student with a more accurate reflection of the day-to-day functioning of the professional counselor within that setting and the anticipated role to be served by a supervisee.

Even Interns Can Effect Change and Define Roles

In the quote with which we opened this chapter, author James Russell Lowell reminds us that the true ideal can be found within the real. The challenge is not only to recognize its presence but to have the ability to bring the elements of the ideal more clearly into the real!

As a student-intern, you may feel as if you are powerless in giving shape to your field placement experience. What you are directed to do or not do has been given form by organizations such as CACREP (2009, 2014) or the American Counseling Association (2014) and most certainly by the rules, regulations, and professional preferences of the site and site supervisor. The Council for the Accreditation of Counseling and Related Educational Programs (CACREP, 2009) notes that the internship should be an experience where the student/supervisee "refines and enhances basic counseling or student development knowledge and skills, and integrates and authenticates professional knowledge and skills appropriate to his or her program and initial postgraduate professional placement" (CACREP, 2009, p. 60).

Thus, one might anticipate that the task assigned and the experiences provided will in fact engage you in the realm of professional practice to the degree that you are capable. This educational goal is, of course, addressed with an eye to the ethics of our profession and particularly the welfare of those whom you serve.

With the proviso of client welfare taking primacy in mind, the question to be considered is, "How does a student/supervisee give shape to the field placement experience to ensure it provides the maximum opportunity for professional growth and development?" Or, perhaps more concisely, "How can a student/supervisee influence the supervisor's attitudes and behaviors in ways that increase the potential value of the field placement experience?"

The answer to the question may be found in understanding and employing the principles of social power. Social psychologists as far back as the early 1960s (e.g., French & Raven, 1959; Raven, 1965) posited that one's attitude and/or behaviors can be influenced by another exhibiting or employing specific forms of social power. For example, a person who is waving a firearm in another's face and demanding that that person relinquish his or her wallet is using coercive power to influence the behavior of another. It can be safely assumed that the person being coerced may have adjusted his or her attitude from one of previously feeling safe and hopeful about the activities of the evening to one now concerned and anxious about his or her own well-being. Similarly, the person's previous behavior of whistling and smiling is now replaced with signs of anxiety and the handing over of his or her wallet. In this case, coercion is a social force that changed the attitude and behavior of another. And although coercive power is neither available to a student/supervisee nor would it be appropriate to employ even if it was, two of the six forms of social power identified by these authors do seem appropriate and potentially useful for students seeking to contribute to the shape of their field experience.

Expert Power

In this case, *expert power* refers to the fact that one has special knowledge or skills that are desired by another yet not possessed by that other. Consequently, the other may be willing to listen to, be directed by, or in other words influenced by the one with that knowledge and skill. Consider a simple example. You have a car that is making some funny noises. Although you have a very limited budget, you also know that the car is essential to your functioning. You take the car to a garage and the mechanic states that he can fix the car at the cost of $200. This is not the news you wanted to hear and you are resistant to engaging the services of this mechanic. As you talk, the mechanic explains in technical yet understandable language exactly what is happening. He explains how failing to address the issue at this point will result in increased damage and increased cost of a future repair. He speaks with authority and is able to technically explain the problem and the problem with waiting. As he explains the details of all that is involved, you take notice of all the special certificates he has hanging on his shop walls. The various certificates provide evidence of his specialized, advanced training with your type of vehicle. Even though the cost of repair is acting as an initial deterrent to fixing the problem, the expert information he is providing and the certificates testifying to his expertise influence your decision and you agree to the service. When individuals perceive or assume that a person possesses superior skills or abilities, they award power to that person (Forsyth, 2010). In this case, your attitude and behavior were changed by the expertise he was able to exhibit.

This perception of expertise and the resulting assignment of expert power can be enhanced by providing indications of advanced education, awards, testimonials, recognitions, or any manifestation of possessing a unique skill set or knowledge base different from and yet desired by another (Parsons & Kahn, 2005). Thus, as a student/supervisee, one way to help give shape to your own field experience is to demonstrate expertise to your site supervisor, especially in those areas in which you would like to increase your engagement.

The first step in this process would be to increase your level of expertise with a particular set of skills or knowledge. This may require extra work on your part. It is important to take advantage of workshops, training opportunities, and enrichment experiences that target specific information or skills applicable to the type of population you will serve in your field placement site. But having the expertise is only one part of the equation. For the expertise to serve as a basis for social power and thus the element of influence for shaping your field experience, you will need to make this expertise public. It is important to provide your supervisor with clear evidence of your increasing expertise. This is not to suggest that you take on an inflated sense of self or a bragging style. Rather, the idea is to find opportunities to simply share what you have learned or experienced. For example, it is helpful to share information you have gained by attending a training session (even something from class that you may feel is "the latest," or unique), or provide the supervisor with copies of materials you gathered or research you have read on a particular topic or area of service. The approach should take the form of a matter-of-fact, collegial sharing rather than that of an opportunity for student to teach the teacher.

Sharing evidence of expertise positions students to take a more active role in defining their field placement experience. Rather than passively waiting to be assigned a task, students seeking to give shape to their field experience will demonstrate their special knowledge (e.g., computer-based tracking of client statistics, working with a particular client demographic [children, women, aged], or gathering behavioral data and performing functional behavioral analyses) and skills (e.g., expertise in anti-bullying programs, the ASCA model, HIPPA, FIRPA, college or career searches, etc.) to the supervisor and ask to use those skills in service of the site's clientele.

Informational Power

A second form of social power available to a student/supervisee is that termed *informational power.* In a lot of ways, this form of social power is aligned with expert power but differs in that it is "independent" of the person exerting the influence. It is the nature of the message provided rather than the personal characteristics of the person that serve as the source of the social power. With informational power, one doesn't have to be an expert; rather, it relies on the strength, logic, and reasoning behind the message—the communication.

Informational power is based on the potential to utilize information. Providing rational arguments, using information to persuade others, and using facts and manipulating information can create a power base. The implication for the student/supervisee is to *stop . . . research . . . reflect . . .* and *reframe* your thoughts and opinions.

In most social settings, we are relaxed and free to interact freely and spontaneously, oftentimes speaking in slang or less than our best English, but it is important as a student/supervisee to remember that you are presenting as a professional and are representing a profession. Therefore, when interacting within the role, it is important to take time to review the issues at hand, gather your thoughts—and when time permits, gather relevant information reflecting research or widely held professional views on the topic, reflect on the goal you wish to accomplish, and reframe your presentation in way that is logical, reasonable, persuasive, and receptive to those you wish to influence. Case Illustration 3.3 provides an example of two counselors attempting to have a client invite her parents into the counseling dynamic. As you will note, the first counselor is succinct and direct. The second counselor employs client data, her own personal sharing, actual facts acquired in session, and a logical presentation to influence the client's attitudes about the decision to bring her parents into the dynamic. To the degree to which this counselor's presentation influences the client's decision, one can argue that the counselor had and employed informational power. Exercise 3.4 invites you to work with a classmate or colleague to engage in the development of such informational power.

CASE ILLUSTRATION 3.3

Gaining Permission to Engage the Parents

Scenario: The counselors engaged in this illustration have been working with a 17-year-old female client, who was self-referred for counseling due to her unexpected pregnancy. The counselor and client have met three times, and it is clear that the young woman is in conflict regarding the many options she has in regards to the pregnancy. She is able to identify the personal "costs" involved with carrying the pregnancy to term, and she is able to articulate the personal costs to considering terminating the pregnancy. Throughout the third session, the counselor has invited the client to consider engaging her parents in the discussion–because their opinion has emerged as pivotal to the client's decision making. The client has been resistant to the idea of inviting them into the session. The counselor in both situations is attempting to invite the client to consider the basis for this resistance and to assess if the basis is founded in any reality-based evidence.

Counselor A (lacking informational power)

Melissa, clearly you are concerned about your parents' reactions to you having become pregnant. If I understand what you are saying, it seems you anticipate that they will be upset and angry and may simply disown you. While I doubt that will happen, I respect your concerns. Since your parents have given no previous evidence of reacting in these ways when you or your siblings have confronted some difficulties, I doubt they will now and really suggest we invite them in.

Counselor B (attempting to frame the discussion more logically–to acquire informational power)

Melissa, I can see how upset you become when thinking about sharing your story with your mom and dad. All that you have shared, and the tears and tone of voice that accompany that sharing, seems to suggest to me that you would love to have their support at this challenging time but that you are also unsure if they will support you? Your nodding seems to support what I am suggesting.

(Continued)

(Continued)

Well—I can see where this could be a risk. But I wonder. While we have only met a couple of times, and I know I haven't heard all of your experiences with your parents, everything you have shared with me about your parents and their previous reactions to any difficulties you or your siblings have encountered suggests that they have been supportive. If I remember correctly, even when your brother was arrested for possession of marijuana, your parents reacted with concern and support and not anger or disappointment. Was that correct? Oh, thanks, so it was? And, the time when you were in high school and you ran away with your boyfriend for a week—I know they grounded you, but did they withdraw their love or begin to treat you in a way that indicated they no longer valued you or wanted to care for and about you? Now, I know these are different situations than that which you are currently experiencing but I wonder—do you think your parents would be surprised about your pregnancy? Would they be concerned about the possible long-term impact of having a baby at this point in your life? They would? Yes, I think you may be right. Do you think that they would be concerned about your health? Yeah . . . I do, too. So if our prediction is that they would be surprised and concerned over your health and well-being—do we have any real evidence that in addition to that loving concern they would be rejecting or dismissing . . . or . . . disowning? No . . . nor do I. So what do you think? Maybe together we can share your story and invite their support?

EXERCISE 3.3

Developing Informational Power

Directions: Informational power requires both the possession of relevant and valuable information and the presentation of that information in clear, logical, and understandable form. In this exercise, you are invited to (a) identify an area of interest/concern for your site supervisor or those with whom you may work; (b) research information regarding a specific target; and (c) reflect on your designated audience, and then formulate (in writing) your presentation of that information in a way that will be clear, concise, reasonable, and logical.

Area of Interest/ Concern	**Relevant Information**	**Form of Communication (incorporate and reference the data and the research and present in non-emotive, logical fashion)**
(Example) Supervisor just completed an	Researching DSM V, you identified a new category of premenstrual	(Speaking with the supervisor) I was thinking about Joann G. and your intake last week. I really

intake of a client. In her presentation, the client shares her own hypotheses about her condition, stating, "I think it is all hormonal and matches up with my cycle."	dysphoric disorder (PMDD). You researched http://www.ask.com/wiki/Premenstrual_dysphoric_disorder?qsrc=3044 and found a good description of the disorder, its etiology, and treatment.	benefitted from watching you gather intake data, especially about her embarrassment of having problems emotionally with her periods. I was wondering if it would help her when she has a better grasp of the possible nature and impact of premenstrual dysphoria. I have gathered some information on the nature of the condition, the fact that it is now included in DSM V—which I think supports the potential disabling impact of this condition and the value of treatment—and some treatment ideas. My question is if it would be appropriate to direct a client to this type of information as a form of bibliotherapy?
Issue you have noted regarding a client		
Issue raised at a team meeting or committee meeting		
Issue regarding site policy or procedures		

To Get Much . . . Much Is Expected

Given all that students are required to do as they progress through their program of study, along with consideration of the fact that most students have been socialized to take direction from their teachers and advisors, it would be totally reasonable to assume that inviting you to take an active role in not only finding but creating your ideal field placement may be unrealistic. Reviewing national standards and formal and informal organizational structures and attempting to employ social power to give shape to your field experience is a lot to ask.

But, as we attempted to explain in Chapter 1, this field experience is unique from all of the previous academic classes you have taken. It is truly the place where you as student transition to you as professional.

The steps we are inviting you to consider in selecting a field placement site are useful for not only that task but also many other tasks that you as a professional will need to accomplish throughout your career. It is you, as professional, who needs to know the evolving standards of our profession or of your specialty and also contribute and give shape to those standards. It is you, as professional, who will experience the reshaping of formal definitions of roles and functions and the creation of job performance evaluations and also you who need to give shape to those ever-changing role and function expectations. Finally, as a professional counselor, yours is a role of social influence. Whether it is working with clients, serving in a work group, engaging as a consultant or facilitating organizational policy and procedure development, your expertise and your ability to frame meaningful professional information will be essential to the contribution of those outcomes desired.

Yes, what we are inviting you to do is a lot. But your role is one that has impact on lives and that role is one of which much is expected. It deserves all that you can give it.

KEYSTONES

- Very few national organizations have provided standards for defining the specific roles and functions to be served by a professional counselor in any one site.
- The American School Counseling Association is one professional body that has attempted to define the expected role and function of a counselor, as well as specifies general parameters for how the counselor should allocate his or her time to specific functions.
- Insight into a general standard of expected role and function of an addictions counselor may be gained by reviewing the report developed by the Department of Health and Human Services, Office of Applied Studies, titled "The National Substance Abuse Treatment System: Facilities, Clients, Services, and Staffing" (2003).
- Those specializing in the area of career counseling may find some direction by reviewing the National Career Development Guidelines (http://ncda.org/aws/NCDA/asset_manager/get_file/3384?ver=47393).
- As organizations develop and respond to the various internal and external challenges to getting things done, these formal structures and processes become adapted by those within the system, often in service of their own subjective interests. The realities encountered by those working within an organization often stimulate the development of shortcuts and creative approaches to the delivery of services, which is typically identified as an informal system.
- In assessing the potential experience to be found in a field placement site, insight can be gained by (a) identifying the formal role and function describing what is to be expected of a counselor within that site, (b) identifying modifications to this formal role and function as evidence of an informal system, (c) assessing the criteria for job performance evaluations as a reflection of the priorities and values given to specific job functions, and (d) noting the degree to which these job functions are in service to the fulfillment of that site's mission.
- Students may be able to give shape to their field placement experience by exhibiting expert and informational social power.

ADDITIONAL RESOURCES

Ashkenas, R. (2010). Simply effective: *How to cut through complexity in your organization and get things done.* Boston, MA: Harvard Business School Publishing.

Carpenter, J. (2013). Five internship secrets from superstar college interns. Retrieved from http://www.cnn.com/2013/07/09/living/ireport-internship-secrets

Levine, R. V. (2003). *The power of persuasion: How we're bought and sold.* Hoeboken, NJ: John Wiley.

Sweitzer, H. F., & King, M. A. (2014). *The successful internship* (4th ed). Belmont, CA: Brooks/Cole.

REFERENCES

American Counseling Association. (2014). *ACA code of ethics.* Alexandria, VA: Author.

American School Counseling Association (2012). *The ASCA National Model: A Framework for School Counseling Programs.* Alexandria, VA: Author.

Council for Accreditation of Counseling and Related Educational Programs. (2009). *CACREP standards.* Retrieved from http://www.cacrep.org/doc/2009%20Standards%20with%20cover.pdf

Council for Accreditation of Counseling and Related Educational Programs (2014). *Draft #2 of the 2016 CACREP standards.* Retrieved from http://www.cacrep.org/wp-content/uploads/2012/07/2016-Standars-Draft-2.pdf

Forsyth, D. R. (2010). *Group dynamics.* Belmont, CA: Wadsworth, Cengage Learning.

French, J. R. P., Jr., & Raven, B. (1959). The bases of social power. In D. Cartwright (Ed.), *Studies in social power.* Ann Arbor: University of Michigan Institute of Social Research.

Gysbers, N. C., & Henderson, P. (2012). *Developing and managing your school guidance program* (5th ed.). Alexandria, VA: American Counseling Association.

Herdman, J. W. (2013). *Global criteria: The 12 core functions of the substance abuse counselor* (6th ed.). Lincoln, NE: Author.

Office of Applied Studies (2003). *Substance Abuse and Mental Health Services Administration Alcohol and Drug Services Study (ADSS): The National Substance Abuse Treatment System: Facilities, Clients, Services, and Staffing.* Rockville, MD, Author.

Parsons, R. D., & Kahn, W. J. (2005). *The school counselor as consultant.* Belmont, CA: Brooks/Cole.

Raven, B. H. (1965). Social influence and power. In I. D. Steiner & M. Fishbein (Eds.), *Current studies in social psychology.* New York, NY: Holt, Rinehart and Winston.

Schiersmann, C., Ertelt, B.-J., Katsarov, J., Mulvey, R., Reid, H., & Weber, P. (Eds.). (2012). Core competences for career guidance and counselling professionals. In *NICE handbook for the academic training of career guidance and counselling professionals* (pp. 41–60). Heidelberg: Heidelberg University, Institute of Educational Science.

4

The Ethics of Practice: More Than Knowing, Being

Action indeed is the sole medium of expression for ethics.

Jane Addams

The topics of professional ethics, codes of conduct, and laws shaping and directing practice are topics that are not new to you. At this point in your professional development, you have most likely heard quite a bit about the American Counseling Association's *Code of Ethics* (ACA, 2014). As a student learning these codes of conduct, you may have had to commit parts to memory and perhaps even apply specific codes to sample cases, all in an effort to help you understand and remember these codes of professional conduct. Knowing the ethical codes of our profession is essential. It is, however, only the beginning.

As the quote attributed to Jane Addams, a social reformer, pacifist, and feminist during the late 19th and early 20th centuries suggests, it is in action that ethics takes on value. The codes are meaningless if they remain merely words on a page or only serve as a response to a test question. For these codes to serve as intended, they must be understood *and* embraced as personal and professional values. As noted in the preamble of the American Counseling Association's *Code of Ethics* (2014), "Professional values are an important way of living out an ethical commitment."

Values inform principles and serve as the foundation for ethical practice. Inherently held values that guide behaviors are deeply ingrained in the counselor and developed out of personal dedication, rather than the mandatory requirement of an external organization.

As a student, you have been challenged to learn these ethical principles. But now, as you transition from student to professional, the challenge is no longer to learn and understand our *Code of Ethics;* the challenge is for you to embrace these standards, these codes, as your own personal and thus professional values. Transitioning from student to professional requires you to move beyond knowing the ethics of practice to embodying the ethics of a professional in all of your professional decisions and actions. It is a transition that will move you from knowing ethics, to being . . . ethical!

This is not an easy task and it is not one that will be completed in one chapter or in one field experience. It will—or it can—be started. And if started correctly, you will soon understand that "ethics isn't what we know or what we do, it is how we are" (Parsons, 2001, p. xiii).

Specifically, after completing this chapter, readers will be able to

- describe the need for and value of a professional code of practice,
- explain the fundamental values serving as the foundation of the *ACA Code of Ethics,* and
- describe challenges to the embodiment of the moral underpinnings of the *ACA Code of Ethics* at their specific field placement site.

The Need and Value of Professional Ethics

Professional codes of ethics stand as articulated values and obeliefs held by those identified with and practicing in a particular profession. Our codes have emerged from the lived experiences of those practicing within our profession. For counselors practicing under a code of ethics created in the 1990s, for example, issues such as cultural sensitivity, responding to clients with HIV/AIDS, having intimate relationships with clients following termination of a formal helping relationship, and confidentiality in light of HIPPA laws were not even on the radar and thus not reflected within the code of ethics. Our codes are continuingly evolving both in anticipation of, and in response to, challenges confronting client welfare and/or the health and well-being of the profession as a whole.

The American Counseling Association's *Code of Ethics* (ACA, 2014) is not intended as a directive for personal morality. This code has developed and is offered as the standard against which to judge professional decisions and actions. The primary goal of these standards is to assist counselors in constructing a professional course of action that best serves those utilizing counseling services. The codes serve as a scaffold supporting decisions that can best serve our clients, while alerting all within the profession to pitfalls that can negatively affect both client and profession. Exercise 4.1 will help highlight the need and value of ethics to our profession and those whom we serve.

EXERCISE 4.1

The Counseling Relationship Demanding Ethical Behavior

Directions: In the table below, you will find "common" forms of interpersonal behavior. It is likely that you have engaged in these behaviors with people you just met or barely know. It is possible that in normal social exchanges, these behaviors are completely acceptable. However, when placed within the context of a counseling relationship, one respectful of the client's needs and committed to doing no harm, these behaviors could be problematic. The second column provides a very brief description of a client. It is suggested that you work with a colleague to identify the potentially negative impact this interpersonal behavior may have on that particular client and the counseling relationship. The final column references at least one of the ethical principles addressing this type of situation. What is important is to attempt to place yourself within the client's shoes and "experience" the impact of this counselor behavior.

Interpersonal Behavior	**Client Characteristics and Experiences**	**Possible Impact of Engaging in the Interpersonal Behavior With That Client in a Counseling Relationship**	**Ethical Principle Guiding Practice Decisions**
Sharing a brief hug and pat on the back as a social greeting	The client is an 18-year-old who is in therapy after attempting suicide due to recently being raped by her stepfather.		A.5.c. Nonprofessional Interactions or Relationships
Sharing a story told to you by another (as in telling a little secret)	The client is apprehensive of coming to counseling, fearing being stereotyped as "crazy."		B.1.c. Respect for Confidentiality
Inviting a person to invest in your business venture	The client is a successful businessperson who is going through a traumatic divorce.		A.5.c. Nonprofessional Interactions or Relationships

Borrowing lunch money	The client presents with extremely low self-esteem and as one who by self-admission states that he cannot say "no" and is a people pleaser.		A.10.d. Bartering
Attempt to pressure a person to allow you to use them as a reference	The client has been in a longstanding abusive relationship.		C.6.d. Exploitation of Others

But the codes are only words on a page until embodied and enacted within practice. And although it would be comforting to assume all who are identified as "counselor" embrace and embody these professional ethical standards, such is not the case.

Situations in which a counselor's physical, mental, or emotional problems may interfere with the ethical performance of his or her duties do exist, and often come to light in the form of legal actions. Malpractice claims are on the rise (NPDB, 2011). A comprehensive review of claims made against counselors during the period of 2003–2012 (see HPSO, 2014) suggests that these claims are most often based on the fact that the practitioner behaved in a fashion inconsistent with the *ACA Code of Ethics,* with complaints ranging from a counselor's failure to employ adequate informed-consent procedures or inadvertent disclosure of confidential information, to more egregious actions such as a counselor's having sex with clients, engaging in embezzlement, or even physically assaulting clients (Reamer, 2003).

As a standard ensuring the public against harm, these codes require each professional to not only embrace and embody the codes but also hold his or her colleagues accountable to do the same. Because of the reality that a minority of practitioners fail to embody the profession's ethical standards in all that they do, the ethics of our practice requires that we serve as agents of accountability, holding one another accountable for giving form to the code in our practices. In addressing the issue of professional impairment, for example (C.2.g,ACA, 2014), the code notes the following: "Counselors assist colleagues or supervisors in recognizing their own professional impairment and provide consultation and assistance when warranted with colleagues or supervisors showing signs of impairment and intervene as appropriate to prevent imminent harm to clients."

This call to accountability requires that each of us be willing to reach out to our colleagues who fall short in embodying the codes of our practice and, when necessary, and in the extreme, to engage our professional association in the censuring of those members who are in violation of these standards (Gladding, Remley, & Hubor, 2001). This is a difficult process but one necessary if we are to protect both our clients and our profession from harm. Case Illustration 4.1 provides a window into the need for this monitoring of professional practice and the ramifications of turning a blind eye toward abuse.

CASE ILLUSTRATION 4.1

Not Comforting

As a practicum student at W. L. B. High School, Carmen was able to shadow the counselors and sit in at many of their department meetings and teacher consultations. Having been in the field only 4 weeks, Carmen had yet to be "assigned" a student with whom to work but was encouraged to "informally" speak with any of the students coming to the Counseling Center seeking college or career information.

Rosa, a junior honors student, was busy working at the computer employing the school's Naviance program to engage in college planning. Rosa appeared to Carmen as if she was having difficulty navigating the program, and because Carmen had just engaged with the program the previous day, she felt that perhaps she could be of assistance.

Rosa was grateful for the assistance and began to freely share with Carmen about her career interests and schools of choice. As they spoke, Carmen suggested that Rosa schedule an appointment with Dr. B., the counselor who specialized in college counseling. Rosa's reaction caught Carmen completely off guard.

While initially providing reasons why she didn't need help, Rosa's reaction quickly escalated. She began to shake and cry. She couldn't catch her breath, and it appeared to Carmen that she was experiencing a panic attack. Luckily, no one else was in the center and Mrs. P., Carmen's supervisor, was in the office with her door open. Carmen invited Rosa to move from the outer office and asked if she would want to go sit with Mrs. P., where it was a bit more private.

The story that unfolded in the office was both shocking and concerning. Rosa went into great detail about her visit during the previous week to Dr. B.'s office. She explained that he had called her down to simply catch up about her college plans and to let her know about upcoming test dates. This was routine for a junior. But as she spoke, she began to cry. With encouragement from Mrs. P., she revealed that during the session, Dr. B. had put his hand on her arm a couple of times and patted her on the knee while making some points about college applications. She also noted that when she was leaving, he placed his arm on her back and rubbed her shoulder. She found the experience to be very upsetting and refused to go back to his office ever again.

> Regardless of the intent of the behavior, the impact was clearly upsetting to Rosa and in this case damaging to her view of the counseling center. Rosa continued to discuss the incident and how it brought back memories of an experience she had as child. She was very open and explained how she had been in therapy and had resolved that previous incident but remained sensitive to what she felt was inappropriate touch.
>
> Throughout the session, Rosa gained her composure and she asked if she could continue to work with Mrs. P., a plan that was easy to ensure. Mrs. P. explained her own concerns about the described behavior and asked if it would be okay for her to talk to Dr. B. about his behavior. Rosa expressed apprehension and the fear that Dr. B. would be upset with her–but she felt that she had described the behavior accurately and, while giving him a benefit of the doubt regarding his intentions, wanted him to know that for some, that behavior was discomforting.
>
> Mrs. P. assured Rosa that she would not be accusatory but would discuss a variety of behaviors that could be upsetting to students and should not be employed within a counseling relationship.

As highlighted by the case illustration (4.1), the goal of protecting the public and our profession from harm cannot be achieved if the code remains merely a document set upon a bookshelf. The words presented in the American Counseling Association's *Code of Ethics* (2014) remain simply that—*words*—until they are embodied in the counselor's decisions and practice behaviors. It is essential that each professional counselor and each counselor-in-training take steps necessary to ensure that these codes are not just understood and embraced in theory, but personally valued and internalized as scaffold guiding practice decisions. It is in making the principles personal values that one will keep the welfare of his or her client primary to all practice decisions.

The requirement to "live" out our professional code *and* serve as an active agent of accountability is certainly a heavy responsibility. It is a responsibility that becomes more challenging when one is in the field as a student-professional. And whereas one could argue that the call to accountability found within the standards speaks to the responsibility of the professional counselor, the student in the field, as one transitioning to professional, should also embrace the intent of these principles. Neither one's status as student-professional nor the degree of difficulty experienced in enacting these principles exempts a student in the field from living out our professional code. The code is clear: "Students and supervisees have a responsibility to understand and follow the *ACA Code of Ethics.* Students and supervisees have *the same obligation to clients as those required of professional counselors*" (F.5.a, Standards for Students, emphasis added).

It is difficult to confront a colleague who is in violation of our professional *Code of Ethics,* regardless of whether that colleague is a fellow student-practitioner or a professional counselor. However, when impairment is apparent and the professional or student-practitioner is exhibiting physical, mental, or emotional problems that are likely to harm a client, confronting that professional or student-colleague is required. Exercise 4.2 is provided to give you an opportunity to consider possible responses to situations calling for professional-to-professional intervention.

EXERCISE 4.2

A Call for Professional-to-Professional Intervention

Directions: For each of the following scenarios involving the actions of a colleague, you are to decide (a) whether intervention is needed and (b) what type of intervention might be employed. It may be helpful to consult with a colleague in regards to steps to be taken in each of the following situations.

Situation	**Response Needed (yes/no)**	**Possible Response**
(Example) Sitting in the lunchroom with a number of nonprofessionals eating lunch, John begins to talk about the "crazy" woman he just saw as an initial intake. John doesn't reveal the name of the client nor any identifying characteristics other than that she was "bipolar, and flying high . . . with all kinds of delusions of grandeur . . . a real head case. . . ."	Yes. Although John is avoiding identifying the client by name or characteristics, he is demonstrating unprofessional and demeaning behavior, which could lead a casual observer to conclude that he is untrustworthy and hypocritical in his "care" for clients, or even that he is judgmental and condescending and that his behavior characterizes that of other professionals.	1. Attempt to redirect the conversation at the moment and talk to John later outside the lunchroom about his public presentation. 2. Intervene at the moment, stating, "John, I'm not sure the lunchroom is a good place to talk about our clients." 3. Proceed to talk with John's supervisor about the behavior.
A colleague leaves a case file at the conference table following a departmental meeting.		
A school counselor who was meeting with a student at the end of the school day offers to drive a student home after school.		
A counselor discloses that he has been giving his client a discount in exchange for his client (a professional house painter) doing some painting at his house.		

A colleague has the habit of terminating each session with all clients (male and female) with a hug.		
A counselor at the local college accepts an invitation from of one his clients to attend her graduation party.		
A counselor is considering taking up an invitation from the parents of a student with whom he has worked to use their beach house.		
Over coffee in a colleague's office, the counselor begins to share the details of the "unusual" sexual practices in which his client engages.		
A colleague comes back to work and scheduled clients—after a two-martini lunch.		
A colleague describes a recent workshop (60 minutes) that she attended on a new technique for working with depressed clients. She expresses interest in trying it out on the next client.		

In addition to holding our colleagues accountable, implicit in the code is the requirement for self-monitoring and holding oneself accountable as circumstances dictate. Thus, if counselors-in-training note that their own physical, mental, or emotional problems are impeding service to clients, it is incumbent on them, as ethical practitioners, to seek assistance for the problems as well as notify their supervisor (ACA, 2014, F.5.b). It may be obvious that conditions of severe physical impairment (e.g., concussion, migraine, temporary hearing loss, etc.), mental difficulties (e.g., inability to concentrate or focus attention), or emotional impairment (e.g., significant grieving or major depression) need to be addressed prior to engaging with a client, but less dramatic conditions might also call for a "time-out" from practice. Exercise 4.3 invites you to consider the potential impact of these less-than-dramatic conditions as they may negatively affect your ability to provide ethical client services.

EXERCISE 4.3

Impaired?

Directions: For each of the following, identify the degree to which the condition may necessitate a student-counselor to take a "time-out" from practice. Also, identify the possible negative effects on clinical decisions and practice if the condition is not resolved. It would be beneficial to share your opinion with a colleague or site supervisor.

Situation	Impaired? Does the condition necessitate a student-counselor time-out from practice? (yes/no/possibly)	Possible Negative Effects if Not Addressed
You are anxious knowing that the supervisor will be reviewing the tape of this session.		
You were recently delivered divorce papers.		
You are hung over from a friend's bachelor party last night.		
You just lost your part-time job and don't have money for the rent due at the end of the day.		
In your supervision session early in the day, you were told that your questioning is often long-winded, compounded, and closed.		
You were up all night studying for a test that you will take later in the afternoon.		
You are anxious about your comprehensive exams, which you will take in 2 days.		
Your previous client expressed suicidal ideation, and you are concerned you did not do enough to assess the risk.		

It appears that while the *ACA Code of Ethics* may be easy enough to understand, its enactment in the world of professional practice is often quite a challenge. However, for those who truly value their client's welfare, the challenges are small in light of the value when the embodiment of the principles presented within our *Code of Ethics* moves from merely a "good idea" to a personal necessity.

The What: In Principle

One could assume that an ethical counselor is one who abides by the *ACA Code of Ethics* (2014). After all, these codes stand as the hallmark of professional practice (Villa, Michael, & Jodi, 2004). However, following the "letter" of the code is important but, in our opinion, not sufficient. The ethical practitioner is one who not only knows the code and follows the specific principles, but has personally embraced and values the underlying moral principles that serve as the foundation for the specific codes.

The American Counseling Association's *Code of Ethics* (ACA, 2014) reflects broadly accepted Western moral principles that have been applied to specific actions and professional decisions (Remley & Herlihy, 2007; Urofsky, Engels, & Engebretson, 2008). And, while it is essential to know, to understand, and to follow the specific codes of conduct found within the American Counseling Association's *Code of Ethics* (ACA, 2014), it is equally important for each counselor and counselor-in-training to understand, value, and embrace the fundamental moral principles that serve as the foundation to our *Code of Ethics*.

As you transition from student to professional, you need to develop those moral dispositions that give evidence of your valuing of (a) the client's autonomy, (b) the desire to do no harm (nonmaleficence), and (c) the desire to do good (beneficence), while being (d) just and (e) faithful in all of your professional practice. These values, as the underpinning for our specific *Code of Ethics*, will be our focus.

Autonomy

Autonomy has been defined as "respect for the inherent freedom and dignity of each person" (Welfel, 2006, p. 32). Counselors who value client autonomy not only allow but encourage client freedom of choice and self-determination. These counselors truly embrace the perspective that they support, promote, and respect the rights of clients to choose their own directions, act in accordance with their beliefs, and control their own lives. Alternatively, this value of respect for client autonomy minimizes the possibility of counselors' fostering client dependency.

The fostering of independent decision making is not done blindly or absolutely. Fostering client autonomy is done in concert with other moral values, such as that directing counselors to do no harm (i.e., nonmaleficence). One would not encourage independent decisions that would likely harm the client or others. Thus, it is incumbent on ethical counselors to encourage client autonomy by first assisting clients in understanding how their decisions affect others as well as how their decisions may be received and reacted to within the context of their community. Ethical counselors encourage their clients to make sound, rational decisions, reflecting their level of development and competence. In short, this respect for autonomy directs counselors to not interfere with a client's decision making when the client genuinely has the capacity to decide.

Respect for client autonomy is a value that permeates the *ACA Code of Ethics* (ACA, 2014). A number of obvious principles found within the code that embody this value are presented in Table 4.1, along with specific examples of counselor behavior manifesting this value.

There are numerous ways this valuing of a client's autonomy takes form in ethical practice. At a minimum, valuing autonomy will direct counselors to obtain informed consent (see ACA, 2014, A.2.a) or, in the case of younger clients, assent, prior to beginning treatment. Seeking informed consent not only engages a client in a collaborative

Table 4.1 Valuing Autonomy

ACA Code of Ethics (2014)	*Counselor's Valuing of Autonomy*
A.1.a. Primary Responsibility The primary responsibility of counselors is to respect the dignity and to promote the welfare of clients.	Understanding that his client remained "embarrassed" about seeing a counselor, Dr. L. provided him the last appointment of the evening to reduce the chances of the client encountering someone in the waiting room, while at the same time inviting him to address this issue.
A.2.a. Informed Consent Clients have the freedom to choose whether to enter into or remain in a counseling relationship and need adequate information about the counseling process and the counselor.	All of the clients coming to K. L. Counseling and Consulting Services received a packet of information titled *Welcome to Our Practice.* The packet provided extensive information about the counselor credentials, the policies and procedures governing the practice, and specific information regarding the typical structure of the counseling sessions. Clients were invited to read the packet, and during the initial session, all client questions were answered.
B.1.b. Respect for Privacy Counselors respect the privacy of prospective and current clients.	Mr. Z. is a middle school counselor. He is well liked and seen as very approachable by students, parents, and teachers alike. Given the structure of the school and school day, Mr. Z. is often seen moving from his office to classrooms or meeting rooms. Because of the ease with which people have access to him, he often finds himself stopped in the hall for a "quick question." In each of these encounters, he is very mindful to invite the questioner to move from the public location to an open, unoccupied room. He believes that both the person who may be the topic of the question and the personal concerns exhibited by the questioner deserve a condition of privacy.

Source: Adapted from the Code of Ethics. American Counseling Association (2014) http://www.counseling.org/

process but gives form to the counselor's respect for the client's autonomous right to make choices. This valuing of a client's autonomy also finds expression in the counselor's respect for and valuing of (a) the confidentiality of client disclosures and (b) a client's right to terminate counseling.

Confidentiality

Confidentiality and the respecting of a client's right to privacy are pivotal to developing trust and establishing a working alliance. Clients, risking deep, personal, and intimate disclosure, have the right to expect that what they divulge will be kept private (Corey, Corey, & Callanan, 2007). But confidentiality is neither an absolute concept nor one that is static and established in concrete. Court decisions and legislative actions (e.g., HIPAA guidelines, FIRPA regulations, etc.) continue to reshape and give form to a counselor's ability to maintain confidentiality. Clients need to be informed of the limits and exceptions to the counselor's ability to maintain confidence. It is in sharing these limits that a counselor gives evidence of his or her respect for the autonomy of the client to engage in counseling under these conditions. Although there are several general and common exceptions to confidentiality (see, for example, Wheeler & Bertram, 2008), there may be additional limits imposed by the organization in which one works, or by the nature of one's professional status (i.e., student in field placement). It is essential as a student in transition that you familiarize yourself with (a) the limits of confidentiality as applied to your work with your clients; (b) the procedures for responding to crisis; (c) the process and procedure for responding to requests, including subpoenas for case notes, and (d) the identification of those within the site who have a "need to know." This information needs to be included, as appropriate, with that offered the client in the process of gaining informed consent.

Right to Terminate

This valuing of autonomy also directs counselors to respect the client's right to terminate counseling. This is true even in the case of clients mandated to attend counseling. Respecting their autonomy directs the counselor to respect their ability to choose not to embrace the mandate. Of course, implicit in this directive to value and respect a client's autonomy is the assumption that the client is capable of understanding the consequences of his or her decisions and is capable of choosing in ways that do not place him or her in a life-threatening situation or result in danger to others. In these cases, the counselor needs to intervene and, even then, the assumption is that the intervention is following the principle of "doing good" (i.e., beneficence) while respecting client autonomy.

The rationale in this situation is that the client is encountering nonautonomous processes that preclude the way the client would choose if not compromised. Consider a client who is in the grips of a psychotic episode. Clearly, the auditory hallucination directing the client to fly off the rooftop is interfering with the client's ability to accurately assess the dangers of such an activity and thus interfering with her ability to choose as she normally would under nonpsychotic conditions. In this case, the counselor needs to intervene to protect the client from the harmful effects of this faulty decision making. But even in this circumstance, the goal for counseling would be to bring the client to a position where she can make more informed decisions, especially in regards to her engagement in the counseling process.

The brief case illustration regarding a client with a psychotic episode is relatively clear-cut, but this is not always the case, and the issue of when and to what degree a counselor should interfere with a client's choice is up for debate (e.g., McLeod & Sherwin, 2000). Exercise 4.4 invites you to investigate this issue of limitations to client autonomy as experienced within your field placement site.

EXERCISE 4.4

Boundaries Defining Client Autonomy

Directions: Interview your site supervisor and/or other professional counselors at your site as to (a) organization policies regarding limiting client autonomy and (b) personal experiences with addressing concerns regarding client autonomy.

I. Policies, Conditions, and Laws

1. What, if any, policies, conditions, and laws exist that may interfere with a counselor's ability to acquire a client's informed consent?
2. Are there any policies, conditions, and laws that exist that interfere with a counselor's ability to maintain confidentiality?
3. What, if any, policies, conditions, and laws exist that would interfere with a counselor's ability to work jointly in devising integrated counseling plans?
4. Do counselors consider the cultural implications of informed consent procedures and, where possible, adjust their practices accordingly?
5. Are there conditions that limit the counselor's ability to ensure that clients understand the implications of diagnosis, the intended use of tests and reports, fees, and billing arrangements?
6. What, if any, policies, conditions, and laws exist that would interfere with a client's ability to refuse any services?

II. Personal Experience

1. How does valuing a client's autonomy give shape to your practice decisions?
2. Have you experienced any conditions that you felt necessitated your limiting of a client's autonomy?

Nonmaleficence

The principle of nonmaleficence, a principle with long standing in the medical profession, directs counselors to *do no harm*. The *ACA Code of Ethics,* A.4.a (ACA, 2014, p. 4), explicitly states, "Counselors act to avoid harming their clients, trainees, and research participants and to minimize or to remedy unavoidable or unanticipated harm."

On face value, this principle appears to be one that would be easy to recognize and implement. Consider, for example, Section C.6.d (ACA, 2014) of the *ACA Code of Ethics,* which refers to the exploitation of others: "Counselors do not exploit others in their professional relationships." More specifically, the *Code* (ACA, 2014, A.5.a) directs counselors against "sexual or romantic counselor–client interactions or relationships with current clients, their romantic partners, or their family members."

Although it may be hard to imagine, sexual exploitation continues to serve as a major reason for malpractice suits. For example, in one study (Stuart, 2007), it was found that 7% of therapists reported having had sex with their clients. Such behavior is clearly unethical, immoral, and, depending on circumstances, illegal. One can hope that such violation is the exception, not the rule, and point to the less than 10% reporting such action, but the truth is that in such a powerful, helping role, such behavior is not only legally and ethically nondefensible but also morally reprehensible.

It is important to be aware of and sensitive to the very fact that the dynamic of a counseling relationship can often invite the unintentional infliction of harm by way of the misuse of counselor power or the subtle imposition of counselor values in service of his or her personal needs. A simple example might be a situation in which a counselor in private practice, seeking to increase her income, extends the number or frequency of the counseling sessions well beyond any value to be accrued by the client. A similar situation is the case of a student in a field placement who makes the decision to extend the number of sessions with a client with the sole purpose of completing a course requirement (e.g., to meet a minimum of six times), with no regard given to the possible impact on the client.

The principle of nonmaleficence calls on us not only to avoid such extreme forms of exploitation but also to engage in any act that risks hurting clients, even inadvertently. For example, a counselor providing services that require knowledge and skill outside of his or her level of competency risks harming clients. Such behavior is not only warned against in our code, which states that counselors "practice only within the boundaries of their competence" (ACA, 2014, C.2.a), but also appears to be the second most frequently reported area of ethical complaint after sexual misconduct (Neukrug, Milliken, & Walden, 2001). This issue of practicing within the boundaries of one's competence becomes a special concern for the student-in-transition.

As a student in the field, your knowledge and skill need to be stretched beyond your current mastery. Therefore, it is essential that those with whom you work understand your "student" status, and within that role of student, the limits to your competency. It is also important to convey to your clients the nature of your relationship with your supervisor and the impact this relationship has on both monitoring your competency and affecting the limits of confidentiality. In gaining that informed consent and in receiving appropriate supervision, you can ethically stretch beyond your current grasp in the hope of further developing your professional knowledge and skill.

Other potential areas where a counselor can unintentionally impose harm on a client is the imposition of values and the insensitivity to other worldviews. Counselors who fail to understand and respect the client's unique experience and worldview and how these can give shape to the client's goals, values, and agendas risk harming not just the process but the client as well (Ryan, Lynch, Vansteenkiste, & Deci, E. L., 2011). Given this possibility, the code is clear to remind us that "Counselors are aware of—and avoid imposing—their values, attitudes, beliefs and behaviors" (ACA, 2014, A.4.b).

The danger of inflicting harm on one's client can emerge from what in many circumstances appear to be normative decisions and behaviors but that, within the uniqueness of any one counseling relationship, could prove harmful. Exercise 4.5 invites you to reflect on the potential harm that could be the inadvertent result of such "normative" counselor decisions and behaviors.

EXERCISE 4.5

The Possibility of Doing Harm

Directions: For each of the following counseling decisions or counselor behaviors, identify (a) potential conditions under which harm to the client could result and (b) steps to take to reduce the possibility of inadvertent harm. As with other exercises, it may prove beneficial to share your reflections with a colleague or site supervisor.

Counseling Decision or Counselor Behaviors	**Conditions Increasing the Possibility of Harm to the Client**	**Steps to Take to Reduce Possibility of Inadvertent Harm**
(Example) Counselor is working with a client who presented with extremely low self-esteem and dependency issues, especially in her relationship with her husband. The counselor engaged the client in CBT, focusing on developing increased assertiveness.	Client's cultural background and religious beliefs position her to view the role of husband as primary authority within a marriage.	Counselor needs to assist the client in identifying what she hopes to achieve as a result of counseling and then discuss with the client the possible impact such a change may have on her, those in her environment, and her relationships (including that with her husband).

Counseling Decision or Counselor Behaviors	Conditions Increasing the Possibility of Harm to the Client	Steps to Take to Reduce Possibility of Inadvertent Harm
Needing to cancel an appointment.		
Volunteering to assist a client in getting home following an appointment, knowing that her expected transportation is unavailable.		
Agreeing to meet the client for an appointment during a time (Sunday) when the office is typically closed.		
Volunteering to coach a community baseball league with the client's spouse.		
Offering to negotiate an alternative payment schedule, including the possibility of bartering, in response to the client's loss of his job.		

Beneficence

Beneficence is the counterpoint to nonmaleficence. This principle calls professional counselors to a higher standard than might be seen as a general norm of doing no harm that is proposed for the society at large. Counselors who embrace the value of beneficence will *actively* pursue actions that are helpful, supportive, and ultimately promoting client health and wellness. Table 4.2 provides a sampling of the specific principles found within the *Code of Ethics* (ACA, 2014), which give form to this moral value of beneficence.

Counselors who have embraced and embody beneficence in their professional practice are proactive in their pursuit of doing good. One form of such proactivity is found in the counselor who serves as an advocate for his or her client. When viewed from the perspective of the American Counseling Association's Advocacy Competencies (Lewis, Arnold, House, & Toporek, 2003), this advocacy includes not only acting on

Table 4.2 Beneficence: A Sampling of the *ACA Code of Ethics*

Code of Ethics (ACA, 2014)	*Description*	*Illustration*
A.7.a. Advocacy	When appropriate, counselors advocate at individual, group, institutional, and societal levels to examine potential barriers and obstacles that inhibit access and/or the growth and development of clients.	A school counselor serves on the school's IEP committee and advocates for students needing specific accommodations.
A.1.c. Counseling Plans	Counselors and their clients work jointly in devising integrated counseling plans that offer reasonable promise of success and are consistent with the abilities and circumstances of clients.	A mental health counselor actively investigates research supporting the effectiveness of various therapeutic strategies and employs this research as a foundation for formulating treatment plans.
C.2.a. Boundaries of Competence	Counselors practice only within the boundaries of their competence, based on their education, training, supervised experience, state and national professional credentials, and appropriate professional experience. Counselors gain knowledge, personal awareness, sensitivity, and skills pertinent to working with a diverse client population.	A licensed professional, who is in the process of changing jobs, experiences an increase in the number of minority clients being served. She contracts with a colleague for ongoing clinical supervision with the hope of increasing her self-awareness of her own worldviews and increase her level of cultural sensitivity.
C.2.f. Continuing Education	Counselors recognize the need for continuing education to acquire and maintain a reasonable level of awareness of current scientific and professional information in their fields of activity. They take steps to maintain competence in the skills they use, are open to new procedures, and keep current with diverse populations and the specific populations with whom they work.	Albeit fully licensed and in possession of the credentials necessary to maintain his job as a clinical mental health counselor, Dr. J. has created his own continuing education program. Each year, Dr. J. identifies a specific target for knowledge and skill development and then creates both a self-directed curriculum (identifying a series of articles and books to read) as well as enrolling in a minimum of four professional workshops or training sessions targeting his learning objectives.
C.2.d. Monitor Effectiveness	Counselors continually monitor their effectiveness as professionals and take steps to improve when necessary. Counselors in private practice take reasonable steps to seek peer supervision as needed to evaluate their efficacy as counselors.	The four counselors at M. L. King High School meet each Friday to (a) review cases and treatment plans, (b) present outcome data reflecting work with students, and (c) seek recommendations for improvement.

the behalf of the client but also empowering the client toward self-advocacy. Such empowerment clearly gives form to the value of beneficence. As noted in Table 4.2, beneficence takes on multiple forms beyond the obvious of explicitly advocating for one's client. For example, beneficence serves as the impetus for a counselor's continuing education, supervision, and self-monitoring and assessment procedures.

The value of beneficence directs counselors to address each client as an individual, not imposing cookie cutter theories, models, or approaches but rather developing treatment plans that reflect the uniqueness of the client (see A.2.c, Developmental and Cultural Sensitivity, ACA, 2014), in line with knowledge of best practice (see C.2.f, Continuing Education). All counselors' efforts to improve their knowledge and skill in service of best practice reflect their desire to do good and their valuing of beneficence.

As a student in the field, you are very likely focused on those tasks assigned by your supervisor or university faculty. This is how it should be. It is possible that the requirements, the assignments, the "have-to" may be both challenging and exhausting. However, as a student transitioning to professional, meeting course requirements is not sufficient. Your embodiment of beneficence needs to direct you to prioritize your time and your energies in service of doing good for your clients. Exercise 4.6 invites you to reflect upon your own practice decisions and the degree to which these embody beneficence and a commitment to "do good" for your clients.

EXERCISE 4.6

Embodying Beneficence

Directions: The current exercise invites you to reflect on your practice actions and decisions, identifying actions that clearly embody beneficence. If your role within your field placement confines you to a "look-see" role rather than a "do" role, your task is to identify places where beneficence could be manifested if you were serving in the role of counselor.

Arena for Embodying Beneficence	**Specific Examples**	**Possible Steps to Be Taken to More Fully Manifest Beneficence**
Participating in a strategic planning committee for a mental health agency	1. Advocate for flexible fee schedules for those in need. 2. Advocate for on-site continuing education for counselors.	1. Study and review steps that could be taken (e.g., marketing strategies) to increase service accountability to members of the community.

(Continued)

(Continued)

	3. Develop process and outcome evaluation measures to provide counselors with feedback on effectiveness.	2. Provide resources for providing community education as a preventive service.
Advocating for system responsiveness to client need		
Supporting and encouraging counselor professional development		
Monitoring "best practice"		
Using data-based decision making		
Supporting employment of evidenced-based treatment		
Making efforts to increase counselor cultural sensitivity		
(other forms of embodying beneficence)		

Justice

Justice requires the counselor's commitment to fairness in professional relationships. Counselors' actions and decisions must be fair to all concerned. As noted in the *Code of Ethics* (ACA, 2014),

> Counselors do not condone or engage in discrimination against prospective or current clients, students, employees, supervisees, or research participants based on age, culture, disability, ethnicity, race, religion/spirituality, gender, gender identity, sexual orientation, marital/partnership status, language preference, socioeconomic status, immigration status, or any basis proscribed by law. (C.5, Nondiscrimination)

Clearly, justice demands equality, which has implications for nondiscrimination and equitable treatment of all clients. But equitable does not mean sameness. The principle of justice directs counselors to treat individuals in proportion to their relevant differences. Consider, for example, the issue of setting fees. Here the code directs the professional counselor to "consider the financial status of clients and locality." In the event that the established fee structure is inappropriate for a client, counselors assist clients in attempting to find comparable services of acceptable cost (ACA, 2014, A.10.b). Thus, equal does not mean sameness. For justice to be present, however, differential treatment, even when applied to fee setting, needs to be done with a rationale that explains the necessity and appropriateness of such differential treatment. Further, in all cases, justice demands that the actions, even when unequal, are engaged with the intent of equally promoting the health and well-being of each client and are appropriate within the counselor/client relationship.

Thus, justice, when guiding treatment planning and practice decisions, directs counselors to take into account the client's current and past cultural environment, especially when it is different from the counselor's. Fairness includes respecting clients' cultural values and refraining from imposing one's personal beliefs when those beliefs are inappropriate. Consider Case Illustration 4.2 as it reflects a counselor's engagement of justice into his decision making.

CASE ILLUSTRATION 4.2

Sensitivity to Client Culture

It was clear that Junita was a bright, achieving, and socially mature college freshman. It was also clear that she was extremely unhappy and stressed following a visit home during a brief fall break. In meeting with the counselor, Junita expressed very strong, yet very conflicting feelings about being at college.

Junita was the first female in her family to attend college. The other children (two older brothers and two older sisters) worked in the family restaurant. Although Junita always dreamed of becoming a physician–a dream that appeared to the counselor to be quite reasonable and realistic, given her academic abilities–her return home resulted in a lot of second guessing. She was feeling very guilty about not following in her siblings' footsteps and helping out at the restaurant.

In her meeting with the counselor, Junita shared comments made by her dad questioning the value of a college education for a female who would most likely "get married and have kids." She also was troubled by questions posed by her mom and siblings, who could not understand why she would want to move away from the family. They even questioned her possible desire to hide her cultural heritage and act "white."

The limited family support and challenges she experienced were not only upsetting but, at a deeper level, causing great internal conflict. Junita was having difficulty reconciling

(Continued)

(Continued)

the conflict between what she felt was her inner direction to continue in college and the felt outer demands.

The counselor valued client autonomy and self-actualization and, as such, was inclined to invite the student to revisit the "realities" of the situation in the hope that she could assert herself and her needs. But as the story unfolded, the counselor became aware that a goal of self-assertion was not, at this point, in service of promoting the client's health and welfare.

The client's cultural values, which were initially inculcated but now were clearly embraced and voluntarily owned, positioned her to value family and collectivist culture as strongly as she valued her own self-actualization. With evidence of the strength of this cultural belief, the counselor realized that targeting the development of her assertiveness in response to these family challenges could be an affront to her family, her society, and her own collectivist values, and thus not in her best interest.

Respecting the uniqueness of the client and being sensitive to these cultural forces, the counselor shifted his focus to assisting the client in her identification of all of these competing values.

Fidelity

The fidelity principle reflects the counselors' call to earn and maintain the client trust within the counseling relationship. Without the client's ability to trust both the counselor and the therapeutic relationship, little growth will occur.

Fidelity is based on counselors' faithful adherence to the promises explicitly made and those implied by the nature of the counseling relationship. Simply put, fidelity requires counselors to honor all of their professional commitments. Counselors need to be faithful to their word and the expectations they have created in their client. Thus, that which was shared with the client in the process of obtaining informed consent—including the parameters marking confidentiality, the nature of the fee structure, the anticipated process to be employed, and so forth—must not only have been shared but consistently enacted.

Perhaps the principle that best illustrates the need for fidelity is the one that addresses counselor abandonment. Principle A.12 (ACA, 2014) states, "Counselors do not abandon or neglect clients in counseling." The idea of client abandonment may seem shocking, especially if interpreted in absolute terms, but the truth is that conditions of life may force or invite the counselor to be unavailable to a client. Consider the situation of normal interruptions to treatment that may occur as a result of counselor vacations, alternative work demands, or illness. Responding to these disruptions with an eye toward fidelity requires a counselor to make appropriate arrangements for the continuation of treatment when such continuation is necessary.

Another challenge to enacting this value of fidelity comes when a counselor recognizes that his or her efforts are proving unproductive in assisting the client. To continue the treatment plan or perhaps even the therapeutic relationship in light of its ineffectiveness would be unethical, at a minimum violating the principle of beneficence and even potentially doing harm to the client and the client's view of counseling as a profession. Thus, while fidelity may direct the counselor to continue in the relationship, the welfare of the client demands termination. In this situation, remaining faithful to the primary directive of counseling, to "promote the welfare of clients" (ACA, 2014, A.1.a, Primary Responsibility) takes precedence and directs appropriate termination. When done appropriately, that is, with the counselor providing pretermination counseling and recommending other service providers when necessary (see ACA, 2014, a.11.c & a.11.d), termination is an embodiment of fidelity. Under these conditions, termination is evidence of a counselor remaining faithful to the primary directive of his or her counseling contract, that is, to promote the welfare of the client.

Maintaining fidelity is not always easy given organizational policies, staffing issues, or even subtle organizational culture influences. Exercise 4.7 invites you to identify challenges experienced by counselors at your field placement site that make the embodiment of fidelity difficult at times, as well as the strategies they employ to address these challenges.

EXERCISE 4.7

Ensuring Fidelity

Directions: Interview your site supervisor and/or other professional counselors at your site. Your task is to identify challenges experienced by counselors at your field placement site that make the embodiment of fidelity difficult at times. Also identify the strategies they employ to address these challenges.

1. What events or conditions (including staff turnover, scheduled vacations, rotation of assignments, etc.) may interfere with a counselor's ability to maintain his or her relationship and counseling dynamic with a client? How are the client's needs addressed during these disruptions?
2. Does early termination and transfer of a client to another counselor ever occur? If so, under what types of conditions might it occur and how is it enacted?
3. What internal or external forces may operate and result in a counselor breaking his or her word to a client? For example, although the parameters of confidentiality may have been discussed during the process of obtaining informed consent, are there times or conditions that require violation of this initial "promise" (e.g., a court order) and/or are there subtle social norms that exist that allow or encourage violation (e.g., open discussion of clients in the lunchroom)?

From the Ideal to the Real

In the previous pages, we identified a number of the principles articulated in the American Counseling Association's *Code of Ethics* (ACA, 2014) and demonstrated how these are outgrowths of five fundamental moral principles: autonomy, nonmaleficence, beneficence, justice, and fidelity. Throughout the chapter, we have attempted to highlight the need for counselors—both professional and those in transition to professional status—not only to understand the *Code of Ethics* and the moral principles serving as their foundation but also to embrace these codes, these moral principles, as personally valued guides to professional practice.

We recognize that this is not always an easy task. The day-to-day demands faced by counselors within the field often present challenges to the full embodiment of these principles. But then, no one said it would be easy. Even with that difficulty as a reality, we know that our clients and our profession demand that we move beyond simply knowing our ethics to engaging them in all of our professional decisions and practices.

We close this chapter with one last exercise (Exercise 4.8). We invite you to sit with your site supervisors and/or other site counselors and identify the challenges they have encountered in embodying these moral principles as well as the steps they have taken to ensure their own ethical practice.

EXERCISE 4.8

The Lived Experience

Directions: As a summary activity, you are invited to interview your site supervisor, as well as other professional counselors working at your site, in order to identify examples of how the five moral principles discussed within this chapter are embodied in their practice decisions along with the challenges they have encountered in their embodiment of these principles.

Autonomy (i.e., respecting client's freedom of choice and consent)

Nonmaleficence (i.e., operating within competency)

Beneficence (i.e., heeding duty to warn or protect)

Justice (i.e., advocating against discrimination)

Fidelity (i.e., showing loyalty to clients)

KEYSTONES

- Professional codes of ethics stand as articulated values and beliefs held by those identified with and practicing in a particular profession.

- The *ACA Code of Ethics* has developed and is offered as the standard against which to judge professional decisions and actions.
- As a standard ensuring the public against harm, the code requires each professional to not only embrace and embody the code's principles but also hold his or her colleagues accountable to do the same.
- Counselors-in-training have a responsibility to understand and follow the *ACA Code of Ethics* and adhere to applicable laws, regulatory policies, and rules and policies governing professional staff behavior at the agency or placement setting. Students have the same obligation to clients as those required of professional counselors.
- The American Counseling Association's *Code of Ethics* (ACA, 2014) reflects broadly accepted Western moral principles that have been applied to specific actions and professional decisions.
- Transitioning from student to professional requires one to develop those moral dispositions that give evidence of the valuing of (a) the client's autonomy, (b) the desire to do no harm (nonmaleficence), and (c) the desire to do good (beneficence), while being (d) just and (e) faithful in all of your professional practice.
- Autonomy has been defined as "respect for the inherent freedom and dignity of each person."
- The principle of nonmaleficence, a principle with long standing in the medical profession, directs counselors to *do no harm.*
- Counselors who embrace the value of beneficence will *actively* pursue actions that are helpful, supportive, and ultimately promoting client health and wellness.
- Justice demands equality, which has implications for nondiscrimination and equitable treatment of all clients. But equitable does not mean "sameness." The principle of justice directs counselors to treat equals equally and unequals unequally but in proportion to their relevant differences.
- Fidelity is based on a counselor's faithful adherence to the promises explicitly made and those implied by the nature of the counseling relationship.

ADDITIONAL RESOURCES

Web Based

American Counseling Association. (n.d.). *Counseling and risk management.* Retrieved from http://www.counseling.org/knowledge-center/ethics/risk-management

Healthcare Providers Service Organization: http://www.hpso.com//mail/counselor-risk-management-v2/?refID=BP1BWi

Resources for Therapists and Counselors. (n.d.). Retrieved from http://www.goodtherapy.org/resources-for-therapists.html

Wheeler, A. M., & Bertram, B. (2012). *The counselor and the law* (6th ed.). Retrieved from http://www.counseling.org/Publications/FrontMatter/72919-FM.PDF

Print Based

American Counseling Association. (2014). *ACA code of ethics.* Alexandria, VA: Author.

Bernstein, B. E., & Hartsell, T. L. (2004). *The portable lawyer for mental health professionals* (2nd ed.). Hoboken, NJ: John Wiley.

Burke, A., Harper, H., & Kruger, G. (2007). Moving beyond statutory ethical codes: Practitioner ethics as a contextual, character-based enterprise. *South African Journal of Psychology, 37*(1), 107–120.

Hodges, S. (2011). *The counseling practicum and internship manual.* New York, NY: Springer.

Welfel, E. R. (2013). *Ethics in counseling and psychotherapy: Standards, research and emerging issues* (5th ed.). Belmont, CA: Brooks/Cole-Cengage.

REFERENCES

American Counseling Association. (2014). *ACA code of ethics.* Alexandria, VA: Author.

Corey, G., Corey, M., & Callanan, P. (2007). *Issues and ethics in the helping profession* (7th ed.). Pacific Grove, CA: Brooks/Cole.

Gladding, S. T., Remley, T. P., & Hubor, C. H. (2001). *Ethical, legal, and professional issues in the practice of marriage and family therapy* (3rd ed.). Upper Saddle River, NJ: Merrill/Prentice Hall.

Healthcare Providers Service Organization. (2014). *Understanding counselor liability risk.* Retrieved from https://www.hpso.com/pdfs/db/CNA_CLS_COUNS_022814p_CF_PROD_ASIZE_online_SEC.pdf?fileName=CNA_CLS_COUNS_022814p_CF_PROD_ASIZE_online_SEC.pdf&folder=pdfs/db&isLiveStr=Y

Lewis, J., Arnold, M. S., House, R., & Toporek, R. (2003). *The advocacy competencies.* American Counseling Association. Retrieved from http://www.counseling.org/docs/competencies/advocacy_competencies.pdf?sfvrsn=3

McLeod, C., & Sherwin, S. (2000). Relational autonomy, self-trust, and health care for patients who are oppressed. In C. Mackenzie & N. Stoljar (Eds.), *Relational autonomy* (pp. 259–279). New York, NY: Oxford University Press.

National Practitioner Data Bank. (2013). *NPDB 2011 annual report.* Retrieved from http://www.npdb-hipdb.hrsa.gov/resources/reports/2011NPDBAnnualReport.pdf

Neukrug, E., Milliken, T., & Walden, S. (2001). Ethical complaints made against credentialed counselors: An updated survey of state licensing boards. *Counselor Education and Supervision, 41,* 57–70.

Parsons, R. D. (2001). *The ethics of professional practice.* Boston, MA: Allyn & Bacon.

Reamer, F. G. (2003). *Social work malpractice and liability: Strategies for prevention* (2nd ed.). New York, NY: Columbia University Press.

Remley, T. P., & Herlihy, B. (2007). *Ethical, legal, and professional issues in counseling* (Updated 2nd ed.). Upper Saddle River, NJ: Merrill/Prentice Hall.

Ryan, R. M., Lynch, M. F., Vansteenkiste, M., & Deci, E. L. (2011). Motivation and autonomy in counseling, psychotherapy, and behavior change: A look at theory and practice. *Counseling Psychologist, 39*(2), 193–260.

Stuart, J. (2007, May 8). Sex on the couch: The therapists who abuse their clients' trust. *The Independent* (UK).

Urofsky, R. I., Engels, D. W., & Engebretson, K. (2008). Kitchener's principle ethics: Implications for counseling practice and research. *Counseling & Values, 53*(1), 67–78.

Villa, M. T., Michael, J. L., & Jodi, L. S. (2004). A comparison of ethical beliefs of certified rehabilitation counselors and national certified counselors. *Rehabilitation Counseling Bulleting, 47*(4), 234–246. Retrieved from http://search.proquest.com/docview/213914071?accountid=7113

Wheeler, A. M., & Bertram, B. (2008). *The counselor and the law: A guide to legal and ethical practice.* Alexandria, VA: American Counseling Association.

Welfel, E. R. (2006). *Ethics in counseling and psychotherapy: Standards, research, and emerging issues.* Belmont, CA: Brooks/Cole.

5

Reflecting on Practice

An unexamined life is not worth living.

Socrates

With apologies to Socrates, the Greek philosopher, it appears that with a minor tweaking of the words, his quote holds value for all professional counselors. Counseling, as an intentional process, demands that counselors examine or reflect on their professional life and practice to ensure that the service they offer is effective and . . . worth doing.

The counselor's ability to reflect on his or her counseling has been identified as an essential component to effective practice (Nelson & Neufeldt, 1998). As will be presented within this chapter, the process of reflecting on one's practice decisions is essential to the ethical and effective practice, whether this reflection takes form in the development of a counselor's case conceptualization and treatment plan or is evidenced by a counselor's in-the-moment adjustment to these plans.

As used here and elsewhere (see Parsons, 2009), a distinction is made between reflection *on* practice and reflection *in* practice. Reflection on practice is a process of looking back over the previous session in the hope of more fully understanding what was intended, what was achieved, and what changes or adjustments need to be made as the counselor and client move forward. Whereas reflection in practice takes place during the session and involves the counselor's ability to attend to his or her own behaviors and counseling decisions and the client's response to those decisions and behaviors. This counselor reflective observation of what was done and what resulted serves as the data for making at-the-moment, "on the run" adjustments to the dynamic occurring at any one point in a session.

The current chapter addresses the nature of reflective practice as it gives shape to the counselor's case conceptualization and treatment planning as well as to his or her within-session decisions. In addition to facilitating readers' understanding and utilization of reflective practice as an essential ingredient to effective counseling, the chapter will assist readers' self-evaluation and planning of the next phase of their professional development as it takes form in their emerging professional identity. Specifically, at the completion of this chapter, readers will be able to

- describe the essentials in the process of reflection on counseling practice,
- explain the moment-to-moment decisions made in the process of reflection in practice,
- describe their intentionality behind what they are doing to increase the efficacy of their decisions and the effectiveness of their helping strategies, and
- articulate the essence of reflection for professional development.

Reflecting *on* Practice: Case Conceptualization

Professional counselors enter a counseling relationship with specific knowledge and skills that allow them to facilitate the client's sharing of his or her story. The counselor will employ skills such as attending behavior, reflections, summarizations, questions, clarifications, and so forth, all in the hope of unearthing the client's concerns, resources, and goals. Under the right conditions, these skills will elicit a large amount of information. This gathering of data, however, is not the end goal.

Like pieces of a very complicated puzzle, the data acquired will provide full value only once they are arranged into a meaningful, consistent, and coherent picture of the client's concerns, goals, challenges, and resources. To develop such a meaningful picture of the client and the client's current experience, a counselor will need to process these data in light of his or her theoretical orientation, knowledge of the research, and extensive professional experience. Through a process of reflection, the counselor will assemble the data into an integrated view of what is, what is desired, and what can be done to assist the client in his or her achievement of his or her goals. This integrated view, or case conceptualization, sets the framework for consideration of strategies and techniques needed to move the client toward the desired outcome (Parsons, 2009).

When attempting to completely understand the client's story, a counselor will need to gather data identifying the behavioral, cognitive, affective, physiological, and sociocultural components of the client's issue (Parsons & Zhang, 2014a). Case conceptualization is a process that guides a counselor's observations, data collection, understanding, and conceptual integration of client behaviors, thoughts, feelings, and physiology from a clinical perspective (Neukrug & Schwitzer, 2006). Consider the simple case of a student who is sent to the school counselor's office because of his failure to complete homework assignments. Although the presenting complaint points to a failure to complete homework, how might a counselor's understanding of the situation change if the client was a second grader or a senior in high school? Would the developmental characteristics associated with these ages color the counselor's understanding? Or consider how the counselor's understanding of the issue might be altered if the student used English as a second language, or had parents who recently went through a very contentious divorce? Understanding the nature of a client's concern in order to develop interventions that will effectively assist the client in achieving his or her desired goals requires a full understanding of all the conditions that affect the client's situation.

Key to effective case conceptualization is the ability of the counselor not only to discern data that is relevant from information that is not but also to integrate those relevant data into hypotheses regarding the causes, precipitants, and maintaining influences of the client's psychological, interpersonal, and behavioral problems. This integration of the data into a meaningful conceptualization of the case is facilitated by the counselor's ability to process the information shared through his or her knowledge of the theory and research addressing all aspects of the human condition. Consider Case Illustration 5.1. The case, while somewhat simplistic, depicts a counselor's adjustment of her case conceptualization as a result of ongoing client disclosure and her knowledge of theory and research explaining the human condition.

CASE ILLUSTRATION 5.1

A Changing Picture

Introduction: The following demonstrates one counselor's thinking about the data presented by a client during an intake interview and how the meaning drawn from the data was adjusted given each new presentation and the counselor's knowledge of the theory and research on the human condition.

Summary of Client Information

The client, Selena, is a freshman business major in her second month at college. Selena came to the University Counseling Center complaining of sleeplessness, loss of appetite, lethargy, and general loss of interest in engaging socially with those in her dorm. Selena expressed concern that her grades were falling off and said she just didn't feel as interested in her classes as she was when she first came to class.

In sharing her history, Selena noted that she was always a good student and had received a scholarship to come to state college. She noted that it was difficult leaving home—especially because her father expected that she, like her two siblings, would graduate from high school and work at the family restaurant. "My dad never did see any value to college—especially for a girl whom he believed would simply become married and pregnant and never use that education." Selena noted that she originally wanted to study pre-med because she excelled at mathematics and science and deeply felt a calling to medicine and the possibility of being of service within her community. Her choice of business as a major was an attempt to gain her father's approval. "I thought he would like the fact that I could return to help in the restaurant."

Selena reported how she simply loved her first 2 months on campus. "The things I was learning were so cool and the new friends I made convinced me this was where I needed

(Continued)

(Continued)

to be." But all that changed. Selena stated that she has been feeling really down for a couple of weeks and that it seemed to have started after her return home for Thanksgiving. In describing the experience, Selena noted how she enjoyed seeing her brother and her extended family and how they were all excited to hear about her experience at school. When asked about her mom and dad, Selena stated that her mom was proud and very emotional about missing her whereas her dad spoke very little about college and just said that he was glad that she was serious about her studies and knew she would do well. "But then he was quick to remind me not to get into all that college partying. I don't know why he had to say that. He knows me—I don't do that. Why can't he just say he's proud?"

Counselor—On *Practice Reflections*

- It's not so atypical to find a freshman showing some difficulty adjusting to the process of being away from home. (I wonder if this is just typical adjustment of an adolescent to an independent adult and the stress and anxiety that elicits?)
- Selena, however, is exhibiting symptoms of depression that would suggest that the stress she is experiencing is more than that typically encountered by a freshman in transition. (Clearly, the intensity of her symptoms and their disruption to her functioning moves this beyond the realm of a typical young adult challenge.)
- There is evidence that she has the academic and social skills necessary to be successful at college and, during the first 2 months of her freshman year, she was experiencing that success. (The fact that she has the skills necessary for successful adjustment and that she has adapted successfully both in high school and during the early months of college seems to dismiss the possibility that this is a personality issue or long-standing pattern.)
- The change seems to coincide with her visit home for Thanksgiving. (This specific event appears associated with the change in mood. I wonder if Selena experienced enough stress over that period to result in the development of these emotional or behavioral symptoms. If so, then we are looking at an adjustment disorder.)
- Selena appears to be having difficulty reconciling what she feels is an inner direction, to be a physician, with what she is expected to do, to work in the family restaurant. (I wonder if breaking away and moving toward independence as an adult are more stressful for those of Latin heritage. I need to do a little research on this issue.)
- Selena's attempt to reconcile these two forces—by embracing a business major—is satisfying neither of these forces, and this incongruency is serving as a source for the stress taking form in her symptoms. (This issue of congruency and incongruency is central for client-centered theory, and I wonder if taking a less-than-directive approach may be helpful here?)
- It appears that although her dad is unconvinced of the value of his daughter's college education, he is taking a wait-and-see attitude and has attempted to provide some support for her work. (I am surprised—I didn't initially expect her dad

to be at all supportive. He is taking a real task focus but I'm not sure that is atypical for many males or many Latin males. Again, I want to check that out.)

- Other family members—mom, brothers, and extended family—are clearly supportive and proud of Selena's college experience. (I wonder, with this level of support, what the source of the stress is? Is it that she is fearful of disappointing them? Or is she now feeling as if she couldn't leave college even if she wanted? No . . . her statements about doing well and envisioning graduate school suggest she is not stressed by these possibilities.)
- With the clear support found both at home and on campus, Selena's unhappiness seems to rest in her need for her dad's approval. (It seems to me that her dad is supportive—he noted he was happy with her hard work and believed she would do well—but clearly she appears to have discounted those comments and was focusing on the absence of any clear statement of pride and valuing coming from her dad. I wonder if taking a cognitive approach to help her look at her thoughts about needing dad's approval might be of assistance to her?)

Case Illustration 5.1 demonstrated a counselor's reflection on practice as she reviewed elements of the story that appeared significant and processed those elements through her knowledge of theory and research in an attempt to identify the theme running through these data and tie them to a coherent picture. In this case, the initial case conceptualization targets the client's possible cognitive distortion regarding her personal values and the need for external approval (specifically that of her father), while being respectful of the unique cultural values and experiences the client is bringing to the practice. It is now your turn. Exercise 5.1 invites you to reflect on client data as it emerges and affects your case conceptualization.

EXERCISE 5.1

Case Conceptualization: An Emerging Picture

Directions: The following exercise will present you with some specific data about a client, Christina. These data are presented in small segments. The focus is for you to allow each piece of information, each piece of this puzzle, to give shape to your working hypothesis about the emerging picture of what is happening and what needs to be done.

You may find that doing this exercise with a colleague or your site supervisor will prove helpful and productive.

Presenting Problem

Christina has not spoken to her mother for more than 4 months. Christina's mother called her a slut during the summer when she dumped her boyfriend in order to date a

(Continued)

(Continued)

married coworker. The relationship with that man lasted only a month, and Christina went back to her original boyfriend. Christina is currently experiencing stress related to her relationship with her mother. She is anxious about the upcoming Thanksgiving holiday, thinking that she may not attend what has been a long-standing family tradition of dinner at Mom's. She is very concerned about how she will handle being in the same room with her mother after 4 months of not speaking to each other.

While it is early in the data collection phase–what might be your initial hypothesis about what is going on here, and what type of treatment plan (goals and strategies) might you be thinking about?

Client Data

Christina is 38 years old and has lived on her own since graduating college at age 20. Christina was actively recruited by a number of pharmaceutical companies following graduation due to her exemplary performance as a dual major in biology and chemistry and a minor in marketing. Christina graduated magna cum laude and took a job, initially as a research scientist for a major pharmaceutical company. Since being hired, Christina has moved up through the ranks and now serves as vice president for east coast sales.

The puzzle taking shape now has new pieces. As you filter this information through your knowledge of developmental theory and life tasks, how might it affect your initial hypothesis and treatment plan (if at all)? How might the new data, the new pieces, give form to a different puzzle picture? A competent woman successfully navigating a tough academic curriculum and business within a highly male-oriented industry and yet . . . she is intimidated about confronting her mother following an extended period of non-contact.

Family Information

Christina's mother, a Kashmiri Hindu, came to the United States when Christina was 6 months old. She left her home in Kashmir as part of a Kashmiri exodus, which saw a massive displacement of Hindus from Kashmir. There were threats and rumors that the Kashmiri Hindus were to be killed, but the incident that served as the impetus for Christina's mother to leave was a vicious attack on her neighbor, who had acid thrown on her because she went out into the marketplace without wearing a headscarf.

Again, as you continue evolving your case conceptualization, this information will serve as new pieces that not only need to fit the overall puzzle but will give shape to it. What, if anything, do you know about Kashmiri Hindus? As Christina's counselor, do you feel ethically responsible to investigate the values of this culture? How might this culture give shape to mother–daughter interactions? How does knowing this cultural information affect your initial hypothesis and treatment plan?

Client History

Christina is an attractive, bright woman who reached puberty at the age of 11. Her years in middle school and high school were marked by success in social context (e.g., being elected student council president), academics (e.g., receiving a 4-year presidential scholarship to an

Ivy League university), and in athletics (e.g., being elected as captain for both the girls lacrosse and softball teams). In addition to these areas of notable success, Christina received a lot of male attention due to her early development. In middle school, her early physical development drew the attention of those not only within her own class but much older (high school) boys. Christina was not allowed to date until she turned 18 (her senior year). Prior to that, she missed out on school formal dances or proms and could only socialize in group settings.

How might your viewing the above information through your knowledge of preadolescent and adolescent development color your current hypothesis? How might the above information—if viewed through an orienting theory such as a psychodynamic, Adlerian, or cognitive theory—color your initial hypotheses and treatment plan?

Recent Developments

In an interview with the counselor, Christina alluded to the fact that she had a history, while in college, of participating in risky sexual behaviors (one-night stands, unprotected sex, promiscuity, etc.). She was hesitant to respond when the counselor attempted to gain more information, stating, "That was the past. I'm different now, even though my mom doesn't think so."

In discussing her current relationship, she noted that she has been with her current boyfriend off and on for the past 3 years. She did note that throughout the past 3 years she has had four secret affairs, all with married men. She quickly added that these occurred only during times when she and her boyfriend were separated. Christina expressed a concern whether or not she could ever settle down with one man or be committed to one monogamous relationship.

Given this pattern of behavior and expressed concerns about interpersonal, intimate relationships, how might your initial hypothesis and treatment plans change?

Client Goals

When asked by the counselor what she hopes to achieve as a result of coming to counseling, the client quite unexpectedly began to cry. This was a change from her previous anger and aggressive style and presentation. She responded, "I can't stand it that my mother is so disapproving of me. Why can't she love me? I'm not a bad child."

Although the response was unexpected by the counselor, and perhaps also by you, how might the response and the tone of the response change the picture that is unfolding and the hypothesis and treatment plan that you were developing?

The formulation of an integrated, consistent view of the client's main issues provides the foundation for developing a coherent plan for change (Eells, 1997). Thus, the effective, competent counselor employs the process of reflecting on practice as a base for the formulation of a case conceptualization. The process requires a counselor to move smoothly from data collection, through organization, and finally to the extraction of meaning as the springboard for formulation and implementation of the treatment plan (Jongsma, Peterson, & McInnis, 2006).

This reflection on practice and the resulting conceptualization and planning is not a one-time process. The effective counselor takes time to reflect on each session, reviewing what he or she did, what he or she anticipated would happen and what in fact happened. This reflection provides the data from which a counselor can assess the current state of the counseling and make adjustments as needed. Reflection on what was done is foundational for deciding what needs to be done. Reflection on practice is what would typically occur following a session. It is the process through which a counselor reviews a session in terms of what was initially expected and hoped for, what occurred, and how the experience gives shape and direction to what needs to happen as the counseling relationship moves forward.

This reflection on practice may occur in the brief time existing between seeing clients or that period between seeing that client and the end of the day, and it is not unusual for counselors who work in a setting where there are a number of professional colleagues to find time during their busy schedules to discuss their sessions with one another. Many counselors have found end-of-week meetings for case review to be a way of both gaining insight about their clients and promoting professional development.

As a student in the field, this reflection on your practice will most likely occur within your field placement class and most certainly with your site supervisor. Whether reflection on practice occurs in isolation or with others, this intentional assessment of the outcome and process of a session provides the counselor the data necessary to make meaningful adjustment to plans and approaches to ensure maximum effectiveness. To maximize the benefit—both for your client and your own professional development—from your own guided reflection on practice, you may want to approach reflection on practice with an understanding of (a) what you did; (b) why you did what you did; (c) the actual impact or client response; and (d) finally and perhaps most important, an openness to the feedback you receive, as it provides possible alternative perspectives on "what happened" and "what needs to be done." The value of reflecting on practice with the help of a colleague or supervisor is highlighted in Case Illustration 5.2.

CASE ILLUSTRATION 5.2

Something Not Quite Right?

The client, Leah, was self-referred to a local counseling center. She explained that her husband had just announced that he was thinking about separating and perhaps filing for divorce. This announcement was both "heartbreaking" and "totally unexpected." She felt that although her marriage of 5 years had some challenges, they were no more severe than those experienced by most of her friends.

Throughout the intake session, Leah described how "devastated" she was and how she simply "could not live without" her husband. Leah noted that her goal for coming to counseling was to find ways to engage her husband in marriage counseling in order to save what she described as a good marriage.

The counselor in this case found that something didn't feel quite right about this focus on marital counseling, but he was unsure what or why. Over lunch, he invited a colleague to provide a perspective on the case. As he shared the information from intake (protecting the identity of the client), it became clear that the client had an agenda and was specific in stating it. Although her initial concern and goal highlighted her desire to engage in marriage counseling and save her marriage, both the counselor and his colleague felt as if something more might be in the mix.

As they discussed the case, the colleague pointed out what appeared to be an unusual level of intensity with which the client not only shared her sadness, but more important, framed that sadness within the context of "desperately" needing to save the marriage. The counselor when reflecting on the case felt that the sadness and her phraseology were appropriate to the fact that they had been married 5 years and the announcement was totally unexpected.

As the two continued to discuss the case, both agreed that it was clear that the client valued her marriage commitment. The counselor's colleague continued to question whether it was possible that her need to stay in the marriage reflected something other than a commitment to and valuing of the marriage. Through the continued reflection on the session, the two identified data, other pieces of this puzzle, that failed to neatly and easily fit the picture of a "good, worth-saving marriage."

Throughout their discussion, attention seemed to keep coming back to the client's presentation of both verbal and nonverbal evidence of experiencing heightened anxiety when considering the possibility of being on her own. The more they reviewed the case, the more the colleague observed that perhaps something other than a desire to save her marriage was in play. The hypothesis that began to emerge was that it was the client's anxiety about being on her own, living as a single person, that was more concerning than the actual fact that her marriage might be ending. As they reflected on the data, it appeared that it was this anxiety about being on her own, even more than sadness, that might be serving as the primary motivation for saving the marriage. With reflection, the counselor began to remember the numerous points throughout the session where the client made note of how she "wasn't sure she could do it on her own" and that she "needed" him or someone on whom she could rely. The client shared how she was sure that "if he leaves me, no one else would want me . . . and then what am I to do?"

These statements of *needing* the relationship versus *wanting or desiring* the relationship seemed to suggest the possibility that low self-esteem and a belief that she needed to rely on others to navigate life successfully promoted a sense of dependency and gave form to the current anxiety. As he began to think about the direction he might like to take during the second session, the counselor was intrigued by a question posed by his colleague. "How might the client's desire to save the marriage be different if she had a better, stronger sense of self and a belief in her own resiliency and ability to thrive outside of this marriage?"

With this question in mind, the counselor decided to use the next session to not only follow up on the original plan of assessing the experience of sharing with her husband about the client's engagement in counseling, but also begin to test out the degree to which the client's self-perception might be coloring her experience of this current situation.

With the two case illustrations demonstrating the process of reflection on practice, you are now invited to engage in this process of reflection on your own practice (see Exercise 5.2 and Exercise 5.3).

EXERCISE 5.2

Considering Salient Elements of the Client Story

Directions: Your task is to identify a client with whom you have had initial contact. If you are not engaging with clients, ask your colleagues or supervisor to share the details of one of their cases. Now, working with a colleague or supervisor, your task is to complete the following.

1. What is/was the client's original presenting concern or goal for coming to counseling (describe here).

   ____

   ____

2. Descibe your working hypothesis about what is happening with the client, identifying the underlying cause, precipitating events, and maintaining elements.

   ____

   ____

3. Review each of the following questions and discuss how the data derived from answering the question may contribute to the unfolding picture of your client's story as well as your evolving working hypothesis.

Question	**How might these data change the nature of the picture emerging?**	**How might these data affect your working hypothesis and case conceptualization?**
What are the developmental characteristics of your client (e.g., cognitive stage of development, moral stage, physical changes, social-emotional tasks, etc.)?		
What is the client's ethnic, cultural, and social background?		
What is the client's family constellation?		
What is the client's current social support network?		

What, if any, physical, emotional, or social challenges or stressors is the client experiencing?		
What is the client's history with this or similar issues?		
What does the research suggest about best practice with this type of presenting concern or goals?		

EXERCISE 5.3

Looking for an Alternative Hypothesis

Directions: The following invites you to reflect on your work with one of your clients. The process is a two-phase process: the first phase is self-directed and the second is engaging your supervisor. The exercise will require you to video- or audiotape one session (with client permission).

Part I: (Self-directed)

1. Describe the client's presenting concerns/goals.

___

___

___

2. Describe your working hypothesis about what is happening with the client, identifying the underlying cause, precipitating events, and maintaining elements.

___

___

___

3. Review the tape recording of the session and complete the following table.

Data Supporting My Hypothesis	Data Failing to Support My Hypothesis

(Continued)

(Continued)

4. Review the data you acquired via review and reflection. Did you find support for your hypothesis? Does an alternative hypothesis appear viable? How will these reflections give form and direction to your next session?

PART II: (An alternative perspective)

After sharing your original hypothesis (number 2, above) with your supervisor, invite your supervisor to review your taped session and complete the table found in number 3 of this exercise. Together, revisit and discuss the data in light of your original and potential alternative hypotheses.

Reflecting *in* Practice: Guiding Moment-to-Moment Decisions

In an ideal world, all counselor responses and interventions would be done with reflection and intentionality. Professional counselors research best practice and sharpen their understanding of theories with the end result that they produce well-designed, well-thought-out treatment plans for their clients. In an ideal world, the counselor would develop a plan and engage in behaviors that systematically moved the client from a first "hello" to the final "goodbye." Each decision and each action employed by the counselor would move the client closer to his or her goal. But this is an ideal, and counselors do not operate within the ideal.

The real world of counseling doesn't always lend itself to such ideal, rational, sequential planning. Each client is unique, and each session brings with it the unexpected. Counseling is dynamic and does not follow a neat script, moving the client in linear steps from what is to what is desired. A solid case conceptualization and treatment plan is a beginning in the process of intentionally effecting change within the counseling relationship. Technical rationality has its limits when applied to the real-world dynamic of the counseling relationship, so a counselor needs to be reflective not only *on* practice, but *in* practice.

Effective counselors, who are reflective *in* the moment, are aware of their intentions and hoped-for effect as well as the actual impact of their moment-to-moment interventions. This knowledge allows them to monitor effectiveness and make adjustment "on the run." This is reflection in practice.

Even the best of plans will need to be fine-tuned and adjusted across and within sessions. Consider the situation described in Case Illustration 5.3, following this paragraph. The counselor in this scenario had created the conditions for making a significant impact on the way the client processed information. She had taken time to help the client understand and embrace a cognitive approach and gained the client's cooperation on gathering data reflecting those times when she found herself angry and hurt. During the current session, the counselor hoped to use the client data to illustrate how her overpersonalization and catastrophizing of her mother-in-law's comments became the source for her intense feelings of anger and hurt. In this segment, the counselor is attempting to confront the client regarding the manner in which she is processing information and making meaning out of her experiences. However, the client initially takes the feedback in a very defensive manner and thus the feedback is ineffective.

CASE ILLUSTRATION 5.3

Midconversation Adjustment

Background: The following exchange occurred during the fourth session. The client had previously shared her upset with her mother-in-law and, through the first three sessions, the counselor has reframed the discussion to focus on the value of cognitively reframing the experience to reclaim the power the client is apparently giving to her mother-in-law. We pick up the exchange as the counselor and client review the client's thought log, in which she has recorded specific situations that accompanied her feelings of anger toward her mother-in-law, along with the interpretations (self-talk) that she employed to make meaning out of these situations. The counselor's goal was to

a. point out the connection of the client's thinking to her feelings,

b. confront the client in relationship to her catastrophizing and personalizing the events, and

c. invite the client to challenge her distortions and reinterpret the situations in ways that were more reflective of the actual data.

Counselor: You did a great job completing your thought log.

Client: Thanks. It was easy since I spent the entire weekend with her. I had a lot to write about.

Counselor: As I'm looking over these situations, it seems that these are very similar to the ones you have shared in the past?

Client: Yeah . . . she's consistent if nothing else.

Counselor: Okay—I think I understand but I'm a bit confused. If she is, as you say, consistent, then what is it about what she is doing that is surprising to you? I mean, I see you wrote down, "I can't believe that she is acting like this!"

Client: Yeah—but how dare she. This is horrible. I can't stand the way she treats me.

Counselor: Clearly you are upset—not just then but even now as you retell the story. But again, I am wondering. She clearly has done this type of thing before and, in fact, up here you wrote down that she was doing it to both your husband and his brother. How did they respond?

Client: You don't get it. They can take it. She targets me.

(Continued)

(Continued)

Counselor Reflection in Session and Adjustment

Clearly, she is having a difficult time detaching emotionally and personally from the situations she has recorded. I am not making any headway in my attempts to point out the role her thinking plays in the creation of her emotional reaction. Her tone of voice is suggesting that she is feeling defensive in response to my questions. I need to back off and shift the conversation to other events.

Post-Adjustment

Counselor: As I am looking at your notes, I am really impressed by all the work you did monitoring those times when you felt angry. I wonder if we could look at a couple of other examples.

Client: Thanks. I tried to do it the best I could.

Counselor: How about this one? This was last Wednesday–you were walking to work and you passed a person who appeared homeless.

Client: Yeah–very sad.

Counselor: But it is kind of interesting . . . look here. So, you described that you walked past him and he made some derogatory . . . very critical . . . comments about the way you looked.

Client: Yeah.

Counselor: But here's what's interesting. You wrote down that you had a little anxiety but mostly felt sad for the man.

Client: I was a little concerned that he might approach me but when he didn't, I just thought of how sad it was that he was homeless and clearly having some psychological problems.

Counselor: So, let me see if I get this. He was being very critical of you–the way you were dressed–and yet, because you processed that criticism through your thinking that he was homeless and struggling psychologically, you didn't seem to take it personally or take it to heart. In fact, look here, you responded to the comment by smiling, continuing to walk, and feeling sad for him.

Client: Yes . . . and I also said a prayer for him.

Counselor: Well, that is certainly a reaction that is clearly different from what you usually have when you are criticized by your mother-in-law.

Client: Huh? I'm not sure what you mean.

Counselor: Well–look here on Friday. You wrote down that she made a comment

	about you wearing jeans and your response was to feel "furious" and angrily walk out of the kitchen. I wonder if you processed her comment through thinking that placed her comments into her pattern of making critical comments. You know—well, there she goes—consistent—attempting to be critical. I wonder if the words would have been taken so personally or so hurtfully?
Client:	(smiling) Maybe if I saw her as having psychological problems it would help? No . . . I understand what you are saying. I am making it more personal and more important than maybe I should. Boy, I wish I could learn not to take it so seriously.
Counselor:	That is something we certainly could work on.

The counselor in this situation engages in reflection in practice. She is able to process her own actions, her expectations of the effect of those actions, and then the actual impact of her actions. With this awareness, she is able to make an adjustment to her approach and as a result facilitate the client's reception of the counselor's feedback.

The counselor's awareness of not only what she did but the disparity between what she expected to be the outcome and what actually resulted positions her to make the adjustments needed to get back on track. Through the process of reflecting *in* practice, counselors will fine-tune their behaviors in order to facilitate the development of a working alliance and the progression of the counseling process toward successful achievement of the counseling goals.

Counselors who are able to monitor their actions and their impact will make not only adjustments to a treatment plan but subtle adjustments within the interaction. The effective counselor will allow the experience of the moment to guide his or her decisions and actions.

With a goal of facilitating the counseling process, counselors will intentionally select actions from those options available to them at any one point in the interaction. Their selection, when effective, will have been guided by their reflection in practice. Do I ask a question or hold it until another point in the interaction? Should I engage the client or for now sit in silence? Is this the time to confront the client or offer my interpretation? Even decisions about what appears to be the more mundane—"Should I offer him a tissue?"—are guided by the data presented at the moment and selected intentionally to facilitate the counseling process.

In the ideal scenario, a counselor should be able to identify each and every decision he or she is making, along with the anticipated impact of those decisions. These data provide the counselor with the picture of what is happening and what needs to be adjusted. Exercise 5.4 invites you to reflect in practice.

EXERCISE 5.4

Why Did I Do That?

Directions: The current exercise will require you to have a video- or audiotaping of a recent session. The goal of this exercise is to help you develop the skill of reflection while in session. Even though the exercise is engaging you in the process of reflection after the fact, it will help to sensitize you to the need and value of engaging purposively, intentionally, and reflectively in session.

It is suggested that you repeat this exercise as often as possible. It is through practice, even after the fact, that your awareness and reflection will be sharpened.

Process:

1. Set a timer or alarm to be sounded every 3 or 4 minutes.
2. Listen and/or observe your session and, as you do, take notes writing down what it is you think you were trying to achieve at any one moment.
3. When the timer goes off, pause the session and write down what you were doing (even if it was remaining in silence) at that moment.
4. (now the hard part) Answer each of the following:
   a. What was I trying to accomplish with my behavior, my response at this moment?
   b. How was the client responding to my behavior, my response at this moment?
   c. Was the client's reaction what I expected and intended?
   d. What, if anything, would I do differently now that I have reflected on this moment and my response in the moment?

Alternative Approach to the Exercise:

You may find it beneficial to engage in this activity with a colleague or supervisor in order to gain an alternative perspective on what occurred and what could have been done differently to achieve your desired outcome.

Reflective Practice: Supporting Efficacy and Accountability

The goal of reflection in and on practice is to increase the efficacy of counselors' decisions and the effectiveness of their helping strategies. Reflective counselors truly know what they are doing—and the intentionality behind it. But more than this, reflective counselors are self-aware and know the impact of what they are doing and the degree to which the actual impact matches what was expected. Clearly, these data serve as the basis for reflective counselors to make those adjustments necessary to increase their effectiveness.

The benefits of reflective practice can be expanded and increased when the practitioner's reflections are systematic and data based (Lederman & Niess, 1997). The reflections can not only improve practice, but also be used to provide accountability to one's stakeholders when based on systematic date collection (Baker, 2012).

The introduction of the concept of *systematic data collection* to the reflective process invites the practitioner into the realm of the researcher. This may, on first view, appear challenging, but counselors need to be aware that "practice and research are not two mutually exclusive activities" (Whiston, 1996, p. 616) and that each benefits from the inclusion of the other.

The intent is not to turn practitioners into researchers but rather to simply assist those in the field in embracing a frame of mind that calls them to accountability through systematic data collection. One relatively simple illustration of this process is found in Case Illustration 5.4, which highlights the effort of one practitioner-researcher to document the effectiveness of her intervention. The case demonstrates one counselor's use of a single subject design (A-B-A) to demonstrate and document the effectiveness of her intervention.

CASE ILLUSTRATION 5.4

Is It Really the Distraction?

The referral simply asked the counselor to observe Bart, a 3rd-grade student who was apparently having difficulty completing his desk work. The counselor decided to observe Bart and collect behavioral data reflecting his time on task during a specific observation period (baseline data collection, absent intervention). Following this data collection, the counselor hypothesized that Bart's on-task behaviors were being affected by his sitting next to a gerbil cage. In discussing this with the teacher, it was clear that the teacher felt that this was too simplified and that there must be something "wrong" with Bart.

The counselor invited the teacher to participate in a mini-experiment. It was proposed that the teacher would move Bart to the other side of the room (away from the noise of the gerbil) and that the counselor would return to the class and make observations of on-task behavior during a similar class time. The teacher was comfortable with the plan but was skeptical.

After one week, the counselor revisited the classroom, during the same day of the week and time of day as during the gathering of baseline data. Once again, data on Bart's on-task behavior were gathered. The teacher reported "feeling" that his work had improved, and reviewing the comparative data appeared to support this feeling. The data revealed that there had been an increase of 22 minutes on task (54 minutes during the 60-minute post-"treatment" observation) over the original baseline of 32 minutes on task during a 60-minute baseline observation period (i.e., prior to adjusting the location of the gerbil cage).

The teacher was pleased with the result but was still skeptical as to the cause for the change. The counselor suggested that it might be instructive to return Bart to his original seat (next to the gerbil) with the hypothesis that if it was the presence or absence of the

(Continued)

(Continued)

gerbil noise that was affecting Bart's performance, returning him to his previous location should result in his on-task behavior returning to its initial baseline levels. Because the teacher regularly moved the children's seats just to have them work with new partners, she was more than willing to continue the experiment. Following the adjustment, data were gathered and, to the teacher's surprise, the on-task behavior, which had improved, did in fact return to the baseline. With these data, the teacher was convinced that the gerbil, as a distraction, was the influencing element. She relocated the gerbil to the back of the classroom where it would no longer be an auditory or visual distraction.

Although one might argue that there are threats to the internal validity of this study, the simple, single-subject A-B-A (i.e., baseline-intervention-return to baseline) design produced data that appeared to confirm the effectiveness of the counselor's intervention.

There are numerous strategies and methods one can use to approach his or her practice with such a frame of reference. Although the discussion of research methods is beyond the scope of this text, interested readers are referred to works such as that of Parsons and Brown (2002) or Stringer (2014), which highlight the value and process of becoming a practitioner-researcher.

Reflection: For Professional Development

The profession you are entering is young among health professions and is constantly evolving as a reflection of emerging theories, ever-expanding research findings, and articulation of best practices. This evolving base of professional practice invites—no, requires—the professional counselor to stay informed or experience "professional obsolescence" (Vitulano & Copeland, 1980, p. 891). The focus of the current chapter highlights the process of reflection as one approach to monitoring and improving effectiveness. The use of reflection as a method for taking steps to improve practice is not only intuitively appealing but responsive to our own ethical principle requiring counselors to monitor effectiveness and take steps to improve when necessary (ACA, 2014, C.2.d).

But beyond this call to reflect in and on the process of their practice, ethical counselors must also reflect on themselves as counselor. Through meaningful self-assessment and self-monitoring of their own level of professional knowledge and skill, ethical professional counselors position themselves to engage in activities that promote continuing education and professional development. This is not just a good idea, it is a response to our ethical mandates. The American Counseling Association's *Code of Ethics* directs counselors to "recognize the need for continuing education to acquire and maintain a reasonable level of awareness of current scientific and professional information in their fields of activity. Counselors maintain competence in the skills they use, are open to new procedures, and remain informed regarding best practices for working with diverse populations." (ACA, 2014, C.2.f)

These ethical directives apply to all counselors, including those who are just entering the field or, like you, are continuing to serve as student-counselors. The direction for self-monitoring, or what has been called self-supervision (Morrissette, 1999), invites you to engage in a systematic process or structured approach to assess, plan, and improve your professional knowledge and skills. This process requires you to observe and assess your current level of professional knowledge, especially as these position you to address the unique needs of your clientele and the expectations of your field placement site.

Assessment

A process of continuing professional development starts with an effective—and useful—self-assessment targeting fundamental helping skills (e.g., use of questioning, reflection of feelings, etc.); competency in managing a counseling process (e.g., case conceptualization); knowledge and skill in the application of best practice interventions (i.e., treatment planning); and ability to address the unique needs, both clinical and cultural, of the clientele seen within a professional setting (e.g., crises needs, psychiatric disorders, addictions, etc.). Exercise 5.5 is provided to guide you in this professional knowledge and skills self-assessment. It is a process that we hope will begin here and will continue throughout your professional career.

EXERCISE 5.5

Directed Self-Assessment

Directions: As noted within the chapter, self-assessment, as a step in the process of continual professional development, is both essential to professional practice and responsive to our ethical mandates. The following invites you to assess the current state of your knowledge and skills as they relate to and affect your current level of practice. The scale we are asking you to employ goes from 5, which represents professional mastery and understanding, to 1, which reflects total absence of the referenced knowledge or skill. These data will be used in the creation of a professional development plan (see Exercise 5.6).

Area	***Knowledge/Skill***	***Level of Proficiency*** **1 = absent, 2 = awareness and understanding but not skilled; 3 = developing skills; 4 = competency; 5 = mastery**
Helping Skills (Building and Maintaining a Working Alliance)	Understanding of the value of establishing a working alliance with clients	

(Continued)

(Continued)

Area	***Knowledge/Skill***	***Level of Proficiency*** **1 = absent, 2 = awareness and understanding but not skilled; 3 = developing skills; 4 = competency; 5 = mastery**
	Counseling skills facilitating the development of a working relationship (e.g., exhibiting warmth, genuineness, attending, valuing, etc.)	
	Facilitation of expression of and exploration of client thoughts, feelings, and nonverbal communication and behaviors through warmth and utilization of listening skills	
	Skills supporting client insight, including such things as questioning, confrontation, and interpretation	
	Skills targeting promoting changes in client affect, thought, or behavior (e.g., goal setting, scaling, modeling, encouragement, increasing awareness and commitments, etc.)	
Session Management and Facilitation	Employment of skills of reflection on practice, including the development of case conceptualization	
	Control of session duration, including starting and ending	
	Skills supporting continuity of focus and work session to session	
	Ability to maintain professional boundaries	
	Maintenance of useful, ethical, and legal client notes and files	
	Knowledge and skill in crises management	

Area	***Knowledge/Skill***	***Level of Proficiency*** **1 = absent, 2 = awareness and understanding but not skilled; 3 = developing skills; 4 = competency; 5 = mastery**
	Knowledge and skill in making and facilitating referral	
Best Practice	Knowledge of research supporting intervention strategies applied to your client's identified problems/goals	
	Knowledge and skills necessary to effectively and ethically engage in therapeutic techniques/strategies appropriate for your client	
	Knowledge and skill necessary to gather both formative (in process) and summative (at conclusion) data demonstrating treatment effectiveness	
	Knowledge of professional ethics guiding practice	
Responsive to Client and System Needs	Awareness of personal values and cultural perspective	
	Sensitivity to and awareness of the unique impact that your client's values and cultural perspective play in the process of counseling	
	Skills and knowledge necessary to effectively counsel the types of presenting concerns found within your site	
	Awareness of and responsivity to the unique system policies, procedures, and values governing the various aspects of a professional counseling relationship	

From Assessment to Development

Starting with self-assessment, a professional development plan will identify specific goals and objectives to be achieved, the activities or strategies to achieve these goals, and ways to monitor progress. As you continue to reflect on yourself—as professional—it is important to begin the process of creating a professional development plan.

This may seem a bit premature because it is very likely that you are continuing in a graduate program, and that alone is developmental. However, professional development planning shouldn't be restricted to graduate education or even those times of renewal of certification and licenses. The professional counselor continually reflects on his or her professional identity, knowledge, and skills and considers ways that these can be improved. This is true even for those engaged in a structured graduate program.

The following steps will guide you in that process.

Step 1: Self-Assessment

The steps of professional development planning start with an accurate, honest self-assessment. We hope Exercise 5.5 has assisted you in beginning this process of self-assessment and the identification of your current strengths and areas of challenge. This process and the profile that emerges can serve as targets of your goal setting and planning.

A reflection on current knowledge and skills is an effective way to begin a self-assessment, but it is not the only data to consider. As you progress through this planning process, it is also important to turn to other sources for identification of areas where personal and professional growth may be desirable.

If you are moving into a field that requires ongoing continuing education for purposes of maintaining your certifications or licenses or merely as a requirement of the job, it would be helpful to contact those agencies or regulatory bodies to identify any mandatory learning requirements that will be imposed. Further, while your assessment has targeted current levels of functioning, it is also important to review your longer term career goals in light of the knowledge, skills, and credentials that may be required to move in those directions. Table 5.1 provides a number of questions that could be used to guide your self-assessment of these broader issues. As you respond to the questions, it is important to be as specific and concrete in your responses as possible. This specificity will be useful in guiding you to identify goals desired as well as strategies to be employed to achieve these goals.

Step 2: Identification of Goals

It is very likely that both in your training and early experience with clients, you have come to understand the need for goals to be clear, concrete, and achievable. Whether it be those set by and for your client or those established for yourself, goals that are vague, overly generalized, or simply unrealistic will prove ineffective and valueless as well as could also result in heightened frustration and a sense of hopelessness (Parsons & Zhang, 2014b).

Table 5.1 Reflecting on Self as Professional

- In reviewing my self-assessment of my proficiency in areas of specific knowledge and skill, which stand out as targets for growth?
- Are there other professional competencies that I should work on in support of my career goals?
- If I were to be employed at my field site, are there specific competencies that I would need to develop? Or strengthen?
- Am I interested in acquiring additional credentials or professional status and, if so, what competencies (skills and cognates) would these require?
- When I think of the profession, which direction does it seem to be going in and what knowledge and skills would I need to navigate that future?
- What specific recommendations for targets for growth do my field supervisor and/or university mentor suggest I consider?
- Are there technical skills that I need to acquire or improve upon?
- Are my communication and interpersonal skills professional and effective in supporting my work with colleagues?
- Am I caring for myself—physically and psychologically—in ways that will allow me to function as an effective professional? What plan should I employ to maintain my health and well-being?

One often-employed model for goal setting (see Locke & Latham, 2002; Parsons & Zhang, 2014b) emphasizes the need for goals to have the characteristics of specificity, measurability, attainability, relevance, and being time bound. These characteristics, often identified with the acronym SMART goals, are those that you want to incorporate in your own goals for professional development. The questions posed in Figure 5.1 may help you in the crafting of your own SMART goals.

Step 3: Identification of Resources

Now that you've set goals, the next step is to begin to identify resources that are available and will help you achieve your goals. For some of your goals, the resources may already be available. But don't simply lock yourself into the same pathways. Consider alternative routes to a goal. Look up professional development courses, events, certifications, and trainings that will help you achieve your goals. Connect with your local, state, regional, and national associations to see what is being offered. Discuss with your supervisor and program advisor the possibilities for continued training that exist on campus or within the community. Consider volunteer opportunities as well as experiences that are offered commercially.

Get the specifics, including costs, schedule, requirements, and so forth, and then align the opportunities with the goals you have identified. Remember—be realistic. You have many things on your plate and can only do so much, so consider other deadlines, other demands, or even other opportunities with friends and family as you begin to target experiences that will foster your professional development.

Figure 5.1 Setting Smart Goals

Goal Characteristics	*Questions to Guide Goal Setting*	*Adjustment to My Goal*
Specific	Does your goal outline exactly what you are trying to achieve?	
Measurable	How will others know if progress is being made or that your goal has been achieved? Can you quantify your progress?	
Attainable	Do you have the needed resources to achieve this goal? Is achieving your goal dependent on the support or actions of others? If so, can you reframe the goals so you can achieve independently from the support or actions of others? Is the goal too big? If so, would it help to break it down into smaller SMART goals? What factors or forces may be existing that could interfere with your achievement of the goal? What plans do you have to remove or navigate these forces?	
Relevant and Produces Results	Is this goal really important to you? Can you see the positive consequences of achieving the goal? How will achieving this goal affect your personal and professional life?	
Time Bound	Have you set a target date? Can you establish markers along the way to use as evidence of progress? Is the timeline reasonable? Flexible? And adjustable?	

Action Steps

The creation of your professional development plan will allow you to explore a variety of learning and developmental opportunities available on the job, online, or in a group setting to help you progress from your current position to where you want to be in the future. To be effective, take into account your individual learning style and preferences. Be creative when developing your plan and consider learning opportunities beyond the traditional classroom setting to help you meet your objectives.

With goals established and resources and strategies identified, it is now time to begin the process of engaging in your professional development plan. As you do, it is important that you track and monitor your progress. This will not only help you stay on schedule, but keep you updated on how close or far you are from reaching your target goal(s). In addition, it is true that the "best laid plans of mice and men" can go awry and that as you engage in your action steps, things may surface that present road blocks or detours to your goal achievement. Monitoring your actions and progress will help you make the adjustment to your initial timeline.

As you begin the process of establishing your own professional development plan, you may find the outline presented in Exercise 5.6 to be helpful. It is also important to understand and embrace the fact that, like most things we do as professional counselors, reflecting on our knowledge, our skill, our competency, and our awareness of our developing profession is not a one-time event.

EXERCISE 5.6

My Professional Development Plan

Date Established: ____________ Date of Expected Completion: ____________

From Data on Exercise 5.5:

Specific area of professional practice being addressed ____________________________

Specific knowledge and/or skills being targeted ________________________________

Current level of proficiency ______________________________________

Level of proficiency anticipated following professional development activities ______________

What new and specific knowledge, skill, or attitude do you need to acquire to achieve target competency?	What specific activities, materials, and personnel will be used to achieve your goal?	How will you evaluate your progress?	What is the target date for completing this phase of your professional development?	(To be completed following your professional development activities) What, if anything, would you like to target for continued development along this same line?

Our practice is evolving and so is our knowledge base from which we make professional decisions. As such, even when you have completed the requirements of your current program and are embraced as a member of the profession, you, like all professional counselors, will remain a student and a professional in development. Regardless of your credentials, degrees, or continuing experience, you will need to remain informed about the evolving nature of your profession and use that information to assist you in responding to the changing demands of your professional life. This plan is but the beginning.

KEYSTONES

- Reflection *on* practice is a process of looking back over the previous session in the hope of more fully understanding what was intended, what was achieved, and what changes or adjustments need to be made as the counselor and client move forward.
- Case conceptualization is an outcome of reflection *on* practice and is the result of a counselor's observations, data collection, understanding, and conceptual integration of client behaviors, thoughts, feelings, and physiology from a clinical perspective.
- The process of reflection *on* practice and the development of a case conceptualization requires a counselor to move smoothly from data collection, through organization, and finally to the extraction of meaning—as the springboard for formulation and implementation of the treatment plan.
- Reflection *in* practice takes place during the session, and involves the counselor's ability to attend to his or her own behaviors and counseling decisions and the client's response to those decisions and behaviors.
- Reflection *in* practice provides data for making at-the-moment, "on the run" adjustments to the dynamic occurring at any one point in a session.
- The benefits of reflective practice can be expanded and increased when the practitioner's reflections are systematic and data based.
- In addition to using reflection in and on as a way of improving service to a client, ethical counselors must also reflect on themselves as counselors in order to continue to develop professional knowledge and skill.
- Through meaningful self-assessment and self-monitoring of their own level of professional knowledge and skill, ethical professional counselors position themselves to engage in activities that promote continuing education and professional development.

ADDITIONAL RESOURCES

Web Based

Council for Accreditation of Counseling and Related Educational Programs (CACREP): www.cacrep.org. Organization promoting the professional competence of counseling and related practices.

The National Board for Certified Counselors and Affiliates (NBCC): www.nbcc.org. An independent not-for-profit credentialing body for counselors.

Print Based

Eells, T. D. (2002). Formulation. In M. Hershen & W. Sledge (Eds.), *The encyclopedia of psychotherapy* (pp. 815–822). New York, NY: Academic Press.

Falvey, J. E. (2001). Clinical judgment in case conceptualization and treatment planning across mental health disciplines. *Journal of Counseling and Development, 79*(3), 292–303.

Hensen, M., & Porzelius, L. K. (2002). *Diagnosis, conceptualization and treatment planning for adults: A step-by-step guide.* Mahwah, NJ: Lawrence Erlbaum.

Schon, D. A. (1983). *The reflective practitioner: How professionals think in action.* New York, NY: Basic Books.

REFERENCES

American Counseling Association. (2014). *ACA code of ethics.* Alexandria, VA: Author.

Baker, S. B. (2012). A new view of evidenced-based practice. *Counseling Today.* Retrieved from http://ct.counseling.org/2012/12/a-new-view-of-evidence-based-practice/

Eells, T. D. (1997). Psychotherapy case formulation: History and current status. In T. D. Eells (Ed.), *Handbook of psychotherapy case formulation* (pp. 1–25). New York, NY: Guilford Press.

Jongsma, A. E., Jr., Peterson, L. M., & McInnis, W. P. (2006). *The adolescent psychotherapy treatment planner* (4th ed.). Hoboken, NJ: John Wiley.

Lederman, N. G., & Niess, M. L. (1997). Action research: Our actions may speak louder than our words. *School Science and Mathematics, 97*(8), 397–399.

Locke, A. E., & Latham, G. P. (2002). Building a practically useful theory of goal setting and task motivation: A 35-year odyssey. *American Psychologist, 57,* 705–717.

Morrissette, P. J. (1999). Family therapist self-supervision: Toward a preliminary conceptualization. *The Clinical Supervisor, 18*(2), 165–183.

Nelson, M. L., & Neufeldt, S. A. (1998). The pedagogy of counseling: A critical examination. *Counselor Education and Supervision, 38,* 70–88.

Neukrug, E. S., & Schwitzer, A. (2006). *Skills and tools for today's professional counselors and psychotherapists: From natural helping to professional counseling.* Belmont, CA: Brooks/Cole.

Parsons, R. D. (2009). *Translating theory to practice: Thinking and acting like an expert counselor.* Upper Saddle, NJ: Pearson.

Parsons, R. D., & Brown, K. (2002). *Teacher as reflective practitioner and action researcher.* Belmont, CA: Wadsworth/Cengage Learning.

Parsons, R. D., & Zhang, N. (2014a). *Counseling theory: Guiding reflective practice.* Thousand Oaks, CA: Sage.

Parsons, R. D., & Zhang, N. (2014b). *Becoming a skilled counselor.* Thousand Oaks, CA: Sage.

Stringer, E. T. (2014). *Action research.* Thousand Oaks, CA: Sage.

Whiston, S. C. (1996). Accountability through action research: Research methods for practitioners. *Journal of Counseling & Development, 74,* 616–623.

Vitulano, L. A., & Copeland, B. A. (1980). Trends in continuing education and competency demonstration. *Professional Psychology, 11*(6), 891–897.

6

Growing Through Supervision

The five steps in teaching an employee new skills are preparation, explanation, showing, observation and supervision.

Bruce Barton

Barton's quote certainly applies to the process of acquiring the knowledge and skills essential to being an effective professional counselor. Your course work has been an arena in which much information has been conveyed—via direct instruction, demonstration, and even illustration. But for your professional development to bloom, the knowledge that has been acquired needs to be applied and, with this application, the feedback you receive via supervision is refined.

Clinical supervision provides you with the supportive and educative activities that help you develop your abilities to apply counseling theory and techniques within a "real world" context. It is evident that supervision is one of the most important learning experiences that counseling trainees will experience in their formation. In counseling supervision, counseling trainees will be able to associate themselves with experienced supervisors both at their college or university and the practicum and internship site. Your experience in the field and the supervision you receive are invaluable in assisting your transition from classroom student to the role of professional.

As a counseling practicum student or intern, you want to fully involve yourself in this supervision process and gain experiences to increase your competence for becoming a professional counselor. When viewing yourself as part of the supervision, participating in the supervision, interacting with others in the supervision, and expressing your uniqueness in the supervision, you will grow and become mature professionally and personally. This participation includes activities such as exposing your vulnerability and sharing your strengths and weaknesses through video sessions, discussions, case conceptualization, and group activities in the process of the supervision. This participation will enrich your counseling knowledge and skills, and through this participation in supervision, you will become aware of the gap between your ideal and the real. Meanwhile, it is during this supervision that you will narrow this gap of yours as well. As a counseling supervisee, you will receive and give feedback and evaluation from and to your supervisors and others who are involved in this supervision process. It is in this counseling supervision that your belief and passion to become a professional counselor will also be attested. Further, your practicum or internship supervision will be another vehicle that carries you into the field of counseling.

This chapter will guide readers in exploring the importance of counseling supervision and its nuts and bolts in the training process. Therefore, after reading this chapter, readers will be able to

- know what is counseling practicum/internship supervision and its importance;
- understand the reasons of having practicum and internship supervision;
- prepare themselves for issues they will encounter in the supervision;
- become familiar with various supervision models and theoretical orientations;
- identify expectations and issues before, during, and after the supervision;
- distinguish the difference between supervision and therapy;
- know supervision evaluation, peer feedback, and self-evaluation; and
- become aware of how to transition from student to professional.

Counseling Supervision

What Is Counseling Supervision?

Perhaps you have heard the adage "do as I say, not as I do"? When applied to developing as a counselor, the guiding principle for supervisors and the experience they provide is "do as I say *and* as I do." Your supervisor and the supervision provided will serve not only as the model, or template, but as the experience that forges your knowledge, skill, and professional identity as counselor.

Counseling supervision is a means of transmitting counseling knowledge, skills, and attitudes of the counseling profession to the next counseling generation (Bernard & Goodyear, 2014). It is also a means of passing on the values and the professional identity of the counseling profession to the new generation in the profession. Stoltenberg and Delworth (1987) conceptualize counseling supervision as a process in which various developmental stages progress for counseling supervisees. In this process, there is also a working alliance between the supervisor and the supervisee in which the supervisee provides an account of his or her work, reflecting on it and receiving feedback and guidance, while the supervisor facilitates the development of therapeutic competence in the supervisee and helps the supervisee acquire appropriate professional behaviors through an examination of the work the supervisee has offered (Hart, 1982; Loganbill, Hardy, & Delworth, 1982).

We believe that supervision is a professional relationship that empowers counseling trainees and counselors to accomplish development and growth professionally and personally. As a result, the counselors become capable of not only providing the best service to their clients but also transmitting the essence of counseling principles, knowledge, and skills to the new generation.

Why Is Counseling Supervision Necessary and Required?

When asked why they take the practicum or internship class, students oftentimes say, "because of the program requirement." The answer is certainly correct at least at the level of course requirements, but the real question is then—why is it required?

As counselor educators whose responsibility is to develop counselors who are fully prepared to function ethically and efficiently with real-world clients, we recognize that clinical supervision is crucial for preparing counselors to function in complex work environments and handle complicated situations (Bernard & Goodyear, 2014). The benefits of counseling supervision include (a) developing greater effectiveness and accountability; (b) enhancing skill development and competencies; (c) increasing feelings of support, confidence, job satisfaction, professional identity development, and self-efficacy; and (d) decreasing feelings of isolation, role ambiguity, and burnout (Herlihy, Gray, & McCollum, 2002; Lambie, 2007; Lambie & Sias, 2009). Supervision has been reported to build supervisees' strengths; ameliorate supervisees' weaknesses; create an environment that fosters supervisees' clinical skill development, self-efficacy, and ethical decision-making; maintain clients' welfare (Falender & Shafranske, 2004); facilitate supervisees' personal growth; and assist supervisees in transitioning from students to professionals. Furthermore, the benefits of clinical supervision extend even beyond the formative values encountered by those in training. Studies have shown that clinical supervision has produced greater staff retention, less burnout, significant reduction in turnover, and improvements of treatment outcomes (Garner, Hunter, Modisette, Ihnes, & Godley, 2012; Knudsen, Ducharme, & Roman, 2008).

On the other hand, those trainees who lack clinical supervision are often troublesome and have low confidence in what they are doing clinically (Bernard & Goodyear, 2014). Studies have demonstrated that the number of hours of formal supervision and the number of supervisors that trainees have had are significantly related to trainees' felt competence (Bradley & Olson, 1980). Consider the reflection shared by a student following a particularly difficult session (see Case Illustration 6.1).

CASE ILLUSTRATION 6.1

Thank God for Dr. L.

I came close to calling it quits. I know this is not a new feeling. I can remember my first taping with a simulated intake during which I felt lost, and did everything wrong, and just felt like, crap, I'll never be a counselor. But today was different. This was a real

> human being—not a simulation. This is not a lab setting but a walk-in clinic. I'm not talking about grades—I'm talking about someone's life and I am not sure I can handle it. I am not sure I am qualified.
>
> Clearly, Dr. L. could tell I was not doing well, postsession—perhaps the fact that I was crying and about to throw up may have given her the first indication? Anyway, thank God she is here!
>
> Yes, she was warm and supportive, but I expected that. But once I was able to focus, she was really able to help me stop generalizing and catastrophizing. We were able to review my goals for the session and the approach I took, or tried to take. We looked at the client's comments (thank God for video), and we objectively assessed the progress—and yes, there was progress made.
>
> I know I have a lot to learn, I have skills I need to hone. But I also now know I need to stop trying to be a perfect student to be more of a trained, caring professional. It wasn't so much what she said but how she approached it. I need to view myself and my performance with the same critical, problem-solving, yet caring and supportive eye, as she gave me and as I give my clients.
>
> Rough day . . . yep . . . but more for me than my client. Thank God for Dr. L.

Evidently, counseling supervision is both an ethical imperative and evidence based. For this reason, almost all counseling and mental health professional organizations, national and international, mandate supervision for both trainees and professionals because clinical supervision has become the cornerstone of quality improvement and assurance. The value of supervision suggests that any client who encounters an intern counselor who is without supervision should perhaps reconsider if he or she is willing to seek help from a student counselor (Bernard & Goodyear, 2014).

When and How Often Is Counseling Supervision Conducted?

Given the benefits of supervision previously described, the simple answer to when and how often supervision is desirable could be "very often and throughout one's professional career." But, more specifically, counseling supervision is needed under four major circumstances: (a) when a person is a counseling graduate student to fulfill necessary requirements for a master degree, (b) when a person with a master's degree in counseling pursues a professional licensure, (c) when a licensed professional counselor needs improvement and education in certain specialty areas, and (d) any time a professional counselor is feeling "stuck" in his or her work with a client.

Because counseling is an applied science, all counseling programs, either master's or doctoral, require all students to be supervised while they see clients. Especially when students take practicum or internship class, they must be supervised by at least one on-site professional who is a qualified counseling supervisor. Here the word *qualified* means the following two aspects: education (e.g., master's or doctoral degree in counseling or related fields, supervision courses, or responsibility exams) and counseling experience (e.g., at least a certain number of years' experience, various from state to state and institutions to institutions). For example, a licensed counseling professional has practiced for at least 2 or 3 years beyond the issue date of the license, completing a graduate course in counseling supervision and successfully passing a required exam. However, to be qualified for supervising a master's student in training, a counseling professional may only need to meet the requirements of holding a master's degree in counseling or related field plus 2 years counseling experience. Exercise 6.1 will invite you to explore counseling supervision with your supervisor and your peer supervisees.

EXERCISE 6.1

Clarifying Expectations

Directions: To master the essence of supervision, you are asked to bring the questions *"What is your counseling supervision? Why is it necessary? What can each of you in supervision contribute and gain?"* to your individual supervision or group supervision and explore these questions with your supervisor or peer supervisees. As a result of the discussion, each party will thoroughly understand the core of counseling supervision and clarify the expectations for each other.

Expectations of Counseling Supervision

Clarifying counseling expectations from both counseling trainees and supervisors is crucial. As a counseling practicum student or supervisee, you want to be clear about your rights (see Table 6.1, Supervisee Bill of Rights) and know what you want out of the counseling supervision or, in other words, what learning experience you expect to have at the time you finish your supervision at the end of the semester or academic year. Specifically, both the supervisor and the supervisee must clarify their expectations from the following aspects of the supervision and specific expectations in the Supervision Agreement (see Table 6.2).

The first expectation is regarding the frequency and attendance of supervision meetings. As a practicum student and an intern, the first thing you want to do is sit down with your supervisors to set up the expectation of how often the supervision meeting will occur and what the attendance policy is. The most commonly used time frequency is weekly, and the length of the supervision session can be one hour or more than one hour depending on individual or group supervision. CACREP 2009 standards require counseling practicum students to receive a minimum of one hour of individual supervision weekly and an average of one and a half hour of group supervision per week (CACREP, 2009). The attendance is imperative because any absence may affect the dynamics of the group or triadic supervision meetings and the quality feedback (Bernard & Goodyear, 2014).

Table 6.1 Supervisee Bill of Rights

Introduction
The purpose of the Bill of Rights is to inform supervisees of their rights and responsibilities in the supervisory process.

Nature of the Supervisory Relationship
The supervisory relationship is an experiential learning process that assists the supervisee in developing therapeutic and professional competence. A professional counselor supervisor who has received specific training in supervision facilitates professional growth of the supervisee through: monitoring client welfare; encouraging compliance with legal, ethical, and professional standards; teaching therapeutic skills; providing regular feedback and evaluation; providing professional experiences and opportunities.

Expectations of the Initial Supervisory Session
The supervisee has the right to be informed of the supervisor's expectations of the supervisory relationship.

The supervisor shall clearly state expectations of the supervisory relationship that may include: supervisee identification of supervision goals for oneself; supervisee preparedness for supervisory meetings; supervisee determination of areas of nonprofessional growth and development; supervisor's expectations regarding formal and informal evaluations; supervisor's expectations of the supervisee's need to provide formal and informal self-evaluations; supervisor's expectations regarding the structure and/or the nature of the supervisory sessions; weekly review of case notes until supervisee demonstrates competency in case conceptualization. The supervisee shall provide input to the supervisor regarding the supervisee's expectations of the relationship.

Expectations of the Supervisory Relationship
A supervisor is a professional counselor with appropriate credentials. The supervisee can expect the supervisor to serve as a mentor and a positive role model who assists the supervisee in developing a professional identity.

The supervisee has the right to work with a supervisor who is culturally sensitive and is able to openly discuss the influence of race, ethnicity, gender, sexual orientation, religion, and class on the counseling and the supervision process. The supervisor is aware of personal cultural assumptions and constructs and is able to assist the supervisee in developing additional knowledge and skills in working with clients from diverse cultures.

Since a positive rapport between the supervisor and supervisee is critical for successful supervision to occur, the relationship is a priority for both the supervisor and supervisee. In the event that relationship concerns exist, the supervisor or supervisee will discuss concerns with one another and work towards resolving differences.

Therapeutic interventions initiated by the supervisor or solicited by the supervisee shall be implemented only in the service of helping the supervisee increase effectiveness with clients. A proper referral for counseling shall be made if appropriate.

The supervisor shall inform the supervisee of an alternative supervisor who will be available in case of crisis situations or known absences.

Source: Reprinted from "Supervisee's Bill of Rights" by M. Giordano, M. Altekruse, and C. Kern, 2000, in *Clinical Supervision in the Helping Professions*, by R. Haynes, G. Corey, & P. Moulton (Eds.), Belmont, CA: Thompson/Brooks Cole.

Table 6.2 Supervision Agreement

Based on the Supervisee Bill of Rights

The supervisory relationship is an experiential learning process that assists the supervisee in developing therapeutic and professional competence. This contract is designed to assist the supervisor and supervisee in establishing clear expectations about the supervisory process.

Supervisee

1. Read the Supervisee Bill of Rights and this agreement. Complete the sections on skills, goals, and professional opportunities and bring this agreement to the initial supervisory session.
2. Prior to the first supervisory session, read the Introduction and Expectations of the Supervisory Experience sections of the American Counseling Association's *Code of Ethics* and Standards of Practice.

Supervisor

1. Introduce yourself and discuss your credentials, licenses, academic background, counseling experience, and supervisory style.
2. Describe your role as a supervisor: teacher, consultant, counselor, and evaluator.
3. Discuss your responsibilities: monitoring client welfare; teaching therapeutic skills; providing regular verbal and written feedback and evaluation; and ensuring compliance with legal, ethical, and professional standards.
4. Ask the supervisee about his or her learning style and developmental needs.
5. Help supervisee develop goals and counseling skills.
6. Review supervisee's progress regarding Professional Practice Portfolio.

Supervisee

1. Introduce yourself and describe your academic background, clinical experience, and training.
2. Briefly discuss information you want to address during the supervisory meetings.
3. Describe the therapeutic skills you want to enhance and professional development opportunities you want to experience during the next three months.

These goals/skills must be formed (written) within the first month of the internship experience at both levels.

List three therapeutic skills you would like to further develop.

1.
2.
3.

List three general goals you would like to attain during the supervisory process.

1.
2.
3.

List three specific counseling or professional development experiences you would like to have during the next three months (e.g., attending a conference, facilitating a group, presentation)

1.
2.
3.

Expectations of the Supervisory Relationship

Supervisor & Supervisee

1. Discuss your expectations of the supervisory relationship.
2. Discuss how you will work toward establishing a positive and productive supervisory relationship. Also, discuss how you will address and resolve conflicts.
3. The supervisory experience will increase the supervisee's awareness of feelings, thoughts, behavior, and aspects of self, that are stimulated by the client.
4. Discuss the role of the supervisor in assisting with this process.
5. Share your thoughts with one another about the influence of race, ethnicity, gender, sexual orientation, religion, and class on the counseling and the supervision process.

Supervisee

Describe how you would like to increase your awareness of personal cultural assumptions, constructs, and ability to work with clients from diverse cultures.

Supervisor

If the supervisee needs to consult with you prior to the next supervision session, discuss how you would like to be contacted. Also, if you are unavailable during a period of time, inform the supervisee of an alternate supervisor who will be available in your absence.

Ethics and Issues in the Supervisory Relationship

1. Discuss the *Code of Ethics* and Standards of Practice. Review key issues not listed in this section.
2. A professional relationship is maintained between the supervisor and supervisee. The supervisor and supervisee do not engage in social interaction that interferes with objectivity and professional judgment of the supervisor.
3. After the initial supervisory meeting, the supervisee and supervisor can reestablish goals and expectations and discuss roles of the supervisory process. The supervisor and supervisee provide one another with regular feedback.
4. During the initial counseling session, the supervisee will inform the client that she or he is in training and is being supervised. If the supervisee wishes to audiotape or videotape, the client needs to give written consent.
5. Discuss confidentiality and the importance of obtaining a written release from the client prior to consultation with other professionals who are serving the client.
6. The supervisor is ultimately responsible for the welfare of the supervisee's clients. During each supervisory session, the supervisee will review each client's progress and relate specific concerns to the supervisor in a timely manner.

(Continued)

Table 6.2 (Continued)

Expectations of the Supervisory Process

Supervisor

1. Describe your theory of counseling and how it influences your counseling and supervision style.
2. Discuss your theory or model of supervision.

Supervisee

1. Discuss your learning style and your developmental needs.
2. Discuss your current ideas about your theoretical orientation.

Expectations of Supervisory Sessions

Supervisee

Discuss your expectations about the learning process and interest in reviewing audiotapes, videotapes, and case notes.

Supervisor

1. Describe the structure and content of the weekly supervisory sessions.
2. Discuss your expectations regarding supervisee preparedness for supervisory sessions (e.g., audiotapes, videotapes, case notes).
3. CACREP (2009) standards require students in their internship experience to receive a minimum of one hour of individual supervision per week and 90 minutes of group supervision each week.
4. The weekly supervisory session will take place face-to-face in a professional environment that ensures confidentiality. Decide the location, day, and time.

Expectations Regarding Evaluation

Supervisee

Discuss your interest in receiving weekly feedback in areas such as relationship building, counseling techniques, client conceptualization, and assessment.

Supervisor

1. Discuss your style of providing verbal feedback and evaluation.
2. Provide the supervisee with a copy of the formal evaluation you will use; discuss the evaluation tools and clarify specific items that need additional explanation.
3. Discuss the benefit of self-evaluation, provide a copy of self-evaluation forms, and clarify specific items that need additional explanation.

____

Supervisor's Signature Date

____

Supervisee's Signature Date

Source: Adapted from M. Giordano, M. Altekruse, and C. Kern (2000). Unpublished manuscript. Adapted by Yolanda Hawkins-Rodgers and Anthony Tasso for the Farleigh Dickinson University's Practicum and Internship Program Handbook.

The second expectation is regarding the supervisory relationship. What are your expectations of a supervisory relationship? Areas to think about may include skills of building an effective and productive supervisory relationship; strategies of addressing and resolving conflicts in supervision; roles that both supervisors and supervisees will take; and multicultural factors such as race, ethnicity, gender, religion, and sexual orientation that may affect the supervisory relationship.

The third expectation is about the process and content of supervision. It is important that both the counseling trainee and his or her supervisor have a clear understanding about the way each supervision session will be conducted as well as the nature of the topics or content that will be reviewed. This also includes clarification about what it is that you want to gain during the supervision sessions. The process and content of supervision meetings may involve discussing the structure and styles of teaching and learning and supervision models and reviewing audiotapes, videotapes, SD cards, case notes, treatment plans, or the case study. The process and content may further consist of case presentation, giving feedback, and case conceptualization. In addition, you may have interest in learning things that you do not typically have opportunities to learn during your tenure of practicum/internship (e.g., mediation, consultation, or alternative medicine). One last task that both supervisees and supervisors expect to see is the evaluation. All these operations will be discussed in detail later in the chapter.

Because the content of supervision is to facilitate the development of the supervisee's therapeutic competence, the specifics concerning the content of supervision may also include using a variety of operations to learn therapeutic skills and techniques based on theories and research outcomes, exploring supervisee's personal issues that may affect the counseling process and the relationship between the supervisee and his or her clients, and addressing issues related to the supervisee's personal and professional growth. Now you're invited to complete Exercise 6.2 to compare the expectations in the Supervision Agreement by Maria A. Giordano, Michael K. Altekruse, and Carolyn W. Kern (2000) to the expectations between you and your supervisors.

EXERCISE 6.2

What Are Our Expectations?

Directions: To make counseling supervision effective, both you as supervisee and your supervisor must have clear expectations from each other. To achieve your goal, you are invited to compare the expectations that you have set up with your supervisor and the expectations that are described in the Supervision Agreement. Identify the similarities and differences and discuss these similarities and differences in your supervision. The questions you will want to ask may include the following: *Why are your expectations similar or different from the ones described in the Supervision Agreement? What have been missing? What have been added? Why?*

Forms of Counseling Supervision

Classroom Versus On-Site Supervision

A parallel process of practicum supervision has been adopted by almost all counseling training programs—classroom supervision and on-site supervision. This parallel form functions as the two legs that help the practicum student walk into the field of counseling profession.

Counseling training programs usually require you, the practicum student, to attend a group supervision provided by a college or university faculty member. This type of supervision is conducted in a classroom with a number of practicum students and serves as a support system processing the practicum students' firsthand experiences and facilitating their professional development. The faculty supervisor plays the role of instructor, consultant, counselor, and monitor, while student peers doing their internships at the same or different sites support each other by sharing their experiences; providing each other with their perspectives on those experiences; coming up with ideas on dealing with conflicts and solving problems; and addressing operational concerns such as site carrying out treatment, staff theoretical orientations, site rules, or ethical practice (Hodges, 2011).

Within such a supportive atmosphere, you as an intern student will feel safe to express your concerns about the site agency or relationship development with the site supervisor and others, address your issues on counseling and personal development, and process your experience gained on site. Your faculty supervisor and peer students will be able to help you achieve your professional development of therapeutic competence.

Parallel to your classroom supervision, you are required to have supervision with your on-site supervisor. The on-site supervision can be either individual or in groups, which will be discussed in the following section. No matter what format is used, the purpose of the on-site supervision is similar to your classroom supervision—to facilitate your development and growth professionally and personally. As has been discussed in the previous section, counseling supervision is designed to create an environment that fosters your clinical skill development, maintain your clients' welfare, facilitate your personal growth, and assist you in the transition from student to professional.

Individual Versus Group Supervision

Supervision has three major forms: individual, triadic, and group supervision. The individual supervision consists of two people, a supervisor and a supervisee; the triadic supervision includes one supervisor and two supervisees; and the group supervision can have one supervisor and more than two supervisees. The most common group supervision has one supervisor and 3 to 12 supervisees. There are no advantages or disadvantages among these forms of supervision; in other words, individual supervision, triadic supervision, and group supervision have no significant difference in terms of their effectiveness (Lawson, Hein, & Stuart, 2009; Newgent, Davis, & Farley, 2005).

Which form is used largely depends on the supervisor's preference, time, and number of trainees. When there is only one trainee, the supervisor would have no choice but to conduct individual supervision. If there are more than three trainees, the supervisor can choose to have individual, triadic, or group supervision. Under such circumstances, the supervisor is most likely to use group supervision unless he or she has enough time for each trainee individually. However, even with multiple counseling trainees, the supervisor may conduct individual supervision due to special situations such as one trainee has a particularly difficult case or situation. If this is the case, the supervisor may provide this trainee individual supervision and have group or triadic supervision with the rest of the trainees.

Process and Content of Supervision

Carroll (1997) outlined seven generic tasks of counseling supervision: teach, evaluate, monitor professional practice (ethical standards), counsel, consult, monitor administrative tasks, and set up a learning relationship. Through the accomplishment of these tasks, the goal of developing the supervisee's initial professional competencies will be achieved. These competencies contain the supervisee's process skills (what you are doing in session), conceptualization skills (how you understand what is occurring in the session), personalization skills (how you interface a personal style with the role of the counselor at the same time that you attempt to keep therapy uncontaminated by personal issues; Bernard, 1979), professional behavior (ethics; Lanning, 1986), and administrative skills (Bernard & Goodyear, 2014). Other practical skills learned in supervision may include diversity, application research, interpersonal relationships, clinical assessment, and interprofessional collaboration (Hatcher & Lassiter, 2007).

To help supervisees develop these major professional skills, the supervisor may use a variety of processing methods. Some popular methods include but are not limited to audio, DVD, SD card, case conceptualization, role-plays, activities and exercises, live observation, joint therapy, discussions and didactic teaching, and feedback.

Audio- and Videotape and Case Presentation

Audio- and videotape of counseling sessions are the most commonly used means in counseling supervision, particularly when they are used for case presentation (Prieto, 1998). These means may be more often used in your classroom supervision than in your on-site supervision because your faculty supervisor does not have access to your on-site facilities. Many on-site supervisors also prefer videotapes because they can have more flexibility during watching the tapes with you; for example, it can be stopped anywhere the supervisor thinks necessary or he or she may want the tape to be played without sound to teach nonverbal skills. On the contrary, live observation does not have such advantages.

As supervisees, there are a number of very practical tasks that you need to attend to in preparing for the audio- or videotaping and the presentation. However, before addressing these, it is important that we—actually *you*—confront any anxiety you may feel about presenting yourself in video.

It is natural to be somewhat self-evaluative when viewing yourself on tape and even to be apprehensive, if not defensive, about the evaluation of your supervisor, but performance on tape needs to be secondary to service to client. Perhaps an illustration outside of the realm of counseling would help.

Imagine if you were interested in learning a sport such as tennis or golf. You can read about the right way to swing a racket or club, but at some point you need to do it. Further, while an observing eye of a trained professional may result in suggestions for adjusting your swing, actually viewing your swing and having a professional point out specifics at any one moment would prove invaluable at improving your game. We imagine that if you hired a professional to help with your game, you would be less concerned about how you dressed or how your hair was or even what mistakes you made. Rather, you would focus on your shortcomings and seek corrective feedback. After all, that is why you are paying your trainer! The same is true as you develop your counseling skills. You have the opportunity to work with a professional—who, with the aid of your videotape, can point out specifics or make on-the-mark recommendations, all for your professional growth. So, before we worry about how to tape, let's embrace the value of taping and put aside your ego in service of your professional development.

Now that this has been addressed, you will want to do well on the following tasks. First, make sure you have a recorder, camera, audio- and videotapes, and DVD or SD card. Some schools and internship sites provide cameras and tapes or SD cards for students to borrow and others may not. If not, you need to get your equipment ready before starting your internship. Second, follow the site's procedures on how to obtain clients' consent and/or guardians' permission for minor clients before you tape any session, and make sure your clients understand all the legal ramifications of taping and that the session on the tape/SD card will be viewed by your classmates and supervisors and *destroyed for clients' privacy after your task is complete.* Third, before you record a session, test the camera and the tape or SD card to make sure of their functionality and the quality of recording. Oftentimes a student will record a session and then bring the tape/SD card to supervision only to find there is nothing on the tape/SD card or the quality is not good. Such a situation can be frustrating and waste your supervisor's and other supervisees' time. As a result, the feedback and evaluation of your presentation or supervision can deviate from what you expected. Fourth, before you show your tape/SD card session in supervision, make sure that your tape/SD card is cued beforehand at the segment(s) you plan to show. Searching for what you want to show during your presentation in supervision can be nerve-racking for you as well as others. Finally, most supervisors often let their supervisees decide what they want to show for supervision. If this is the case, you may want to balance between your strengths and areas in which you need improvement of your clinical skills. In this way, you will be able to get constructive feedback. Alternatively, you might show only the areas where you need improvement. However, in that case, you need to prepare for the feedback. If all feedback is negative, you may feel discouraged. Particularly for those who have just begun their internship, negative feedback may make them doubt their ability to succeed in the field. On the other hand, if you present only what you do well, you may not get what you really need to improve your skills. Showing successful sessions in supervision can help you master what you have done effectively and build your confidence, whereas reviewing the sessions that you don't think are ideal will help you expand your counseling skills (Baird, 2002). That is why we suggest a balanced presentation of counseling sessions in supervision.

Case Conceptualization

Case conceptualization refers to the process in which the counselor understands his or her client's presenting concerns or explains the client's symptoms, emotions, cognitions, behaviors, personality, and interpersonal aspects in the context of a particular theory or integration of theories (Loganbill & Stoltenberg, 1983). Such understanding and explanation of presenting concerns will lead to the formulation of therapy goals and objectives, treatment plans, and intervention strategies.

You may have learned case conceptualization skills in your theory and basic counseling skill classes. Further implementation of this skill is a major emphasis in your internship and internship supervision. As you know, the same case can be conceptualized differently by different counseling theorists due to the aspect of client experience they emphasize. The same thing is true when different counselors, coming from different theories and experiences, view the case materials. As such, discussing your case conceptualization in supervision invites another perspective on the what and why of the client's unfolding story and, with those varied perspectives, the identification of a variety of paths and strategies to pursue. The following exercise (6.3) helps illustrate how case conceptualization is actualized by way of supervision.

EXERCISE 6.3

How Is Case Conceptualization Actualized in My Supervision?

Directions: Your task is to observe how your supervisor helps you with the case conceptualization. How does your supervisor handle the following questions? *What does your client say about what his or her problems are? Where are his or her problems coming from (e.g., learned problematic behaviors, irrational thinking, unhealthy relationships, etc.)? How did he or she come to have these problems? What are the goals for counseling that are identified? What specific interventions are used to address these problems? How are your client's strengths used in the process of the interventions?* Then compare the similarities and differences between your and your supervisor's case conceptualization approach.

Role-Play

The concept of role-play is not foreign to you at this point as it may have been used in the counseling classes you took earlier. Role-play is a very common method and a fundamental component of counselor education (Ivey & Ivey, 2007; Smith, 2009).

Although specific instructions for using role-play in group or individual supervision are still sparse (Smith, 2009), role-play has become one of the important tools frequently used by counseling supervisors (Borders & Brown, 2005).

Role-play is used in counseling supervision (e.g., individual, triadic, or group) for counseling interns to learn or refine a counseling skill (Borders & Brown, 2005). Borders and Brown listed the following ways that role play is used in counseling supervision: (a) the intern plays the role of the counselor and the supervisor plays the role of the client to learn a new skill or improve a learned skill; (b) the supervisor plays the role of counselor to model a specific skill; (c) an intern assumes the role of the client while the supervisor plays the role of the counselor to help the intern work on his or her skill of empathy; (d) the intern plays the role of the counselor and another intern in the same group supervision assumes the role of the client to practice a new skill or theoretical perspective; and (e) after watching a tape segment, the intern plays the role of the counselor while other interns in the supervision group take the roles of the client and a family member. After each role-play, the supervisor will process what has happened with you, the intern. Particularly after the role-play in the group supervision, each person will talk about his or her experience and the intern is helped by hearing the many possible perspectives. The two case illustrations (see Case Illustrations 6.2 and 6.3) created by Allison L. Smith (2009) below show you how role-play is used in both individual and group supervision.

CASE ILLUSTRATION 6.2

The Use of Role-Play in Supervision: Mary

During the check-in at the start of group supervision, supervisee Mary explained she was struggling with a client. The supervisor suggested that the group do a creative supervision activity to explore the struggle, along with any other struggles that members might have. The supervisor asked the group to split into dyads and for each to draw an image that depicted a challenge he or she was facing at the internship site. Supervisees Mary and Joshua paired up and began drawing. After the dyads completed the drawing activity, the supervisor asked Mary about her drawing. Mary reported that she had struggled with a new client, Robert, during a recent intake session at her internship site. She had depicted this in her drawing and explained what each part of the drawing represented. The supervisor then asked Mary to assume the role of her client, Robert, while her partner Joshua took on the role of counselor. The supervisor asked Mary to arrange the chairs in the supervision room according to how they were arranged at her internship site. The supervisor also instructed Mary to assume the gestures, mannerisms, posture, and tone of voice that her client, Robert, assumed. Next, the supervisees started the role-play. As the session began, Joshua assumed the counselor role. Mary shifted from her talkative and bright demeanor to a more withdrawn and awkward role as Robert. Joshua and "Robert" discussed Robert's hobbies and his struggles with meeting women. Robert answered the questions but appeared uncomfortable.

After the role-play, the supervisor encouraged group members to share their observations. Group members pointed out that Robert seemed uncomfortable talking to Joshua about his struggle with meeting women and that talking about his hobbies was much easier. Members also noted that Robert avoided eye contact when Joshua asked him questions. The supervisor then asked Joshua about how it felt in the counselor seat. Joshua remarked, "The more he resisted answering questions, the more uncomfortable I felt as the counselor. When I felt this discomfort, I got nervous and started asking more and more questions!"

When the supervisor asked Mary about her experience as she role-played her client, Robert, Mary explained that she felt uncomfortable answering questions, especially about meeting women. She reported the more questions that Joshua asked, the more her discomfort grew. She also said she wanted Joshua to tell her more about him in order to build a strong relationship. "I felt as though my counselor wanted to know so much about me, and I didn't know anything about him!" The supervisor then asked Mary if she had any new insight into her struggle after engaging in the role-play. Mary stated, "I didn't realize that Robert might be feeling this way. I think I might have overlooked the need for relationship building. Maybe I need to back up and take more time developing our relationship." The supervisor processed this in more depth with Mary, and then proceeded with other group members who wished to explore a struggle. (Smith, 2009)

Source: Adapted from Smith, A. L. (2009). Role play in counselor education and supervision: Innovative ideas, gaps, and future directions. *Journal of Creativity on Mental Health, 4,* 124-138.

CASE ILLUSTRATION 6.3

Sarah

Supervisee Sarah explained a case to her peers during group supervision. The videotaped session that Sarah wished to present was a recent meeting she had with Anna (client) and Patrice (client's mother). Before showing the tape, Sarah described the client. Anna, age 13, had been acting out in school and at home, prompting her mother, Patrice, to seek family counseling. Sarah shared that she had an ongoing struggle with keeping Patrice from dominating the conversations in session and getting Anna to speak at all. Sarah asked group members to assume the roles of mother, client, and counselor.

The group watched the tape and, afterward, group members offered feedback to Sarah in first person and present tense (see Borders, 1991). The group member who assumed the role of Anna exclaimed, "Why won't anyone treat me like an adult? Everyone talks *about* me and not *to* me and I can't stand it anymore! Doesn't anyone care what I think?" The group member who assumed the role of Patrice stated, "I just don't understand what's going on with Anna. She's always been so well-behaved. Now, all of a sudden, she turns 13 and everything changes—problems in school, fighting at

(Continued)

(Continued)

home. I'm not prepared for this. Plus, I have no one to talk to except you since all my friends have *good* kids." The group member who watched the session in the role of counselor noticed Sarah's struggle to keep Patrice on track. Speaking from Sarah's point of view, this group member stated, "I just can't seem to get Patrice to refrain from telling stories related to Anna's problems at school. Whenever I try to redirect, she finds a way to get off-topic. I don't know how we can make progress if all she wants to do is tell me about behavior problems. I may as well give up and just let her talk."

From the feedback, Sarah was able to understand more clearly the dynamics of the session: Anna wanted to be heard, but Patrice needed to vent about behavior problems. This, along with Sarah's struggle to redirect, interfered with the productiveness of the session. In Sarah's next session with the family, she established a few simple ground rules about taking turns so that everyone could speak. These rules assisted with Anna's need to feel heard and Sarah's need to direct the session so that Patrice did not dominate. (Smith, 2009)

Source: Adapted from Smith, A. L. (2009). Role play in counselor education and supervision: Innovative ideas, gaps, and future directions. *Journal of Creativity on Mental Health, 4,* 124-138.

Feedback and Evaluation

Feedback and evaluation are two major elements of supervision, and feedback can be either oral or written, but evaluation is most often given to supervisees in writing. As a practicum student or intern, you will frequently get feedback at different occasions during your supervision. In your university supervision, both group and individual, you may receive feedback from both your peers and supervisor during or after you present a case, show a counseling session on video-/audiotape, or conduct a role-play. During your on-site supervision, you may be given feedback by your supervisor and peers on various occasions of your performance. Your performance may include but not be limited to case presentation; observation of your counseling sessions using either video-/audiotapes or live observation; management of administrative matters; and dealing with personnel issues, workshops, outreach programs, or your paperwork. The feedback on all these matters is often provided orally and in a constructive manner.

We have noticed that in the feedback-giving process, it is beneficial for students to be in control. As a reflection of the students' increased responsibility for directing their own professional development, they should enter supervision with a clear understanding of those areas of professional practice for which they desire supervisory feedback. Most supervisors may ask the practicum student what kind of feedback he or she wants, and this type of question puts the practicum student in the driver's seat. As the practicum student, you want to get feedback on both what you do well and areas in which you want to see improvement. Again, if we return to our simple illustration of developing skills in tennis or golf, it is clear that the "student" has some insight into what is not exactly right or the way he or she wants to perform and thus will request specific feedback from the trainer. The same is true in developing our counseling. As a student, you will know areas where you feel stuck, or lost—or simply feel that it didn't go as well as you desired. Bring these specific concerns to your supervisor and ask for his or her concrete feedback and suggestions.

Evaluation is pretty much about the formal feedback, which is often in writing and which the practicum student receives in the middle or at the end of a semester. There are two kinds of evaluation here, the site supervisor's evaluation and the grade given by the faculty supervisor. In almost all circumstances, the site supervisor will provide some written evaluation about the practicum student's overall performance, which includes strengths and areas that need improvement. The site supervisor's evaluation may be factored into the faculty supervisor's final grade for the student.

The supervisor's evaluation should not be a surprise. Prior to starting your field work, it is important that you discuss with the supervisor both the areas of expected functioning and the methods by which your functioning will be assessed. If there is a particular scale or form, ask to see it. Be sure to understand the components that go into your evaluation and, as you progress through your experience, seek feedback as to your performance on those evaluative measures.

There are a few important things that are necessary for the intern to know about the evaluation. These things include that evaluation is a tool used to help the intern to grow, to reflect the unknown aspects of self, and to become more open-minded or less defensive. In addition, the intern should know that he or she can direct communication about unfairness of evaluation to the supervisor.

The faculty supervisor also gives the intern a final evaluation, which can be an academic grade plus a formal written evaluation that reflects all the tasks the intern performed in the on-campus supervision. The faculty supervisor's grade often includes both the work done by the intern in the on-campus supervision and the on-site supervisor's evaluation. As intern, you want to understand the relationship between the two evaluations.

Counseling Supervision Models

In an almost parallel way, just as theories of counseling provide an orientation or template within which to view client issues and engage in a helping process, so does a supervisor's model of supervision provide a conceptual framework for the supervisor to address the supervisees' needs (Bernard & Goodyear, 2014). Through using supervision models, counseling supervisors build a supervisory alliance with their supervisees, in which the supervisees gain competence and obtain confidence and the ability to be creative in order to offer the best service to their clients.

There are many instructional supervision models for classroom supervision. Your faculty supervisor may choose an instructional supervision model or format that he or she sees fits a certain group of counseling trainees for their development of counselor skills and personal growth. For example, your faculty supervisor may adopt an empirically supported model such as structured group supervision (SGS) by Wilbur, Roberts-Wilbur,

Morris, Betz, and Hart (1991; 1994) for your practicum class. This is a commonly used model by college/university faculty supervisors. The SGS includes five phases: case presentation, readings, goal setting, discussion of articles, and review and critique of counseling sessions by peer practicum students and faculty supervisor. In addition, a recent study of CACREP-accredited programs by Prieto (1998) showed that faculty supervisors tend to use a collegial and relationship-oriented approach in practicum classes regardless of the level of practicum class being taught.

Numerous models have been created for clinical supervision. Supervision models are generally conceptualized from three major perspectives: psychotherapy theories–based, developmental, and integrative. The psychotherapy-based supervision models are a natural extension of counseling theories used by counselors (e.g., psychodynamic, humanistic-relationship, cognitive-behavioral, systemic, constructivist, narrative, and solution-focused theories; Bernard & Goodyear, 2014). The developmental supervision models focus on progressive stages of supervisee development from novice to expert with discrete characteristics and skills (Haynes et al., 2003). The processing models of supervision "emerged from an interest in supervision as an educational and relationship process" (Bernard & Goodyear, 2014, p. 51).

Because each model or approach has a special focus and will influence the nature and direction of the clinical supervision received, it is important to discuss the model or models employed by your site supervisor and how these address your unique needs as a supervisee.

Issues and Dilemmas in Supervision

As with counseling, the relationship and the dynamic that occur in supervision are not without challenge. The very personal, as well as professional, nature of supervision requires supervisees to take close look at themselves, as people and as counselors, and to challenge themselves in ways that are sometimes difficult. This all happens within the boundaries of supervision—boundaries that at times are difficult to maintain.

Conflicts in Supervisory Relationships

Conflicts are not uncommon in all human relationships. Supervisory relationships cannot be an exception. Supervision occurs in a supervisory relationship, so conflicts are inevitable. As a counseling trainee, you will encounter a process of building multiple relationships in your field practice: the relationship between you and other counseling professionals (your supervisor's colleagues), between you and your peer practicum students, and particularly between you and your supervisors. The dynamics that these relationships create will facilitate your growth and development as a counseling professional and protect the welfare of your clients. As we discussed in the previous chapters (e.g., Chapter 1), field experience is an opportunity for you to construct and strengthen your relationships with yourself and with the external world and to gain confidence in your belief of becoming a counseling professional.

The relationships in your supervision area are a small portion of the relationship between you and the external world. However, they can affect your other relationships, either positively or negatively. If this relationship is managed well, it will compensate your other areas of relationship (e.g., your relationship with self, clients, peers, and even friends and family). If not managed well, it can cost the gain in your other areas of relationship. For example, negative supervision experience affected supervisees' clinical skills (e.g., less strong relationships with clients), training satisfaction, career aspirations, and overall supervisory relationship (Ramos-Sanchez et al., 2002). Further, Burkard and his colleagues (2006) have found that such negative supervision experiences have an impact on future supervision experiences. Therefore, building a strong supervisory relationship is crucial. This requires devotion, trust, and confidence. It also calls for, on your part, a strong professional ethic, open and honest communication, reliability, and behavioral predictability/consistency.

Conflicts in supervision can directly rise in the supervision process or be brought into the supervision process from other aspects of practicum and internship. Some examples of direct conflicts are when supervisees arrive late, leave early, do not come prepared for supervision, are reluctant to record or show tapes, or do not accept feedback. Other conflicts might be supervisors throwing students into counseling situations that are too serious and involve more skills and experience than their current level of experience (e.g., assigning supervisees' clients who are in crisis or at risk for lawsuit). Some supervisors might treat practicum students more as office assistants than counselors-in-training, which means they do not always supervise or let trainees do the activities that faculty supervisors give as assignments, or they fail to include supervisees in important activities and meetings. Some supervisors do not let supervisees count hours if they are not present on the site. All these can result in the trainees' not getting enough hours to meet the requirements of the graduate program. Some supervisors do not spend enough time with practicum students and fail to provide proper delegation of duties and adequate supervision (e.g., they are busy with many other administrative tasks or meetings, come late, leave early, or take prolonged vacation or personal leave without designating a substitute supervisor for trainees). In addition, research has identified examples of conflicts caused by supervisors such as some supervisors dismissed supervisees' ideas and emotions (Gray, Ladany, Walker, & Ancis, 2001), did not invest themselves in the supervisory alliance, avoided responsibility for conflictual actions (Nelson & Friedlander, 2001), and displayed racial microaggressions (Constantine & Sue, 2007).

There are also supervisors who role-model inappropriate professional behaviors. These behaviors include but are not limited to talking about clients with others who are not involved in the case in front of trainees, frequently taking phone calls during meetings, discussing personal matters during supervision, using trainees as confidants by talking about other colleagues' shortcomings, or taking advantage of trainees by asking trainees to do things that have nothing to do with work or training. Consider the situation experienced by one intern, as illustrated in the case of "needing a sitter" (Case Illustration 6.4).

CASE ILLUSTRATION 6.4

Needing a Sitter

Emma just finished her practicum of 100 hours in the counseling center at one of the Big Ten universities in the past semester. She felt the experience she gained at her practicum was beneficial and interesting and something she wanted to continue with her internship. Unfortunately, the counseling center where she did her practicum was not able to take her as an intern due to its commitment for more predoctoral interns, so she found her internship site in a counseling center at a community college nearby. Emma was excited about this opportunity and began her internship as it was scheduled. At the beginning of the semester, Emma gave her supervisor, Elizabeth, the internship requirements from her university faculty supervisor. Her supervisor was very responsive and promised Emma that there would be no problem for her to complete all her 300 hours and other requirements. However, after 2 weeks, Emma had not done much more than become very familiar with her supervisor's 5-year-old daughter, Ava. Elizabeth divorced before her daughter was born and she had remained single since. For some reason, her daughter could not go to the kindergarten for longer hours and Elizabeth had to bring Ava to work and watch her when she did not see clients in the afternoon. After Emma began her internship at the counseling center as her supervisee, Elizabeth often asked Emma, "Can you watch Ava for a minute and I'll be back soon?" She left no matter whether Emma agreed or not, leaving Emma no choice but to watch Ava. In addition, Elizabeth often told Emma about some of the issues she had in her previous relationship with her ex-husband. Emma felt frustrated and did not know what to do.

Moreover, there are situations in which supervisors do not always give credit to the students for the work they do or do not spend enough time with practicum students to provide proper delegation of duties and supervision needed for feedback. In addition, many site supervisors have never taken any supervision courses or trained to be supervisors. They do not understand what practicum students should be doing and what they as supervisors should be doing. For example, some school counselors do not know or use American School Counselor Association (ASCA) model.

Conflicts can occur due to miscommunication or mismatched expectations and normative processes (Bernard & Goodyear, 2014). Evaluative feedback is one of the major tasks of supervision, which can cause tension, even obstruction, to the supervisory relationship between the supervisee and the supervisor. The normative processes occur in response to the supervisee's developmental level. Although counseling trainees are soon becoming professionals, many still have feelings of insecurity and lack the confidence to behave as professionals. These feelings of insecurity and lack of confidence can also cause obstruction in the supervisory relationship. Some other specific conflicts may arise in areas such as different theoretical orientations, supervision style (structure vs. no structure), values clash, ethical violations, and personality conflicts.

Resolving Conflicts in Supervisory Relationships

Moskowitz and Rupert (1983) have found that all trainees in their study expected their supervisors to address the conflict openly when a conflict was present. However, these researchers also discovered that more than 80% of trainees who experienced conflicts reported their own initiation of discussion about the conflict. Therefore, this study tells us that as counseling trainees, you want proactively to address a conflict when it is present. Direct intervention is the better option to address either misunderstandings or incongruent expectations in the supervision process (Bernard & Goodyear, 2014).

Besides bringing the conflict to your supervisor and making your supervisor become aware of it, you may want to consult your peers or other counseling professionals to make sure about your approach. If the conflict arises in your supervision on site, you may seek a different perspective by taking the issue to your supervision class or faculty supervisor at the university. Finally, the Internet is also a wonderful resource to discover how other people deal with similar situations.

Brian Baird (2002), a long-time experienced internship supervisor, has identified six principles for interns to use to deal with conflicts effectively in supervision. The first principle is to have a positive attitude toward conflicts. The author believes that if you, as the intern, have an attitude of learning from a conflict rather than an attitude of anger, fear, or avoidance, the resolution of the conflict and the way you deal with the situation will be more positive and effective. The second principle is to define the nature of the conflict, which means that you need to identify what a conflict is really about before raising it with your supervisor. Third, you honestly and thoroughly explore what your actions and reactions are to better understand your role in the conflict. If you find it difficult to identify your part, you may want to get a third party's objective perspective. Baird suggests that the purpose of seeking an outsider's perspective is to understand what has happened instead of to assure others of your supervisor's fault or to prove you're right. The fourth principle is to see the situation from your supervisor's perspective. In other words, stepping into your supervisor's shoes is another critical step to resolve the conflict. The fifth principle is to clarify what you really want to be different and what change would make you satisfied. The final principle is when the mutual satisfaction of resolving the conflict cannot be reached, a switch of supervisor or placement might be considered. This change can be mediated by a neutral third party, for example, another supervisor or instructor who can help you and your supervisor find the satisfactory alternatives. In Exercise 6.4 we would like to challenge you to identify a conflict or issue and the resolutions or strategies you have used to resolve this in your supervision.

EXERCISE 6.4

My Style of Resolving Conflicts

Directions: Now you have an opportunity to use some of Baird's principles to identify a major conflict you had and how you resolved it.

Step 1: What was the conflict (issue or situation)?
Step 2: Who were involved?
Step 3: What was your attitude toward the conflict?
Step 4: What was the nature of the conflict?
Step 5: What was your role in the conflict (action or reaction)?
Step 6: What was the other party's position?
Step 7: What conflict resolution strategy did you use to resolve the conflict?
Step 8: What was the "ideal situation"?

Boundaries: Supervision Versus Therapy

Counseling supervision is not personal therapy. The focus of the counseling supervision is mainly on the counseling trainee's professional development and personal growth. This professional development and personal growth may include but not be limited to the trainee's counseling skills, knowledge and implementation of ethical and legal standards, and delivery of minimum quality of care to clients. It is a unique intervention that occurs at a different level than therapy (Bernard & Goodyear, 2014). To some extent, a counseling supervisor may do therapy with his or her trainees in order to help the supervisee "examine aspects of his or her behavior, thoughts, or feelings that are stimulated by a client, particularly when these may act as barriers to the work with the client" (Bernard & Goodyear, 1992, p. 5). However, the purpose of this type of therapy with a supervisee is to help the supervisee become more effective with his or her clients. Along this line, the supervisor may also help the supervisee become aware of his or her personal issues that may interfere with his or her efficacy in the counseling process.

Your own issues. It is expected that supervisees reflect on the impact of their own history and issues on the work with clients. To bring this into discussion as appropriate, you and your supervisor need to distinguish the difference between supervision and therapy. If your own issues began to be the main focus or to interfere with your work with clients, you would want to seek therapy for yourself. Consider the following case illustration (Case Illustration 6.5).

Transference and Countertransference

Transference and countertransference are two concepts gleaned from psychoanalysis to describe the projection of intense feelings that may occur in the process of

CASE ILLUSTRATION 6.5

Losing Perspective

Jennie is a second-year graduate student in a counseling program at a large state university in the Midwest of the United States. Currently, she is doing her internship in the practicum clinic of the university. As a graduate intern and supervisee, Jennie is observed during each counseling session that she conducts with an actual client from the local communities. One of Jennie's clients has issues of PTSD and severe depression. Each session after the intake, the client began crying when the topic touched her relationship with her stepfather. However, Jennie quickly shifted the topic to other issues every time the client brought up her relationship with her stepfather. The supervisor noticed what was happening while he was observing the sessions on the other side of the mirror and pointed out what was going on during the supervision with Jennie. Jennie then admitted that she was sexually abused by her father when she was little, and she was scared to go in that direction with the client. As a result of this supervision meeting, Jennie was counseled to seek therapy for herself because her issue had become an interference to her work with her client.

counseling or therapy. Freud (1933) noted that clients would transfer personal thoughts or feelings that perhaps they held for other significant individuals in their life or their past onto a therapist. Whereas the analysis of such transference was viewed as therapeutic, the occurrence of countertransference, that is, the process by which the therapist transfers his or her own personal feelings, desires, wishes, and fantasies onto the client, was not. Clearly, any personal feelings or fantasies experienced by a counselor in session cannot be acted on and need to be resolved in the counselor's own supervision so they do not influence or leak into the treatment relationship. Therefore, addressing the importance of countertransference feelings is considered a professional and ethical responsibility of the counselor.

But beyond the experience of both transference and countertransference in a counseling session, it is also possible to experience these within the dynamic of supervision. Perhaps, for example, one is resisting supervision feedback because the feedback threatens the strong countertransference you feel for a client (Epstein, 2001), or your supervisor mirrors your client's attitude and behavior—transference may occur within the supervision process in what has been called a parallel process (Bernard & Goodyear, 2014).

Baird (2002) suggests that understanding transference and countertransference in supervision can be helpful for you as a counseling supervisee to make the most out of supervision and gain greater awareness of processes you are likely to observe and experience in therapy. Transference reactions within supervision may present as a form of resistance to supervisory feedback, or your expectations and reactions to supervisory feedback may be distorted given the nature of that feedback. Baird (2002) suggests that a supervisee consider the following question as a way of making possible points of transference conscious: "If you were to anticipate a transference reaction toward a supervisor based on someone from your own past, who most likely would the person be? Why?"

Supervision and Multiculturalism

In most counseling programs, interns and practicum students are required to take at least one class on multicultural issues in counseling. The exposure to multicultural issues in counseling in one class is far from enough. As we will discuss in the next chapter on practice in multicultural settings, increasing multicultural awareness, knowledge, and skills is a lifetime task for all counselors. Multiculturally sensitive clinical supervision can be a cornerstone toward enhancing competence in practice for counseling interns. It is the responsibility of the supervisor to assure that multicultural issues receive attention in supervision (Bernard & Goodyear, 2014). This does not mean that you as the intern have no obligation. You want to make sure multicultural issues and issues related to multicultural supervisory relationships are addressed during your supervision; this is vital to interns' professional and personal growth and development (Brown & Landrum-Brown, 1995; Constantine, 1997), especially racial/ethnic minority supervisees, who also need to integrate their ethnic and professional identity (Vasquez & McKinley, 1982).

Issues that you and your supervisor want to address are on four dimensions: the intrapersonal dimension of identity; the interpersonal dimension of expectations, bias, and prejudice; the interpersonal dimension of cultural identity and behavior; and the sociopolitical dimension of privilege and oppression (Bernard & Goodyear, 2014). To fully understand these four dimensions, we ask you to complete Exercise 6.5.

EXERCISE 6.5

Multicultural Dimensions in Supervision

Directions: Complete the following questions under each dimension and then take the questions and your answers to your supervision meetings for discussion with your supervisor and peer supervisees.

Intrapersonal Dimension of Identity

1. How do you identify yourself in terms of race, gender, sexual orientation, national, cultural, etc.?
2. How does the way you identify yourself affect your sense of self in relationship to others?

Interpersonal Dimension of Expectations, Bias, and Prejudice

1. What are your expectations, bias, and prejudice toward others based on their membership in a particular group (e.g., racism, sexism, classism, heterosexism, ageism, ableism, etc.)?
2. How do you categorize the world and the peoples populating in the world?

Interpersonal Dimension of Cultural Identity and Behavior

1. How do you view people from different cultures? Do you view them as essentially the same or different?
2. Do you believe that culture can produce effects on interactions between you and your clients and your supervisor? If so, in what ways? If not, why not?

Social Political Dimension of Privilege and Oppression

1. In what ways and in what situations have you been either privileged or oppressed due to your race/ethnicity, gender, sexual orientation, age, social economic class, religious belief, nationality, or other characteristics?
2. How did the experience that you had in Question 1 affect your identities and behavior?

Through addressing multicultural issues in supervision, interns will increase their abilities in overall case conceptualization (Gainor & Constantine, 2002), abilities to include multicultural issues in client treatment conceptualization (Ladany, Inman, Constantine, & Hofheinz, 1997), personal awareness of cultural issues (Toporek, Ortega-Villalobos, & Pope-Davis, 2004), satisfaction in supervision (Gatmon et al., 2001), and multicultural competence (Constantine, 2001). Therefore, as interns, it is best to be proactive in the aspect of addressing multicultural issues in supervision.

Transitioning From Student to Professional Counselor in Supervision

A final value of field experience is that it is a valuable opportunity for students to more fully transition to the role and identify as professional counselors. The supervision one experiences throughout his or her field work serves as one of the most important vehicles that will guarantee the counselor trainee a quality transition from student to professional. The practicum supervisors, both on site and on campus, are the gatekeepers of the counseling profession. They are obligated to facilitate the occurrence of a high-quality transition that takes place at two major levels—interpersonal functioning and intrapersonal functioning.

In conclusion, the purpose of supervision is to facilitate the development, growth, and maturity of counseling interns in the areas of counseling skills, theories, techniques, research, multicultural competence, and capability of professional practice. The purpose of supervision further includes helping counseling interns fully understand their professional roles, set clear boundaries of professional behavior, abide by professional ethics rules, and improve service quality. Finally, counseling supervision assists in improving counseling interns' mental health and personality and helps them become role models.

KEYSTONES

- Counseling supervision is a professional relationship that empowers counseling trainees and counselors to accomplish their development and growth professionally and personally; as a result, counselors become capable of not only providing the best service to their clients but also transmitting the essence of counseling principles, knowledge, and skills to the new generation.
- Counseling supervision is both an ethical imperative and evidence based, and it has become the cornerstone of quality improvement and assurance.
- Clarification of counseling expectations from both counseling trainees and supervisors is essential; it benefits all parties and facilitates supervisory outcome.
- The focus of the process and content of counseling supervision is to achieve the goal of developing the supervisee's initial professional competencies, which include the supervisee's process skills, conceptualization skills, personalization skills, professional behavior and administrative skills, and other practical skills.
- Counseling supervision model is a framework with which the counseling supervisor helps the supervisee gain competence to offer the best service to his or her clients.
- Issues and dilemmas in counseling supervision are necessary challenges that can be opportunities for the supervisee to grow.
- Counseling supervision is an important vehicle that, with many others, will guarantee the counselor trainee a quality transition from student to professional.

ADDITIONAL RESOURCES

Web Based

American Counseling Association (ACA). (2014). *2014 ACA code of ethics.* Retrieved from http://www.counseling.org/docs/ethics/2014-aca-code-of-ethics.pdf?sfvrsn=4

Association for Counselor Education and Supervision: http://www.acesonline.net/resources/

Heimsch, K. A. (2013). *A development theory for the clinical supervision of counselors encountering suicidal clients* [video]. Retrieved from http://www.youtube.com/watch?v=23AfQXWxXWw

Heimsch, K. A. (2013). *The benefits of supervision for counselor development part 1* [video]. Retrieved from http://www.youtube.com/watch?v=rj0D4Jkr74E

Heimsch, K. A. (2013). *Therapist countertransference and supervision* [video]. Retrieved from http://www.youtube.com/watch?v=hUQiq1mou78

Print Based

Borders, L. D., & Brown, L. L. (2008). *The new handbook of counseling supervision.* Mahwah, NJ: Lawrence Erlbaum.

Fukuyama, M. A. (1994). Critical incidents in multicultural counseling supervision: A phenomenological approach to supervision research. *Counselor Education and Supervision, 34*(2), 142–151.

REFERENCES

Baird, B. N. (2002). *The internship, practicum, and field placement handbook: A guide for the helping professions* (3rd ed.). Upper Saddle River, NJ: Prentice Hall.

Bernard, J. M. (1979). Supervisor training: A discrimination model. *Counselor Education and Supervision, 19,* 740–748.

Bernard, J. M., & Goodyear, R. K. (1992). *Fundamentals of clinical supervision.* Needham Heights, MA: Allyn & Bacon.

Bernard, J. M., & Goodyear, R. K. (2014). *Fundamentals of clinical supervision.* Upper Saddle River: Pearson.

Borders, L. D., & Brown, L. L. (2005). *The new handbook of counseling supervision.* Mahwah, NJ: Lawrence Erlbaum.

Bradley, J. R., & Olson, J. K. (1980). Training factors influencing felt psychotherapeutic competence of psychology trainees. *Professional Psychology, 11,* 930–934.

Brown, M. T., & Landrum-Brown, J. (1995). Counselor supervision: Cross-cultural perspectives. In J. G. Ponterotto, J. M. Casas, L. A. Suzuki, & C. M. Alexander (Eds.), *Handbook of multicultural counseling* (pp. 263–286). Thousand Oaks, CA: Sage.

Burkard, A. W., Johnson, A. J., Madson, M. B., Pruitt, N., Tadych-Contreas, D., Kozlowski, J. M., . . . Knox, S. (2006). Supervisor cultural responsiveness and unresponsiveness in cross-cultural supervision. *Journal of Counseling Psychology, 53,* 288–301.

Carroll, M. (1997). Clinical supervision: Luxury or necessity? In I. Horton & V. Varma (Eds.), *The needs of counselors and psychotherapists* (pp. 135–151). Thousand Oaks, CA: Sage.

Constantine, M. G. (1997). Facilitating multicultural competency in counseling supervision: Operationalizing a practical framework. In D. B. Pope-Davis & H. L. K. Coleman (Eds.), *Multicultural counseling competencies: Assessment, education and training, and supervision* (pp. 310–324). Thousand Oaks, CA: Sage.

Constantine, M. G. (2001). Multiculturally-focused counseling supervision: Its relationship to trainees' multicultural counseling self-efficacy. *The Clinical Supervisor, 20,* 87–98.

Constantine, M. G., & Sue, D. W. (2007). Perceptions of racial microaggressions among black supervisees in cross-racial dyads. *Journal of Counseling Psychology, 54,* 142–153.

Council for Accreditation of Counseling & Related Educational Programs. (2009). *CACREP 2009 standards.* Retrieved from http://www.cacrep.org/wp-content/uploads/2013/12/2009-Standards.pdf

Epstein, L. (2001). Collusive selection inattention to the negative impact of the supervisory interaction. In S. Gill (Ed.), *The supervisory alliance: Facilitating the psychotherapist's learning experience* (pp. 13–163). Northvale, NJ: Jason Aronson.

Falender, C. A., & Shafranske, E. P. (2004). *Clinical supervision: A competency-based approach.* Washington, DC: American Psychological Association.

Freud, S. (1933). *New introductory lectures on psychoanalysis.* New York, NY: W. W. Norton.

Gainor, K. A., & Constantine, M. G. (2002). Multicultural group supervision: A comparison of in person versus web-based formats. *Professional School Counseling, 6,* 104–111.

Garner, B, R., Hunter, B. D., Modisette, K. C., Ihnes, P. C., & Godley, S. H. (2012). Treatment staff turnover in organizations implementing evidence-based practices: Turnover rates and their association with client outcomes. *Journal of Substance Abuse Treatment, 42*(2), 134–142.

Gatmon, D., Jackson, D., Koshkarian, L., Martos-Perry, N., Molina, A., Patel, N., & Rodolfa, E. (2001). Exploring ethnic, gender, and sexual orientation variables in supervision: Do they really matter? *Journal of Multicultural Counseling and Development, 29,* 102–113.

Giordano, M. A., Altekruse, M. K., & Kern, C. W. (2000). *Supervisee bill of rights.* Unpublished manuscript. Retrieved from http://www.grace.edu/files/uploads/webfm/pdfs/Supervision%20Training%20Manual%20081009.pdf

Gray, L. A., Ladany, N., Walker, J. A., & Ancis, J. R. (2001). Psychotherapy trainees' experience of counterproductive events in supervision. *Journal of Counseling Psychology, 48,* 371–383.

Hart, G. M. (1982). *The process of clinical supervision.* Baltimore, MD: University Park Press.

Hatcher, R. L., & Lassiter, K. D. (2007). Initial training in professional psychology: The practicum competencies outline. *Training and Education in Professional Psychology, 1,* 49–63.

Haynes, R., Corey, G., & Moulton, P. (2003). *Clinical supervision in the helping professions: A practical guide.* Pacific Grove, CA: Brooks/Cole.

Herlihy, B., Gray, N., & McCollum, V. (2002). Legal and ethical issues in school counselor supervision. *Professional School Counseling, 6,* 55–60.

Hodges, S. (2011). *The counseling practicum and internship manual: A resource for graduate counseling students.* New York, NY: Springer.

Ivey, A. E., & Ivey, M. B. (2007). *Intentional interviewing and counseling: Facilitating client development in a multicultural society* (6th ed.). Belmont, CA: Brooks/Cole.

Knudsen, H. K., Ducharme, L. J., & Roman, P. M. (2008). Clinical supervision, emotional exhaustion, and turnover intention: A study of substance abuse treatment counselors in the Clinical Trials Network of the National Institute on Drug Abuse. *Journal of Substance Abuse Treatment, 35,* 387–395.

Koltz, R., & Champe, J. (2010). *A phenomenological case study: The transition of mental health counseling interns from students to professionals.* Retrieved from http://counselingoutfitters.com/vistas/vistas10/Article_31.pdf

Ladany, N., Inman, A. G., Constantine, M. G., & Hofheinz, E. W. (1997). Supervisee multicultural case conceptualization ability and self-reported multicultural competence as functions of supervisee racial identity and supervisor focus. *Journal of Counseling Psychology, 44,* 284–293.

Lambie, G. W. (2007). The contribution of ego development level to burnout in school counselors: Implications for professional school counseling. *Journal of Counseling & Development, 85,* 82–88.

Lambie, G. W., & Sias, S. M. (2009). An integrative psychological developmental model of supervision for professional school counselors-in-training. *Journal of Counseling and Development, 87*(3), 349–356.

Lanning, W. (1986). Development of the supervisor emphasis rating form. *Counselor Education and Supervision, 25,* 191–196.

Lawson, G., Hein, S. F., & Stuart, C. L. (2009). A qualitative investigation of supervisees' experiences of triadic supervision. *Journal of Counseling and Development, 87,* 449–457.

Longanbill, C., Hardy, E., & Delworth, U. (1982). Supervision: A conceptual model. *The Counseling Psychologist, 10*(1), 3–42.

Loganbill, C., & Stoltenberg, C. (1983). The case conceptualization format: A training device for practicum. *Counselor Education and Supervision, 22,* 235–241.

Moskowitz, S. A., & Rupert, P. A. (1983). Conflict resolution within a supervisory relationship. *Professional Psychology: Research and Practice, 14*(5), 632–664.

Nelson, M. L., & Friedlander, M. L. (2001). A close look at conflictual supervisory relationships: The trainee's perspective. *Journal of Counseling Psychology, 48,* 384–395.

Newgent, R. A., Davis, H., Jr., & Farley, R. C. (2005). Perceptions of individual, triadic, and group models of supervision: A pilot study. *Clinical Supervisor, 23,* 65–79.

Prieto, L. R. (1998). Practicum class supervision in CACREP-accredited counselor training programs: A national survey. *Counselor Education and Supervision, 38*(2), 113–223.

Ramos-Sanchez, L., Esnil, E., Goodwin, A., Riggs, S., Touster, L. O., Wright, L. K., . . . Rodolfa, E. (2002). Negative supervisory events: Effects on supervision and supervisory alliance. *Professional Psychology: Research & Practice, 33,* 197–202.

Smith, A. L. (2009). Role play in counselor education and supervision: Innovative ideas, gaps, and future directions. *Journal of Creativity in Mental Health, 4,* 124–138.

Stoltenberg, C., & Delworth, U. (1987). *Supervising counselors and therapists.* San Francisco, CA: Jossey-Bass.

Toporek, R. L., Ortega-Villalobos, L., & Pope-Davis, D. B. (2004). Critical incidents in multicultural supervision: Exploring supervisees' and supervisors' experiences. *Journal of Multicultural Counseling and Development, 32,* 66–83.

Vasquez, M. J. & McKinley, D. L. (1982). Supervision: A conceptual model. Reactions and an extension. *The Counseling Psychologist, 10*(1), 59–63

Wilbur, M. P., Roberts-Wilbur, J., Morris, J. R., Betz, R. L., & Hart, G. M. (1991). Structured group supervision: Theory into practice. *Journal for Specialists in Group Work, 16,* 91–100.

Wilbur, M. P., Roberts-Wilbur, J., Morris, J. R., Betz, R. L., & Hart, G. M. (1994). Structured group supervision: A pilot study. *Counselor Education and Supervision, 33,* 262–279.

7

Multicultural Counseling in Practice

Multiculturalism without strong research risks becoming an empty political value, and evidence based treatment (EBT) without cultural sensitivity risks irrelevancy.

Eduardo Morales and John C. Norcross

The above statement by Morales and Norcross reflects the true nature of multiculturalism in counseling practice, and it further alerts us counselors of the necessity and urgency of becoming multiculturally competent while we serve our clients with cultural backgrounds that are different from our own. Therefore, training multiculturally competent counselors has become an imperative obligation for counselor educators, and this call comes from the awareness of counseling professionals, the requirement of the counseling profession (e.g., ACA, APA, and CACREP), the society, and ultimately the need of our clients.

Up to this point as interns, you most likely have taken courses with some components of multiculturalism, and some of you may have taken a required course on multicultural counseling. In this chapter, we will emphasize the value of approaching each of your clients through a multicultural perspective. After completing this chapter, readers will be able to

- understand the necessity of becoming multiculturally competent;
- become more sensitive while they serve clients with multicultural backgrounds;
- become more aware of their function and impact as counselors in the process of multicultural counseling;
- understand the necessity to adapt traditional counseling interventions for meeting the needs of multicultural clients;

- select culturally appropriate counseling skills and techniques and assessment tools when working with multicultural clients;
- develop culturally sensitive treatment plans for multicultural clients;
- understand that becoming multiculturally competent is a component of the counseling professional identity; and
- understand that developing multicultural competency is a lifelong professional commitment.

Multiculturalism in Counseling

Although multicultural issues and diversity in counseling have been addressed in the literature for more than a half century and emphasized by almost all counseling professional organizations and accreditation bodies for almost two decades, some counselor educators may be still in the process of developing their own awareness, knowledge, and skills in this area (D'Andrea, Daniels, & Heck, 1991). The picture of the infusion of multicultural information into practicum and internship is favorable, but almost 70% of CACREP counseling programs do not require multicultural counseling training before practicum and only 18% require students to counsel clients from ethnic minority populations, which suggest that limited multicultural counseling instruction has been delivered before and during students' practicum training (Bradley & Fiorini, 1999). These researchers have made further interpretation that counselor educators may perceive multicultural counseling as supplemental to traditional theories and assumptions and are not convinced that multicultural counseling is the essence of the counseling process. This last point, we feel, needs to be reiterated!

For some, multicultural counseling is viewed as *supplemental* rather than pivotal or core to the counseling process. However, whether we know it or not, all competent counselors, both those with formal multicultural training and those without, incorporate some level of multicultural competency within their practice. It is not possible to be ethical and effective without such integration and incorporation. Perhaps before we discuss the fundamentals of the what, why, and how of multicultural counseling, it is important to invite you to take time to look at your own *valuing* of the need for multicultural competency. Exercise 7.1 invites you to take time to reflect on some very simple and yet poignant questions that each counselor needs to answer.

EXERCISE 7.1

A Matter of Values

Directions: The directions for this exercise are relatively simple:

For Part I: Read the "context" being presented and then respond—honestly—to each of the questions posed. It is important to take time to reflect on each question and write out your response in as much detail as possible.

For Part II: Discuss the questions and your responses with your colleagues, classmates, and site or campus supervisor, focusing on how the specific cultural (in the broadest sense) variables "color" your perspective on the nature of a client's presenting concern and even the approach you may take to assist that client.

Context:

Imagine that you are about to meet with a client for the first time. The referral handed to you states that the client has expressed concerns over feeling depressed and has identified what is felt to have been a trigger for this depression. The trigger is the recent loss of employment.

Part I

Reflections

1. Prior to meeting with the client, what are your pre-notions, theories, or assumptions about what may be going on? (For example, are you wondering about possible biological connections to familial depression? Or beliefs, such as hopelessness, that may be contributing?)
2. How would the client's age affect your assumptions? For example, what if the client were a preteen? A young adult? A person in his or her 70s?
3. Would the client's gender and/or role identity influence your perspective on the presenting issue and conditions offered as triggers?
4. How might knowing the clients' socioeconomic status affect your viewpoint? Would the trigger be seen differently for one from a low SES as opposed to a client operating at the upper boundaries of the socioeconomic categories?
5. Would knowing the client's religious, theological, or philosophical views influence your perspective (e.g., if the client's religion espoused strong sanctions against suicide? other values?)
6. How might knowledge of the client's familial values, as tied to issues such as productivity, independence, achievement, interdependence, responsibility, and status, affect your perspective on the presenting concern?
7. Would your initial views of the presenting concern and even the approach to counseling be affected by knowledge of the client's racial identity (being same as or different from yours) or cultural heritage (and whether they are generations removed from their ancestors' immigration to the U.S.)?
8. Would knowing that the client presented with some physical, cognitive, social, or emotional challenges affect your view of the presenting problem and the approach to be taken?

Part II (Discuss with colleagues, classmates, and site or campus supervisors)

Does knowing the unique cultural (again in the broadest sense of that word) profile of your client affect your perspective on the nature of the presenting concern and the approach to be taken? What might this suggest about the need and value for developing multicultural competency?

Although we hope you understand the importance of the core value of multicultural competency to our practice as counselors, we cannot, given the information provided by the research cited above, assume that all practicum and intern students have been exposed to multicultural and diversity issues and have obtained multicultural training in the program they have more than half completed. For this reason, we will begin this chapter with some basic concepts and issues before discussing your application with clients of the knowledge and skills obtained from all your course work.

Issues in Multicultural Counseling

Multiculturalism or multicultural issues in counseling were addressed in literature as early as the 1950s (Jackson, 1995), but training multiculturally competent counselors did not emerge on the center stage of the counseling profession until the 1990s (Ponterotto, 2008). It was during this decade that multicultural counseling began to expand and became mature from the narrow concept—cross-cultural counseling (Black vs. White)—to an enriched concept, multicultural counseling. Multicultural counseling has, since then, endorsed a broad definition referring to a complex array of cultural variables such as racial/ethnic heritage, sexual orientation, religious/spiritual orientation, disability, and other defining cultural characteristics of one's identity (Fukuyama, 1990).

The presentation on multicultural theories and research has significantly affected the enhancement of multicultural counseling development and training on multicultural counseling-competent counselors (Ponterotto, Casas, Suzuki, & Alexander, 2010). For example, one major issue identified by the research early on was the underutilization of mental health services and high dropout rates by racial, ethnic, and cultural minority clients (Atkinson & Thompson, 1992). Moreover, the fast-changing demographics in the United States have ensured a client population more diverse than ever (Sue & Sue, 2013). Counselors' competence and effectiveness have been questioned on their ability to help their multicultural clients without the awareness of their own sociocultural backgrounds, values, assumptions, biases, and perspectives with regard to their multicultural clients (Chandras, 1997). Counselors' effectiveness becomes questionable when they lack an understanding of their feelings about their own social class; racial, ethnic, and religious characteristics; and points of convergence with or divergence from their clients (Wintrob & Harvey, 1981). Here we ask you to complete Exercise 7.2 to examine your biases.

CULTURAL EXERCISE 7.2

Cultural Encapsulation

Directions: Below you will find five questions related to cultural encapsulation. Your task is to respond to each and then take both the questions and your answers to your supervision meetings for discussion.

1. In what ways have you seen that the same hypothetical normal standard of behavior is applied to all clients in your practice?

2. In what ways have you seen individualism presumed to be more appropriate than a collectivist perspective in your practice?
3. In what ways have you seen that dependency is considered to be an undesirable condition?
4. In what ways have you seen that the client's support system is not normally considered relevant in analyzing the client's psychological health?
5. In what ways have you seen that only linear-based "cause-effect" thinking is accepted as scientific and appropriate in your practice?

Counseling individuals with a different cultural background from the Western culture becomes ethically problematic because all theories of counseling and psychotherapy are based on the values and assumptions of theorists from the Western culture, and the intervention techniques for change are Western-values oriented (Corey, 2012). The profession's response to this situation has to increase focus of counselor education on issues of diversity and multicultural counseling. Multicultural counseling competence has been recognized as one of the major counseling competencies and emphasized as one of the core components of curriculum of almost all counseling training programs by counseling professions and accreditation bodies (e.g., ACA, 2014; ASCA, 2010; APA, 2013; CACREP, 2014).

Ethics and Working With Multicultural Clients

The American Counseling Association (2014) requires that all counselors must uphold the practice standards to "recognize diversity and embrace a cross-cultural approach" and "maintain awareness and sensitivity regarding cultural meanings of confidentiality and privacy." The American School Counselor Association (2004) expects all school counselors to acquire interpersonal skills to "recognize, accept and appreciate ethnic and cultural diversity." We invite you to read Case Illustration 7.1, which is an actual case with the client's demographics modified.

CASE ILLUSTRATION 7.1

Why Does He Want to Know That?

Jin Yang is a 35-year-old female Asian international student who studies social work at a state university in the Midwest of the United States. In the first semester, Jin Yang was very happy and excited about the things she had never seen before. However, starting in the middle of the spring semester, Jin Yang begins to feel down and has low energy.

(Continued)

(Continued)

Oftentimes she can't turn in her assignments on time. She feels that she misses her parents and other family members in her home country. She studies social work and has learned some knowledge about counseling, so she decides to give counseling a chance.

After calling the university counseling center, Jin Yang was offered an appointment a week later. She thought that she might feel better then. To Jin Yang's surprise, she seemed to be feeling worse on the day she visited the counseling center. After she waited for a few minutes in the waiting room, a man walked over to her and identified himself as Dr. Sterling. Dr. Sterling appeared very friendly, reaching out his hand to Jin Yang for a handshake. Jin Yang was a little hesitant but shook hands with Dr. Sterling anyway. Right after they both sat down, Dr. Sterling began to share with her about confidentiality and what would happen in counseling. Jin Yang saw that what Dr. Sterling was doing was similar to what she was taught in some classes. After they discussed her relationships with her parents and siblings, Dr. Sterling asked Jin Yang if she had a boyfriend. Jin Yang told Dr. Sterling she did not have a romantic relationship at the present. Dr. Sterling then asked if Jin Yang was a virgin. Jin Yang was a little surprised and remained silent for almost half a minute and then said "I don't have a romantic relationship." From then on, Jin Yang was reluctant to share much of her life experience and focused only on her academic stress.

Right after Jin Yang walked out of the building where the counseling center was located, she burst into tears. She felt insulted and embarrassed. She cried in her room for hours, asking herself, "Why does he want to know that?"

What are the ethical considerations involved in this case? What might you have done differently? What can you learn from this case as you move forward in your own clinical development?

This case demonstrates how the counselor's awareness and insensitivity regarding cultural meanings of confidentiality and privacy may cause mistrust from and harm to clients. A woman's virginity in some Asian cultures is considered private and confidential. Asking a woman about her virginity is disrespectful and rude.

To meet its standards for accreditation, the American Psychological Association (APA, 2013) requires that internship programs provide culturally relevant training (i.e., knowledge and practical experience). Further, the Council for Accreditation of Counseling and Related Educational Programs (CACREP, 2014) in its standards requires all counseling programs seeking accreditation to train their students from a multicultural perspective and to develop their students' multicultural competency. As noted in these standards (CACREP, 2014), trainees should not only know the efficacy and applicability of counseling theory to multicultural populations, but also have experience in applying multicultural competencies to case conceptualization, diagnosis, treatment, referral, and prevention of mental and emotional disorders. The directives posed by both APA (2013) and CACREP (2014) should serve as beacons to your own goals while engaging in field work. Experiencing clients from diverse backgrounds and gaining the knowledge and skills necessary for working with such diverse populations are essential to your field work and professional formation.

When concerning working with multicultural clients, the American Counseling Association (ACA) has set its specific standards for all professional counselors. Its *Code of Ethics* (2014), approved by the ACA Governing Council, explicitly stipulates its requirements on what professional counselors should do in the aspect of respecting client rights and conditions of assessment administration, as well as responsibilities of counselor educators. But what does this actually mean? Exercise 7.3 invites you to review the methods, materials, policies, and procedures that guide the decisions and actions made within your field placement as they reflect cultural sensitivity and valuing of multicultural competency.

EXERCISE 7.3

Practice Reflecting Sensitivity

Directions: Below you will find three specific ethical principles articulated by the American Counseling Association (ACA, 2014) in reference to counselor multicultural competence and sensitivities. Your task is to discuss with your site supervisor specific ways practice, policies, and procedures employed at your site reflect adherence to these principles.

Ethical Principles	**Site Policies**	**Counselor Practice**	**Training Opportunity**
A.2.c. Developmental and Cultural Sensitivity: Counselors communicate information in ways that are both developmentally and culturally appropriate.			
When clients have difficulty understanding the language used by counselors, they provide necessary services (e.g., arranging for a qualified interpreter or translator) to ensure comprehension by clients. (A.2.c)			
In collaboration with clients, counselors consider cultural implications of informed consent procedures and, where possible, counselors adjust their practices accordingly. (A.2.c)			

(Continued)

(Continued)

Ethical Principles	Site Policies	Counselor Practice	Training Opportunity
E.5.b. Cultural Sensitivity: Counselors recognize that culture affects the manner in which clients' problems are defined.			
Clients' socioeconomic and cultural experiences are considered when diagnosing mental disorders. (E.5.b)			
E.6.c. Culturally Diverse Populations: Counselors are cautious when selecting assessments for culturally diverse populations to avoid the use of instruments that lack appropriate psychometric properties for the client population.			

It is clear that our professional ethics demand that we develop our multicultural counseling competencies, and those in counselor education have attempted to respond to this call by the inclusion of specific training in multicultural issues and counseling competencies. The importance of this training can be attested in the fact that one accrediting body, the Council for Accreditation of Counseling and Related Educational Programs (CACREP, 2014), includes social and cultural diversity as one of the eight common core curricular areas. The expectation is that all students will have an understanding of the cultural context of relationships, issues, and trends in a multicultural society (see CACREP standards, 2014). Some specific expectations for students to acquire diversity awareness, knowledge, and skills include the following:

a. "Demonstrates the ability to modify counseling systems, theories, techniques, and interventions to make them culturally appropriate for diverse populations of addiction clients." (Sect. III, Addiction Counseling Subsection, F3)

b. "Understands the effects of racism, discrimination, sexism, power, privilege, and oppression on one's own life and career and those of the client." (Sect. III, Clinical Mental Health Counseling Subsection, E.2)

c. "Demonstrates an ability to help staff members, professionals, and community members understand the unique needs/characteristics of multicultural and diverse populations with regard to career exploration, employment expectations, and economic/social issues." (Sect. III: Career Counseling Subsection, F2)

d. "Demonstrates appropriate use of culturally responsive individual, couple, family, group, and systems modalities for initiating, maintaining, and terminating counseling." (Section III: Mental Health Counseling Subsection, D5)

e. "Designs and implements prevention and intervention plans related to the effects of (a) atypical growth and development, (b) health and wellness, (c) language, (d) ability level, (e) multicultural issues, and (f) factors of resiliency on student learning and development." (Sect. III, School Counseling Subsection, D3)

It is very clear that all the organizations listed above have committed themselves to diversity and professional counselors' multicultural counseling competence. Each organization and accreditation body has a genuine belief that achieving multicultural counseling competencies for professional counselors is a fundamental responsibility of the counselor educator and the counseling trainee. Further, each organization in its own way has highlighted the need and desire to make the product of counselor education relevant to the reality of diversity in the world. As a result, a meaningful and high-quality service will be provided for the underrepresented populations seeking mental health assistance. As you continue in your own professional development, it is important to target those areas of deficiency that you need to address. Exercise 7.4 invites you to consider the standards of multicultural competency and your own levels of competency. The goal is not to find fault or dwell on areas where growth is needed, but rather to target specific goals and objectives for your ongoing professional development.

EXERCISE 7.4

What Does the *Code of Ethics* Say About MCC?

In this exercise, you are asked to review the section(s) of the *Code of Ethics* of ACA and American Association of Multicultural Counseling and Development (AAMCD) on multicultural counseling competencies (see Additional Resources). As you review the standards, write down which competency or competencies of multicultural counseling have been addressed in your course work and which competency or competencies of multicultural counseling you have gained training on (e.g., you have been required to counsel multicultural clients). Finally, set up goals and objectives for yourself to work on the multicultural counseling competencies you have not been exposed to and had training on. You could use these goals as targets for your field work experience.

Multicultural Counseling Competence

As a counseling graduate student, you have most likely been required to take courses that encompass multiculturalism and address evidence-based practice (EBP). While doing your course work concerning multiculturalism, you may have been expected to participate in some multicultural events and even write papers reflecting your awareness and multicultural knowledge. However, translating and implementing what you have learned from classroom lectures and books into reality begins to take shape now while you are engaging in field work. If we viewed your professional development from the perspective of engaging in the process of change, then we would assume that gaining knowledge in the classroom reflects the stages of awareness and preparation, whereas the process of engaging in practicum and internship becomes your action stage. During the action stage, your practice must attend to the culture and the culturally sensitive. Without cultural sensitivity, your counseling would be irrelevant and your service would not be evidence-based practice (Morales & Norcross, 2010).

Client population becomes more and more diverse and virtually every counseling-therapy interaction can be viewed as more or less cross-cultural (Sue et al., 1982, p. 47); just consider your previous responses to Exercise 7.1. So, without multicultural awareness, multicultural knowledge, and multicultural counseling skills, counselors will not be able to provide the service their clients need. Without cultural competence developed in clinical training, psychotherapists become irrelevant at best, and guilty of cultural malpractice at worst (Hall, 1997).

Counseling Competence Versus Multicultural Counseling Competence

Although much of the literature discusses the need and value of multicultural counseling competency, a question might be raised: how does one demonstrate counseling competency (in general) in the absence of multicultural competency? Can one really be separated from the other?

Consider what it means to be a competent counselor. To be competent, one has the knowledge and ability to engage with another in the dynamic process of counseling. This would include competency in skills of exploration, developing and maintaining therapeutic alliance, engaging in processes of change, and managing the processes through to successful outcome (Eriksen & McAuliffe, 2003). When one considers the specific knowledge and skills needed to perform in this way, a model of competency emerges, one that has been articulated by Ridley, Mollen, and Kelly (2011). These authors identified what they deemed to be therapeutic competencies, including (a) self-appraisal/self-evaluating, (b) structuring the therapy, (c) building a therapeutic alliance, (d) applying a conceptual map of therapeutic change, (e) using therapeutic techniques, (f) self-correcting, (g) surmounting obstacles, (h) leveraging opportunities, (i) managing special situations, (j) working with other systems of care, (k) consulting other sources, and (l) terminating therapy (p. 20).

Even a cursory glance at these competencies reveals the truth to their statement that "counseling competence is multicultural counseling competence" (Ridley et al., 2011, p. 17). We strongly affirm this assertion that counseling competence is multicultural counseling competence because culture is an invisible but imperative participant in all counseling (Draguns, 2008), and counseling competence is a multidimensional construct of which multicultural counseling competence is an aspect (Constantine, 2002). Again, review your responses to Exercise 7.1 and consider this question: Can culture be removed from your understanding of the nature of the problem, and/or the means for assisting the client with that problem?

As interns, you may encounter a client population that is composed of individuals with diverse cultural backgrounds, and this diversity gives you the opportunity to gain experience in multicultural counseling with people who may be different from you in terms of values, beliefs, or worldviews. This opportunity of working with the underrepresented client population will be the gatekeeping experience that is used by your professors and supervisors to determine your competence to practice independently as a counseling professional (Holloway & Roehlke, 1987).

As you may see, multicultural counseling competence intertwines with counseling competence because an effective professional counselor must work in a culturally competent manner with a broad range of cultural variables, which can be simultaneously as relevant to clients as do their presenting concerns (Coleman, 2006). Without multicultural counseling competence, your counseling competence is crippled and your ability to perform necessary counseling skills and to function as a professional counselor is inept. For this reason, all your practicum and internship experience is multicultural in nature, and the process of your development of counseling competence is a process of developing multicultural counseling competence.

A Model Guiding the Development of Competency

The goal throughout your field experience is not merely to "experience." Rather, it is to approach each encounter, each task, and each client as an invitation for your own personal and professional development. This is certainly true as applied to the development of your own multicultural counseling competencies.

We suggest that you familiarize yourself with the following tripartite model of multicultural counseling competence as it serves as a template to your own pursuit of increased competency. The value of this model lies in the fact that the tripartite model of MCC is the most widely recognized framework guiding research and training (Xie, 2015). As you may have noticed in the section Ethics and Working With Multicultural Clients in this chapter, most counseling professional organizations and accreditation bodies created their code of ethics and standards on multicultural counseling competence development based on the tripartite model of MCC (e.g., ACA, APA, ASCA, and CACREP). In addition, the tripartite model of MCC has been extensively researched (Malott, 2010) and finally, is expansive, including not only racially and ethnically different populations, but also a wide variety of other underrepresented individuals (Xie, 2015). It is our belief this model is applicable in practice and will provide you a framework you will find useful in the process of developing your multicultural counseling competence during your practicum and internship.

The tripartite model contains three dimensions of cultural competence: (a) awareness, (b) knowledge, and (c) skills (Sue et al., 1982). *Awareness* deals with counselors' beliefs and attitudes about multicultural individuals and biases and stereotypes toward multicultural persons, meanwhile developing a positive orientation toward multiculturalism and becoming cognizant that their values and biases may hinder effective multicultural counseling. The *knowledge* means multiculturally competent counselors understand their own worldviews and possess specific knowledge of the multicultural client populations they work with and further understand sociopolitical influences on both counselors and clients. The *skills* dimension deals with specific skills, such as intervention techniques and strategies needed to work with multicultural clients.

Arredondo and associates (1996) revised this tripartite model by extending its original focus on racial/ethnic issues to more human diversity dimensions such as gender, sexual orientation, social economic status, religion, and disability. This revised partite model included three dimensions of counselor characteristics and identified nine competence areas with 31 specific competencies. Later on, the American Association of Multicultural Counseling Development (AAMCD) fully approved this model and adopted all these multicultural counseling competencies, which are also firmly endorsed by the American Counseling Association. You may easily find all these multicultural counseling competencies online (see link for AAMCD Multicultural Counseling Competencies in Additional Resources at the end of the chapter).

Developing Multicultural Counseling Competence

As noted throughout this textbook, the goal is not solely to increase the reader's knowledge, but rather to stimulate professional development and identity formation. Therefore, it is not sufficient just to know or understand the tripartite model or the ethical reasons for multicultural competency. It is essential to engage in processes that further foster your own development of multicultural competence, including (a) increasing awareness of your own cultural values and biases, (b) increasing awareness and valuing of a client's culture and worldview, and (c) increasing your knowledge of and skill with culturally relevant interventions.

Counselor Awareness of Own Cultural Values and Biases

Each intern is in a different place in terms of his or her development of multicultural competencies at the time of beginning the internship (Ponterotto, Fuertes, & Chen, 2000; Sevig & Etzkorn, 2001). Some may be more advanced in the area of awareness; some may have developed certain multicultural counseling skills; and others may have had few opportunities to expose themselves to multicultural issues. No matter where you are in terms of your level of multicultural counseling competencies, developing multicultural competence is a lifelong journey, which you may have just started. We present Case Illustration 7.2 to help you on your journey of multicultural awareness.

CASE ILLUSTRATION 7.2

Confronting My Own Ethnocentrism and Racism

I am a White man who is about to reveal a part of my soul to the world, and I am frightened by the risk I am taking. You see, the subjects I am about to discuss—ethnocentrism and racism, including my own racism—are topics that most Whites tend to avoid. We shy away from discussing these issues for many reasons: We are racked with guilt over the way people of color have been treated in our nation; we fear that we will be accused of mistreating others; we particularly fear being called the "R" word–racist–so we grow uneasy whenever issues of race emerge; and we tend to back away, change the subject, respond defensively, assert our innocence and our "color blindness," denying that we could possibly be ethnocentric or racist.

I have felt this way most of my life. For the longest time, I didn't consider myself to be ethnocentric or racist in any shape or manner. After all, I genuinely abhorred the Ku Klux Klan. I had a couple of African American and Cuban American friends as a boy. I was a nonviolent youngster who had never hurt any ethnic or minority individuals. I admired Martin Luther King, Jr. I always supported Democrats who fought for the oppressed.

Nevertheless, I had no clue that I was ethnocentric and, to some extent, racist–yes, racist–and that I missed out on much of what life has to offer because of my "isms" and the racist world that surrounded me as a boy and a young man. I am hoping that you will listen to my story with understanding, because it is scary and difficult to divulge some of my human frailties in public. But I remain hopeful that my disclosure may provide some glimmer of insight into the process of confronting one's own racism. So I will speak from my heart, entrusting you with the intimate details of a very personal, often painful, and always growth-producing journey.

It may help to preface my story by providing you with a descriptive picture of me, for I now realize that my physical appearance has greatly affected my experience of the world and, in some respects, shaped the story you are about to read. I am a 40-year-old White man, a very White man, about as White as a person can appear. I have blond hair, blue eyes, and fair skin. I am long and lean, standing 6 feet tall. Although my ancestry is half Slovak and half Irish, I have been told at varying times that I look German, Scandinavian, or Polish.

I never realized until I was in my late 20s how much privilege my physical appearance afforded me, even though all of my ancestors were poor and I was born into a lower-middle-class, blue-collar neighborhood. Throughout my early years, I also was totally unaware that my appearance alone could evoke a wide range of emotional reactions, including fear, envy, and admiration, from people who were culturally different from me. Surprising as it may sound, understanding the implications of my physical appearance has helped me to appreciate that the degree of comfort and opportunity provided to people in this nation is partially determined by skin color. It is to this issue of skin color that I would now like to turn my attention, for my gradual recognition of this issue sparked a process of self-reckoning through which I learned that I had, on the one hand, identified with the oppressed and, on the other hand, behaved in ethnocentric and racist ways. (Kiselica, 1999, p.14)

Questions to ponder:

What privileges do you have? How have your privileges affected your experience of the world? What does ethnocentrism mean to you? In what ways have you identified with the oppressed and how have you behaved in an ethnocentric way?

Source: Kiselica, M. S. (1999). Confronting my own ethnocentrism and racism: A process of pain and growth. *Journal of Counseling and Development, 77(1),* 14–17.

This is a portion of a true story by a counseling professional, and you may read the entire story by Kiselica (1999) in *Journal of Counseling and Development*. We think this story may be useful as an example to help you develop your awareness, moving you from being culturally unaware to being aware and sensitive to your own cultural heritage and to valuing and respecting differences, and gradually you can develop awareness of your own values and biases and how they may affect minority clients.

However, on the issue of awareness: Some may feel guilty, miserable, and painful about the mistreatment done to minorities in history, as Mark stated in his story, and others may tend to ignore it for fear of being considered as racist. Either way, this is not helpful to the issue we face at the present. The only choice left for us is to accept the responsibility and "find a realistic, constructive, and, importantly, a personal way to deal with the reality of the past within the context of the present" (Baird, 2002, p. 90). This responsibility is for individuals from both the majority and minority cultures because each of us lives and is educated in an ethnocentric cultural system.

Developing multicultural awareness also means to explore historical influences of self that may affect counseling practice, therapeutic relationship, and subsequently the client's well-being. One layer of historical influences of self includes becoming self-aware of the influence of personal biases and values in working with diverse client populations, and the other layer is engaging diversity and difference in practice (Negi, Bender, Furman, Fowler, & Prickett, 2010). This suggests that before eliminating historical influences of personal biases and values in working with minority clients, counselors must become aware of their potential influence of personal biases and values on their clients. If the awareness of historical influences of self in multicultural counseling has not been achieved, engaging diversity and difference in practice would do the opposite of helping.

Again, we invite you to engage in Exercise 7.5 to further your self-awareness by exploring your roots. This exercise, created by Negi and associates (2010), will help you know your roots and examine the unique experiences of your parents, grandparents, great-grandparents and beyond, or other significant caregivers who have shaped your path in life. If you did this exercise before, we invite you to go back to review what you did and consider how you apply what you have learned to your practice with your multicultural clients.

EXERCISE 7.5

Exploring My Ethnic Roots

In this exercise, you are asked to interview some of your family members to gather family histories on their processes of immigration. They can be your parents, grandparents, great-grandparents, or other significant caregivers. In your interview, you may include questions regarding race, ethnicity, immigration, and acculturation. After you collect the facts, you are expected to assign meanings to those facts by incorporating theory about acculturation processes. Moreover, examining your thoughts, feelings, and perspectives in the process of this interview is critical. After you complete the interview, you are asked to answer this question: "What conclusions do you personally draw about your own current status of assimilation based on your ethnic roots, socialization, and personal experiences and its implication for cultural sensitivity and culturally competent practice?" (Negi et al., 2010, p. 234)

(This exercise is adapted from the assignment created by Negi and colleagues)

To develop multicultural awareness, Sue and Sue (1990) suggested counseling training should use exercises that can help students get in touch with their own values, biases, and perspectives about other cultures, religions, and human behavior. We believe that some of you may not feel comfortable because such a critical self-examination will involve your beliefs, biases, and feelings related to cultural differences. Now we challenge you to complete Exercise 7.6 by answering a set of questions about your identities, values, and awareness.

EXERCISE 7.6

Self-Awareness Assessment

The following are some questions that assist you to increase your self-awareness. Answer these questions as honestly as you can.

1. What are some of my most important identities, for example, gender, race/ethnicity, religion, sexual orientation, social economic status, etc.?
2. Which identity/identities identified in Question 1 allow me to experience privileges?
3. Which identity/identities identified in Question 1 expose me to oppression?
4. How do I feel about these experiences?
5. What are some of my major values, for example, ideas (beliefs, opinions, ways of seeing things), things (people, materials, relationships etc.), and experiences (activities and events)?
6. What are my biases, assumptions, and beliefs about people whose social, cultural, and ethnic backgrounds differ from my own?
7. What certain stereotypes or impressions do I hold about people from other cultural groups than my own?

Source: Sue & Sue 2013.

Counselor Awareness of Client's Worldview

Developing multicultural competence is a change process. The awareness is of paramount importance for the change to occur. As you know, if there is no awareness, there is no action; if there is no action, there is no change. Cultural awareness has two aspects: awareness and understanding of one's own culture, which includes values, beliefs, and biases; and awareness and understanding of others' cultures. This further means one understands one's worldview and others' worldviews. Worldview is our perception of the world based on our experiences as well as the socialization processes of our interaction with members of our reference group (e.g., culture; Gladding, 2001). Each of us has a worldview, and our worldview affects how we perceive and evaluate situations and how we determine appropriate actions based on our appraisal (Sue & Sue, 2013). This suggests that a counselor may affect a client positively or negatively due to his or her worldview. If a counselor does not have awareness of his or her worldview, he or she may do harm to the client, for example, unintentionally delivering microaggressions to clients who are minorities. Microaggressions are "brief and commonplace daily verbal or behavioral indignities, whether intentional or unintentional, that communicate hostile, derogatory, or negative racial slights and insults that potentially have a harmful or unpleasant psychological impact on the target person or group" (Sue, Bucceri, Lin, Nadal, & Torino, 2007). Case Illustration 7.3 shows how the counselor's worldview may be different from that of the client's and how it has consequently affected the client and the counseling relationship.

CASE ILLUSTRATION 7.3

Is She Really Helping?

Todd is a 35-year-old Asian American male graduate student in a counselor education program on the East Coast of the United States. He was born in a town in the northern part of New York and has been living on the East Coast most of his life. Todd was accepted into a graduate program in counseling at a college and is currently in his second semester of a 2-year program.

Todd is one of two adult children in his family. Both of his parents are in their 60s and work for a retail industry. At home, Todd speaks Korean with his parents but he can't read Korean at all.

Although Todd got all As and Bs for the courses he took in the first semester, he feels exhausted and begins having doubts about his ability to graduate from such a rigorous program. Besides handling all the course work, he has to work a full-time job to finance his education and pay his other living expenses. In addition, he started dating someone at the university during the holiday break.

At this point, Todd decides to take advantage of the university counseling center. He called the university counseling center and scheduled an appointment without any hesitation because the messages he has received in the counseling program have informed him that all counseling professionals are well trained with multicultural competence. Todd came to the counseling center and completed all the necessary paperwork. He was then told that he had been assigned to have Dr. Johnson as his counselor. Dr. Johnson is a licensed counseling professional with more than 10 years' practice experience. After a few minutes, Todd is welcomed into Dr. Johnson's office.

Dr. Johnson: Hello, hello! Welcome, and take a seat please.

Todd: Where should I sit?

Dr. Johnson: Take whichever one you feel comfortable (there are two chairs and a couch besides Dr. Johnson's chair).

Todd: (picking up one of the chairs and sitting down)

Dr. Johnson: You're Todd, right?

Todd: Yep.

Dr. Johnson: I assume you speak another language, Chinese, Korean?

Todd: Sort of Korean.

Dr. Johnson: Teach me how to say hello in Korean.

Todd: (reluctantly) 안녕하세요 (*Anyoung haseyo*)

Dr. Johnson: *Ahnyoung haseyo.* Am I correct?

Todd: Yep.

Dr. Johnson: I reviewed your paperwork and see that you're in a counseling program. I'm impressed.

Todd: Why?

Dr. Johnson: As I have noticed, Asians students prefer to major in math or science.

Todd: Well, I'm a little bit odd.

Dr. Johnson: No, no, I think you're unique. So, tell me what brought you in today?

Todd: I feel a little bit overwhelmed.

Dr.Johnson: What do you feel overwhelmed about?

Todd: School, job, and a relationship.

(Continued)

(Continued)

Dr. Johnson:	You named three. Which one do you want to talk about first?
Todd:	I don't know, all of them.
Dr. Johnson:	Okay. Tell me more about your relationship?
Todd:	I started a relationship during the holiday break and was excited at the beginning. After a few weeks, I started feeling frustrated.
Dr. Johnson:	I hear you're saying you started a relationship during the holiday break and felt good about it initially and frustrated now.
Todd:	Exactly.
Dr. Johnson:	Can you tell me more about it, for example, who is your girlfriend, what are you frustrated about?
Todd:	(paused a little bit) Well, my partner . . .

After reading the case illustration, your task is to identify the multicultural issues that occurred during the interaction between Dr. Johnson and her client Todd. What issues do you see? Is Dr. Johnson multiculturally competent? If not, why not? What themes were in Dr. Johnson's behavior? What microaggressions did she present? What messages might be sent via her microaggressive behaviors? If you disagree on what Dr. Johnson has done, what would you do differently?

Getting familiar with minority identity development models is also important for culturally competent counselors because "culturally skilled counselors possess specific knowledge and information about the particular group with which they are working" and "to accomplish this goal the counselors need to be aware of the life experiences, cultural heritage, and historical background of their culturally different clients" (Arredondo et al., 1996). Identity development models include but are not limited to W. E. Cross's Black identity development model, J. Kim's Asian American identity development model, A. S. Ruiz's Latino/Hispanic American identity development model, D. W. Sue and D. Sue's racial/cultural identity development model, K. McNamara and K. M. Rickard's feminist identity development model, and R. R. Troiden's homosexual identity development model. Each of these models suggests that identity resolutions directly affect the development of attitudes and interpersonal and social behaviors (Helms, 1995).

Sue and Sue (2013) suggest that identity development models make contributions to counseling in the way that they help counselors (a) avoid stereotyping their minority clients and acknowledge their possible differences in attitudes, beliefs, and behaviors (e.g., preference for a racially or ethnically similar counselor is influenced by racial/ethnic identity); (b) make accurate diagnosis (reaction to counseling, the counseling process, and counselors is related to cultural/racial identity); and (c) acknowledge sociopolitical influences in shaping minority identity.

Now we ask you to read Case Illustration 7.4 and then answer the questions concerning the client's attitude and behavior toward the counselor and counseling. Remember to keep the racial/ethnic identity development model in mind while you assign meaning to the client's reactions.

CASE ILLUSTRATION 7.4

Alda

Alda is a 21-year-old Latino American female college student who is about to graduate in the next few months. She was born in Allentown, Pennsylvania, and has never had a chance to travel out of the state in her life. Alda's parents immigrated to the United States from the Dominican Republic 25 years ago and worked in restaurants first and then switched to retail stores. The family has three children and Alda is the one in the middle.

Alda's friends are exclusively White, and she hasn't made a single friend with Latino American culture. Occasionally she interacts with a couple of Asian American students at college. Currently, Alda has some issues regarding her career and relationship, so she made contact with the university counseling center and wants to see a counselor for help. At the reception desk, Alda asked the receptionist if her counselor is White. The receptionist looked at her and said "yes" and then asked her why. Alda responded, "That's good." The following is the conversation between Alda and her counselor, Christine.

Alda:	(while sitting down) I'm so pleased to have you as my counselor.
Counselor:	Thank you. Your name is . . .
Alda:	Alda. I hate my name. I wish my parents named me Jennifer, Karen, or something better than a Latino name. I'm afraid, who's going to hire me when they see my name in my résumé."
Counselor:	Your name is beautiful and unique. Nowadays industries look for minority individuals to diversify their work force. Do you speak Spanish?
Alda:	I can understand a little bit but can't read or write since my parents speak Spanish to each other, but I hate them talking to me in Spanish. I don't need to speak Spanish and all my friends are White and they don't speak Spanish but English. All my teachers speak English. There is no need to speak Spanish.

After reading the case, how do you conceptualize Alda's behavior? Where do you see Alda is in terms of her racial/ethnic identity development? As a counselor, how do you see her identity issues are intertwined with her other issues such as her career and relationship? What will be your approach to Alda?

Culturally Appropriate Intervention Strategies

Developing culturally appropriate intervention strategies is another category of multicultural counseling competencies. In this category, the competencies require a culturally skilled counselor to demonstrate his or her ability in three areas (awareness, knowledge, and skills) and 15 aspects (see AMCD MCC). As you see in AMCD MCC, some key elements of cultural competencies include the following:

1. Awareness of respecting client's beliefs and values, opening to indigenous helping, valuing bilingualism.
2. Knowledge about (a) limitation of traditional counseling; (b) bias in assessment and using procedures and interpreting findings with consideration of characteristics of minority clients; and (c) minority individuals' values, beliefs, family structures, and hierarchies.
3. Skills in communication style, institutional intervention, seeking consultation with healers or spiritual leaders, taking responsibility for interacting in language requested by clients, use of traditional assessment and testing instruments, and eliminating bias when conducting assessment and interpreting test results (Arredondo et al., 1996).

The following case illustration is about culturally skilled counselors' awareness in respecting clients' beliefs and values and knowledge of values and beliefs in developing culturally appropriate intervention strategies. We ask you to finish reading Case Illustration 7.5 first and then answer all the questions at the end of the case illustration before you continue reading.

CASE ILLUSTRATION 7.5

A Case of Child Abuse

Kelly graduated from a counseling program 5 years ago and was hired by a school on the East Coast as a school counselor. As a graduate, Kelly did very well in all her course work and completed her practicum and internship with all A's. As a certified school counselor, Kelly's expertise lies in the area of working with kids whose ages range from 6 to 12. As an employee, Kelly has been very conscientious and goes above and beyond. For this reason, she is liked by teachers and students alike. Because of her busy schedule and her kids and family, Kelly never has had time to attend workshops to advance her knowledge and skills.

One day, the English teacher, Mrs. Christopher, referred a student in her class named Robert, a 9-year-old boy, to Kelly, saying that Robert was struggling with his English homework and was not able to concentrate in the class. Robert was born in Vietnam. After his father died, his mother married a Chinese-Vietnamese American man and brought Robert to the United States at about the age of 5. Robert was always quiet and doing okay in all other classes but English.

When Robert was brought to Kelly's office, he showed some nervousness. As an experienced counselor, Kelly was confident she could place Robert in a chair and calm him down quickly. However, while Robert was walking toward the chair and scratching his back with his right hand over his left shoulder, Kelly noticed some bruises on the back of his neck. "What is that on your neck?" asked Kelly. Instead of responding verbally, Robert "asked" what by opening his eyes wider. "The bruises I see on the back of your neck? Can I take a look?" asked Kelly. Robert was a little bit reluctant but said "okay." Robert bent his neck while pulling his shirt down from the back, showing Kelly the back of his neck and some part of his back. Kelly saw some bruises on Robert's neck and on the part of his back that she could see. To see more, Kelly asked Robert to pull his shirt a little bit up and Robert did it. Kelly opened her eyes widely when she saw bruises all over Robert's back. "What happened, Robert? Who did it?" asked Kelly. "Hm . . . Mom," said Robert.

At this point, what action do you think Kelly should take? Why? What would you do if you were the school counselor? Why?

As you may have predicted, Kelly reported the case immediately to the law enforcement department and Robert was sent to a foster home and his parents were arrested. What had happened to Robert was that when he caught a cold his mother used *gua sha* in Chinese, or *cao gió* in Vietnamese, meaning "scraping *sha*-bruises" a traditional Chinese medical treatment in which the skin is scraped to produce light bruising. Those who use this method believe *gua sha* (Gua Sha, 2014) releases unhealthy elements from injured areas and stimulates blood flow and healing. When the treatment was brought to Vietnam and translated into Vietnamese, it roughly means "to scrape wind." In Vietnamese culture, "catching a cold" or having a fever is often referred to as *trúng gió*, "to catch wind." Unfortunately, Robert's parents did not speak fluent English and Robert was too young to understand what it meant to him and his parents when he showed his back to Kelly.

A few implications can be made from this case. First, counselors need to constantly advance their cultural knowledge and skills to meet the professional standards. Otherwise, they will do harm to their minority clients. As in Kelly's case, not reporting suspected child abuse is unethical or illegal, but doing harm to Robert's family is as unethical as not reporting it. Second, when having doubt in an area they are not familiar with, counselors need to consult peer professionals (e.g., school nurses or other counselors) specialized in that area. As a counselor-in-training, you always want to consult your site supervisor whenever you have uncertainty. Finally, institutions need to hold the counselors accountable by providing them opportunities for further training.

Cross-cultural differences have created challenges for counseling professionals in all areas of the service assessment, in particular since it "is a two-way street, influenced by client and therapist variables" (Sue & Sue, 2013, p. 346). For example, Eurocentric culture typically values the primacy of the task (e.g., completing the MMPI-A) whereas some minority cultures value the primacy of the relationship (e.g., African American culture, American Indian culture; Rosenberg, Almeida, & MacDonald, 2012). To have an accurate diagnosis, the counselor and the client must collaborate in the assessment process. This is a process in which the counselor demonstrates not only awareness of his or her stereotypes about minority clients and their cultures but also vigilance of common diagnostic errors such as confirmatory strategy, attribution errors, judgmental heuristics, and diagnostic overshadowing (Sue & Sue, 2013). Case Illustration 7.6 is the reflection of a counseling professional after she successfully completed the assessment with one of her clients.

CASE ILLUSTRATION 7.6

Cocreating Meaning

William knew the streets. He knew life in the African American community. He explained his life to me from those perspectives and pulled for a certain kind of attention during our work together. He demanded a relationship. Throughout the assessment, I struggled to balance the "objective" or "value-free" position of an assessor with the importance of developing a relationship with William that had a social and cultural context. I struggled between Eurocentric culture that typically values the primacy of the task (e.g., completing the MMPI–A) and African American culture that values the primacy of the relationship. In the final feedback session with William, we discussed ways for him to begin to build a positive identity in the midst of his personal and cultural trauma. We talked about power, empowerment, and writing rap songs with positive political messages. We talked about increasing his involvement in the men's group at school and vocational opportunities that would increase his self-esteem. We also discussed the need for William to have a full neurological exam by a medical doctor (given his previous neurological symptoms) as well as a psychiatric evaluation for possible medication. When I left his apartment for the last time, William stood by the old wooden gate and watched me walk to my car. Before I got in, he said, "Hey, I will miss seeing you." I replied, "I will miss seeing you, too."

> What I learned from my relationship with William is that we were able to cocreate and co-constitute meaning throughout the assessment process. As the focus alternated between task completion and our therapeutic alliance, a tension emerged that could not be ignored. It was in these moments where meaning making occurred, because I wanted to learn and communicate more than I wanted to be the person who had some "absolute" knowledge of another. In this way, a rich cultural tapestry became the matrix for understanding the actual test data. Or, to paraphrase Hook (2004), multicultural assessment postulates that subject and object, self and other, psyche and culture, person and context, figure and ground, practitioner and practice, live together, require each other, and dynamically, dialectically, and jointly make each other up. (Rosenberg et al., 2012, p. 230)

Source: Rosenberg, A., Almeida, A. & MacDonald, H. (2012). Crossing the cultural divide: Issues in translation, mistrust, and cocreation of meaning in cross-cultural therapeutic assessment.. *Journal of Personality Assessment, 94(3),* 223–231.

Multicultural Counseling Competence and Professional Identity

Your career path is one that is leading to your full engagement in the helping professions as a professional counselor. Our profession, counseling, not only recognizes the pluralistic nature of our society but has committed to advocacy for the rights of the socially disadvantaged groups. It is in this context that multiculturalism has become a significant component in counseling practice.

Upholding the dignity of all served by our profession and respecting the uniqueness of each individual and his or her worldview is the clarion call to all who become counselors. Your embracing of the value of multicultural competency reaches beyond your development as a student and touches the core values that will give shape to your identity as a professional.

Ours is a profession that manifests the best of our scientific knowledge as well as the core of our professional values. Ours is not a "recipe"-type practice where one approach fits all or one intervention applies equally well. Although empirically supported treatments have been identified for a significant number of mental disorders, these treatments have not been adequately validated for minority clients because clinical trials like these often miss culturally different individuals (Bernal & Sáez-Santiago, 2006). Given this fact, counselors will be called on to employ knowledge of diverse worldviews, the impact of developing racial and ethnic identities, and the lived experience of those with diverse backgrounds to adapt existing treatments when working with minority clients (Sue & Sue, 2013). Although there is clear evidence that counselors need to be culturally competent before they serve their socially disadvantaged clients, a point of special concern for you currently working with disadvantaged populations, the truth is cultural competency is counselor competency and increases the efficacy of all counselors.

Becoming a multiculturally competent counselor is a lifelong commitment. Along with your ongoing pursuit of knowledge of the emerging research and the issues confronting our profession, your developing multicultural competency gives form to your professional identity.

It is impossible to touch base with all aspects of multicultural competency development due to the limited length of one chapter. So, to conclude this chapter and help you make the adventure of developing your multicultural counseling competence more exciting, we will ask you to respond to our final exercise, Exercise 7.7. We hope your answers to these questions will be enlightening and go beyond what you have read to inspire you for further exploration on your journey to become a multicultural competent counselor.

EXERCISE 7.7

Moving Forward

Directions: One of the goals we have set for this chapter (as well as for the entire book) is to take that which may appear academic and make it more personal, more relevant, and more meaningful to your own professional development. As we end this chapter, we invite you to (a) reflect on each of the following and (b) identify the implications your responses have for your own continued development.

For Reflection and Direction

- How much am I aware of my biases, assumptions, stereotypes, and prejudice toward culturally different individuals?
- How much am I aware of my values, beliefs, worldview, and communication style?
- How much am I aware that my behaviors are mainly based on my values, beliefs, and worldview, which consequently make impact on others around me and my clients in particular?
- How much knowledge do I have about my clients' values, worldviews, and their experiences in being stereotyped and discriminated against, which continue to impact their current life and the issues they have at the present?
- How well do I understand the complexity of individual cultural identity in the process of counseling?
- What knowledge do I have to understand the impact of social inequality on individuals' psychological functioning and well-being?

- How well am I prepared to advocate on behalf of those who are directly and indirectly affected by social inequalities if I'm aware of my responsibility to do so?
- In what degree is my practice based on evidence?
- How prepared am I to conduct a successful cross-cultural collaborative assessment?
- To what extent are my interventions culturally appropriate?
- How prepared am I to operate as a professional counselor in an international context with the increasing influence of globalization?
- Am I culturally competent when serving all my current and future clients?
- What does multicultural counseling involvement in practice mean to me?

KEYSTONES

- Although multicultural issues in counseling have been addressed in literature for decades, integration of multiculturalism in counseling and counselor training remains controversial.
- Counselors' multicultural competence is the key to their multicultural counseling effectiveness.
- Counseling multicultural clients without multicultural awareness, knowledge, and skills can become ethically problematic for today's counselors.
- The counseling profession and its organizations and accreditation bodies have committed to the public to hold all their members ethically accountable for the service they provide.
- Multicultural counseling competence intertwines with and is one aspect of counseling competence.
- A scientific model guiding the development of multicultural competency is tripartite, which includes increasing awareness of the counselor's own cultural values and biases, increasing awareness and valuing of a client's culture and worldview, and increasing the counselor's knowledge of and skill with culturally relevant interventions.
- Developing multicultural competence is a lifelong commitment and a professional identity construction as well.

ADDITIONAL RESOURCES

Web Based

AMCD Multicultural Counseling Competencies: http://www.counseling.org/docs/competencies/multcultural_competencies.pdf

Audio-Visual Materials

Confronting Racial and Gender Difference: Three Approaches to Multicultural Counseling and Therapy: Available from Microtraining Associates, 80:43 mins

Multicultural Competence: Awareness, Knowledge & Skills: Available from Microtraining Associates, 2004, 38:49 mins

Multicultural Counseling: Intake and Follow Up: Available from Alexander Street Press, 2011, 72:08 mins

Multicultural Counseling/Therapy: Culturally Appropriate Intervention Strategies: Available from Microtraining Associates, 2003, 69:52 mins

Multicultural Supervision: Available from Microtraining Associates, 2010, 93:25 mins

White Privilege: Available from Alexander Street Press, 2011, 24:42 mins

Print Based

Arredondo, P. (1999). Multicultural counseling competencies as tools to address oppression and racism. *Journal of Counseling & Development, 77*(1), 102–108.

Arredondo, P., Toporek, R., Brown, S. P., Sanchez, J., Locke, D. C., Sanchez, J., & Stadler, H. (1996). Operationalization of the multicultural counseling competencies. *Journal of Multicultural Counseling & Development, 24*(1), 42–78.

Ortiz, S. O. (1999). You'd never know how racist I was, if you met me on the street. *Journal of Counseling & Development, 77*(1), 9–12.

Weeks, W. H., Petersen, P. B., & Brislin, R. W. (1998). *A manual of structured experiences for cross-cultural learning.* Yarmouth, ME: Intercultural Press.

REFERENCES

American Counseling Association. (2014). *Code of ethics and standards of practice.* Retrieved from http://www.counseling.org/Resources/aca-code-of-ethics.pdf

American Psychological Association. (2013). *Guidelines and principles for accreditation of programs in professional psychology.* Retrieved from http://www.apa.org/ed/accreditation/about/policies/guiding-principles.pdf

American School Counselor Association. (2010). ASCA school counselor competencies. Retrieved from http://www.schoolcounselor.org/asca/media/asca/home/SCCompetencies.pdf

Arredondo, P., Toporek, M. S., Brown, S., Jones, J., Locke, D. C., Sanchez, J. & Stadler, H. (1996). *Operationalization of the multicultural counseling competencies.* Alexandria, VA: AMCD.

Atkinson, D. R., & Thompson, C. E. (1992). Racial, ethnic, and cultural variables in counseling. In S. D. Brown & R. W. Lent (Eds.), *Handbook of counseling psychology* (2nd ed., pp. 349–382). New York, NY: John Wiley.

Baird, B. N. (2002). *The internship, practicum, and field placement handbook* (3rd ed.). Upper Saddle River, NJ: Prentice Hall.

Bernal, G., & Sáez-Santiago, E. (2006). Culturally centered psychosocial interventions. *Journal of Community Psychology, 34,* 121–132.

Bradley, C., & Fiorini, J. (1999). Evaluation of counseling practicum: National study of programs accredited by CACREP. *Counseling Education & Supervision, 39*(2), 110–119.

Chandras, K. V. (1997). Training multiculturally competent counselors to work with Asian Indian Americans. *Counselor Education & Supervision, 37*(1), 50–59.

Coleman, M. N. (2006). Critical incidents in multicultural training: An examination of student experiences. *Journal of Multicultural Counseling and Development, 34,* 168–182.

Constantine, M. G. (2002). Predictors of satisfaction with counseling: Racial and ethnic minority clients' attitudes toward counseling and ratings of their counselors' general and multicultural counseling competence. *Journal of Counseling Psychology, 49,* 255–263.

Corey, G. (2012). *Theory and practice of counseling and psychotherapy* (9th ed.). Belmont, CA: Brooks/Cole.

Council for Accreditation of Counseling and Related Educational Programs. (2014). *Draft #2 of the 2016 CACREP standards.* Retrieved from http://www.cacrep.org/wp-content/uploads/2012/07/2016-Standars-Draft-2.pdf

D'Andrea, M., Daniels, J., & Heck, R. (1991). Evaluating the impact of multicultural counseling training. *Journal of Counseling & Development, 70*(1), 143–150.

Draguns, J. G. (2008). Universal and cultural threads in counseling individuals. In P. B. Pedersen, J. G. Draguns, W. J. Lonner, & J. E. Trimble (Eds.), *Counseling across cultures* (6th ed., pp. 21–36). Thousand Oaks, CA: Sage.

Eriksen, K. P., & McAuliffe, G. J. (2003). The counseling skills scale: A measure of counselor competence. *Counselor Education and Supervision, 43,* 120–133.

Fukuyama, M. A. (1990). Taking a universal approach to multicultural counseling. *Counselor Education and Supervision, 30,* 6–17.

Gladding, S. T. (2001). *The counseling dictionary: Concise definitions of frequently used terms.* Upper Saddle River, NJ: Prentice Hall.

Hall, C. C. I. (1997). Cultural malpractice: The growing obsolescence of psychology with the changing U.S. population. *American Psychologist, 52,* 642–651.

Helms, J. E. (1995). An update of Helms's White and people of color racial identity models. In J. G. Ponterotto, J. M. Casas, J. A. Suzuki, & C. M. Alexander (Eds.), *Handbook of multicultural counseling* (pp. 181–198). Thousand Oaks, CA: Sage.

Holloway, E. L., & Roehlke, H. J. (1987). Internship: The applied training of a counseling psychologist. *The Counseling Psychologist, 15*(2), 205–260.

Kiselica, M. S. (1999). Confronting my own ethnocentrism and racism: A process of pain and growth. *Journal of Counseling and Development, 77*(1), 14–17.

Jackson, M. J. (1995). Multicultural counseling: Historical perspectives. In J. G. Ponterotto, J. M. Casas, L. A. Suzuki, & C. M. Alexander (Eds.), *Handbook of multicultural counseling* (pp. 3–16). Thousand Oaks, CA: Sage.

Malott, K. M. (2010). Multicutural counselor training in a single course: Review of research. *Journal of Multicultural Counseling and Development, 38,* 51–63.

Morales, E., & Norcross, J. C. (2010). Evidence-based practices with ethnic minorities: Strange bedfellows no more. *Journal of Clinical Psychology, 66*(8), 821–829.

Negi, N. J., Bender, K. A., Furman, R., Fowler, D. N., & Prickett, J. C. (2010). Enhancing self-awareness: A practical strategy to train culturally responsive social work students. *Advances in Social Work, 11*(2), 223–234.

Ponterotto, J. G. (2008). Theoretical and empirical advances in multicultural counseling and psychology. In S. D. Brown & R. W. Lent (Eds.), *Handbook of counseling psychology* (pp. 103–120). Hoboken, NJ: John Wiley.

Ponterotto, J. G., Casas, J. M., Suzuki, L. A., & Alexander, C. M. (Eds.). (2010). *Handbook of multicultural counseling* (3rd ed.). Thousand Oaks, CA: Sage.

Ponterotto, J. G., Fuertes, J. N., & Chen, E. C. (2000). Models of multicultural counseling. In S. Brown & R. Lent (Eds.), *Handbook of counseling psychology* (3rd ed., pp. 636–669). Hoboken, NJ: John Wiley.

Gua Sha. (n.d.). In *Wikipedia*. Retrieved October 14, 2014, from http://en.wikipedia.org/wiki/Gua_Sha

Ridley, C. R., Mollen, D., & Kelly, S. M. (2011). Beyond microskills: Toward a model of counseling competence. *The Counseling Psychologist, 40*(3), 1070–1077.

Rosenberg, A., Almeida, A., & MacDonald, H. (2012). Crossing the cultural divide: Issues in translation, mistrust, and cocreation of meaning in cross-cultural therapeutic assessment. *Journal of Personality Assessment, 94*(3), 223–231.

Sevig, T., & Etzkorn, J. (2001). Transformative training: A year-long multicultural counseling seminar for graduate students. *Counseling and Development, 29*(1), 57–72.

Sue, D. W., Bernier, J. E., Durran, A., Feinberg, L., Pedersen, P., Smith, E. J., & Vasquez-Nuttall, E. (1982). Position paper: Cross-cultural counseling competencies. *The Counseling Psychologist, 10,* 45–52.

Sue, D. W., Bucceri, J., Lin, A. I., Nadal, K. L., & Torino, G.C. (2007). Racial microagressions and the Asian American experience. *Cultural Diversity and Ethnic Minority Psychology, 13,* 72–81.

Sue, D. W., & Sue, D. (1990). *Counseling the culturally diverse: Theory and practice* (2nd ed.). Oxford, England: John Wiley.

Sue, D. W., & Sue, D. (2013). *Counseling the culturally diverse: Theory and practice* (6th ed.). Hoboken, NJ: John Wiley.

Wintrob, R. M., & Harvey, Y. K. (1981). The self-awareness factor in intercultural psychotherapy: Some personal reflections. In P. P. Pealersen, J. G. Draguns, W. J. Lonner, & J. E. Trimble (Eds.), *Counseling across cultures* (rev. ed., pp. 79–87) Honolulu: University Press of Hawaii.

Xie, D. (2015). Multicultural considerations: Within and beyond traditional counseling theories. In R. D. Parsons & N. Zhang (Eds.), *Counseling theory: Guiding reflective practice* (pp. 27–54). Thousand Oaks, CA: Sage.

8

Crisis Prevention and Intervention: Suicide and Homicide

Every problem has two handles. You can grab it by the handle of fear or the handle of hope.

Margaret Mitchell

Crisis such as suicide or homicide is often a problem for not only those who are in it but also those who try to intervene with it. Sadly, the experience of having a client "in crisis" is not uncommon, and in fact, for some counselors, it has become a routine within their professional daily life. Although it is our hope that this has not been your experience as a student in the field, neither those in field placement nor those newly entering the profession are immune to these experiences, and thus it is essential to learn how to recognize and then manage a client in crisis.

Although encountering a crisis situation and dealing with such crisis is not something pleasant or joyful, as an intern, learning how to manage crisis with your site supervisor's support may give you, the future counselor, a sense of personal satisfaction and build your confidence and professional competence. In addition, although crisis is clearly a challenge to both the client and the counselor, crisis also can provide opportunity for growth.

The current chapter will cover crisis such as dealing with suicide and homicide. Specifically, after completing this chapter, readers will be able to

- understand what crisis means and describe a client's suicide or homicide situation,
- know all the major warning signs and risk factors of suicide and homicide,
- know which population is at risk for suicide,
- describe the steps and procedures they need to take in a suicide or homicide crisis situation,
- know how to assess a client's suicide or homicide situation,
- describe the ethical and legal ramifications concerning clients with intention to harm self and others, and
- know what action to take during a crisis.

The Nature of Crisis and Crisis Intervention

From a psychological perspective, the definition of crisis is truly in the eye of the individual in crisis. It is not always directly accounted for by the events or the conditions being presented but rather by the client's experience of being overwhelmed by these conditions. James and Gilliland (2001) have described crisis as a perception or experience of an event or situation as an intolerable difficulty that exceeds the person's current resources and coping mechanisms. One of the pioneers in community counseling, Gerald Caplan (1961), described a crisis as a short period of psychological disequilibrium in a person who is confronted by an important problem that he or she can neither escape nor solve with his or her customary problem-solving resources. The elements of importance presented in both these depictions of crisis are that, regardless of the surrounding events, the client experiences a disequilibrium and the inability to cope.

For those in crisis, the need is for a quick resolution. They seek actions that will restore them to their pre-crisis levels of functioning. Individuals in crisis do not have the luxury of engaging in extended in-depth therapy or counseling but rather seek immediate relief. Thus, counselors engaging with those in crisis will employ strategies and techniques that serve as emotional first aid, reducing the immediate pain, engaging client strengths, and later targeting strategies of prevention.

This approach is somewhat unique to that in which you may have been trained. Although still requiring the counselor to engage his or her skills of attending and observation, as well as responding with empathy, genuineness, respect, and nonjudgmental caring (James & Gilliland, 2001), crisis intervention places the counselor in a more action-oriented and problem-solving role. Less focus is placed on the process and questions that are exploratory. There is less emphasis and need for seeking answers to questions of history, development, and causation. Rather, the focus is on the present and the "here and now," with the goal being to provide clients with the immediate support necessary to survive the moment and regain awareness of their resources that will carry them out of the moment.

Because the experience of crisis is one of loss of control, it is essential for counselors to help clients reengage their power and control. This typically takes the form of assisting clients to establish short-term, concrete goals regarding specific behaviors that can be achieved within a short time frame. The overarching nature of these goals is to reduce the immediate pain and instill a sense of safety, control, and hope.

Phases of Crisis and Counselor Response

Research (e.g., Yassen & Harvey, 1998) suggests that there is a cyclical progression through a series of phases of a crisis reaction. Although noted as phases, it is important to realize that any one client, in any one unique experience, may cycle back through phases in his or her progression out of crisis. The value of this schema is that it helps counselors to recognize what is happening and, at the same time, understand how best to respond. These phases have been identified as *acute, outward adjustment,* and *integration.*

Acute Phase

The acute phase marks the client's initial response to the experience of crisis. Most often clients will feel overwhelmed, with intense anxiety, a sense of disorientation, and loss of control. The client may respond to this initial phase of intensity by becoming volatile or agitated or, conversely, may present as if all systems have shut down by becoming subdued—eerily calm.

Counselors intervening at this point of the crisis will want to help the client

- talk about his or her difficult emotions like guilt feelings and fears;
- feel heard, cared for;
- begin to understand the facts of what is as distinct from his or her belief or perceptions of what is;
- consider an alternative, more objective view of the crisis as presented by the counselor;
- have the time and supportive space to think about what has occurred and bring order to his or her thoughts and feelings;
- believe that he or she will be supported, even coached, through the next steps of resolution;
- begin to identify the resources available for resolution; and
- set small, achievable goals to move out of the crisis.

It is important for the counselor to be not only present, interested, and attentive but also a resource for identifying and connecting the client to real, even if short-term, relief. It is also essential that the counselor accurately assesses the potential of the client to respond to the crisis with violence toward self (i.e., suicide) or others (i.e., homicide) and of course take those steps necessary to protect all involved.

Outward Adjustment Phase

Clients, in their own attempt to reestablish normalcy and stability, may begin to act as if things are back to routine. It is not unusual for the client to not want to talk about the crisis event and consequently not be open to counseling.

As counselors assist clients through the acute phase and some sense of calm returns, it is important to engage in psychoeducation to help the client begin to understand the impact of crisis and the fact that often denial or dismissal occurs. It is important for a client to understand that while reengaging in his or her daily life, it is possible that these behaviors belie an underlying stress and tension that reflects the psychological crisis that is continuing.

Counselors can be of assistance by following up with a client after the initial intervention in order to (a) assess that the crisis has been resolved and the client has actually returned to pre-crisis functioning and (b) serve as a resource should the client be "stuck" in this phase of responding. Counselors may be able to help the client embrace the reality that for some who have experienced a major crisis, this initial period of calm and apparent normalcy gives way to feelings of anxiety, depression, and anger. Further, it is important for a counselor to assist the client in knowing that should there be a reappearance of these feelings and concerns, the counselor or other resources are available to assist him or her through the experience. It is useful to provide the client with contact information for these support services.

Integration Phase

The final phase in one's progression from crisis is not only to make sense out of what just happened but to begin to implement those changes in self or situation that will increase the possibility of preventing reoccurrence. Clearly, engaging in a longer term counseling relationship would position the client to understand what occurred and to take steps to engage those resources and changes necessary to both reduce the possibility of a reoccurrence and promote the personal resources that will help the client navigate through life's many challenges.

Before discussing particularly concerning forms of crises, those in which harm to self and/or others takes center stage, we invite you to engage in Exercise 8.1, which will help you understand the possibility of crisis among that population served at your field setting as well as the protocol followed by the counselors at your setting.

EXERCISE 8.1

A Snapshot of Crisis Intervention

Directions: You are asked to interview the counselors working at your field setting to gather answers to the following questions. It may prove helpful to share your findings with your colleagues/classmates to note differences in experience and procedures followed.

1. Have you worked with a client "in crisis"? If so, what was the nature of the crisis and how was the client presenting?

2. What steps did you take in working with this client (these clients)?
3. Is there a formal protocol that counselors working at this setting are supposed to follow? If so, what is it?
4. What would your advice be to a new counselor in regards to crisis and crisis intervention?

SUICIDE

As noted while describing the nature of crisis, the experience is one in which the client feels that all of his or her copings have failed. As such, clients in the state of crisis may turn to extreme and sadly devastating actions as problem-solving strategies. One such action is suicide.

Given the statistics, the realities of suicide may be something with which you are all too familiar. It is estimated that almost 1 of every 60 Americans has experienced the loss of a loved one who has committed suicide (Westefeld et al., 2000). It is one of the leading causes of deaths in the United States. There were 38,364 suicides in the U.S. in 2010 (105.1 suicides per day, or 1 suicide every 13.7 minutes; American Association of Suicidology, 2014).

Myths About Suicide

Perhaps the first step that needs to be taken in responding at this time of crisis is for you as a counselor-in-training to embrace the reality of suicide and reject the myths often surrounding the issue of suicide. These myths can be misleading and even detrimental to your client's wellness if they are not being acknowledged. There are many such myths, but the most often repeated are

- discussing suicide will cause the client to do it;
- suicide peaks in winter holidays (whereas the numbers suggest it is spring);
- teenagers are at greatest risk (whereas research suggest it is older people);
- depression is always the cause of suicide;
- poor people have higher rates of suicide;
- there are more suicides now than years ago;
- people who attempt suicide do not reach out for help;
- most suicides occur on weekends;
- if people really want to die, you can't do anything about it;
- those who talk about suicide don't mean it but rather are trying to get attention;
- people who survived a suicide attempt won't try suicide again;
- discussing with suicidal clients about methods of suicide would give them ideas for suicide;
- suicidal clients won't kill themselves when they feel better;
- there is not much correlation between alcoholism and drug abuse and suicide; and
- clients who threaten suicide don't do it.

Once the myths have been debunked, it is important to become knowledgeable and skilled at identifying clients who are at risk and engage in those steps to intervene at times of crisis.

Identifying Risk: Common Characteristics of Suicide

Although many people are at risk of suicide and there are some common characteristics shared among individuals who make suicide attempts or commit suicide, there are no existing testable theories that can be used to differentiate between those who make suicidal attempts and those who commit suicide. At best, counselors need to be knowledgeable on the issues of risk identification, suicide assessment, intervention, and prevention.

To be an effective counselor in the area of suicide intervention and prevention, you want to possess all necessary knowledge about suicide. Here we present some common characteristics of suicide: (a) people aged 45–54 have the highest suicide rates; (b) people aged 85 or above have higher suicide rates than all those younger than 85; (c) Caucasians have higher rates (14.13 per 100,000) of suicide completion than African Americans (5.1 per 100,000); (d) suicide is the third-leading cause of deaths among young Americans aged 15–24; (e) suicide rates are the highest among the divorced, separated, and windowed and lowest among the married; (f) firearms are the most commonly used method of completing suicide; and (g) males have 3.7 times higher rates suicide completion than females but females make more suicide attempts than males (American Association of Suicidology, 2014). In addition, research (e.g., Westefeld et al., 2000) has noted cultural factors involved in suicide behavior. These authors point out that people in cultures that value competitiveness and goal directedness have higher suicide rates; American Indians have the highest suicide rates followed by European Americans, Asian Americans, and Latino Americans. Black or African Americans have the lowest suicide rates. Gay and lesbian people have higher suicide rates than heterosexual individuals, and the stress of coming out appears to be the better predictor of suicide than sexual orientation.

Additional factors have been identified as characterizing increased risk of suicide, including such things as having mental disorders, especially depression; having drug and alcohol dependency; and being socially isolated or disconnected. The Association of American Suicidology (2014) has compiled an extensive list of *The Risk Factors for Suicide,* which we have adapted and included in Table 8.1. It is clear that counselors-in-training and in the field, as well as those practicing, need to be knowledgeable of these factors and be alert to their presentation by their clients.

Exercise 8.2 invites you to use the listing of common risk factors for suicide and suicide behaviors as a template to view the characteristics, and thus risk, of clients at your field placement site.

Table 8.1 Risk Factors for Suicide and Suicidal Behaviors

Contributory Risk Factors

- Firearm ownership or easy accessibility
- Acute or enduring unemployment
- Stress (job, marriage, school, relationship, etc.)

Predisposing Conditions

- Demographics: White, American Indian, male, older age, separation or divorce, early widowhood
- Presentation of psychiatric disorder
- History of suicide attempts, especially if repeated
- Prior suicide ideation
- History of self-harm behavior
- History of suicide or suicidal behavior in family
- Parental history of
    - Violence
    - Substance abuse (drugs or alcohol)
    - Hospitalization for major psychiatric disorder
    - Divorce
- History of trauma or abuse (physical or sexual)
- History of psychiatric hospitalization
- History of frequent mobility
- History of violent behaviors
- History of impulsive/reckless behaviors
- Low self-esteem/high self-hate
- Tolerant/accepting attitude toward suicide
- Exposure to another's death by suicide
- Lack of self or familial acceptance of sexual orientation
- Perfectionism (especially in context of depression)

Acute Risk Factors (If present, these increase risk in the near term)

- Demographics: Recently divorced or separated with feelings of victimization or rage
- Suicide ideation (threatened, communicated, planned, or prepared for)
- Current self-harm behavior
- Recent suicide attempt
- Excessive or increased use of substances (alcohol or drugs)
- Psychological pain (acute distress in response to loss, defeat, rejection, etc.)
- Recent discharge from psychiatric hospitalization
- Anger, rage, revenge-seeking behavior

(Continued)

Table 8.1 (Continued)

- Aggressive behavior
- Withdrawal from usual activities, supports, interests, school, or work; isolation (e.g., lives alone)
- Anhedonia
- Anxiety, panic
- Agitation
- Insomnia
- Persistent nightmares
- Suspiciousness, paranoia (ideas of persecution or reference)
- Severe feelings of confusion or disorganization
- Command hallucinations urging suicide
- Intense affect states (e.g., desperation, intolerable aloneness, self-hate)
- Dramatic mood changes
- Hopelessness, poor problem solving, cognitive constriction (e.g., thinking in black-and-white terms, not able to see gray areas or alternatives), rumination, few reasons for living, inability to imagine possibly positive future events
- Perceived burdensomeness
- Recent diagnosis of terminal condition
- Feeling trapped, as though there is no way out (other than death); poor problem solving
- Sense of purposelessness or loss of meaning; no reasons for living
- Negative or mixed attitude toward receiving help
- Negative or mixed attitude by potential caregiver to individual
- Recklessness or excessive risk-taking behavior, especially if out of character or seemingly without thinking of consequences; tendency toward impulsivity

Precipitating or Triggering Stimuli (Heighten Period of Risk if Vulnerable to Suicide)

- Any real or anticipated event causing or threatening
    - Shame, guilt, despair, humiliation, unacceptable loss of face or status
    - Legal problems (loss of freedom), financial problems, feelings of rejection/abandonment
- Recent exposure to another's suicide (e.g., friend or acquaintance, celebrity through media)

Source: Adapted from "Facts and Statistics" by the American Association of Suicidology, 2014. Retrieved from http://www.suicidology.org/resources/facts-statistics. Copyright 2014 by American Association of Suicidology. Adapted with permission.

EXERCISE 8.2

Interviews

After reviewing all the risk factors for suicide and suicide behaviors, you are asked to interview your supervisor and two other senior counseling professionals about their experiences with suicide intervention and prevention in their professional lives. Your task through the interviews is (a) to see if there is a theme in these three professionals' experiences on suicide intervention and prevention, (b) to identify if there are any risk factors for suicide and suicide behaviors described above represented by the clients of these three counseling professionals, (c) to see what lessons they have learned and what experiences they have gained through their crisis intervention and prevention experiences, and (d) to see what suggestions they can give you.

Assessment: The First Step in Intervention

Knowing the signs associated with increased risk of suicide will alert you of the potential danger confronting your client and engage you in what could be seen as the first step of intervention—assessment. One model by Juhnke (1994) for assessment, in our opinion, is quite useful and involves three levels of data collection: face-to-face interview, empirical evaluation, and consultation.

Face-to-face interview. The focus for the counselor's interview is to assess the client's cognitive, emotional, and psychosocial status. The cognition or mental state refers to the client's thinking about suicide, for example, whether the client plans to end his or her life. Furthermore, the client's thought of suicide can be brief, fleeting, intense, or pervasive, and making a determination on his or her thought of suicide is important. The emotional component identifies the client's feeling, or mood, which can alter the client's suicidal behavior, whereas the psychosocial context refers to the client's relationships with others and the environment.

As you continue in your field work, it is important to begin to practice with each of the above components of assessment. Therefore, it would be helpful for you not only to review the previously presented risk factors (see Table 8.2), but to employ the acronym SAD PERSONS to guide your interviews with clients. The acronym reflects 10 research-based suicide risk factors: Sex, Age, Depression, Previous attempt, Ethanol abuse, Rational thinking loss, Social supports lacking, Organized suicidal plan, No spouse, and Sickness. You may also use the SAD PERSONS Scale (SPS) as an empirical evaluation component tool as well as a means to organize a case summary with proposed clinical disposition for consultation purposes (see the form in Table 8.2).

Beyond looking for these indicators of increased risk, it is important not only to attend to the client's responses but also to be cognizant of the behaviors the client presents while disclosing. Attending to not only the words, but also the tones and manner in which the client engages may alert you to the potential of suicide. Table 8.3 provides another mnemonic for remembering the warning signs of suicide. This mnemonic, IS PATH WARM, reflects a listing of warning signs generated by internationally renowned clinical researchers coordinated by AAS (2003).

Empirical evaluation. The second element of this model of assessment is to gather empirical data by the use of suicide prediction scales, suicide checklists, and psychological instruments to determine immediate suicide risk. Counselors-in-training may also use other established personality instruments such as the Minnesota Multiphasic Personality Inventory-2 (MMPI-2), the Beck Hopelessness Scale (BHS), the Beck

Table 8.2 SAD PERSONS Scale

S—Sex: 1 if male; 0 if female (more females attempt, more males succeed)
A—Age: 1 if < 20 or > 44
D—Depression: 1 if depression is present
P—Previous attempt: 1 if present
E—Ethanol abuse: 1 if present
R—Rational thinking loss: 1 if present
S—Social supports lacking: 1 if present
O—Organized plan: 1 if plan is made and lethal
N—No spouse: 1 if divorced, widowed, separated, or single
S—Sickness: 1 if chronic, debilitating, and severe

Guidelines for action with the SAD PERSONS scale	
Total points	Proposed clinical action
0 to 2	Send home with follow-up
3 to 4	Closely follow up; consider hospitalization
5 to 6	Strongly consider hospitalization, depending on confidence in the follow-up arrangement
7 to 10	Hospitalize or commit

Source: This article was published in *Psychosomatics 24(4),* Patterson, W. M., Dohn, H. H, Patterson, J, Patterson, G. A. Evaluation of suicidal patients: The SAD PERSONS scale. 343–345, 348–349, Copyright Elsevier (1983).

Depression Inventory (BDI), and Reynold's Adolescent Depression Scale (RADS). These scales are not specifically designed to address suicide, but they provide information about suicide potential (Westefeld et al., 2000). For example, the Beck Hopelessness Scale (BHS) is a good predictor of suicide.

Specific suicide questionnaires include the Scale for Suicide Ideation (SSI; Beck, Kovacs, & Weissman, 1979), the Modified Scale for Suicide Ideation (SSI-M; Miller, Norman, Bishop, & Dow, 1986), the Self-Rated Scale for Suicide Ideation (SSI-SR; Beck, Steer, & Ranieri, 1988), the Suicidal Ideation Scale (SIS; Rudd, 1989), the Suicide Behaviors Questionnaire (SBQ; Cole, 1988; Linehan, 1981), the Suicide Ideation Questionnaire (SIQ; Reynolds, 1987), the Brief Reasons for Living Inventory (RFL-B; Ivanoff, Jang, Smyth, & Linehan, 1994), the College Student Reasons for Living Inventory (CSRLI; Westefeld, Cardin, & Deaton, 1992), the Suicide Status Form (SSF; Jobes, Jacoby, Cimbolic, & Hustead, 1997), Fairy Tales Test (FT; Orbach, Feshbach, Carlson, Glaubman, & Gross, 1983), the Multiattitude Suicide Tendency Scale (MAST; Orbach et al., 1991), and the Suicide Probability Scale (SPS; Cull & Gill, 1982). These specific suicide questionnaires can provide you with precise information that might be

Table 8.3 IS PATH WARM

I—Ideation: Expressed or communicated ideation

- Threatening to hurt or kill him/herself, or talking of wanting to hurt or kill him/herself; and/or
- Looking for ways to kill him/herself by seeking access to firearms, available pills, or other means; and/or
- Talking or writing about death, dying or suicide, when these actions are out of the ordinary

S—Substance Abuse: Increased substance (alcohol or drug) use

P—Purposelessness: No reason for living; no sense of purpose in life

A—Anxiety: Anxiety, agitation, unable to sleep or sleeping all the time

T—Trapped: Feeling trapped (like there's no way out)

H—Hopelessness: Hopelessness

W—Withdrawal: Withdrawal from friends, family and society

A—Anger: Rage, uncontrolled anger, seeking revenge

R—Recklessness: Acting reckless or engaging in risk activities, seemingly without thinking

M—Mood Change: Dramatic mood changes

Source: Adapted from "Know the Warning Signs of Suicide" by the American Association of Suicidology, 2003. Retrieved from http://www.suicidology.org/resources/warning-signs. Copyright 2003 by American Association of Suicidology. Adapted with permission.

useful in your comprehensive assessment of client suicide in the counseling process (Westefeld et al., 2000).

These empirical evaluation instruments can help all counselors, but particularly those new to the field or those still in training and who are less confident in this area of assessment. Although the listing is impressive, it is only as good as it is useful. Exercise 8.3 invites you to become more familiar with some of these personality instruments and specific suicide questionnaires.

EXERCISE 8.3

Which Questionnaire Should I Use?

Your task is to identify two to three suicide assessment questionnaires and thoroughly examine their clinical applicability. Then you may ask your supervisor or the person who is in charge of assessment at your internship site about what specific suicide questionnaires are used by the site staff. If other than the ones you have identified are used, you may ask why those suicide questionnaires are used, and not others.

Consultation

If, while working with a client, you notice any of the signs included under the rubric IS PATH WARM, consultation with your site supervisor would be an important next step. It is important to discuss that client with your supervisor and engage in a more formal risk assessment. This consultation is the final part of this three-step model of assessment, and serves multiple purposes, including (a) promoting a multi-faceted approach and decreasing "the probability of suicide from a flawed treatment intervention," because the etiology of suicide is often a complex process; and (b) helping in insulating "counselors from certain liability issues that may result from either a misguided intervention plan or a faulty perception of client risk" (Juhnke, 1994, p. 53).

Although you have been ingrained with the understanding of the importance of confidentiality in the counseling relationship and thus might be concerned about the violation of this confidentiality and whether you should choose to consult, it is important to note that disclosure under these conditions is allowed and even may be mandated. Both the American Counseling Association (ACA) and the American School Counseling Association (ASCA) direct counselors to breach confidentiality when clients present danger to themselves and others. The general requirement that counselors keep information confidential does not apply when disclosure is required to protect clients or identified others from serious and foreseeable harm or when legal requirements demand that confidential information must be revealed. Such disclosure is permitted under our codes of ethics, but different organizations have policies that govern the "when," the "what" and the "to whom" of such disclosures and therefore you want to check with your field placement supervisor to understand your site's policies governing such disclosures. Also, when questioning the validity of an exception, counselors should always consult with their supervisor, other counselors, or even their state organizations for guidance.

Although the focus of the previous discussion is on assessing signs of risk, it is also important to assess the presence of factors that have been found to be associated with lower risk. Factors such as the following have been found to serve as potential protective factors, buffering or reducing the risk of suicide:

- positive relationships with family members, friends, or co-workers;
- marriage;
- sense of responsibilities for family members or others;
- religious beliefs;
- social support; and
- resilience during past personal crisis.

Timing of Assessment

The question of who is at risk of suicide is often difficult to answer. So, the question of the appropriate time to approach clients concerning risky behavior on suicide and suicide assessment becomes critical because clients do not always present suicidal signs or directly tell you they are suicidal in counseling. It is our practical experience that at the beginning of each counseling session or intake, in addition to discussing confidentiality issues, the counselor needs to ask his or her clients the procedural questions regarding their dangerous behaviors. For example, the counselor could say, "Just now we discussed the confidentiality in counseling. I also ask all my clients a couple of procedural questions. Do you have any thought of harming or killing yourself? Do you have any thought of harming others?" When the client's answer presents no crisis, the counselor may proceed in assisting the client to address his or her major concerns for seeking help; when a crisis presents after these procedural questions, the counselor must conduct a thorough assessment of the crisis. Needless to say, suicide assessment is not restricted to the initial intake. Counselors must be attentive to the appearance of any of the at-risk signs at any point in their work with a client. Case Illustration 8.1 presents one scenario of how the counselor approached the client on suicide assessment.

CASE ILLUSTRATION 8.1

It's Difficult for Me to Go On

(This conversation occurs after 10 minutes of the first therapy session between a counselor-in-training and a client. The client is a 57-year-old Asian American male, who is divorced with two kids and is a senior director in a pharmaceutical company)

Ken: My life's terrible.

Counselor: What do you mean?

Ken: I don't think I can go on anymore.

Counselor: I'm still not clear. Can you elaborate a little bit more?

Ken: One of my supervisees quit early this week. He did not talk to me about it before he quit but to my boss. I got to know he left the company from my boss. There's no respect for me. Now I have to do my job and his job before I can hire another person. Evidently they are doing something behind my back. I know my boss doesn't like me. He wrote a nasty e-mail message not long ago. You know, he even didn't say "Happy New Year" to me when he saw me the first time in the new year. I said "Happy New Year" to him and he responded without looking at me much. I can tell he has attitude toward me. I feel he wants to get rid of me. I'm 57 years old. Who wants me if this company fires me?! I have worked for this company for most of my life and reached this point in my life, and it appears this guy is going to ruin it. I'm terrified to see the sad ending. I have had depression for almost 8 years and doubt I can recover from it. I'm not sure what the point of living is . . .

(Continued)

(Continued)

Counselor:	I appreciate how difficult this situation must be for you at this time of your life. A client of mine who had similar problems expressed to me his thought about ending his life. I wonder if you have similar thought about harming or killing yourself?
Ken:	(Pause) Yes.
Counselor:	When did you begin to have suicidal thoughts?
Ken:	Three years ago, after I divorced.
Counselor:	When was the last time you had such thoughts?
Ken:	I began to think about it a few weeks ago and my thoughts became intense.
Counselor:	Do you have a plan to end your life?
Ken:	I'm thinking about either hanging or taking some sleeping pills.
Counselor:	Do you have sleeping pills?
Ken:	I have been depressed for years and have never seen a therapist until this point. Each time when I felt worse, I asked my family doctor to give me some sleeping pills. Actually I did not take much of them.
Counselor:	Do you mean you have sleeping pills that accumulated from the past?
Ken:	Yep.
Counselor:	How many?
Ken:	Quite a bit.
Counselor:	Ken, I wonder if you would be willing to sign a contract for safety with me?
Ken:	What is that?
Counselor:	It is a simple documentation in which you agree that you will not harm yourself during a certain period of time. You sign it and I sign it as well.
Ken:	I'm not sure what that can do for my situation. (It seems client shows no interest in signing a contract at this point.)
Counselor:	Ken, I appreciate your sharing. As I told you at the beginning of the session about confidentiality as well as my function as a counselor-in-training, for the sake of your wellness I have to ask my supervisor to step in to help you at this point. I hope you don't mind.

Suicide assessment is a crucial step in prevention of suicide and client treatment. In order to become a competent counselor, you need to master the basic suicide assessment skills. The following exercise (8.4) will provide you an opportunity to practice suicide assessment interview skills.

EXERCISE 8.4

Role-Play

In this exercise, we ask you to do a role-play of a suicide assessment interview. Form a group of three and conduct a 10-minute suicide assessment interview. One person plays the counselor role and one plays the client. The third person will observe the interview and provide feedback after the interview is over. Rotate the role of counselor and client and observer until everyone has an opportunity to play the role of the counselor. The person who plays the counselor needs to conduct a thorough suicide assessment, asking as many suicide assessment questions as possible. If time permits, you may try the three different scenarios.

Document

Document, document, and document: This is what you, as an intern or professional counselor, must do. When you encounter suicidal clients, you should document everything you do with your clients. Document as clearly as possible the data you have collected that support your concern, along with the steps you have taken, including discussion with supervisors or colleagues and the clear rationale for your approach. Simply, it is essential to explain why you chose what you chose to do and why you did not choose other alternatives. This documentation must be written with concise language.

When Harm Is Other Directed

As noted at the beginning of the chapter, crisis is by definition experienced as a time when the normal coping mechanisms are failing and consequently the client may turn to radical and dangerous solutions. One "solution" is to escape the crisis by way of suicide. Another "solution" is to lash out at the perceived source of the pain being experienced. Under these conditions, the client may contemplate harming another.

It is important for counselors to be able to identify those at risk of violence and doing harm to others and to understand counselors' ethical and legal responsibilities.

Prevalence and Potential for Violence

Violence at schools, colleges, and communities is not a new phenomenon. According to the national violent death report of 16 states (Parks, Johnson, McDaniel, & Gladden, 2010), the homicide rate for males is four times more than for females; the highest rate of homicide was among those aged 20–24, followed by those aged 25–29; the lowest homicide rate was among those aged 5–14 and 65–74; the highest homicide-caused deaths by women (4.3 deaths per 100,000 population) were among infants aged younger than 1 year old. A study of 20,507 students at 39 colleges and universities in the United States showed that 31% of students were physically or sexually assaulted within the previous 12 months (Haines et al., 2007). And additionally, Hayes, Crane, and Locke (2010) found that 7% of clients from 66 university counseling centers expressed strong fear of acting violently (Hayes et al., 2010). And within just 14 months, from December 15, 2012, to February 10, 2014, 44 school shootings occurred in 24 states across the United States (Mayors Against Illegal Guns, 2014).

With all these hard facts as the background, it becomes clear that counseling interns and all helping professionals need to take this matter seriously and make assessing clients with potential threat to others an important procedural component in their helping process.

Predictors of Violent Behavior

Similar to predictors of suicide, one of the most salient predictors of violent behavior is the occurrence of violence in the past. In addition to evidence of previous violent behavior, other predictors include experience of abuse in childhood, victimization, and parental history of criminal behavior and substance abuse (Elbogen & Johnson, 2009). Expanding on this list is the inclusion of factors that predict fear of acting violently, including irritable feelings, having harmed another in the past, experiencing nightmares or flashbacks, and engaging in frequent arguments (Hayes et al., 2010).

Assessment: The First Step

When meeting a client in the first session, you may tell the client that you have procedural questions that you ask every client, and one of them is if the client has any thought of harming others. Or, when any of the predictors of violent behavior presents, you may want to ask the client if he or she has the thought of harming others. If the answer is positive, you will need to violate confidentiality and take the steps necessary to protect the third party. It is important to check if the client has a specific plan and access to weapons to implement his or her plan. It is also important to obtain identifying information about the possible victim, including name(s) and location(s) of the third party, time, and date to implement the plan.

After the first session, it is impossible for you to ask the client this type of question each time you meet. What you can do instead is to pay attention to the predictors of violent behavior and the predictors of fears of acting violently listed above and to use their appearance as an invitation to engage in direct questioning regarding intent to harm.

Step Two: Intervention

Intervention begins when the client indicates dangerous thoughts of harming others. First, be honest and frank with your client, telling him or her that you may have to disclose the information to the authority. Second, encourage the client to disclose the information to the third party. Third, immediately contact your supervisor or the authority identified in your site crisis management policy procedures if and when the client refuses to inform the thirty party of his or her intention.

If the client has access to weapons and is willing to give information about his or her intention to the third party, confirm with the client about when and how he or she is to inform the third party. Meanwhile, you need to make an arrangement for the following: (a) to take away the weapons from the client; (b) to schedule a psychiatric evaluation for the client; (c) to screen the client for medication or drugs if necessary; (d) to ask the client to sign a contract to not execute his or her violent behavior; (e) to write down the names, time, date, locations, and all other specific information of the threatened party or parties; (f) to document everything you have done with the client during the session; and (g) to consult with your site supervisor or the crisis intervention team (if there is any). When the client indicates that he or she has no access to weapons (e.g., guns or knives), you may continue counseling but be cautious about his or her near-future thoughts and behaviors.

Of special concern are the conditions under which you may need to violate confidentiality and warn the identified victim. The precedent for such violation of confidentiality was established in a now-famous case of Tarsasoff. The case involved Prosenjit Poddar, an international graduate student from India studying at the University of California, Berkeley, who started to date another student named Tatiana Tarasoff. In the fall of 1968, Poddar met Tatiana and they saw each other throughout the fall. Poddar perceived that they had an intimate relationship. However, when Tatiana learned of his feelings toward her, she told him that she was dating other men and not interested in getting into a serious relationship with him. This rejection caused him to become emotionally depressed.

Because of his depression, Poddar sought help from Dr. Lawrance Moore, a psychologist at the university's hospital in 1969. During his visit with Dr. Moore, Poddar confided his intention to kill Tatiana Tarasoff. Dr. Moore wrote to the campus police, indicating that Poddar had a severe mental disorder and requesting that Poddar be put into a psychiatric hospital. The campus police interviewed Mr. Poddar but released him shortly after because they saw Poddar as rational. In addition, Poddar promised them that he would stay away from Tatiana Tarasoff. Later, Dr. Moore's supervisor, Dr. Harvey Powelson, ordered that the letter to the police be destroyed and Poddar not be subject to further detention.

During the summer of 1969, Tatiana visited her aunt in Brazil. After she returned, Poddar stalked her and killed her. Tatiana's parents sued the regents of the University of California for failing to warn them that their daughter was in danger. However, the trial court did not support the plaintiff because at that time, health providers did not have responsibility for a third party. In 1974, Tatiana's parents appealed to the California Supreme Court, and the Court reversed the previous decision. This 1974 decision mandated all mental health providers to warn the individuals in danger, and the hearing of the same case by the California Supreme Court in 1976 called for a "duty to protect" the threatened persons.

Since then, the supreme courts in most states have concurred with the Tarasoff decision and mandated mental health professionals' warning the threatened individuals to protect the intended victim against such danger. As a result to discharge this duty, mental health professionals must do one or more of the following: warn the intended victim, report to the law enforcement authorities, and take reasonable steps to protect the intended victim.

Although the court did not specify when a counselor should know a potential threat his or her clients may make to a thirty party, it did conclude that "the protective privilege ends where the public peril begins" (Tarasoff v. the Regents of the University of California, 1976, p. 337). According to the court decision, helping professionals have a duty to warn and protect the public when there exist the following factual conditions: (a) a special relationship, (b) a reasonable prediction of conduct that constitutes a threat, and (c) a foreseeable victim (Gehring, 1982).

This precedent court case has been used as a legal reference when helping professionals encounter issues of confidentiality concerning a client's potential dangerous behavior threatening others (Gray & Harding, 1988). Even though you are a student-in-training, your field experience brings you into the "special relationship" of counseling and thus opens you to the same mandates as professional counselors when addressing the need to protect (Gehring, 1982; Gray & Harding, 1988).

Step Three: Following Up

The third step of responding with a client expressing a desire to harm another is to follow up and/or monitor the progression of the case and the intervention. Your responsibility does not cease until the danger is over. As a field student, it is essential to work in close collaboration with your site supervisor and any other authorities who have been engaged in the response plan.

AIDS: A Special Challenge

The duty to protect a third party from intended harm by your client has been firmly established by court rulings. However, when the potential harm being directed to a third party is infection with the AIDS virus, the picture becomes somewhat less clear.

Confidentiality limits with clients who have the AIDS virus are different from confidentiality limits with clients who have potential danger to self and others physically. Health-care professionals are allowed to disclose confidential information about a potentially dangerous patient with the AIDS virus to protect the third party's safety in some areas of the United States (Gray & Harding, 1988). However, the laws in other states do not explicitly give health-care professionals the right to disclose confidential information when they work with AIDS patients. The inconsistency of this practice in the United States as a whole still exists and puts helping professionals in a difficult spot.

This partially defined application of legal limits has made ethical standards unclear for counselors. The question of what kind of response is appropriate when counselors work with AIDS clients who do not inform their sexual partners remains (Gray & Harding, 1988). For example, "When clients disclose that they have a disease commonly known to be both communicable and life threatening, counselors may be justified in disclosing information to identifiable third parties, if they are known to be at demonstrable and high risk of contracting the disease. Prior to making a disclosure, counselors confirm that there is such a diagnosis and assess the intent of clients to inform the third parties about their disease or to engage in any behaviors that may be harmful to an identifiable third party" (ACA, 2005, B.2.b). Although the ethics of our profession directs appropriate disclosure as noted, state law or even organizational policies may present another barrier. It is important to understand the laws and organizational policies governing such disclosure of clients serviced at your field placement site. The decision whether to disclose and what to disclose is not at all clear-cut. Table 8.4 provides some specific guidelines for counseling clients with HIV/AIDS, but Case Illustration 8.2 highlights the legal and ethical issues that often confront counselors engaged in such practice.

Table 8.4 The Process of Helping the Client Take Responsibility for Informing a Sexual Partner(s)

Educating

Once a counseling relationship has been engaged, counselors must assume the role of "educator" when working with a client who has the AIDS virus. It is important that information on specific transmission processes and current medical advice on the use of condoms be clarified during sessions. Specific sexual activities in which there is no exchange of body fluids, such as masturbation and parallel masturbation, must be discussed. Pregnancy decisions and possible in-utero infection to the fetus must be explored.

Consulting

Efforts at working with the client's primary health-care provider in order to address the client in a holistic fashion and use medical resources and expertise should be considered. This should be done after gaining client consent. If a client does not give permission to talk with her/his physician, then the counselor may need to consult with another physician to gain general medical information that would pertain to this health condition.

Active Supporting

Support for the client may require going beyond empathy and positive regard to active rehearsal of difficult communication situations. This might include practicing with the client about how and when to inform her/his potential and/or current sexual partner(s) about the infectious condition. Counseling may also focus on the feelings of potential defensiveness, fear, embarrassment, and rejection. Counselor availability to see the client with her/his partner is also an effective and supportive intervention.

Source: Reprinted from "Confidentiality Limits With Clients Who Have the AIDS Virus" by L. A. Gray and A. K. Harding, 1988, *Journal of Counseling and Development, 66,* pp. 219–223. Copyright 1988 by Wiley. Reprinted with permission.

CASE ILLUSTRATIONS 8.2

Where Is the Way Out?

Ashley, a 16-year-old high school student, comes to counseling with anxiety and depression because of the tension between her and her parents. Ashley's parents divorced when she was 7 years old and she has been living with her mother and her stepfather ever since. Ashley does not get along well with her stepfather, who often abuses her mother, and Ashley does not feel she's ever been loved. She has had a couple of dates and regularly engages in sexual intercourse with her boyfriends. The most recent intimate relationship began in her first year of high school, and she loves her boyfriend very much. In the course of the first session, Ashley reveals she has been diagnosed with HIV and has not told anyone yet, her boyfriend in particular because she's afraid of losing him.

Dave is a 40-year-old man who has been married for 15 years with three children. Dave comes to counseling to deal with his relationships with his wife and a man he loves. Dave reveals that he came to the realization of being gay a few years after he got married and began dating men after he and his wife had their first child. Recently, he has been diagnosed with HIV, but both his wife and the man he is dating have no knowledge about it. Dave feels guilty because he is doing something behind his wife's and children's backs. Meanwhile, he is hiding his secret from the man he loves.

After reading these two cases, what would you do if you were the counselor? Discuss your approach with your peers and share it with your supervisor and see what they think about your approach.

Site Policy on Crisis Procedures

We have emphasized the importance of understanding the specific policies and procedures governing crisis intervention at your site, but it is such an important piece of your education that we want to end this chapter with one final exercise. The following exercise (8.5) offers you an opportunity to get to know your internship site's policy and procedures of crisis intervention and prevention.

EXERCISE 8.5

Site Policy and Procedures

In this role-play exercise, you are asked to demonstrate both your factual knowledge and your interpersonal skills through an intervention of a suicidal client. To perform this assessment, you must follow your internship site's policy and procedures of crisis intervention and prevention.

Step one: Speak with your immediate site supervisor and discuss the site's crisis intervention and prevention policy and management procedures.

Step two: After you thoroughly understand the site crisis intervention and prevention policy and management procedures, ask one of your peers or your immediate supervisor to assist you in conducting a role-play of crisis intervention.

Step three: You play the role of a counselor and your peer plays the role of a suicidal client. During the role-play, you are required to follow the site policy and crisis management procedures as well as to use some of the suicide assessment knowledge and skills presented in this chapter.

Step four: After you complete the role-play, ask your peer to give you honest feedback about your performance during the role-play.

Step five: Reverse the roles this time; you play the suicidal client and your peer or supervisor plays the role of the counselor. During this round, observe how your peer or supervisor performs the suicide assessment.

Step six: Discuss the similarities and differences between your assessment and the assessment of your peer or supervisor, particularly discussing how the factual knowledge and interpersonal counseling skills are used during the role-play.

KEYSTONES

- Suicide does not discriminate, it occurs in all walks of life, and it is one of the leading causes of deaths in the United States.
- Some common characteristics of suicide risk include age, gender, marriage, sexual orientation, culture, race and ethnicity, and use of firearms.
- Ethical standards and legal statutes require all counselors to reveal confidential information when a client poses danger to self or others.
- Suicide assessment consists of three major components: a thorough face-to-face clinical interview, an empirical evaluation, and consultation.
- It is crucial for counseling interns to be cognizant with clients who have suicidal ideation and to pay attention to warning signs in the counseling process.
- Suicide assessment is a crucial step to prevention of suicide and client treatment, and counseling interns need to master all the basic suicide assessment skills.
- "The protective privilege ends where the public peril begins" has become a legal reference for helping professionals to breach confidential information when their client's behavior may have potential threat to a third party.
- Working with clients who may be a threat to others with the AIDS virus is a very complicated task because there is no explicit uniformity or consistency between the ethical standards and the state laws concerning breach of confidentiality.

ADDITIONAL RESOURCES

Web Based

Addressing suicidal thoughts and behaviors in substance abuse treatment. http://www.youtube.com/watch?v=1n2QZlheuzc

American Association of Suicidology: www.suicidology.org

National Suicide Prevention Lifeline: http://www.suicidepreventionlifeline.org/
Suicide.org: Suicide prevention, awareness, and support. http://www.suicide.org/suicide-org-websites.html

Print Based

Godleski, L., Nieves, J. E., Darkins, A., & Lehmann, L. (2008). VA telemental health: Suicide assessment. *Behavioral Sciences and the Law, 26,* 271–286.

Klott, J., & Jongsma, Jr., A. E. (2004). *The suicide and homicide risk assessment and prevention treatment planner.* New York, NY: John Wiley.

Liebling-Boccio, D. E. (2013). The current status of graduate training in suicide risk assessment. *Psychology in the Schools, 50*(1), 72–86.

REFERENCES

ACA. (2005). ACA Code of Ethics. Retrieved from: http://www.ncblpc.org/Laws_and_Codes/ACA_Code_of_Ethics.pdf

American Association of Suicidology. (2003). *Know the warning signs of suicide.* Retrieved from http://www.suicidology.org/resources/warning-signs

American Association of Suicidology. (2014). *Facts and statistics.* Retrieved from http://www.suicidology.org/resources/facts-statistics

Beck, A., Steer, R., & Ranieri, W. (1988). Scale for suicide ideation: Psychometric properties of a self-report version. *Journal of Clinical Psychology, 44,* 499–505.

Beck, A. T., Kovacs, M., & Weissman, A. (1979). Assessment of suicidal ideation: The scale for suicide ideation. *Journal of Consulting and Clinical Psychology, 47,* 343–352.

Caplan, G. (1961). *Prevention of mental disorders in children.* New York, NY: Basic Books.

Cole, D. A. (1988). Hopelessness, social desirability, depression, and parasuicide in two college student samples. *Journal of Consulting and Clinical Psychology, 56,* 131–136.

Cull, J. G., & Gill, W. S. (1982). *Suicide probability scale manual.* Los Angeles, CA: Western Psychological Services.

Elbogen, E. B., & Johnson, S. C. (2009). The intricate link between violence and mental disorder: Results from the National Epidemiologic Survey on Alcohol and Related Conditions. *Archives of Genetic Psychiatry, 66,* 152–161.

Gehring, D. D. (1982). The counselor's "duty to warn." *Personnel and Guidance Journal, 61,* 209–210.

Gray, L. A., & Harding, A. K. (1988). Confidentiality limits with clients who have the AIDS virus. *Journal of Counseling and Development, 66,* 219–223.

Haines, M., Haubenreisser, J., Dollinger, R., Frazier, L., Gordon, K., Havasi, A. . . . Leino, E. (2007). *National college health assessment executive summary.* Baltimore, MD: American College Health Association.

Hayes, J. A., Crane, A. L., & Locke, B. D. (2010). Save me from myself: College students' fears of losing control and acting violently. *Journal of College Student Psychotherapy, 24,* 181–202.

Ivanoff, A., Jang, S. J., Smyth, N. F., & Linehan, M. M. (1994). Fewer reasons for staying alive when you are thinking of killing yourself: The Brief Reasons for Living Inventory. *Journal of Psychopathology and Behavioral Assessment, 16,* 1–13.

James, K. J., & Gilliland, B. E. (2001). *Crisis intervention strategies.* Pacific Grove, PA: Brook/Cole.

Jobes, D., Jacoby, A., Cimbolic, P., & Hustead, L. (1997). Assessment and treatment of suicidal clients in a university counseling center. *Journal of Counseling Psychology, 44,* 368–377.

Juhnke, G. A. (1994). Teaching suicide risk assessment to counselor education students. *Counselor Education and Supervision, 34*(1), 52–57.

Linehan, M. M. (1981). *Suicidal behaviors questionnaire* [Unpublished inventory]. Seattle: University of Washington.

Mayors Against Illegal Guns. (2014). *Analysis of school shootings.* Retrieved from https://s3.amazonaws.com/s3.mayorsagainstillegalguns.org/images/SchoolShootingsReport.pdf

Miller, I., Norman, W., Bishop, S., & Dow, M. (1986). The Modified Scale for Suicide Ideation: Reliability and validity. *Journal of Consulting and Clinical Psychology, 54,* 724–725.

Orbach, I., Feshbach, S., Carlson, G., Glaubman, H., & Gross, Y. (1983). Attraction and repulsion by life and death in suicidal and in normal children. *Journal of Consulting and Clinical Psychology, 51,* 661–670.

Orbach, I., Milstein, I., Har-Even, D., Apter, A., Tiano, S., & Elizur, A. (1991). A Multi-Attitude Suicide Tendency Scale for adolescents. *Journal of Consulting and Clinical Psychology, 3,* 398–404.

Parks, S. E., Johnson, L. L., McDaniel, D. D., & Gladden, M. (2014). Surveillance for violent deaths: National violent death reporting system, 16 states, 2010. *Surveillance Summaries, 63*(1), 1–33.

Patterson, W. M., Dohn, H. H., Patterson, J., & Patterson, G. A. (1983). Evaluation of suicidal patients: The SAD PERSONS scale. *Psychosomatics, 24*(4), 343–345, 348–349.

Reynolds, W. M. (1987). *Suicide Ideation Questionnaire: Professional manual.* Odessa, FL: Psychological Assessment Resources.

Rudd, M. D. (1989). The prevalence of suicidal ideation among college students. *Suicide and Life-Threatening Behavior, 19,* 173–183.

Tarasoff v. the Regents of the University of California, 17 Cal. 3d 424, 551 p.2d. (1976).

Westefeld, J., Cardin, D., & Deaton, W. (1992). Development of the College Student Reasons for Living Inventory. *Suicide and Life-Threatening Behavior, 22,* 442–452.

Westefeld, J. S., Range, L. M., Rogers, J. R., Maples, M. R., Bromley, J. L., & Alcom, J. (2000). Suicide: An overview. *The Counseling Psychologist, 28,* 445–510.

Yassen, J., & Harvey, M. R. (1998). Crisis assessment and interventions with victims of violence. In P. M. Kleepies (Ed.), *Emergencies in mental health practice* (pp. 117–143). New York, NY: Guilford.

9

Reducing Risk

Risk is like fire: If controlled it will help you; if uncontrolled it will rise up and destroy you.

Theodore Roosevelt

The field experience is designed as a reciprocal arrangement where counseling students exchange their work for on-the-job training and experience in the field. The experience provided should be structured to allow counseling students to apply basic knowledge, skills, and professional values to actual practice settings specific to the emphasis of their program of study. The on-site field experience provides an opportunity to integrate theory and practice and thus facilitates the transition from student to professional.

Although this is how it should be and most likely is what you hope it to be, implicit in the above is the idea that as a person operating in the field, you will be immersed in the reality of the professional experience encountered by those serving in that setting. As a participant in the professional world and work of a counselor, you will experience the challenges presented, the joys encountered, . . . and the risk of professional practice that comes with that territory.

The current chapter will discuss the real physical and legal risks that a counselor can encounter along with the steps he or she can take to manage that risk. Specifically, after completing this chapter readers will be able to

- describe the early indicators to potential client violence;
- explain steps to be taken when confronted by escalating client violence; and
- describe the importance of knowing their clients, managing confidentiality, gaining informed consent, managing dual boundaries, and practicing within their competency as steps to reduce the possibility of legal action.

The Risk of Physical Harm

As you are called to provide care and support for another, your function as a counselor could place you in harm's way, which may seem incomprehensible. Sadly, this was the reality for New York City psychologist Kathryn Faughey, PhD, who at the age of 56 was stabbed to death in her office. The man charged with her murder had been in and out of psychiatric facilities since his early 20s. The truth is that although this is both a dramatic and extremely rare situation, violence against mental health professionals is more common than one might first think.

Client aggression can be scaled on a continuum of verbal abuse, covert threats, overt intimidation, and physical assaults. The most frequently occurring physical assaults included grabbing, pushing, kicking, damaging property, and holding. The most common incidents of psychological violence included intimidation, harassing telephone calls, and a statement of intent to harm a person (Arthur, Brende, & Quiroz, 2003). Aggression is more likely for those new to the profession as a result of their inexperience and reduced awareness of the cues of violence, as well as their tendency to set fewer limits on aggressive behavior, thus inadvertently allowing the aggression to escalate.

The risks of encountering violence in any one setting can vary considerably, depending on things such as the nature of the setting, the amount of personnel and support on site, and the type of client typically seen.

Reducing the Risk

There are a number of steps one can take to reduce, although unfortunately not eliminate, the risk of experiencing physical harm at the hands of a client. This reduction of risk starts with the acceptance that the possibility of being a victim is real. Further, it is essential to learn to recognize the indicators of potential violence and engage in personal and systemic steps aimed at preventing violence and de-escalating violence that may occur.

Indicators of Potential Violence

Most would suggest that violence rarely occurs in a vacuum or without early indications and, as such, it is helpful to assess clients for potential violence as well as to understand the behaviors that most often precede violence. Because violence is most often preceded by behavior that indicates a potential for violence, the best single predictor of potential for violence may very well be the extent of a history of aggressive behavior. But this doesn't mean that a client without such a history is not a potential risk.

Most research attempting to identify the indicators of potential violence has focused on static factors that are predictors of violence (Elbogen, Huss, Tomkins, & Scalora, 2005; Harris, Rice, & Camilleri, 2004). The factors that have been found to serve as early indicators of a client's potential for violence include positive symptoms of schizophrenia, medication noncompliance, active drug or alcohol use, mandated clients, a history of violence, and a history of dangerous impulsive acts (Weinger, 2001). Table 9.1 provides a more extensive listing of factors that have been found to be indications of elevated potential for client violence.

Table 9.1 Warning Signs of Potential Client-Initiated Violence

- Complain regularly about provision of services
- Refuse to cooperate
- Demonstrate "cries for help" in some way
- Indicate a heightened level of anxiety or depression
- Have rapid breathing, clenched fists/teeth, flared nostrils, flushing, loud talking or chanting, restless repetitive movements/pacing; make semi-violent gestures, for example, pointing
- Swear excessively and/or use sexually explicit language
- Threaten or verbally abuse workers
- Have noticeable mood swings and/or unprovoked outbursts
- Have a condition that has been associated with an increased potential for violence, for example, paranoid schizophrenia
- Tend to be solitary with few social contacts; unstable family life
- Sexually harass staff
- Blame others for all difficulties
- Cause anxiety or unrest through aggressive behaviour
- Argue frequently and intensely
- Blatantly disregard organizational policies and procedures
- Throw, sabotage, or steal equipment or property
- Have a substance abuse problem
- Send violent or sexual comments via phone, e-mail, or letter
- Make strange or exotic claims (losing touch with reality)
- Have a fascination with weapons and/or military hardware
- Have a history of violence
- Make verbal threats to hurt workers or other clients
- Tell other clients about their plans to initiate violence
- Destroy property
- Have physical confrontations
- Display and/or use weapons
- Commit sexual assaults or arson
- Talk about self-harm or suicide

Source: Mayhew, C. (2000). Preventing Client-Initiated Violence: A Practical Handbook. Australian Institute of Criminology, Research and Public Policy Series, No. 30, Appendix 7.

EXERCISE 9.1

Environmental Assessment and Prevention Measures

Directions: Identify the degree to which each of the following characteristics exist in your work setting and community. In discussion with a colleague or your site supervisor, identify steps that can be taken (or have been taken) to decrease the likelihood of harm.

Area	Factors to Consider	Preventive Measures
The Geographic Area	What is the incidence of recent community violence?	
	Is it a known drug or gang area?	
	How are "outsiders" viewed in the area?	
	Is parking protected?	
	Is the route from source of transportation (car, bus, etc.) to the site safe?	
	Is the setting isolated or a busy and highly populated area?	
Site	Is the setting well lit?	
	Is access to the building protected?	
	Is the counselor isolated from others in the building?	
	Are there policies, procedures, and protocols in place for responding to threat?	
	Are there policies and procedures in place that allow for the use of double teaming in the case of concern about a specific client?	
	Does the clinical office allow for ease of counselor exit?	
	Are there staff meetings or supervisor sessions that afford counselors the opportunity to share concerns about potential client violence?	
	Are clients assessed at intake for history of violence, acute symptomatology, and evidence of drug or alcohol use?	
	Is there a policy in your office about signaling emergencies, and that staff are authorized to call into your office during a session or to interrupt with a knock on the door if they hear anything that is worrisome in terms of safety?	

Although knowledge of these factors and assessment of their presence with any one client will position a counselor to take those steps necessary to reduce the risk of physical harm, aggression can also occur even when these conditions are absent. A number of cumulative stresses or even the experience of frustration and/or bad luck outside of the counseling can serve as the tipping point for an otherwise rational and controlled client to lose control.

Preventive Measures

When it comes to the issue of client violence toward his or her counselor, the adage that an ounce of prevention is worth a pound of cure certainly holds true. Prevention and the reduction of risk of physical harm starts with an assessment of the environment of your site and the community in which it is located. Such an assessment can help in the employment of commonsense steps to reduce the likelihood of experiencing violence. Exercise 9.1 invites you to engage in such an environmental assessment.

Further, when it has been determined that a counselor will be working with a client who presents with a high potential for violence, it is important to engage with the client in an area (e.g., room with glass windows) that, while ensuring confidentiality of the information shared, provides the opportunity for others to observe from a distance.

De-escalation

Although it is important to be sensitive to the early warning signs and risk factors and take appropriate steps to reduce the likelihood of violence, it is also important to prepare yourself for ways to respond to potentially dangerous situations. If you believe that a client is dangerous or likely to be of harm to you, it is essential that you speak with your supervisor, and if he or she is unavailable, consult with a coworker. It is important *not* to try to address a potentially dangerous situation by yourself.

In agencies or in private practices in which counselors treat clients with symptoms or histories of violence, the counselors should have in place safety features such as office or body alarms and safe words that others would recognize when assistance is needed (Arthur et al., 2003). Having someone else present provides the psychological, if not physical, structure to assist the client in becoming more compliant.

If you feel that the client is escalating toward violence and you are unable to gain the presence of a colleague, you need to find a way to remove yourself from the situation without alarming the client. Stating that you have to go to the bathroom or check on a form that you left out front, or any other plausible explanation accompanied by a comment such as "sorry, but I'll be right back," may give you the opportunity to exit the situation and seek assistance without arousing further escalation.

If the violence erupts and you are unable to either seek assistance or remove yourself from the situation, the directive most often given and yet difficult to follow is to remain calm and focused. Clearly this is good advice, but implementing it in the face of possible violence will be difficult if one has not trained for remaining calm under duress (Tunnecliffe, 2007). If you can remain calm, the demonstration of empathy reflecting your awareness of the client's frustration, irritation, annoyance, or anger and a genuine expression of your desire to be of help may help de-escalate the situation. Such an empathic response will hopefully invite dialogue that may allow you to offer an alternative solution to the current situation.

Other practical steps to take include the following:

1. Stand outside the client's personal space and immediate reach.
2. Position yourself on the client's nondominant side (if he or she wears a watch, it is often on the nondominant side).
3. As noted above, be calm.
4. Be respectful in tone and content of speech.
5. Offer suggestions rather than be directive.
6. Do not use rapid hand movement or pointing gestures.

As a student in field placement, the possibility of being harmed or experiencing violence at the hand of a client may be the farthest thing from your mind. Sadly, reality demands that you seriously consider the possibility and discuss with your supervisor the plans employed to assess, prevent, and, when necessary, intervene with violent clients. Even when the history of the setting is such that the possibility of violence seems to be low, a workplace violence prevention/intervention plan should be in place.

Reducing Legal Risks

As a student in a field placement, you might assume that you are immune from any legal action a client or a client's representative may take in response to what he or she feels is a violation of professional ethics or existing law. Such is not the case. Evidence of the real possibility that even as a student in the field you may be a target for legal action can be found in the fact that all major professional organizations, for example, the American Counseling Association (ACA), the American Mental Health Counselors Association (AMHCA), the National Association of Alcohol Drug Abuse Counselors (NAADAC), and the American Psychological Association (APA), offer liability insurance for students.

Although most graduate programs require students to have liability insurance, the truth is that even if your program does not require such insurance, it is a bad decision to begin your field work without it. Most students cannot afford to defend themselves in court if there's a claim against their professional services. Not having professional liability insurance can put your finances and your career at risk. However, even though insurance provides some protection, it is much better to take those steps necessary to avoid legal actions rather than attempt to cope after the fact.

As you engage in your inaugural experience as a counselor, you, like all professional counselors, should reflect on and take the steps necessary to ensure ethical, efficient practice, thus reducing the risk of legal action. The directive to engage in ethical and efficient practice as a way of avoiding or at least reducing the risk of legal action is clear and logical, but it is not always that easy to apply. Most often, counselors who find themselves in legal hot water got there not by way of a massively bad and obviously unethical practice or practice decision. Quite often, it is not a single decision or failure to act that has caused the difficulty. More often than not, those who find themselves legally challenged got there as a result of a number of unwitting actions, lapses in oversight, or failures to act that have simply spiraled out of control. To avoid such stumbling into legal action, it is essential that you understand and employ informed consent, documentation, and consultation as "part of your forethought, thought and after thought processes" (Bennett et al., 2006, p. 34).

These principles are particularly important and relevant to each of the following areas of practice and professional behavior, areas that are often fertile ground for legal action.

Confidentiality

The need to respect the rights of the client to have his or her information held in confidence is something that, we are sure, is not new to you. But as noted above, violation of ethical principles typically don't occur in the obvious, but in the subtle. Consider the following case illustration of a student-intern conferring prior to her evening class (see Case Illustration 9.1).

CASE ILLUSTRATION 9.1

Case Conferencing

It was a routine that she had followed for the past year and half. Meeting with Joanna and Thomas in the graduate student coffee area prior to classes served as a time to unwind, to discuss class projects and upcoming tests, and now that they were in the field, to confer about cases in preparation for their seminar.

Mary Theresa's field placement was unique from that of Joanna's or Tom's, in that the counselors at her site often worked with self-referred young adults who presented with concerns about unwedded pregnancy, alcohol and drug issues, or, given their proximity to the university, conflicts with parents regarding school. The case with which she was working was that of a 19-year-old sophomore who was a walk-in client and who presented with concerns about his blacking out, which he connected to his binge drinking. Mary Theresa was receiving quality supervision at the site and felt that she was establishing a solid working relationship with the client. She noted that a recent event highlighted the seriousness of his drinking and helped motivate him to embrace the recommendation that he take a leave of absence from the university and engage in a residential program.

It was a direction that was supported by her supervisor and now embraced by her client. At that particular time, she felt quite pleased with the relationship and the direction of the counseling and therefore was not seeking any input or advice from her colleagues. However, the extent of her client's drinking and the details of the escapades in which he engaged during his binges were absolutely foreign to Mary Theresa as an intern. So as she sat having coffee with her two classmates, she began to.relate, in graphic detail, one of the most recent episodes in her client's saga.

While never identifying the client by name, she provided graphic detail of the date, time, and place of his most recent episode. She described how he entered a sorority house at 2:00 a.m., stripped off his clothes, pulled the fire alarm, and waited at the front door to "direct" the girls to their safety. A number of the girls in the sorority knew him and interceded on his behalf so that no one in the house filed a report or complained to the campus police. The severity of his behavior and the fact that he had no recollection of the events that led up to this display were extremely upsetting to the client and served as the motivation for his acceptance of the therapeutic recommendation.

Engrossed in the story being shared, all at the table failed to recognize the fact that a woman and her daughter, sitting at the next table, where also listening to the tale. As was later discovered, the girl sitting at the table with her mother was a member of the (named) sorority and not only observed the events being described but also was one of the individuals interceding on the client's behalf. She knew the client as a high school classmate and was concerned about him being kicked out of school and his parents' reactions. When pressed by her mother for details, she disclosed the name of the client to her mother. The fact that her mother knew the client and his family resulted in a disclosure of his drinking behavior to his parents.

Although it could be argued that the student-intern in our case (Case Illustration 9.1) had no intention or expectation of violating the student's confidentiality, the public location and the specific details shared invited just such violation of confidentiality. Sadly, the circumstances of this violation are not all that unusual. As you continue in your field placement and/or hear of events from colleagues in other settings, you may note that client and case details are often discussed in settings such as the staff lunchroom, the hallway, an elevator, or even the bathroom. These are settings that fail to provide the privacy needed to maintain confidentiality and open counselors to the violation of their professional ethics. Other violations of ethical practice can occur as a result of inadvertently sending an e-mail with client information to someone other than the client or one for whom disclosure has been granted. Or, similarly, there is the potential to violate confidentiality when one leaves a telephone message, even confirming an appointment, to which other, non-appropriate recipients may have access. These are all threats to the maintenance of confidentiality.

When disclosing information, even under conditions that are secure, it is important for you to be aware of the basis upon which you are choosing to make that disclosure. Generally, disclosure should be *on a need-to-know basis,* with the specifics being disclosed reflecting the minimum information necessary to provide service, to protect one from harm, or to obtain supervision or appropriate consultation. It is helpful to consider if the disclosure is mandated by law or at a minimum permitted by law. But even here, when disclosure is mandated or permitted, it is ethical practice to make a good faith effort to gain client permission and to explain the specifics to be disclosed, the person or persons to whom the information will be shared, and why.

The parameters of confidentiality are not static. Because legislative actions and court decisions continually reshape the parameters defining what is and is not confidential and under what conditions can or must confidentiality be broken (Wheeler & Bertram, 2008), counselors, especially those in field practice, should consult with their supervisors prior to making any disclosure. Knowing the laws and policies that govern confidentiality and disclosure for your site is a must—both for you as practitioner and for your client—to be able to make an informed consent for treatment. Exercise 9.2 invites you to gather information necessary to ethically manage client data.

EXERCISE 9.2

When to Break Confidentiality

Directions: There are a number of federal laws governing the maintenance of confidentiality and disclosure of information (e.g., HIPPA, FIRPA), and there may be unique statutes governing those populations with whom you may be working (e.g., minors, HIV clients, elderly, etc.) or settings in which you are working (e.g., drug and alcohol rehabilitation centers). It is important to understand the laws and policies governing confidentiality and disclosure for clients with whom you will work in your field placement. You are invited to speak with your site supervisor to gain answers to each of the following questions. Further, where possible, ask your supervisor to direct you to the specific law, statute, policy, or principle governing confidentiality and disclosure.

1. Under what conditions am I to disclose client information? What is the extent of the data to be disclosed?
2. To whom am I required to disclose client information? And to what purpose is such disclosure made?
3. What are the limits to the confidentiality of client records (including those I keep)? Who has access to client records?
4. What are the organization's policies regarding acquiring client consent before breaking confidentiality or for informing the client of the necessity of such breaching of confidentiality?
5. What specific "threats" to violating laws and policies of confidentiality would you (the supervisor) emphasize as needing my special attention?

Identify the Client

Although identifying one's client may not be immediately clear and obvious in practice, as counselor you want to know who your client is because knowing who your client is will help reduce the risk of legal action. This may seem a bit strange as an issue that could reduce the risk of legal action.

Consider the situation of a counselor working in a public school. Is the counselor's "client" the student sitting in his or her office or is it that student's parents or even the school itself? The answer to that question can affect the rules of maintaining confidentiality or gaining informed consent . . . or even providing service. Let's consider the case of a counselor working with a couple. If only one partner is seeking assistance in saving the marriage, whereas the other is hoping to have the counselor assist in the development of a plan for a civilized divorce, which partner is the client? Is either? Or, is there a third party—the "couple"—that is the client? Or, finally, consider the situation of a counselor in private practice who is seeing a minor. Are the parents who brought the child and who are paying the bill the client?

It is possible that under some situations a counselor could be providing service to multiple clients in any one counseling contract. There could be a legal client, as may be the case when a counselor is working with a person mandated to counseling, where legally the counselor will be required to provide reports to the court while ethically being sensitive to the needs of the person in his or her charge. It is important that a counselor know who it is that he or she is serving, the possible constraints legally and ethically on providing service, and, finally, the nature of the services that he or she is to provide.

Respect Client's Autonomy

Essential to any counseling dynamic is the counselor's respect for the client and client's autonomy. This most often takes form in the counselor's efforts to provide essential information that will help the client give his or her informed consent to engage in counseling. Legal problems often emerge as a result of a counselor failing to provide the client the information needed to truly make an informed decision to engage in counseling. This includes such things as informing the client about the limits of confidentiality and mandatory reporting or the nature and extent of records kept.

The need for providing such information extends even to those client populations (for example, young school children or those with cognitive challenges) for whom understanding the information may be difficult. In these cases, the legal directive is to achieve consent from those who are the legal representative or guardian of the client, whereas the ethical principle continues to direct the counselor to engage the client in the decision making as far as that is possible.

This eliciting of informed consent is not a one-time process. It is important to view the provision of informed consent as an ongoing, interactive process (Bennett et al., 2006). Because the course of counseling is dynamic, there may be decisions to be made regarding adjustment to the course of treatment, even including the decision of if, when, and how to terminate treatment. Exercise 9.3, Respecting Client Autonomy, invites you to gather information regarding the way counselors in your field placement setting demonstrate respect for their clients' autonomy.

EXERCISE 9.3

Respecting Client Autonomy

Directions: Although the principle of respecting client autonomy is clear as both an ethical directive and as a way of reducing the likelihood of legal action, the way that principle takes form can vary from setting to setting and even counselor to counselor. Your task is to discuss each of the following with your site supervisor so that you can get a clearer picture of how respect for the client's autonomy takes form in the policies, procedures, and practice employed at your site.

1. What policies, procedures, and processes are employed that reflect the valuing of the client's autonomy?
2. Discuss the procedures for obtaining informed consent:
   a. How is informed consent documented?
   b. Are there special conditions (e.g., age of client, developmental challenges, diagnosis, etc.) that require alternative methods for gaining informed consent?
   c. Are there procedures to be followed in updating and documenting treatment plans?
3. Discuss how termination of counseling is handled:
   a. Is participation in counseling always voluntary?
   b. Are clients allowed to terminate counseling whenever they choose, even if considered unadvisable by the counselor or legally responsible party?
   c. Are there policies, procedures, and processes followed when engaging in termination? How do these reflect the valuing of the client's autonomy?

Professional Boundaries

When applied to professional relationships, the term *boundary* refers to that which distinguishes one's professional role and function from those actions and decisions made to serve one's personal needs. A professional boundary serves as a metaphorical construct that defines the limits of one's professional identity and prescribes the boundaries to the relationship encountered in a professional exchange. Professional boundaries not only support a counselor's efforts to remain caring and therapeutic with a professional sense of objectivity and emotional distance, but also protect the client from inappropriate intrusion by a counselor.

The boundaries separating the counselor's professional from the personal are not impermeable. There are multiple conditions and circumstances that invite a counselor to shift from the professional role to a personal role, thus traversing the professional boundary. Boundary crossing and boundary violations are two terms that refer to any deviation from the traditional, strict, professionally objective demeanor and practice expected of a professional counselor.

Boundary Crossing

As a student in the field, it is quite possible, especially if you live in the same community in which you are doing field work, that a client is a person you know as a neighbor or a relative of a friend, or even as a contact from another organization to which you belong. The question is, "Does your multiple relationships with this individual (e.g., friend and counselor, or neighbor and counselor) restrict your ability to engage professionally as a counselor?"

Understanding the nature of multiple relationships is not always an easy process. When engaged in a multiple relationship, one question that must be considered is, "Whose needs are being met?"

Although it is suggested that it is safer to simply avoid these multiple relationships, this is not always possible. The middle school soccer coach who is also the only school counselor cannot refuse to see the student standing in her doorway, even when that student is her star soccer player. These conditions bring the counselor into an arena in which the professional role of counselor could intrude on the decision of soccer coach or, conversely, the role of coach could make an appearance in the counseling office.

Although boundary crossings need to be a matter of concern, they are not in and of themselves unethical. We now recognize that there are conditions when moving away from the typical in-office role and demeanor can be an integral part of a treatment plan. For example, a counselor who steps into the role of flying companion with a client who suffers from a fear of flying, or who becomes a lunch buddy with a client who is anorexic, or who engages a depressed patient in a vigorous walk or shooting basketball in the gym is crossing from the "typical" role of counselor but with the goal and intention of servicing the client. Under these conditions, it is the need of the client and not the needs of the counselor that serves as the motivation for the change in role. This potential value of engaging in nonprofessional roles has been recognized by all major professional associations (e.g., ACA, APA, NASW, and NBCC) as not unethical.

For example, the 2014 revision of the *ACA Code of Ethics* acknowledged that multiple relationships (referred to as "nonprofessional interactions or relationships" in the ethics code) need to be avoided. "Counselors avoid entering into nonprofessional relationships with former clients, their romantic partners or their family members when the interaction is potentially harmful to the client. This applies to both in-person and electronic interactions and relationships" (Standard A.6.e). A major concern is that extending boundaries beyond the conventional parameters may impair a counselor's ability to remain objective, and thus boundary crossing is discouraged and when it does occur, the rationale along with the potential benefit and anticipated consequences need to be documented (Standard A.6.c). For example, consider the situation of a counselor working with a depressed individual who is also that counselor's son's teacher. Might he feel compelled to ask about his son's performance while in session or, conversely, check on the teacher's status at a parent-teacher conference? Might he experience concern about the impact of the depression on the competency of his client, as teacher? If so, how might these affect his clinical judgments and ability to remain both empathic and objective?

As a student in the field, it is important to review your potential caseloads and discuss any possibilities of multiple relationships and boundary crossings with your supervisor so that provisions can be made to reduce the potential that this multiple relationship could impair your professional practice and result in harm to your client.

Boundary Violations

Unlike boundary crossings, boundary violations are always unethical in that they are, by definition, harmful to our clients. Boundary violations are typically exploitive of the relationship in service of the counselor's needs and ultimately at the expense of the client's well-being. This is most clearly evident in situations where a counselor exploits the client's vulnerabilities or the power of the counseling dynamics for his or her own sexual need or satisfaction.

Although it may be easy to simply suggest that only counselors who have serious emotional problems or questionable moral standards violate boundaries, the truth is that boundary violations can occur anytime a counselor displaces or confuses his or her own needs with those of the client. Such loss of professional objectivity can occur in situations where the counselor (a) has a direct personal involvement with the client, as would be the case of counseling one's family member, close friend, or fiancée; (b) personally identifies with the client and the client's situation, as would be the case of a counselor who is going through a painful divorce while attempting to work with a couple who are experiencing marital conflicts; or (c) when the counselor has deeply unresolved emotional issues that are coming into play in a particular counseling relationship. This last condition, reflecting issues of countertransference, presents a special risk and challenge to boundary maintenance, principally because the issues are most often below the counselor's level of conscious awareness.

The specific definition of countertransference has and continues to be debated, but most agree that it involves a response to a client that may have been prompted by something occurring in session but is primarily based on the counselor's past significant relationships and in service of the counselor's needs, rather than those of client. For example, a counselor who has unresolved issues stemming from his own experience of being abused as a child may push a client to confront his or her own abuse well before the client is ready or, conversely, may discourage the client from talking about the issue, because such a discussion is too conflictual and painful for the counselor. Obviously, under these conditions, effective treatment is severely diminished.

Whether a counselor has a personal relationship or identifies, consciously or unconsciously, with the client's issues, loss of professional objectivity invites unethical violations of professional boundaries and must be avoided. It is important for counselors to work through their own unresolved issues as a step toward reducing the possibility of countertransference and boundary violation, but regular monitoring of one's professional style and decision making may be the most important step for reducing the possibility of boundary violation. Simply stated, *anytime a counselor experiences a departure from his or her usual practice*—for example, extending a session beyond a typical time frame, meeting a client in a location different than the professional office, or perhaps choosing to "barter" for services or adjust a fee structure—he or she needs to step back and give careful consideration to the underlying motives for such modification. It is essential to ensure that all such adjustments from "normal practice" are in service of the client and the client's therapy and not in service of the counselor's personal needs. In addition to such monitoring, it is also important to continue to seek supervision and professional support as a way of engaging an outside, professional perspective on one's professional decisions.

Practice Within Competence

Competence in knowledge, skill, and emotional state is clearly a prerequisite for performance at a professional level. Principle C.2.a of the *American Counseling Association Code of Ethics* states, "Counselors practice only within the boundaries of their competence, based on their education, training, supervised experience, state and national professional credentials and appropriate professional experience" (ACA, 2014).

The question that could be asked—especially for one who is now engaging with "real" clients for the very first time—is, "How does one become competent, if not initially applying his or her knowledge and skill as a novice?" If you return to the *ACA Code of Ethics,* C.2.a (ACA, 2014), you will note that it directs one to practice within the boundaries of competency as a reflection of his or her current level of education, experience, and supervision. Thus, even as a novice—a neophyte in counseling—you bring to the counseling relationship a professional knowledge base and skill set, which, while not yet complete, can, with the guidance of a supervisor, prove beneficial to those with whom you will be working.

Practicing within your level of competence not only directs you to stay within the parameters of service selected in consultation with your supervisor but informs your client of the existence of these parameters. It is essential that, as part of the informed consent procedure, your client is informed of your student-counselor status and the fact that you are being closely supervised.

As a student-in-training, the legal responsibility for treatment technically resides with your supervisor. It is the responsibility of your supervisor(s) to ensure that the work assigned is what you could be reasonably expected to perform competently given your level of education, training, and experience and the level of supervision provided. It is suggested that, prior to being assigned a client as part of a caseload, you meet with your supervisor to discuss your experiences, goals, concerns, and questions. This should be a continual process. It is important to engage in ongoing self-evaluation and reflection in order to identify those areas of strength, those of perhaps "mastery," and those in development. Sharing these data with your supervisor will not only ensure the safety and well-being of your clients but also allow for your continued development as a professional.

Document, Document, and Then Document

When in professional practice, you may find that documentation can be your best ally when presented with ethical and legal challenges. As a general rule, records are needed to facilitate continuation of service, ensure compliance with law, and meet institutional requirements. In addition, good record keeping has been found to be useful for supporting professional decisions and documenting ethical practice when legal action has been taken. Documentation "reflects your competence and demonstrates that you are delivering service in accordance with a reasonable standard of care" (Bennett et al., 2006, p. 45).

As a measure of risk management, it is important to create comprehensive records that address each of the following:

1. Obtain documentation of informed consent (i.e., for treatment, disclosure of information) and the nature and extent of the professional relationship and of duty owed with regard to the client. In this informed consent documentation, it is important to provide evidence of informing the client of your student-intern status.
2. Provide documentation detailing professional decision making, problems encountered in working with the client, engagement with supervisor, and the professional response to crises and other special or problem situations.
3. Keep a record of information that will support the adequacy of the clinical assessment, the appropriateness of the treatment/service plan, and the application of professional skills and knowledge in the provision of professional services, again with evidence of supervisory involvement.
4. Document details of the treatment/services provided and the results of such treatment/services.
5. Document all supervision/consultation obtained in relation to the assessment and treatment of the client, particularly with regard to crises or other special or problematic situations that arise.

The above are meant to serve as a general template for documentation. However, it is important to gather the specifics regarding the data and information that are to be gathered and recorded as required by your placement site and your supervisor. The specific nature and extent of the records you are to maintain along with the rules governing maintenance, dissemination, storage, and disposal are given shape by federal and state laws as well as organizational policies. Exercise 9.4 directs you to reach out to your supervisor to gain clarity about parameters of documentation at your local site.

One final note on documentation—it is highly suggested (see Bennett et al., 2006) that you create records with the expectation that the client or a third party may someday read them. This will guide your decisions on not only what to include, but how to phrase, describe, and reference the information included.

EXERCISE 9.4

Documentation

Directions: You are invited to discuss each of the following with your site supervisor and, where possible, gather specific reference or documentation regarding federal, state, and local laws or organizational policies governing practice.

1. What is the minimum documentation required when working with a client?
2. What are the data to be included in my clinical/counseling records?
3. Are there special provisions for keeping records regarding minors, those with disabilities, or the aged? Are there special provisions based on presenting issues (e.g., drug and alcohol abuse, physical abuse, STD, suicidal/homicidal risk, or other mandated, etc.) or federal and state laws such as HIPPA (Health Insurance Portability and Accountability Act) or FERPA (The Family Educational Rights and Privacy Act)?
4. What are the policies regarding storage, maintenance, and disposal of records?
5. Are there any other policies/practices at the field location governing documentation?

Postscript

We think it is safe to suggest that most of those who enter the counseling profession do so with a high degree of idealism. Most counselors believe in the human spirit and the potential for wellness.

It is likely that you enter your field experiences with a similar sense of optimism about the goodness of the human condition and the value of counseling as a process promoting growth and wellness. Therefore, it may have been a bit disconcerting to read in this chapter of the real possibility that risk of harm, both physically and legally, could await you.

The intent of this chapter is not to shake your idealism, nor cause undo anxiety. Rather, in concert with the quote provided by Theodore Roosevelt that opened the chapter, we believe that risk, if controlled, can help you. The steps needed to reduce the potential for risk and/or manage the risk that is present will help you not only be safer but become a more ethical and effective provider of service. So, as we complete this chapter, we invite you to engage in one last exercise (Exercise 9.5), which invites you to identify your own personal areas of vulnerability and begin to plan those steps necessary to reduce risk to your physical and professional well-being.

EXERCISE 9.5

A Personal Plan for Risk Management

Directions: The following exercise should be completed in discussion with your site supervisor, or with your university advisor if you are not yet at a field placement site. The goal of the exercise is to help you begin to identify targets for the development of your own personal risk management plan. Discuss each of the following questions for reflections with your site or faculty mentor and identify steps you can take to manage the risk in a way that increases your personal safety and professional efficacy.

Part 1: Identifying Points of Vulnerability

1. Environmental Concerns

What are the elements of a work setting (e.g., being isolated, working at night, working in a dangerous geographic location, being alone in the office, working in a setting with unexpected walk-ins, working in a setting with high levels of foot traffic, etc.) that elevate your sense of physical vulnerability?

2. Population Concerns

Although it may be hard to admit, it is possible that as a result of one's lived experience or as a reflection of a personal prejudice and bias, certain types of individuals or even presenting concerns arouse feelings of physical vulnerability. What, if any, client characteristics or presenting problems do you feel may arouse a sense of personal vulnerability in you (e.g., clients with a history of violence; clients with impulse control problems; clients presenting with alcohol or drug abuse issues; clients with a history of abuse or domestic violence; clients of a particular age, gender, social economic status, or racial/ethnic background; clients of a particular physical stature; etc.)?

3. Concerns Regarding Professional Practice

As you anticipate entering the "world of the professional counselor" and all that entails, are there areas of professional practice in which you feel ill-prepared and thus vulnerable to the possibility of legal action (e.g., ability to maintain confidentiality; recognizing and managing multiple relationships; providing competent service; managing records and documentation; knowing specific laws, policies, and practices governing ethical and legal practice at your site; etc.)?

Part II: Embracing Risk and Formulating a Growth Plan

For each of the areas of concern and vulnerability identified in Part I, identify steps you can take to reduce the actual source of threat as well as increase your ability to respond to the risk that may be presented.

1. Addressing Environmental Concerns
2. Addressing Population Concerns
3. Addressing Concerns Regarding Professional Practice

KEYSTONES

- Prevention and the reduction of risk of physical harm starts with an assessment of the environment of your site and the community in which it is located.
- The factors that can serve as indicators of increased potential for violence include positive symptoms of schizophrenia, medication noncompliance, active drug or alcohol use, mandated clients, a history of violence, and a history of dangerous impulsive acts. If you feel that the client's aggression is escalating and you are unable to gain the presence of a colleague, you should find a way to remove yourself from the situation without alarming the client.
- If the client becomes violent and you cannot escape, it is important to remain calm and demonstrate empathy. Reflecting your awareness of the client's frustration, irritation, annoyance, or anger, and a genuine expression of your desire to be of help may help de-escalate the situation.
- When it comes to the risk of legal action, student status does not make one immune.
- Although one might assume legal action comes as a result of some gross ethical violation, such is not usually the case. More often than not, those who find themselves legally challenged got there as a result of a number of unwitting actions, lapses in oversight, or failures to act that have simply spiraled out of control.
- Three areas deserving special attention as areas of high risk for legal action are (a) conditions surrounding the attainment of informed consent, (b) the establishment of documentation that details ethical practice, and (c) the use of supervision/ consultation.

ADDITIONAL RESOURCES

Web Based

AAMFT: https://www.aamft.org/imis15/content/membership/Student_liability_FAQS.aspx
ACA: http://www.counseling.org/Students/ACA_Student_Coverage_FAQs.pdf
ACA Insurance Trust Student Liability Insurance: http://www.1855professionalliabilityinsurance.com/aca-insurance-trust-professional-liability-insurance-company-4.html

Print Based

Caudill, O. B. (2002). Risk management for psychotherapists: Avoiding the pitfalls. In L. VandeCreek & T. L. Jackson (Eds.), *Innovations in clinical practice: A sourcebook.* Sarasota, FL: Professional Resource Press.

Foxhall, K. (2000). How to protect your practice from fraud and abuse charges. *Monitor on Psychology, 31*(2), 64–66.

Haas, L. J., & Malouf, J. L. (2002). *Keeping up the good work: A practitioner's guide to mental health ethics* (3rd ed.). Sarasota, FL: Professional Resource Press.

Meloy, J. R. (2000). *Violence risk and threat assessment: A practical guide for mental health and criminal justice professionals.* San Diego, CA: Specialized Training Services.

Wheeler, A. M., & Bertram, B. (2012). *The counselor and the law: A guide to legal and ethical practice.* Alexandria, VA: American Counseling Association.

REFERENCES

American Counseling Association. (2014). *ACA code of ethics.* Alexandria, VA: Author.

Arthur, G. L., Brende, J. O., & Quiroz, S. E. (2003). Violence: Incidence and frequency of physical and psychological assaults affecting mental health providers in Georgia. *Journal of General Psychology, 130*(1), 22–45.

Bennett, B. E., Bricklin, P. M., Harris, E., Knapp, S., VandeCreek, L., & Younggren, J. N. (2006). *Assessing and managing risk in psychological practice: An individualized approach.* Rockville, MD: The Trust.

Elbogen, E. B., Huss, M., Tomkins, A. J., & Scalora, M. J. (2005). Clinical decision-making about psychopathy and violence risk assessment in public sector mental health settings. *Psychological Services, 2,* 133–141.

Harris, G. T., Rice, M. E., & Camilleri, J. A. (2004). Applying a forensic actuarial assessment (the Violence Risk Appraisal Guide) to nonforensic patients. *Journal of Interpersonal Violence, 19,* 1063–1074.

Mayhew, C. (2000). *Preventing client-initiated violence: A practical handbook* [Australian Institute of Criminology, Research and Public Policy Series, No 30]. Retrieved from http://www.aic.gov.au/documents/F/5/5/%7BF55AACC1-68CB-4DF6-8A34-CFCE6407D183%7DRPP30.pdf

Tunnecliffe, M. (2007). *A life in crisis: 27 lessons from acute trauma counseling work.* Palmrya, Western Australia: Bayside.

Weinger, S. (2001). *Security risk: Preventing client violence against social workers.* Washington, DC: NASW Press.

Wheeler, A. M., & Bertram, B. (2008). *The counselor and the law: A guide to legal and ethical practice.* Alexandria, VA: American Counseling Association.

10

Documentation and Record Keeping

The first and fundamental need of any organised society is the regulation of its network of relationships by means of objective, consistent, meaningful and useable documentation.

Luciana Duranti

The quote from Luciana Duranti points to the value of documentation as a means of regulating a society's network of relationships. We in the helping profession understand that objective, consistent, meaningful, and usable documentation serves as an essential element in ethical and effective practice. Record keeping and documentation for those in professional practice is an ethical mandate, a legal requirement, and a guide to effective practice. As will be described below, the maintenance of accurate records and documentation of one's practice decisions ensures that counselors follow the rules, regulations, and standards for health care set by the counseling profession and the state laws and federal regulations.

As you may anticipate, documentation and record keeping are an important part of your internship training. As counselor-in-training, you will begin to receive information about documentation and record keeping as it takes form and practice within your field site. The specific nature of the records to be maintained and the exact format to be used will often be site specific, but the general principles guiding record keeping cut across the specifics of any one locale or practice, and these will be discussed within this chapter. After completing this chapter, readers will be able to

- describe the nature and value of clinical documentation and record keeping,
- explain the ethical and legal requirements on documentation and record keeping,

- detail what should be included in progress notes,
- describe the common elements/formats of clinical note taking,
- describe issues involved in documentation and record keeping, and
- give details about the strategies to write clinical documentation.

Purpose of Documentation and Record Keeping

Professional counselors are ethically mandated to "create, safeguard, and maintain documentation necessary for rendering professional services" (ACA, 2014, A.1.b). The maintenance of clinical records and documentation ensures the ethical application of standard of care, provides a means for effective communication among all helping professionals, and serves as the data from which to respond to ethical and/or legal challenges.

Standard of Care

Standard of care in mental health professions is reflected in two aspects: what we do, that is the services provided, and the qualification of the provider to engage in those activities. As directed by our *Code of Ethics,* "Counselors practice only within the boundaries of their competence, based on their education, training, supervised experience, state and national professional credentials, and appropriate professional experience." (ACA, 2014, C.2.a). The documentation of activities with any one client serves as the data from which counselors can demonstrate that they have been engaging in those activities that fall within their level of competence and current supervision. But beyond demonstrating that counselors are providing the services they are competent to provide, the clinical record and documentation when listing dates and types of service, as well as evidence of outcomes achieved, serve to demonstrate that this counselor is engaging in the highest standard of care by employing best practice procedures with demonstrated effectiveness.

Communication

The second purpose and value of good documentation and record keeping is that it allows for meaningful exchange and professional communication regarding client treatment or clinical practice. Clearly, there will be times when you wish to engage other professionals in the treatment of a client or perhaps arrange for a referral to a specialist. Sharing of clinical documents, with client permission, will facilitate the ongoing nature of care. Beyond concern for continuation of care, professional documentation is necessary when communicating with third party payers and professionals from accreditation bodies, or in case of legal questions.

As an intern, you will need to review your work and your cases with your on-site supervisor. The records you create, as directed by your site and your supervisor, will be useful when seeking and receiving supervision. It is important to check with your supervisor in order to understand the depth, breadth, and format for the records you are to keep.

Desirable Defense Against Litigation

Although a counselor's intent may be notable and his or her efforts to provide the best service may be commendable, it is not unusual for a client to be dissatisfied and even to file a complaint to the Division of Professional Licensure or state board of registration. This is certainly true in those cases where the mental health counselor failed to maintain acceptable standards of competence and integrity.

The possibility of legal action is a reality. Each year there are significant numbers of complaints filed to state boards of registration against mental health professionals, and the chance of lawsuits against mental health professionals has been high (Sanders, 2006; Slovenko, 2006). Obviously, the best defense against such legal action is to be proactive in reducing and managing one's risk. But in situations where defense is necessary, the presence of accurate documentation depicting the types and level of services provided, along with supervisory notations, will serve as the foundation for that defense. Good, accurate record keeping provides a good foundation for counselors against legal issues and ethics violation claims (Mitchell, 2007).

The value of keeping and maintaining documentation and records cannot be overemphasized. As you continue in your field training, it is important to become informed about the types of data you are to record as well as the format for reporting and maintaining those data. Not only is this a training requirement during your internship, but also an obligation in your lifelong profession. While doing your internship and becoming a competent counselor, you want gradually to build this part of counseling practice into your professional identity.

Ethical and Legal Ramifications

Learning about ethical and legal ramifications of clinical documentation and record keeping during your internship is as crucial as developing your competence in other areas of counseling or counseling psychology. As you know, documentation serves as a road map of clinical treatment that the counselor provides, and record keeping is the only way that reflects the contact between the counselor and the client has been made. Due to the essential function of documentation and record keeping, all health professions have created codes of ethics to govern their members' professional behaviors, and counseling is no exception. As a counselor, one must know the requirements of the *ACA Code of Ethics* concerning clinical documentation and record keeping. As noted in our *Code of Ethics* (ACA, 2014),

> Counselors create, safeguard, and maintain documentation necessary for rendering professional services. Regardless of the medium, counselors include sufficient and timely documentation to facilitate the delivery and continuity of services. Counselors take reasonable steps to ensure that documentation accurately reflects client progress and services provided. If amendments are made to records and documentation, counselors take steps to properly note the amendments according to agency or institutional policies. (ACA, 2014, A.1.b)

In reviewing this guideline, a number of concepts emerge as requiring special attention. Counselors *create* and *safeguard sufficient* and *timely* documentation to facilitate the delivery of continuity of services and also take reasonable steps to ensure *documentation accurately reflects client progress and services* provided. Table 10.1 contains a list of specifications of the *Code of Ethics* by the ACA (2014) concerning documentation and record keeping.

The mandate to keep and maintain records is not limited to those associated with the American Counseling Association. Although it does not provide specific procedures on how to document, the American School Counseling Association (ASCA) requires the following:

> The professional school counselors: (a) Maintain and secure records necessary for rendering professional services to the student as required by laws, regulations, institutional procedures, and confidentiality guidelines. (b) Keep sole-possession records separate from students' educational records in keeping with state laws. (c) Recognize the limits of sole-possession records and understand these records are a memory aid for the creator and in absence of privilege communication. (ASCA, 2010, A8)

Further, the American Psychological Association (APA, 2010) requires its members to

> create, and to the extent the records are under their control, maintain, disseminate, store, retain, and dispose of records and data relating to their professional and scientific work in

Table 10.1 *ACA Code of Ethics* on Documentation and Record Keeping

Counselors ensure that records and documentation kept in any medium are secure and that only authorized persons have access to them. (B.6.b)
Counselors take reasonable precautions to protect client confidentiality in the event of the counselor's termination of practice, incapacity, or death and appoint a records custodian when identified as appropriate. (B.6.i)
Counselors provide reasonable access to records and copies of records when requested by competent clients. Counselors limit the access of clients to their records, or portions of their records, only when there is compelling evidence that such access would cause harm to the client. (B.6.e)
When clients request access to their records, counselors provide assistance and consultation in interpreting counseling records. (B.6.f)
Counselors store records following termination of services to ensure reasonable future access, maintain records in accordance with federal and state laws and statutes such as licensure laws and policies governing records, and dispose of client records and other sensitive materials in a manner that protects client confidentiality. (B.6.h)
Counselors maintain electronic records in accordance with relevant laws and statutes. Counselors inform clients on how records are maintained electronically. (H.5.a)

Source: Code of Ethics. American Counseling Association (2014).

> order to (1) facilitate provision of services later by them or by other professionals, (2) allow for replication of research design and analyses, (3) meet institutional requirements, (4) ensure accuracy of billing and payments, and (5) ensure compliance with law. (APA, 2010, 6.01)

In addition to these, other mental health professions, such as the American Association for Marriage and Family Therapy (AAMFT) and the National Association of Social Workers (NASW), articulate the same ethical requirement for documentation and record keeping.

Our professional organizations have directed the creation and maintenance of clinical records for a long time, but record keeping took on a new dimension with the enactment of HIPAA (1996). The Federal Health Insurance Portability and Accountability Act of 1996, known as HIPAA, was passed to establish a national framework for security standards and protection of confidentiality with regard to health-care data and information. HIPAA also has specific regulations stipulating health professionals' behaviors in terms of documentation. As it states in its Simplification Regulation Text about documentation standards, health professionals "(i) maintain policies and procedures implemented to comply with this subpart in written (which may be electronic) form; and (ii) if an action, activity or assessment is required by this subpart to be documented, maintain a written (which may be electronic) record of the action, activity, or assessment" (Department of Health and Human Services, 2013, Sect. 164.316 b). Furthermore, HIPAA requires that documentation is reviewed periodically and updated as needed and such documentation kept for 6 years from the date of its creation or the date when it last was in effect, whichever is later. In addition to HIPAA, each state also has laws governing health professionals' actions on documentation and record keeping. All practicing counselors need to be aware of and in compliance with the federal and their state guidelines.

As an intern, you may have received ethics training on documentation and record keeping. The purpose of your training and discussing ethics on documentation and recording keeping in your internship class is to help you reduce unethical behaviors and become more aware of ethical conflicts in your work. With that training, you will be able to work through potential conflicts or correct unethical behaviors to reach more morally responsible decisions while you create clinical documentation and maintain records. Exercise 10.1 invites you to do a thorough search on policies and regulations on clinical documentation and record keeping of your internship site and the state where you intend to work after you graduate.

The "What" of Case Documentation

The specific form and details to be included in one's treatment plan and progress notes may vary according to the nature of the work one is doing and the site at which it is being done. However, having said that, there are some general considerations on the what and how of case documentation that cut across these specifics.

EXERCISE 10.1

A Preliminary Search

Directions: In this exercise, you are asked to do a preliminary search on the documentation and record-keeping requirements of your internship site and the laws and regulations of the state where you intend to work after you graduate.

	Internship Site Policies and Requirements	**Your Professional Organization's Standards and Requirements**	**Your State Law**	**Similarities & Differences Among Three**
Documentation	1. 2. 3.	1. 2. 3.	1. 2. 3.	1. 2. 3.
Record Keeping	1. 2. 3.	1. 2. 3.	1. 2. 3.	1. 2. 3.

Treatment Plans

The articulation of a treatment plan is another component of your clinical writing and case documentation. However, this does not happen as frequently as writing your session notes. Institutions and agencies may have different requirements in terms of time and frequency for the development of clinical treatment plans. Some may require the counselor to complete the treatment plan after he or she sees the client two or three times and update it every 3 or 6 months. Others may be more flexible.

It is important for you to inquire about the nature, format, and frequency of developing or adjusting treatment plans at your site. Further, because it is an ethical requirement that we engage our clients in the development of such plans as well as receive their informed consent acknowledging their understanding of what will occur, the development and modification of treatment plans within session can prove useful. Doing the treatment plan during the session may have a few advantages. First, it obviously saves you time. You can finish this piece of paperwork in session instead of out of session. Second, you meet the requirement of the accuracy and timely efficiency of documentation. Finally, it allows for your client's full participation and your ability to check for the reasonableness of the plan as detailed. As with the process of recording session progress notes, engaging in the development and subsequent modification of a treatment plan in session with the client will, with repetition, become a professional habit giving form to your developing professional identity. You are invited to complete Exercise 10.2, My Habit of Clinical Documentation.

EXERCISE 10.2

My Habit of Clinical Documentation

Directions: In this exercise, you are asked to explore your habit of documenting the service you have provided. After you finish it, identify if there is a pattern in your behavior of clinical writing and paperwork completion.

1. The number of clients that I have seen in the past 2 weeks is ________.
2. The number of clients that I have seen a day in the past 2 weeks is __, __, __, __, __.
3. I completed the progress note immediately after the session ________ times.
4. I completed the progress note by the end of the day ______times.
5. I completed the progress note the next day ______ times.
6. I completed the progress note within 2 days ______ times.
7. I completed the progress note within 3 days ______ times.
8. I completed the progress note within 4 days _______ times.
9. I completed the progress note by the end of the week _____ times.
10. I completed the progress note in the following week ______ times.

Progress Notes: A Fundamental and Practical Form of Recording

You may have heard of the 50-minute hour. For many in clinical practice, a session is one that extends for 50 minutes. The value of such timing is that it allows the clinician to take time at the end of a session to reflect on what just occurred and consider the directions to be taken in the next session with that client. It is often during this 10-minute interval that a clinician will record his or her session notes. Session notes can be easy when they are done immediately after each session is over. One can imagine how confusing and burdensome it would be to try to recreate session notes for all clients at the end of a day or, worse yet, a week. Imagine what it would look like if this counselor accumulates his or her unfinished session notes, treatment plans, test interpretation, and so forth for a week. Because of counselors' tendency to value the interaction and the human element in our counseling, it may be tempting to see our note taking as administrative, bothersome, and even unrelated to "real" treatment. Such a perspective toward note taking can be problematic if counselors are not supervised or audited periodically. Case Illustration 10.1 is a real example about how a senior counseling professional managed his clinical writing. Sadly, such behavior may not be that rare.

CASE ILLUSTRATION 10.1

A Real Surprise

Jim is a licensed professional counselor and has practiced for more than 15 years at a state college counseling center. As the only senior staff, Jim supervises two other professional counselors and he reports to the Dean of Students at the college. Once in a while, Jim also acted as supervisor for one or two master's-level interns and provided them weekly supervision. Besides some administrative work, Jim saw four or five clients each day. Jims enjoyed working with his clients and always pleasantly taught the interns in supervision. His colleagues and students loved him in all areas that he did but one—paperwork. The interns and the two counselors he supervised often complained that Jim did not complete their evaluations in a timely manner. Particularly when Jim promised the interns to write them letters of recommendation, he did not do it. Although Jim liked where he was, he was still looking for other places to work because there was no position for him to be promoted to at the college counseling center. Recently, he received a job offer from a state university as director of the counseling center. Because he was leaving, two other counselors would take over all his cases. After the two counselors accessed Jim's clients' files, they were very much surprised to find that he had not done his paperwork—case notes, treatment plans, and so forth—for 2 years.

The importance of accurate, immediate recording is seen in the American Psychological Association (APA, 2007) requirement that its members "make efforts to see that legible and accurate entries are made in client records as soon as is practicable after a service is rendered" (p. 995).

It is important to use this time during your field experience to begin to develop your professional habit of documentation and record keeping. With practice, the creation of meaningful and useful records will become as natural to your practice as the skills of attending and will eventually become part of your professional identity. The development of your habit of recording the service you provide serves to highlight your professionalism and your intention of doing no harm to your clients. Your good habit of documenting the service you provide builds a solid foundation for the high quality of care.

As noted previously, if allowed within your agency, it is useful to schedule your appointments so that you have safeguarded 10 minutes at the end to reflect on the session and make legible and accurate entries of the service provided and perhaps the directions to be taken. If for some reason you can't finish your session notes before your next appointment, you will want to finish your case notes either before your lunch or before you leave the office at the end of the day. Further, if there is a time when your client fails to attend a session, we suggest that you use that time to review your notes and clarify and expand as needed. Although you may find that various pressures make it difficult to develop your notes immediately following the end of a session, it is essential that you commit to not leaving the process of recording session notes until the next day.

Perhaps this directive "not to wait until tomorrow" appears reactive, but there are a few issues of concern that exist if you leave your session notes for the next day. First, we all know how memory decays as time moves on. Your ability to recall what happened in sessions can be restricted the next day. Second, after you go home, anything can happen. If something happens at home, you may not be able to come to work, or the event(s) at home can interrupt your ability to recall what happened in your sessions. Third, when you see multiple clients, sometimes the clients and client issues can be similar, which may confuse you while you recall during the next day. Both the second and third situations can make your accuracy of documentation questionable.

Recommendations for Case Notes Writing and Record Keeping

We are very positive that you will receive quality training at your internship site and from your faculty supervisor about documentation and record keeping. We also believe both your site supervisor and faculty supervisor are experienced in clinical practice and will be able to provide you with tips and recommendations for case notes writing and knowledge about record keeping based on their clinical experiences. In addition to those resources, we also offer you some suggestions on case notes writing gained from our professional practice. We hope you will find these useful as you engage in your field work and even in your future practice.

1. Write your case notes in a timely fashion.

Case notes are the key tracking records that provide (a) evidence of your client's treatment, progress, or lack of progress; (b) evidence of your decisions and actions taken during treatment; (c) a rationale and defense for you should the case become a legal one; and (d) evidence that you follow the best practice (Hodges, 2011). The timing of taking case notes has both ethical and legal implications, and events recorded immediately reflect more accuracy than events recorded later on. Therefore, you want to develop a good habit of writing your case notes immediately after the session or as soon as possible.

2. Include essential elements in your case notes.

The content of case notes is crucial because it reflects the treatment of standard care, and there is the potential that the case notes may be reviewed by professionals from a variety of fields and your clients. How much to include in your case notes is a decision you need to make based on whether the information is a necessary part of the session you have conducted. Table 10.2 contains some examples of essential elements that should be included in case notes. We urge you to review them and keep them in mind while writing your case notes.

Table 10.2 Examples of Essential Elements That Should Be Included in Counseling Case Notes

- Times that a counseling session starts and stops
- Treatment modalities
- Progress or lack of progress
- Treatment plan made or modified
- Results of clinical tests
- Diagnosis or symptoms
- Functional status
- Danger to self/others
- Child abuse or elder abuse involved
- Actions taken on emergencies
- Consultation or teamwork with other health professionals
- Compliance or lack of compliance from clients
- Recommendations made
- Issues related to fees
- Issues related to informed consent
- Treatment compliance or lack of compliance
- Issues related to termination
- Referral made

3. Use concise language and accurate terminology.

Clarity is key for any documentation, and counseling case notes are not an exception. When writing case notes, counselors need to make good choices of words that are specific, explicit, clear-cut, and precise, because "clear, specific, unambiguous, and precise wording enhances the delivery of services" (Reamer, 2005, p. 330). While taking case notes, you need to do your best to limit words that are vague such as "*something, someone, someplace, nice, soon, late, terrible, miserable, interesting, simple, furniture*" and so forth. For example, instead of saying that *client was late for today's session,* you may want to make your statement precise, such as *client arrived 20 minutes after the originally scheduled time for today's session.* Another example can be instead of saying *client looked tired in today's session,* you may want to state your observation as *client yawned with watery eyes about every half-minute, and each time after he yawned, he said, "I'm so sorry and this is rude."* When some clients are not as cooperative as you expect, avoid saying *client was very resistant* to describe the client's behavior while you take your case notes. You may want to be specific in describing his or her behavior, for example, *Client neither responded directly to almost all the questions asked, nor did the homework assignments as agreed in the previous session.*

4. Keep in mind an audience while documenting.

While writing your case notes, keep in mind who, besides yourself, may be reviewing these notes. Generally speaking, people who possibly read your case notes can be counselors, other health professionals (e.g., nurses, doctors, and psychiatrists), lawyers, judges, auditors, clients, and clients' parents. No matter who is reading your case notes, the person expects the information to be arranged in a consistent and systematic manner. If you use a certain case notes format, strictly follow that format. For example, if you use SOAP format (see the following section on case notes format), you should always follow the format to arrange your case notes in the order of subjective, objective, assessment, and plan. When you write the subjective part, you describe in a consistent manner your client's feelings, concerns, plans, goals, thoughts, and so forth. While writing the objective part, you arrange your observation in the order of appearance, affect, behavior, strengths, weaknesses, and so forth (see Table 10.3).

Because your case notes might be read by other health professionals and professionals from other disciplines, avoid including political, religious, and racial views, as well as avoid using defamatory language about other counselors or health professionals (Cameron & turtle-song, 2002); rather, write your case notes in a constructive, simple, and objective fashion (Baird, 2002).

5. Always ask when you feel uncertain.

The golden rule is, always ask when you feel uncertain. Agencies, institutions, and schools oftentimes cover general situations in their policies and regulations. As an intern, it is common that you may have questions regarding areas and situations that are not specified in the policies of your internship site. Your site supervisor and senior counselors are your resources and assets for things you are unsure about.

The "How," or Format, of Case Documentation

As we have discussed earlier in this chapter, the purpose of documentation is to give full care to clients, to communicate with other health professionals, to meet professional standards, and to protect clients and counselors themselves legally. Progress notes are an essential portion of clinical documentation, which demonstrate the counselor's day-to-day care for his or her clients. Writing progress notes in a consistent manner in terms of format and content can be crucial in this process of care. As you may know, form always follows the content. So does the form of counseling session notes. Counseling or psychotherapy session note form is designed for the counselor to focus on certain aspects of the counseling process and "to facilitate the formulation of inferences and hypotheses on the basis of clinical data" (Presser & Pfost, 1985, p. 11).

Although there are many systems or methods for taking and recording case notes (e.g., Individual Educational Programs [IEP] and Functional Outcomes Reporting [FOR]), we are going to introduce you to four standard formats of counseling progress notes, (a) SOAP, (b) IPSN, (c) DART, and (d) DAP, for your consideration while you practice at your internship site. You may want to check with your internship site supervisor about the internship site's guidelines regarding record keeping and make sure that you follow those guidelines. If your internship site does not have a requirement for its health professionals to use a specific notes format, you may consider one of these formats based on your personal preference.

SOAP Notes

The first format to be discussed, SOAP notes, is probably the most commonly used standard format across all health professions. SOAP notes originated in the medical field and are part of the problem-oriented medical records (POMR), which are commonly used by medical and other health professionals. SOAP is an acronym that stands for Subjective, Objective, Assessment, and Plan, a system created by Lawrence L. Weed (1964). The counselor's progress notes are structured within the framework of these four components, that is to say, after your individual session is over, you as counselor may follow this structure to write your case notes if you choose to use this case notes system. An excellent review of the use of SOAP notes was written by Susan Cameron and imani turtle-song (2002), and their review serves as the basis for the discussion that follows.

Subjective

In the SOAP notes system, *subjective* means the information from the client and the client's family members, friends, teachers, or anyone who provides information about the client and the client's issues. More specifically, the information may include the client's thoughts, feelings, behaviors, or points of view that negatively or positively affect the client's significant relationships.

Objective

The word *objective* in the SOAP notes system means facts or factual information. This information comes from the observations of the counselor or others. The information in this section may contain the client's appearance, smell, affect, behaviors, thought processing, relationship with the counselor, strengths, weaknesses, response to treatment, compliance with medication, results of physical tests, or observations from other health professionals. The counselor's objective observations must be evidence based instead of personal opinions, judgments, labels, or values-laden language. The wording must be precise and descriptive. Words such as "appear" or "seem" should not be used. If they are used, the counselor needs to provide justification with observational evidence.

Although it may appear useful to include client quotations as part of the "objective" data, such inclusion should be done with caution. As a general rule, the inclusion of client quotes should be kept to a minimum. According to Cameron and turtle-song (2002), the inclusion of too many quotes may make it difficult for clinicians to view the client themes and track the therapeutic intervention effectiveness. Moreover, the counselor also needs to be mindful about the appropriateness of the content while writing his or her progress notes. Because your progress notes are read by other professionals, you may not want to repeat the client's inflammatory statements and you may want to omit information about insidious family life, political, religious, and racial views unless these are the focus of therapy, because this information can be interpreted negatively about the client and his or her behaviors. Ultimately, it may risk the client's care from other health professionals. Client quotations or identification of key words or phrases are used to highlight, emphasize, or provide additional support to a notation. This may be particularly useful when documenting a client's aggressive behaviors and abusive languages, which might suggest potential threat toward the counselor. An additional area in which the use of direct quotation may be of value is when noting client's confusion of time, space, or people.

Assessment

The assessment section is where the counselor summarizes and synthesizes the subjective and objective data. This section also reflects the counselor's clinical impressions concerning the client's presenting issue or issues. Generally the assessment is stated in the form of diagnosis based on DSM-V (American Psychiatric Association, 2013), which is included each time the counselor writes his or her case notes. The authors indicated that some counselors may resist a DSM diagnosis, but third party payers and accrediting bodies have such expectation.

Two major points need to be kept in mind when the counselor writes the assessment section. One is that the assessment must be based on the data collected in the subjective and the objective section. When a diagnosis is made and the counselor is not confident about the diagnosis, insufficient data may have been collected. In this situation, the counselor needs to consult a senior colleague. The other point is the counselor's clinical impression, which is made in the progress notes when there is lack of sufficient data in the subjective and the objective sections to support a particular diagnosis. In such a case, the counselor needs to summarize the existing information in the subjective and the objective sections and make a clear conclusion for future counselors or health professionals to follow his or her reasoning in order to reach a final diagnosis.

Plan

The plan section of the SOAP notes system covers the parameters of counseling interventions that have been used. Specifically, this section includes the action plan as well as the prognosis. In the action plan, the counselor writes about the date of the appointment for the upcoming counseling session, intervention(s) used during the complete session, homework or assignment, treatment progress, consultation, and treatment direction for the upcoming session. The client's prognosis or progress assessment included in this section is a forecast for future gains given what the client has been treated with.

As Cameron and turtle-song (2002) state in their article, the plan brings the SOAP notes and treatment direction full circle. As counselor, you document not only all the interventions used in the session that you have just completed with the client but also possible interventions that may be used by other counselors or health professionals. In addition, you use words such as *poor, guarded, fair, good,* or *excellent* to make the progressive assessment with supportive explanations.

Table 10.3 provides a summary of SOAP definitions and examples as provided by Cameron and turtle-song (2002). Table 10.4 presents guidelines for the creation of progress notes. Finally, we invite you to practice using SOAP notes (see Exercise 10.3).

Table 10.3 A Summarization of SOAP Definitions and Examples

Section	*Definitions*	*Examples*
Subjective (S)	What the client tells you What pertinent others tell you about the client Basically, how the client experiences the world	Client's feelings, concerns, plans, goals, and thoughts Intensity of problems and impact on relationships Pertinent comments by family, case managers, behavioral therapists, etc. Client's orientation to time, place, and person Client's verbalized changes toward helping
Objective (O)	Factual What the counselor personally observes/ witnesses Quantifiable: what was seen, counted, smelled, heard, or measured Outside written materials received	The client's general appearance, affect, behavior Nature of the helping relationship Client's demonstrated strengths and weaknesses Test results, materials from other agencies, etc., are to be noted and attached
Assessment (A)	Summarizes the counselor's clinical thinking A synthesis and analysis of the subjective and objective portion of the notes	For counselor: Include clinical diagnosis and clinical impressions (if any) For care providers: How would you label the client's behavior and the reasons (if any) for this behavior?
Plan (P)	Describes the parameters of treatment Consists of an action plan and prognosis	Action plan: Include interventions used, treatment progress, and direction Counselors should include the date of next appointment Prognosis: Include the anticipated gains from the interventions

Source: Reprinted from "Learning to Write Case Notes Using the SOAP Format" by S. Cameron and i. turtle-song, 2002, *Journal of Counseling & Development, 80,* p. 290. Reprinted with permission.

Table 10.4 Guidelines for Subjective, Objective, Assessment, Plan (SOAP) Noting

Do	*Avoid*
Be brief and concise. Keep quotes to a minimum. Use an active voice.	Avoid using names of other clients, family members, or others named by client. Avoid terms like seems, appears.

Do	*Avoid*
Use precise and descriptive terms. Record immediately after each session. Start each new entry with date and time of session. Write legibly and neatly. Use proper spelling, grammar, and punctuation. Document all contacts or attempted contacts. Use only black ink if notes are handwritten. Sign-off using legal signature, plus your title.	Do not use terminology unless trained to do so. Do not erase, obliterate, use correction fluid, or in any way attempt to obscure mistakes. Do not leave blank spaces between entries. Do not try to squeeze additional commentary between lines or in margins.

Source: Reprinted from "Learning to Write Case Notes Using the SOAP Format" by S. Cameron and i. turtle-song, 2002, *Journal of Counseling & Development, 80,* p. 291. Reprinted with permission.

EXERCISE 10.3

Session Notes (SOAP Notes)

Directions: This exercise offers you an opportunity to practice the SOAP notes format. You are asked to write up a session of one of your cases. After you complete your notes, check to see if you have followed the guidelines offered by Cameron and turtle-song. Session Notes (SOAP Notes)

Counselor: ______________ Session Date: ___________ Time: ___to_____

Client(s) Name: ____________________________ Session #: ______

****

Client Description:

Subjective Complaint:

Objective Findings:

Assessment of Progress:

Plans for Next Session:

Needs for Supervision:

Counselor Signs:

By now, you may see some advantages of the SOAP notes system, for example, its well-designed structure, consistency across all your documentation, care with a problem focus, a nature of combination of subjective and objective perspectives from both the counselor and the client with supporting evidence, easy-to-retrieve information, and so forth. However, it also has its disadvantages. These disadvantages include but are not limited to (a) it has a medical background with terminology ambiguity and rigid guidelines (Baird, 2008); (b) the problem focus may reduce the probability of the client's problems being resolved because in many situations clients have no control over the problems they face in their lives; and (c) it categorizes the client with a diagnosis label(s), which is contradictory to the belief of many counselors. Given these advantages and disadvantages, we suggest you choose your progress notes system based on your counseling theoretical orientation and the requirements of your state laws or third party payers if the organization, agency, or school you work for does not require you to follow a specific format.

A number of other systems, which specifically address the needs of counselors and therapists, have been developed, including the Individual Psychotherapy Session Note format (IPSN), described below.

Individual Psychotherapy Session Note (IPSN)

IPSN, or the individual psychotherapy session notes format, was developed by Nan R. Presser and Karen S. Pfost (1985). As these authors described in their article, this format of session notes was especially useful for counseling and counseling psychology novices. Presser and Pfost indicated that they developed this session notes format based on three principles: (a) encouraging counselor attendance to several specific, relevant aspects of the therapeutic process; (b) being atheoretical so it is useful for counselors adhering to most theoretical orientations; and (c) being simple, not time consuming, and user friendly.

IPSN's format includes eight sections: brief summary of session, client, therapist, therapist-client interaction, problem addressed, progress made, plans, and other. The first section includes a narrative overview of the session with a sequential account of major events within the session. In the second section, the counselor objectively records the client's verbal and nonverbal behavior, including the counselor's hypotheses and inferences, with emphasis on the speculative nature of such inferences and desirability of testing of hypotheses later. The third section consists of the counselor's overview of his or her own behavior. This information helps the counselor both to examine and to increase awareness of his or her own behavior with a purpose of altering the counselor's perspective so he or she can be subjective and objective. The information in this section can also be used to evaluate the consistency of the counselor's behavior, correspondence to a theoretical stance, and evolution of the counselor's own style. The fourth section is about the interaction between the counselor and the client. The focus of this section is on the interpersonal dynamics, not on the individuals. The information in this section can be used to evaluate the therapeutic relationship. The fifth section is the place where the problems are addressed. The problems are the ones that are addressed within the session. In the sixth section, the counselor will record the assessment of the progress that the client has made. This assessment also provides legitimacy for the continuation of the therapy and a need for movement within therapy. The seventh section is about the plans, which include information about the transition from the current session to the future ones. In this section, the counselor may plan therapeutic alternatives and conceptualize issues that the client will work on in the subsequent sessions. The last section includes information that may not logically belong in any of the previous session, such as test data or relevant correspondence. Table 10.5 includes a sample of this format of progress notes as developed by Presser and Pfost.

Table 10.5 Individual Psychotherapy Session Notes (IPSN)

I. BRIEF SUMMARY OF SESSION:

Pt. had a recent argument with her parents regarding lack of progress in finding another job led into discussion of pervasive feelings of inadequacy and hopelessness. She feels incapable of attaining the standards which her parents have set for her, but still she refuses to acknowledge any anger toward them. She appears more depressed and reports increased incidence of self-destructive behaviors. Does not appear to be suicidal at this time.

THERAPIST'S OBSERVATIONS OF:	THERAPIST'S INTERPRETATIONS AND HYPOTHESES:
II. CLIENT: At the beginning of session, pt. talked slowly and softly with infrequent pauses; slumped in chair; rarely made eye contact. Later, many self-deprecating statements as she discussed parents' expectations. Raised voice when discussing these, but denied anger. Reported drinking and contact with ex-boyfriend. Hinted re suicide, but denied intent.	Appears moderately depressed; turning anger inward? May be exacerbated by drinking. Seems threatened by suggestion that she might feel angry toward parents. Overidealization of them is impediment. Presents self as victim and seems stuck in this role; assumes it with ex-boyfriend and parents. Could hints about suicide and drinking be to elicit rescuing by therapist?
III. THERAPIST: Early in session felt tired, looked at watch frequently. Interventions primarily reflective and clarifying. Tone of voice gentle, soothing.	Initially impatient and bored. Am I becoming tired of her helplessness? Approach is relatively client-centered, with only mild confrontations. Is this avoidance of confrontation my issue (helpless behavior annoys me) or is it due to wanting to avoid recapitualization of victimization?

(Continued)

Table 10.5 (Continued)

IV. THERAPIST-CLIENT INTERACTION: When pt. appears helpless or distressed, therapist is still responding supportively rather than confronting. Pt. asked if therapist was disappointed in her lack of progress and reported surprise at the negative reply; this was discussed vis-a-vis her father.	Does pt. typically elicit rescuing, or at times the opposite (frustration and alienating others with her helplessness)? Relationship with therapist is beginning to parallel relationship with father, particularly re projection of negative evaluation onto therapist and expectation of criticism.
V. PROBLEMS ADDRESSED: 1. Pt.'s feelings of unworthiness and despair re attaining the standards which she has injected. 2. Relationship with parents. 3. Expectations of negative evaluations.	VI. PROGRESS MADE: Displays more insight into the connection between internalized standards and her depression. Beginning to express some of the anger that she has heretofore turned inward. Her expectation that therapist would also judge her negatively was examined. Therapeutic alliance solidified by discussion of her reaction to therapist.
VII. PLANS: In supervision, bring up my reaction to her helplessness and consider reacting differently (first explore if this is my issue and, if not, how best to respond to her). Look for more signs of anger and point these out as they occur. Explore idealization of parents. Continue to monitor suicidal ideation.	VIII. OTHER: Will soon need to discuss my absence due to vacation.

Source: Reprinted from "A Format for Individual Psychotherapy Session Notes" by N. R. Presser and K. S. Pfost, 1985, *Professional Psychology: Research and Practice 16*(1), pp. 13–14. Reprinted with permission.

While being particularly useful for novice counselors, IPSN has a number of other advantages. These advantages include (a) clear distinction among all aspects of each counseling session, (b) an atheoretical nature, (c) a focus on interaction or dynamics between counselor and client, (d) minimization of diagnosis, (e) inclusion of counselor behaviors, and (f) a process orientation. However, there are major disadvantages with IPSN. One is that the format seems lengthy (although the authors claimed it is not time consuming), and the counselor may not be able to complete it within 10 minutes before he or she starts the next session. When a counselor has a full schedule for the day, accumulation of unfinished session notes can be cumbersome. The other disadvantage is that logging counselor behaviors such as being tired or not being able to concentrate in session in the client's permanent file may not be desirable. Counselors may be concerned that in any legal action, such notes may suggest that they were ill-prepared or in some way unable to provide the best care. Perhaps the best way to assess any system is to employ it. As such, you are invited to complete Exercise 10.4, which offers you an opportunity to use IPSN to write one of your cases.

EXERCISE 10.4

Session Notes (IPSN notes)

Directions: This exercise offers you an opportunity to practice the IPSN format. You are asked to write up a session of one of your cases with IPSN format. After you complete your notes, check to see if you have followed the guidelines offered by Presser and Pfost.

Counselor: _______________ Session Date: ___________ Time: ___to_____

Client(s) Name: ____________________________ Session #: ______

****

Brief Summary of Session:

Client:

Therapist:

Therapist-Client Interaction:

Problems Addressed:

Progress Made:

Plans:

Others:

Counselor Sign:

Data, Assessment, and Plan (DAP)

DAP is another session notes format commonly used by health professionals at agencies and institutions. DAP, which is the acronym for Data, Assessment, and Plan (or sometimes Description, Analysis, and Plan) has been found to be useful for mental health providers.

Data (Description)

Data (or Description) refers to the section in which factual information or data collected by the counselor during the session is presented. This factual information or data contains what the client and the counselor said on specific topics about the client's concerns or issues. The descriptions included may target the client's emotions, thoughts expressed, behaviors, experiences or observations, points of view, and reactions to any treatment, as well as the counselor's perception and impression of what happened in the session. In other words, this section includes both objective findings and subjective impressions. The subjective data is the information (verbal or nonverbal) provided by the client, whereas the objective data is the information about the client observed by the counselor during the session, which may include the client's appearance, affect, mood, speech, attitude, behaviors, or reaction to homework or activities. This section may further comprise the information about the general content and process of the session, which include interventions (goals and objectives worked on), education, review of homework if there is any, or consultation.

Assessment (Analysis)

In the Assessment (Analysis) section, the counselor records his or her understanding of the client's problem(s) along with the hypotheses that the counselor has developed. Information from initial screening, test results, and any other forms of assessments are included in this section. Also included within this section would be the client's current response to the treatment plan, the client's progress or stage of change, and how this particular session relates to the overall treatment.

Plan

The final section is the Plan. In this section, the counselor documents any need for revision of the treatment plan that may be necessary as a result of the client's response to the initial plan. The counselor would likely make adjustment to the established goals and objectives and/or the strategies and techniques to be used. Additional information included in this section would be a recording of the goals and objectives that were addressed in the session, along with any action steps that will be taken following the session. Finally, the counselor would list the date of the next session and the client's commitment to any homework assignment or action step to take, as well as any referral made during the session. Again, as a way of helping you get a "feel" for this system, we invite you to engage in Exercise 10.5, which provides a demonstration of DAP session notes.

EXERCISE 10.5

DAP Session Notes

Directions: For this exercise, you are asked to write up the case notes for one of your cases with DAP session notes format. You may use the following questions as a guideline for your session documentation.

Data:

What are your client's thoughts, observations, experiences, or direct quotes?

What have you observed during the session about the client's mood, feelings, appearance, attitude, behaviors, and reaction to homework or activities?

What interventions have you used and what goals and objectives have you worked on?

Have you reviewed homework or consulted anyone?

Assessment:

What are your hypotheses?

What is your understanding of the client's presenting issue(s)?

What are the results of the assessment (e.g., testing results), if there are any?

What are your client's responses to the current treatment plan?

Plan:

What goals and objectives have been addressed during this session?

What adjustment is needed based on your client's reaction to the treatment plan?

What are you going to do with the client in the coming session?

What is the date of this client's next session?

Counselor: ________________ Session Date: ____________ Time: ___to_____

Client(s) Name: ______________________________ Session #: ______

****

Data (Description):

Assessment (Analysis):

Plan:

Counselor signs:

Description, Assessment, Response, and Treatment Plan (DART)

DART is a progress notes system created for mental health professionals by Brian N. Baird (2002). The author created the DART system because he felt that other systems, specifically SOAP, with its use of medical terminologies, were problematic for those working in psychological settings.

Description

The first section of this system is a detailing of the client and client situation. To develop a good description, the clinician should answer the four "W" questions: when, where, who, and what. The question of when refers to the date and time that the event occurred; where indicates the location of the event; who is the person who played a significant role in or observed the event; and the what is the event that was observed. The sequence of the clinician's progress notes would be the presentation of time, location, people, and event or incident. Among the four Ws, the event or incident is the most flexible part, which means "the more significant the event, the more space will be dedicated to the corresponding progress notes" (Baird, 2002, p. 115).

Assessment

Assessment is the section in which you as the clinician need to answer the "why" question and document what you have observed and the meaning you have subscribed to those observations. Although it is not necessary to give elaborate explanations or offer profound insights about the event, the clinician needs to provide his or her understanding of the client's response (e.g., client's behaviors and emotions) to the event. Any client behavior or response that does not immediately seem interpretable should also be documented for later consideration or in the event the counselor seeks to consult about the case. In this section, the clinician uses his or her knowledge of the client to develop hypotheses about the events and the best way to assist the client in addressing these events.

Response

In the Response section, clinicians record how they respond to what they have observed based on their understanding or assessment of what they have observed. In other words, this is what the clinician did when he or she heard what the client did and said. As Baird suggests, "In this process, the clinician is recording not only the action taken but the reasons for taking or not taking an action" (pp. 115–116). It is suggested (Baird, 2002) that the clinician document accurately, including important details, in a way that supports a well-founded and rational treatment approach and counseling decisions. In this section, include data such as descriptions of rationale for referral; types of test or measures employed and why; consultations and their results; and, in terms of clients who present at risk, specific measures taken to ensure the safety of all. The rationale for the clinician's responses is important to have articulated, especially in the event of future legal action where the clinical judgment may be under question.

Treatment Plan

The final section includes an articulation of the treatment plan. This may be as specific as stating when the next follow-up session will be along with the "homework" assigned to the client (e.g., the clinician invites the client to bring artwork to the next session for discussion). The description of the plan moving forward might also include the rationale for including other service providers or even preparing the client for referral to another clinician. In all cases, the "what" needs to be described, as does the rationale behind the counselor's decisions. Case Illustration 10.2, Jeff Gates, is a demonstration of the DART notes system.

CASE ILLUSTRATION 10.2

Jeff Gates

D (description): 10 a.m. to 10:50 a.m., Monday, 8/11/2014; Individual Therapy: Jeff came to session on time and began speaking about his insomnia, caused by the conflict between him and his wife. According to Jeff, he felt very bad on the weekend and last night in particular. He remarked that he kept thinking about why his wife was doing this to him—allowing her three adult children to ruin their life and his life. Jeff stated that all his wife's three adult children don't have jobs and are dependent on his wife and him. "We not only give them money but feed them as well; the more I was thinking about it, the angrier I became," said Jeff. Client indicated that while he was angry, he had butterflies in his stomach and then felt terrible and could not fall asleep. He added that he did not have any other problems with his wife but the problem of her children, whom she could not let go. When asked about other areas of life, Jeff reported he had a hard time concentrating on his work, had less appetite than before, and did not want to see anybody but drank by himself.

A (assessment): Client appears to have mild depression due to conflict between him and his wife over her adult children. Symptoms of depression include insomnia, reduced appetite, problems with concentration at work, and diminished interest in social life. Though client reports no suicidal or homicidal thoughts, he has been using alcohol to cope with his frustration and depression.

R (response): During the session, client was asked to verbalize his anger and his depressed mood. He was further helped to become aware of the relationship between these two feelings, which in turn affected his thoughts and behaviors, his drinking behavior in particular. Through sharing his feelings, Jeff gained some insights on how the value differences between him and his wife on raising children have caused him to feel angry and depressed.

T (treatment): Homework of listing pros and cons of client's marriage was assigned. BDI and AUDIT will be used to make a further assessment on client's depression and alcohol consumption in the session on Monday, 8/18/2014, which has been scheduled with client.

Signed, Gordon Wood, M.A., Date, 8/11/2014

Concluding Thoughts

We hope, as you read through the chapter, you were able to see and embrace both the need and the very practical value of good documentation and clinical records. Documentation is more than an administrative function. Record keeping and documentation safeguard ethical and legal practice and, perhaps most important, are useful in the provision of best practice standard of care.

It is important to become familiar with the various systems of documentation while familiarizing yourself with the system employed at your field setting. In this chapter, we have introduced four formats of progress notes systems for your consideration. Each format has its advantages and disadvantages. You may want to try all of them to see which one fits your style and your work environment. Of course, you may have no choice if you are required to use a certain format by your agency, institution, or school. No matter which system you use, it is important to be clear and legible and avoid spelling and grammatical errors. Not only do these errors detract from the validity of the session notes, but present a less-than-professional image of the clinician. To avoid these problems, you want to develop a good habit of notes taking from the very beginning of your practice.

KEYSTONES

- The purposes of clinical documentation and record keeping are to ensure standard of care, enable effective communication between health professionals, and provide a desirable defense for litigation.
- The ethical practice of documentation and record keeping facilitates the counselor's clinical choices and reflects the dignity and integrity of the counseling profession.
- All mental health professions have developed ethical guidelines for their members to follow in the aspect of clinical documentation and record keeping.
- HIPAA regulations, as well as any other state, local, or organizational requirements, need to be considered when establishing a system of record keeping and maintenance.
- Most case notes formats share more commonalities than differences, and counselors may choose the one that best fits their style and organizational needs.

ADDITIONAL RESOURCES

Web Based

Documentation Tips and Guidelines: http://www.school-counseling-zone.com/documentation.html
Healthcare Providers Service Organization (HPSO): http://www.hpso.com/resources/article/233.jsp

Print Based

Mitchell, R. W. (2007). *Documentation in counseling records: An overview of ethical, legal, and clinical issues* (3rd ed.). Alexandria, VA: American Counseling Association.

Wheeler, A., & Bertram, B. (2012). *The counselor and the law: A guide to legal and ethical practice* (6th ed.). Alexandria, VA: American Counseling Association.

Zukerman, E. L. (2010). *The clinician's thesaurus: The guide to conducting interviews and writing psychological reports* (7th ed.). New York, NY: Guilford.

REFERENCES

American Counseling Association. (2014). *ACA code of ethics.* Alexandria, VA: Author.

American Psychiatric Association. (2013). *Diagnostic and statistical manual of mental disorders, fifth edition (DSM-5).* Washington, DC: American Psychiatric Association.

American Psychological Association. (2007). Record keeping guidelines. *American Psychologist, 62,* 993–1004.

American Psychological Association. (2010). *Ethical principles of psychologists and code of conduct.* Retrieved from http://www.apa.org/ethics/code/principles.pdf

American School Counseling Association. (2010). Ethical standards for school counselors. Retrieved from http://www.schoolcounselor.org/asca/media/asca/Resource%20Center/Legal%20and%20Ethical%20Issues/Sample%20Documents/EthicalStandards2010.pdf

Baird, B. N. (2002). *The internship, practicum, and field placement handbook: A guide for helping professions* (3rd ed.). Upper Saddle River, NJ: Pearson.

Baird, B. N. (2008). *The internship, practicum, and field placement handbook: A guide for helping professions* (5th ed.). Upper Saddle River, NJ: Pearson.

Cameron, S., & turtle-song, i. (2002). Learning to write case notes using the SOAP format. *Journal of Counseling & Development, 80,* 286–292.

Department of Health & Human Services, USA. (2013). *HIPAA administrative simplification: Regulation text* (§ 164.316, Policies and procedures and documentation requirements).

Hodges, S. (2011). *The counseling practicum and internship manual: A resource for counseling graduate students.* New York, NY: Springer.

Mitchell, R. W. (2007). *Documentation in counseling records: An overview of ethical, legal, and clinical issues* (3rd ed.). Alexandria, VA: American Counseling Association.

Presser, N. R., & Pfost, K. S. (1985). A format for individual psychotherapy session notes. *Professional Psychology: Research and Practice, 16*(1), 11–16.

Reamer, F. G. (2005). Documentation in social work: Evolving ethical and risk-management standards. *Social Work, 50*(4), 325–334.

Sanders, R. K. (2006). Serving with care: Ethical issues to consider when faced with high risk situations. *Journal of Psychology & Christianity, 25*(1), 63–67.

Slovenko, R. (2006). Patient and non-patient spouse lawsuits for undue familiarity. *The Journal of Psychiatry & Law, 34,* 567–578.

Weed, L. L. (1964). Medical records, patient care, and medical education. *Irish Journal of Medical Science, 39*(6), 271–282.

11

Termination and Closure

Everything has to come to an end, sometime.

L. Frank Baum

The quote by L. Frank Baum certainly has universal application, and it is clearly true when applied to the counseling relationship. If we consider counseling termination as a process, then its beginning would breed the birth of its termination. From a developmental perspective, termination in counseling is the counselor's attempt to help the client extend what has happened in counseling or internalize the outcome of therapy (Quintana, 1993). Although termination causes the client loss of contact, it may help the client gain independence. Moreover, it becomes a new beginning for both the client and the counselor. In fact, termination in a therapeutic relationship is more than an act (Pearson, 1998). With the internalized outcome of counseling, the client will be able to function independently and complete all his or her daily tasks without therapy.

Termination is an important component in the counseling process, and the issues of termination for all parties involved must be addressed adequately and appropriately. These issues are essential to the client, the counselor, and the incoming counselor. These issues may include but are not limited to ethical/legal ramifications; assessment of goal completion; learning transferring; and closure of the therapeutic relationship, which may cause disturbance of emotion in both the client and the counselor. Termination is an integral part of the counseling process and can make significant contribution to the client's overall success in treatment when handled appropriately (Barnett, MacGlashan, & Clarke, 2000).

In addition to terminating therapeutic relationships with clients, interns also need to terminate their relationships with their supervisors and other counseling staff. "Just as it is important at termination to consider the progress a client has made, a comparable process is equally important to the work of concluding supervision" (Baird, 2002,

p. 168). Moreover, many interns establish not only professional relationships but also personal relationships at their internship sites. Terminating these relationships at the end of the internship can be beneficial for the intern, the supervisor, and counseling staff at both professional and personal levels. As a result, formally terminating the relationship with the supervisor and the counseling staff will help the intern grow as a mature professional.

In this chapter, we will discuss counseling termination and issues involved in its process from a variety of aspects. So, after completing this chapter, readers will be able to

- describe what is termination and abandonment,
- articulate the essence of professional ethics concerning counseling termination,
- describe the specifics in the process of counseling termination,
- explain the common issues involved in termination,
- describe the crucial steps taken to achieve successful termination, and
- depict the essentials of terminating relationships with their supervisors and other counseling staff.

Terminating the Counseling Relationship

Counseling Termination Defined

"Counseling is a professional relationship that empowers diverse individuals, families, and groups to accomplish mental health, wellness, education, and career goals" (ACA, 2010). When clients reach their goals, the professional relationship reaches its end and termination becomes necessary and an intentional process. Therefore, termination is defined as "an intentional process that occurs over time when a client has achieved most of the goals of treatment, and/or when psychotherapy must end for other reasons" (Vasquez, Bingham, & Barnett, 2008, p. 653). Termination also means "the ethically and clinically appropriate process by which a professional relationship is ended" (Younggren & Gottlieb, 2008, p. 500), whereas abandonment means the failure of a counselor to take the clinically indicated and ethically appropriate steps to terminate a counseling relationship (Younggren & Gottlieb, 2008). We believe termination is a therapeutic process in which the counselor ends the counseling relationship ethically and professionally as clinically indicated appropriate.

An End That Starts at the Beginning

It may seem strange to suggest that it is at the beginning of the engagement of a counseling relationship that the process of termination or ending is set into action. But think about it. We enter our relationship with clients with a clear intention of moving them from their current state to a state that is more desired. Our intent is to employ the process of counseling in a way that facilitates the client's growth so that he or she can move beyond the counseling relationship. Simply put, we engage at the beginning with our eye toward the end.

It is not possible to talk about termination without knowing the beginning of a counseling relationship, because if there is no beginning there is no end. The beginning and the end of the counseling relationship is a coin of two sides; one exists in the other. As counselors, we all have a clinical responsibility to clarify these two major boundaries within the professional counseling relationship (Vasquez et al., 2008).

Because counseling is a relationship that occurs between a counselor and a client, as mentioned above, it is necessary to understand the defining point of its beginning before terminating it. Questions regarding a counseling relationship may involve who initiates the relationship, who accepts or rejects the relationship, and when it happens. The majority of us may agree that most counseling relationships are initiated by clients, and the counselor either accepts or rejects the relationships. Table 11.1 includes some examples of common engagement between a counselor and a client that imply the beginning of the professional relationship.

Once the counseling relationship is established, the counselor then has both ethical and legal responsibilities for and to the client.

The Ethics of Termination

Successful termination is essential to effective and ethical counseling. Termination is part of the growth-filled process of counseling and thus ethically cannot occur without client notification and engagement. Many counselors may think that termination occurs when a client has achieved his or her goals in a counseling relationship or when

Table 11.1 Times When Therapist-Client Relationship Begins

Online consultation or treatment
Giving advice to prospective patients, friends, and neighbors
Making psychological interpretations during an independent evaluation
Providing advice during an evaluation for a third party (e.g., pre-employment, medical-legal, workers' compensation, etc.)
One's role as a supervisor
Having a lengthy telephone conversation with a prospective client
Correspondence by mail, email, texting that includes advice/treatment
Giving a prospective client an appointment
Telling a walk-in prospective patient that he or she will be seen
Acting as a substitute therapist
Providing treatment during an evaluation

Source: Deardorff, William W. Difficult Therapy Termination Issues [Ethics Risk Management]

a client does not want therapy anymore for whatever reason. However, termination can happen at any time and any point of a counseling relationship.

The American Counseling Association's *Code of Ethics* (2014) highlights elements that contribute to ethical termination, including (a) competence within termination and referral, (b) values within termination and referral, (c) appropriate termination, and (d) appropriate transfer of services.

Competence

The first condition talks about counselor competence. When a counselor does not possess the expertise for the assistance that a client requests, the counselor avoids continuing the counseling relationship; instead, he or she terminates the counseling relationship by referring the client to appropriate services. Such termination can occur at the very beginning or later in the counseling relationship. For example, the client makes the request of assistance on an eating disorder via a phone call or e-mail but you as counselor have no training in this area, or the client comes in to work on issues in his or her marital relationship and suddenly raises his or her issue of substance addiction but you as counselor have no knowledge or experience in treating this problem. When encountering competence issues such as these, you will want to refer the client to appropriate services or provide the client with appropriate clinical resources. The emphasis here is on referral to *appropriate* services, and therefore all counselors need to be aware of those resources available within their communities that can be called upon when special support is needed. To assist you in this process, we invite you to complete Exercise 11.1. This exercise directs you to identify those clinical resources that your internship site has provided its staff for appropriate referral.

EXERCISE 11.1

Resources in My Reach

Directions: Your task is to identify clinical resources in the following areas at your internship site:

- the site professional counselors' areas of expertise;
- resources for referral of children, adults (men & women), and seniors;
- resources for referral that support multicultural individuals;
- clinical resources for referral of issues such as child abuse, domestic violence, addiction, crisis, divorce, child custody, or cultural adoption; and
- resources for referral of facilities such as hospitals, law firms, career centers, community mental health services, women's centers, health centers, police departments, and crisis hotlines.

Values

The second condition focuses on the counselor's values involved in termination and referral. The key point on this condition is that

> counselors refrain from referring prospective current clients based solely on the counselor's personally held values, attitudes, beliefs, and behaviors. Counselors respect the diversity of clients and seek training in areas in which they are at risk of imposing their values onto clients, especially when the counselor's values are inconsistent with the client's goals or are discriminatory in nature. (ACA, 2014, A.11.b)

This stipulation of the *Code of Ethics* charges you, the counselor, to abstain from imposing your values onto the service you provide to the client, or your decision of not providing the client with counseling is discriminatory. In other words, termination and referral should not be based on your potential client's personal characteristics that are inconsistent with your values. However, implementing this code of ethics in reality has been challenging. We invite you to read Case Illustration 11.1. You may find it valuable to discuss with your professors, supervisor, or colleagues your response to the case and, perhaps more important, what you would do in a similar situation.

CASE ILLUSTRATION 11.1

Ward Versus Wilbanks

Julia Ward was a graduate student in the school counseling program at Eastern Michigan University (EMU). EMU's school counseling program is accredited by CACREP and it follows the *Code of Ethics* of the American Counseling Association (ACA). In Ms. Ward's first practicum, she was assigned a client who was gay. Ms. Ward claimed that because of her religious belief, she would not be able to work with a client whose sexual orientation was different from hers, so she decided to refer the client. She also stated a further refusal to counsel any clients with views about premarital sex that differed from hers. After she refused to work with a prospective client who is gay, she was dismissed from the school counseling program for failing to adhere to the *Code of Ethics* of the American Counseling Association (ACA).

Ms. Ward disputed the university's decision and filed a lawsuit claiming that EMU had violated her constitutional right of freedom of speech and that the *Code of Ethics* of ACA gives counselors permission to make referrals. In addition, her lawyer said public universities should not force students to violate their religious beliefs to get a degree.

Questions for Discussion:

1. Under what circumstances can a counselor terminate a client and make a referral?
2. When it comes to termination, which should be protected, the counselor's values (religious belief) or the client's welfare?
3. What does the *Code of Ethics* really mean about counselor competence where the decision of termination and referral is concerned?

Appropriateness

The third condition is that you as counselor make *appropriate termination* of a counseling relationship "when it becomes reasonably apparent that the client no longer needs assistance, is not likely to benefit, or is being harmed by continued counseling," (ACA, 2014, A.11.c). Here there are three situations in which counselors may terminate counseling: (a) the client does not need help anymore, (b) counseling does not benefit the client anymore, and (c) continued counseling may do harm to the client. The determination of these situations is based on your, the counselor's, clinical or professional judgment. Other situations in which you as counselor may terminate counseling include when you are in jeopardy of harm by your client or by another person with whom your client has a relationship, or when your client does not pay fees as agreed upon (ACA, 2014, A11.c). *ACA Code of Ethics* also requires you as counselor to provide pretermination counseling and recommend other service providers to your clients when necessary. To help you further understand this code of ethics, we present you Case Illustration 11.2, I'm Happy With the Therapy.

CASE ILLUSTRATION 11.2

I'm Happy With the Therapy

Dr. Davis is a licensed counselor who has been practicing for over 20 years. In her private practice, Dr. Davis sees clients with a variety of issues and treats them with cognitive-behavioral therapy (CBT). Peter is one of her clients with social phobia and general anxiety. Dr. Davis has seen him for more than 6 months. Peter attends his weekly therapy meeting and seems satisfied with what happens in sessions. Dr. Davis has given Peter homework assignments, one after another, but Peter has not done any of them. Each time Dr. Davis makes an assignment, Peter says he will do it, and that he's happy with the therapy. When Dr. Davis challenges Peter multiple times, pointing out the discrepancy between what he says and what he does, Peter apologizes each time, indicating he will do it. However, nothing happens. Dr. Davis strongly believes CBT is effective with social phobia and anxiety problems and continues to look for ways to work with Peter.

1. What action do you think Dr. Davis should take at this point?
2. What would you do if you were in Dr. Davis's position?

Process

The fourth condition is "when counselors transfer or refer clients to other practitioners, they ensure that appropriate clinical and administrative processes are completed and open communication is maintained with both clients and practitioners," (ACA, 2014, A11.d). Here the *Code of Ethics* requires you, the counselor, to follow appropriate procedures and communicate the transfer or referral with both your clients and the health professionals to whom you transfer or refer your clients. As an intern, you are most likely to transfer your clients at the end of your internship. To ensure you are aware of and understand the clinical and administrative processes, you may want to check what procedures you must follow at your internship site when you transfer or refer a client.

In addition, the *Code of Ethics* also requires that "counselors do not abandon or neglect clients in counseling," instead "making appropriate arrangement for the continuation of treatment, when necessary, during interruptions such as vacations, illness, and following termination" (ACA, 2014, 12A). The *ACA Code of Ethics* (2014) defines abandonment as "the inappropriate ending or arbitrary termination of a counseling relationship that puts the client at risk" (p. 20). It is clear that any termination of a counseling relationship that puts the client at risk is abandonment. Besides illness and vacations of the counselor, many other situations of a counselor's life change can cause inappropriate termination occur, for example, job termination (maternal leave, end of internship, dropping school, etc.), not being able to collect fees from insurance, relocation, role change in an institution, or a threatening client. See Case Illustration 11.3, Debt Collection. After reading the case illustration, you may take it to your group supervision for discussion.

CASE ILLUSTRATION 11.3

Debt Collection

You are a licensed counselor who just started your private practice 2 years ago. Almost all of your patients are referred by insurance companies. For 2 years, you have never had a problem with fee collection. However, one of your clients was suddenly laid off by his company so his benefit came to an end. Because the client came to therapy for a substance abuse issue, he did not mention anything about his job termination. After a while, the accounting service notified you that this client's benefit was ended due to job termination. You then discussed the fee issue with your client. The client apologized for not informing you of his job situation and promised to pay you. However, the fee had accumulated to over $1000 dollars and the client still did not send you the payment. You discussed this issue with the client and informed the client you would not be able to schedule any more appointments. The client indicated that he would pay you when he found another job, but he did not know when he could find one. You were doubtful about his ability to find a job soon and insisted that you could not provide him any more therapy. The client complained to the state board, alleging that you abandoned him, and threatened a malpractice action.

Factors Involved in Appropriate Termination

We consider that termination in counseling is a process, so it can then occur at any point and time when the goal of counseling is achieved or according to the agreement or treatment plan made between the counselor and the client. Termination under these conditions is considered a successful or appropriate termination. Successful or appropriate termination

> is determined by mutual agreement among the parties involved when the goals of psychotherapy have been accomplished and/or no longer require attention. In successful termination, the consumer is a full participant, understands the decision, agrees with the reasons for ending psychotherapy, and is satisfied with the outcome. (Younggren & Gottlieb, 2008, p. 501)

Moreover, as you may know, trust, power, and caring are major ingredients in the counseling process (Pope & Vasquez, 2007), and appropriate termination prevents harm and abuse of power, avoids betrayal of the trust, and conveys caring (Vasquez et al., 2008). Therefore, appropriate termination safeguards the nature of counseling and supports the counselor's professional identity as one who is caring and trustworthy.

Although the client should fully participate in the termination process, the power and responsibilities appear not evenly distributed. It is the counselor's responsibility to ensure that this process of termination is elected with the best interest of the client in mind. With this as a beacon to counselors' decision making, a counselor may find times when he or she helps the client see that termination at this or that particular time may not be in his or her own best interest or, conversely, that it is. Obviously, the counselor plays a significant role in the process of termination. To have an appropriate or successful termination as counselor, you must play an active role in this process. Exercise 11.2 offers you an opportunity to do a self-assessment on how you have approached termination in your practice.

EXERCISE 11.2

My Action on Termination in Counseling

Directions: Answer the following questions and then take your answers to your supervision for discussion.

1. Have you discussed termination in your intake or your first counseling session?
2. Have you discussed termination while you set up goals with your clients?
3. Have you discussed termination during treatment planning?
4. Have you discussed termination periodically in the process of counseling?
5. How do you allow your clients to own and internalize the work of therapy?
6. How have you periodically assessed your clients' gains in counseling?
7. What have you done to prevent client dependence in counseling?
8. Have you assessed your clients' expectations for how long therapy will take?
9. What have you done with your clients to prepare for a forced termination?
10. How will you know that the treatment is ready to end?

As may be obvious from the previous discussion, successful, ethical termination is a process that develops across the counseling relationship (see Quintana, 1993). Research has demonstrated that termination is viewed by most clients as a positive transition rather than a loss, and during the ending period of therapy both clients and counselors have a sense of accomplishment, pride, calmness, and health (Hardy & Woodhouse, 2008). Such positive feelings are largely due to the open discussion counselors have with their clients about the termination and the therapeutic relationship (Marx & Gelso, 1987). Therefore, as counselor, you want to actively and frequently have discussions about current status; progress; and, by implication, termination with your clients. Table 11.2 presents a list of recommendations by Vasquez and colleagues (2008) for your reference and consideration when you counsel clients.

Table 11.2 Twelve Recommendations for Practice

The following 12 recommendations may be helpful for ensuring the clinically appropriate and effective termination of each client.

1. Provide patients with a complete description of the therapeutic process, including termination; obtain informed consent for this process at the beginning of treatment, and provide reminders throughout treatment.
2. Ensure that the psychotherapist and client collaboratively agree on the goals for psychotherapy and the ending of psychotherapy.
3. Provide periodic progress updates that include discussions of termination and, toward the end of psychotherapy, provide pretermination counseling.
4. Offer a contract that provides patients with a plan in case the psychotherapist is suddenly unavailable (including death, or financial, employment, or insurance complications).
5. Help clients develop health and referral plans for posttermination life.
6. Make sure you understand termination, abandonment, and their potential effects on patients.
7. Consider developing (and updating) your professional will to proactively address unexpected termination and abandonment, including the name(s) of colleagues who will contact current patients in the case of your sudden disability or death.
8. Contact clients who prematurely terminate via telephone or letters to express your concern and offer to assist them.
9. Use the Ethics Code (e.g., ACA, 2014; APA, 2002), your state practice regulations, and consultation with knowledgeable colleagues to help guide your understanding and behavior in regard to psychotherapy termination.
10. Review other ethics codes for discussions of abandonment. The American Counseling Association (http://www.counseling.org/Resources/CodeOfEthics/TP/Home/CT2.aspx) and the American Mental Health Counselors Association (http://www.amhca.org/code/) contain prohibitions against abandonment.

11. Make the topic of termination a part of your regular continuing education or professional development.
12. Be vigilant in monitoring your clinical effectiveness and personal distress (e.g., Baker, 2003; Norcross & Guy, 2007). Psychotherapists who self-monitor and practice effective self-care are less likely to have inappropriate terminations or clients who feel abandoned.

Source: Reprinted from "Psychotherapy Termination: Clinical and Ethical Responsibilities" by M. J. T. Vasquez, R. P. Bingham, & J. E. Barnett, 2008, pp. 661–662), *Journal of Clinical Psychology, 64*(5). Reprinted with permission.

Challenges to Effective and Ethical Termination

As we all know, while oftentimes counselors face many challenges in building a trusting therapeutic relationship in counseling, they may face more challenges in terminating the trusting relationship they have established with their clients. Questions we ask regarding what factors affect appropriate termination may include the following: When is the appropriate time to terminate a therapeutic relationship? How should a therapeutic relationship be terminated? Who should initiate the termination process?

It is widely agreed among professional counselors that premature termination negatively affects both clients and counselors and is particularly problematic for clients who have not gained the full benefit of therapy (Roe, 2007). The negative effects for clients may include ambivalence about end, anxiety about maintaining therapeutic gains, sadness related to separation and loss, pain associated with unresolved attachments or losses, fears of abandonment and rejection, betrayal, and anger; for counselors, the negative effects can be countertransference, anxiety, guilt, and anger (Pearson, 1998; Pekarik, 1985; Penn, 1990). Denial of their own negative feelings by counselors further obfuscates the termination process (Pearson, 1998).

Termination of a counseling relationship can be initiated by either the client or the counselor. But the issue of who's supposed to make the decision of termination has never been clarified. It was found in two studies that more counselors thought that termination decisions were mutual, whereas clients thought that terminating therapy was the counselor's decision (Manthei, 2007; Metcalf, Thomas, Duncan, Miller, & Judd, 1996). Evidently, the issue of the termination decision should be discussed, understood, negotiated, and clarified at the very beginning of the therapy.

Reasons for terminating a therapeutic counseling relationship can be the client's dissatisfaction, lack of financial ability, and other personal life circumstances (e.g., illness or relocation); or the counselor's job termination, relocation, role change, lack of specialized competence, illness, sudden death, and completion of an internship. However, how to avoid inappropriate termination remains a critical issue for counseling and counseling psychology professionals. In the following paragraphs, we will discuss some commonly seen terminations.

Termination Due to Lack of Progress

The goal of counseling is to help clients improve their current unsatisfactory life situations. To achieve this goal, the counselor conducts intake, develops the treatment plan, implements the treatment plan, makes assessment, and terminates the counseling relationship when therapeutic goals in the treatment plan are all achieved. In this entire process, tasks set for the client must be accomplished and progress must be made. When the client does not make any progress, the counselor is ethically obligated to terminate the therapy. But how to handle the termination seems as important as to obey the ethical obligation. Case Illustration 11.4 demonstrates one situation in which the counselor terminates the therapy due to lack of progress.

CASE ILLUSTRATION 11.4

Lack of Progress

Henry Chen is a 24-year-old Asian American male who graduated from a prestigious university 2 years ago. After graduation, Henry stayed at home playing computer games pretty much every day. Often, Henry stayed up until 4:00 a.m. in the morning and then went to bed, sleeping until 1:00 or 2:00 p.m. in the afternoon. When his mother asked him about what his plan was next, Henry became very angry, telling his mom to stay away from his business. His mother worried so much about Henry's situation that she obtained a referral for him to a professional counselor. Initially Henry refused to go, but to avoid his mom's nagging, he finally went to therapy.

Henry's counselor has practiced for more than 10 years and had experiences working with individuals from different cultural backgrounds. Her theoretical orientation is cognitive-behavioral. Henry was diagnosed with mild depression and given a dozen assignments to regulate his eating, sleeping, and social behaviors. Henry did not complete any homework assigned by his counselor, but he seemed to enjoy going to therapy and talking with his counselor. After 2 months seeing Henry make no progress, the counselor told Henry she had to terminate the therapy due to lack of progress. Henry thought therapy was all about talking and did not expect to have to do anything. So, he was upset because he felt he was being abandoned.

Termination Due to Being Out of Area of Competence

As a professional counselor, one must be competent at what one is doing. When lacking competence, a counselor may do harm to his or her clients. The *ACA Code of Ethics* requires that counselors are knowledgeable about the work they are doing with clients. "If counselors lack the competence to be of professional assistance to clients, they avoid entering or continuing counseling relationships. Counselors are knowledgeable about culturally and clinically appropriate referral resources and suggest these alternatives" (ACA, 2014, A.11.a.). A counselor may claim himself or herself to be competent in a specialized area if he or she has been formally trained in that area, which includes having mastered the knowledge and skills of that area and having applied the knowledge and skills to clients under clinical supervision. With this in mind, the counselor may know when the appropriate circumstance is to terminate a counseling relationship. Case Illustration 11.5 is a counseling termination situation which involves the counselor being out of his or her area of competence.

CASE ILLUSTRATION 11.5

Out of Area of Competence

Brenda Wood is a licensed professional marriage and family counselor who has practiced for more than 25 years. Currently, Ms. Wood has seen a couple who have been married for 7 years. Two years after they got married, the husband moved out because he could not tolerate his wife's three adult children who constantly interrupted their life. For example, none of these adult children were financially independent and they often asked for money from their mother, who owns a small business. They came to the couple's house to eat more than 2 days a week. Moreover, they did not wash dishes or help clean the house. As a result, their stepfather, the husband, became the one who did the cleaning. The husband told the wife that she needed to let her children become independent, but the wife did not listen. So, the husband decided to separate. He moved out and rented an apartment. During the 5 years since he moved out, the couple has continued to visit each other and make love as they did before. Up until now, Ms. Wood has seen them for more than eight sessions and they three have had a very good working alliance. However, in the last session the husband suddenly disclosed that he has been addicted to substances (alcohol and marijuana) since he separated from his wife. She had no knowledge about it. Ms. Wood has never had training in substance abuse and believes that she has to make a quick decision.

1. Because Ms. Wood has no training in substance abuse or addiction clients, what do you think she should do?
2. How would you handle this situation if you were in her position?

Terminating Due to Fee Issue

Client fee-for-therapy service is critical in practice, private practice in particular. In reality, some counselors or psychotherapists accept insurance and others do not. Those who accept insurance are either in network or out of network. Those who are in the network usually have an agreement with the insurance company to accept a fixed pay rate, which means it doesn't matter how much the counselor charges for his or her service, the insurance company only pays a certain amount of the charge and the counselor agrees not to charge the client the unpaid portion. However, those who are out of network may handle fees differently. The counselor may charge the client's insurance for his or her service, but the insurance company may only pay a portion of his or her charge. At this point, the counselor has a choice—he or she may charge the client for or waive the remaining balance. For counselors who do not accept insurance, they have much flexibility in terms of service fees. Many counselors use sliding-scale fees, which are variable costs for their services based on the client's ability to pay. In other words, the counselor reduces fees for those clients who have lower incomes or less money to spend after their personal expenses regardless of income. Due to these fee variations, the counselor and the client must be on the same page when coming to a fee agreement, and these details must be discussed and presented as part of gaining client informed consent. Case Illustration 11.6 presents a situation in which the counselor uses the sliding-scale fees.

CASE ILLUSTRATION 11.6

Sliding-Scale Fees

Mr. Sam Burton is a professional licensed counselor who has practiced for more than 10 years. Currently, Sam associates with a group of psychologists and one psychiatrist in a local community center. Sam sees about 25 clients each week, and he uses the sliding-scale fees for those who are from lower income families. One of his clients is Jennifer White, whom he has seen for more than half a year on a weekly basis. Jennifer works as a custodian and gets paid at an hourly rate. Her husband is a veteran who claims social security due to his disability. They have two kids, who are 11 and 13 years old. Because of Jennifer's family situation, Sam was willing to discount 75% of her fees. However, in recent sessions, Jennifer disclosed that she has bought each of her kids an iPhone as their birthday gifts; in addition, the families have booked their Florida vacation. Jennifer said that the last time they visited Disney World was 5 years ago. After hearing about Jennifer's recent purchases, Sam began to question his decision of sliding-scale fees for Jennifer—after all, he himself does not have an iPhone yet. He thinks, *Why can't she pay me while she can afford such expensive luxury items for her kids and a luxury vacation for her family?* After debating with himself, Sam decided to stop offering Jennifer the sliding-scale fees. He told Jennifer she needs to pay the full fee rate for her future sessions; otherwise, he can't see her anymore. Jennifer is not happy with it, saying she still wants the service with the sliding-scale fees. She also remarked that she would report Sam to the state board for abandonment if Sam refuses to provide her the service.

Questions:

1. What would be the most appropriate approach for Sam?
2. How would you handle this situation if you were Jennifer's counselor?

After reading the case illustration, we ask you to answer the questions at the end of the case illustration and discuss the fee issues on termination in your individual or group supervision.

Termination Due to Counselor's or Client's Life Circumstances

Termination due to personal life circumstances of either counselor or client is often abrupt or forced. Forced termination is one kind of premature termination and refers to the fact that the counselor ends the counseling relationship with the client before the work is completed. For example, the counselor suddenly becomes seriously ill (e.g., hospitalization or death) and cannot continue his or her ongoing work with the client; the counselor or his or her spouse receives a job offer and the family has to relocate; or an intern has to finish his or her internship and move on to the next stage of his or her life. A forced termination is when the counselor chooses to end the counseling relationship and imposes premature endings by virtue of his or her personal choice.

No matter what the causes are, clients are given no choice but to end a meaningful therapeutic relationship in which they have put a great deal of effort and investment—they have to work through a difficult termination that is not dictated by their own timing or needs (Penn, 1990). Case Illustration 11.7 demonstrates one scenario in which a counseling relationship is abruptly terminated without the client's consent.

CASE ILLUSTRATION 11.7

No Longer Objective

Elizabeth Davis is a 35-year-old White female who has been in therapy for more than 3 years with her current counselor, Dr. William Ball. In therapy, Elizabeth has been dealing with her bipolar disorder. In the years that she has been working with Dr. Ball, Elizabeth feels the therapeutic relationship established has been strong and, with a combination of medicine and therapy, she has made much progress to stabilize her mental condition, which she has struggled with for almost 7 years. Elizabeth believes that she has invested a great deal into this relationship and is very hopeful about making further improvement because her mental health is important to not only her but also her children and family.

Dr. William Ball is a professional licensed counselor who has practiced for more than 15 years. Dr. Ball sees 20 to 25 clients at a college counseling center and enjoys his good reputation as a counseling professional. However, in the past 2 years, Dr. Ball has been struggling with his marriage. During the past 2 months, Dr. Ball has often been distracted while talking with his clients. In the last week's counseling session, Dr. Ball suddenly told Elizabeth that he is no longer objective, and he has received permission to take an unpaid leave from his supervisor, who is also the center director.

From Case Illustration 11.7, you can imagine the reaction of Elizabeth to the sudden termination of her therapy by Dr. Ball. Because Dr. Ball chose to leave and end the therapy without considering the timing and needs of the client, his ability to consider his client's readiness for termination has been eliminated. Due to lack of time and strategies to facilitate an appropriate termination, Dr. Ball's forced termination presents quite a challenge to Elizabeth and himself.

Client reactions to forced termination often include anger, feelings of anxiety, self-blame, and initial reluctance to express feelings, whereas counselor reactions to abrupt termination may include anxiety over the separation, sadness over the losses, anger over the necessity to terminate clients (Penn, 1990), and fear of abandonment and rejection (Kramer, 1990). As a counseling or counseling psychology intern, you will probably have multiple forced terminations due to the end of your internship. It is impossible to match the end of your internship with the termination of each of your cases. Therefore, you need to prepare for all the terminations you may have ahead of time. The following are some strategies for addressing the realities of potential forced termination.

Strategies may include (a) informing the client before the start of treatment, (b) leaving time for discussion, (c) facilitating expression of feelings, (d) recognizing indirect expressions of reactions (Penn, 1990), (e) reviewing progress and accomplishments, (f) preparing the client for transferring, and (g) making all transitional procedures as easy and clear as possible. While discussing practical strategies for managing multiple terminations brought on by the counselor's departure, Quinn M. Pearson (1998) offered a list of forced termination strategies based on her personal experience and review of literature (see Table 11.3).

Table 11.3 Practical Strategies for Forced Termination

1. Accept and work through your own intense feelings. Acknowledging the fact that one's own personal decisions are imposing premature endings takes an emotional toll on the departing counselor. Faced with such feelings as sadness, guilt, anger, fear, and helplessness, counselors tend to feel embarrassed, thinking that such intense feelings are inappropriate (Fair & Bressler, 1992; Mathews, 1989). It is critical, however, that counselors normalize and work through these feelings rather than deny them or act them out in session.
2. Reflect on each client and imagine how it will be to end this relationship permanently. This self-reflection enables counselors to recognize the particular loss of each counseling relationship. Moreover, personal reflection is warranted to guard against the possibility that counselors are confusing clients' reactions with their own. By putting each loss into perspective, counselors can better differentiate feelings associated with the real loss from counter-transferential feelings related to individual client's dynamics. As a result, counselors are likely to grieve more effectively and to predict clients' reactions more accurately.
3. Maintain physical energy levels through adequate rest, nutrition, and exercise. Terminating counseling with multiple clients is emotionally and physically draining. In order to maintain the necessary energy to be fully present with each client, it is imperative that counselors take care of their physical needs.

4. Seek professional and personal support. Through consultation or supervision, colleagues can provide both professional support for the emotional strain and an objective view regarding potential countertransference. Additionally, telling significant others of the emotional struggles (without discussing specific cases) can provide emotional support.
5. Review each client's therapeutic progress, previous reactions to separation and loss, common defenses, and typical emotional expressiveness. A number of questions may facilitate this review: How disruptive is the timing of termination related to the client's current work in counseling? How dependent is the client on the counseling relationship? What significant losses has the client experienced? How has the client coped with previous losses? To what degree is abandonment a significant part of the client's dynamics? How does the client typically respond to disappointment or conflict in relationships? What feelings are most comfortable and least comfortable for the client? Asking such questions when reviewing each case prepares counselors for clients' probable responses and helps counselors to interpret unexpected reactions.
6. Tell clients that you are leaving as soon as possible once your decision is final. Counselors should neither delay the announcement nor announce their departure before the decision is final. On the one hand, a premature announcement that does not materialize could create insecurity and burden clients with the nagging awareness that their counselor could decide to leave at any time. On the other hand, informing clients as soon as possible communicates respect for the counseling relationship.
7. Give clients information about where you are going and why you are leaving. Withholding such information leaves clients with many unanswered questions. Because of clients' tendency to personalize or fantasize about the answers, it is advisable for counselors to be open about why they are leaving and where they are going (Penn, 1990; Siebold, 1991).
8. Allow clients initially to respond spontaneously in their own ways. While some clients react almost immediately, others need time to absorb the news (Penn, 1990; Siebold, 1991). It is helpful to keep in mind that clients' reactions seem to come in layers as the reality of ending and its consequences register at various levels. As a result, clients should be allowed to incorporate the news at their own pace.
9. Respond empathically and listen closely for implied messages in clients' initial and subsequent reactions. As stated earlier, forced terminations often generate intense emotions and the subsequent tendency to deny or minimize such reactions. Advanced empathy is a powerful means for helping clients express and work through the range of their emotions. Clients seem to benefit from having some time (at least one session) to assimilate the news of termination on an emotional level before moving on to the task of discussing therapeutic progress.
10. Assess each client's therapeutic progress as well as the need and motivation for continued counseling. Before discussing post-termination plans with clients, counselors are advised to make their own assessments outside of the counseling sessions.
11. Encourage clients to assess their progress and review together in session both their accomplishments and areas which need further work (Penn, 1990). Just as it is helpful for counselors to reflect on clients' progress outside of the sessions, it is beneficial for clients to engage in personal reflection on their own.
12. Actively facilitate the transfer/referral process if further counseling is indicated. Discussing the client with the new counselor (with client consent) and introducing them to each other are two ways to be an active facilitator of the transition. Assisting in either a transfer or a referral to another counselor is a critical step in adhering to the ethical prohibition against abandoning clients (American Counseling Association, 1995).

(Continued)

Table 11.3 (Continued)

13. Give clients a forwarding address. When giving clients your forwarding information, it is important to state clearly that you are not requesting them to contact you but welcome correspondence if they want to report on progress or need assistance in obtaining a referral. Fears of clients abusing this invitation seem unwarranted. Not only is the literature (e.g., Penn, 1990; Siebold, 1991) absent of problematic accounts regarding client follow-ups, but in the eight-month period since my departure, only 3 of 23 clients have corresponded. Giving forwarding information seems to ease clients' initial feelings of panic and abandonment and also allows for real closure.
14. Say goodbye and end the relationship. Assuming that counselors have worked through their own reactions to ending, they are in the perfect position to model saying goodbye in appropriate, meaningful ways. It is helpful for counselors to use immediacy, communicating in a genuine way about how they have been impacted by each relationship and its ending. Pointing out unique qualities or specific ways that each client has affected you as a professional or a person can communicate the significance that each relationship deserves. Additionally, rituals that arise out of this immediacy or that symbolize the counseling process can help to bring final closure to the relationship.

Source: Pearson, Quinn, M. (1998). Terminating before counseling has ended: Counseling implications and strategies for counselor. *Journal of Mental Health Counseling, 20(1),* 55–63.

Transferring Clients to Another Counselor: A Special Form of Termination

Transferring clients to other counselors does not happen unless it is necessary. A counselor must transfer his or her client to another counselor if he or she has not completed the work of counseling with the client but has to depart. Like counseling termination, the process of transitioning presents a number of challenges (Baird, 2002). When reviewing literature on transferring clients, Williams and Winter (2009) summarized some common issues about transferring clients. These issues include client reactions and departing counselor reactions. The client reactions include the client's feelings of abandonment, loss, increased anxiety in response to the separation, rage, helplessness, depreciation of therapy, urges to quickly get everything out to quickly finish treatment, vengeful self-defeating behavior, and increases in symptoms. Some clients could potentially react with depression, regression, and acting out.

The departing counselor's reactions may include feelings of loss or feelings of guilt for having "used" and "abandoned" the client for academic purposes. The departing counselor may also deny his or her importance to the client and underestimate his or her own bereavement over the loss. In addition, the departing counselor may feel insecurity or shame at exposing himself or herself to the incoming counselor, who will see his or her written work, theoretical knowledge, and relationship with the client. This feeling of vulnerability may hinder the departing counselor to handle the transfer appropriately. Another major issue for the departing counselor is countertransference.

For this issue, the departing counselor may handle the transfer inappropriately by terminating the client prematurely, informing the client about the transfer in the last session, making social arrangements with the client, or doing favors for the client.

Williams and Winter (2009) also identified some recommendations in the literature for addressing these issues. The common recommendations to address the client's issues are (a) preparing the client for the transfer in advance, (b) seeking suggestions for termination from the client, (c) getting the client involved in the transferring process, (d) recapitulating the client's progress and focusing on the client's assets and gains, (e) assisting the client to process both negative and positive feelings about the impending loss, and (f) setting up a joint appointment with the client and the incoming counselor to facilitate the transition.

The recommendations for the counselor include (a) using clinical supervision to address countertransference issues; (b) having the clinical supervisor model a willingness to clarify, confront, and interpret issues and resistances; (c) maintaining an introspective attitude about the transfer processes; and (d) discussing overt feelings of sadness and bereavement in supervision.

To further understand the transfer and develop strategies for transferring clients and counselors, we ask you to identify your clients' needs, your needs, the incoming counselor's needs, and strategies to meet the needs of each by completing Exercise 11.3.

EXERCISE 11.3

Needs of the Transfer

Directions: Review all the cases you have and identify all the transfer needs and strategies of your clients, you as the departing counselor, and a potential incoming counselor.

Clients	Needs:	Strategies:
Departing Counselor	Needs:	Strategies:
Incoming Counselor	Needs:	Strategies:

Steps Toward Effective and Ethical Termination

Termination of counseling or psychotherapy is one of the most important components in the counseling process. An appropriate termination is also a representation of a successful outcome of therapy, which is determined by a mutual agreement between the client and the counselor (Younggren & Gottlieb, 2008). For this outcome, the counselor needs not only to understand the termination but also to use appropriate strategies to achieve it.

Ward (1984) conceptualized counseling termination with three functions: (a) assessing client readiness for the end of counseling and consolidating learning, (b) resolving remaining affective issues and bringing about appropriate closure of the significant and intense relationships between the client and the counselor, and (c) maximizing transfer of learning to increase the client's self-reliance and confidence in his or her ability to maintain change after counseling has ended. After reviewing the literature on termination, the author identified themes and tasks of termination. Those themes and tasks include separation, loss, sadness, grief, increased self-efficacy, autonomy, personal power, reviewing, summarizing, consolidating, transferring of learning, and saying goodbye.

To manage these themes and tasks of termination, Donald Ward suggested that the counselor needs to identify signs of the approach of termination from the client. These signs demonstrated by the client can be missed appointments, lateness for appointments, joking, acting out, withdrawal, denial, apathy, inadequacy, less mature behavior, expression of anger, or abandonment. When seeing these signs, the counselor may need to initiate the process of termination followed by the evaluation of termination readiness. Eight areas for client readiness to terminate counseling are necessary for evaluation. The counselor evaluates (a) whether the client's initial problems or symptoms have been reduced or eliminated, (b) whether what motivated the client to seek for help has dispelled, (c) what the client's increased coping ability looks like, (d) if the client's understanding and valuing of self and others have been increased, (e) what the client's increased levels of relating to others and of loving and being loved are, (f) what the client's increased abilities to plan and work productively look like, (g) what is the client's increased capacity to play and enjoy life, and (h) whether the client has confidence to continue to live effectively without counseling (Ward, 1984).

Clearly, exploring the various options of advantages and disadvantages of termination and processing both negative and positive feelings related to termination are beneficial for all parties involved in the helping process (Bostic, Shadid, & Blotcky, 1996). To do this, we suggest that you take the following steps when terminating a client. These steps are (a) identifying signs of termination; (b) discussing issues of termination (affective and relationship); (c) examining and assessing goal achievement and client learning; (e) deciding to do the right thing (follow *Code of Ethics*); and (f) terminating with care for all parties—the client, the counselor, and the incoming counselor. Exercise 11.4 invites you to review your current caseload and identify relevant termination issues for each of your counseling relationships

EXERCISE 11.4

My Caseload Review

Directions: In this exercise, you are asked to review all the cases you have and find out if termination has been addressed between you and your clients.

Client	Signs Identified Yes/No	Issues Discussed Yes/No	Goals/ Learning Examined Yes/No	*Code of Ethics* Followed Yes/No	Care for All Parties Given Yes/No
1					
2					
3					
4					
5					
6					

Terminating Other Relationships at Internship

After the discussion of termination with your clients, we also want to address the issues involved in the process of terminating your relationships with your supervisors and other counseling or counseling psychology staff at the internship site. Besides terminating your relationships with your clients, you must have a professional closure with your supervisor(s) and other counseling or counseling psychology staff in the process of completing your internship. "As completion of the final internship is a critical step in the education of future counselors, field supervisors and interns should ensure ample time is set aside for evaluation and discussion of the intern's development before termination occurs" (Hodges, 2011, p. 169). Unfortunately, terminating these relationships is not as sufficiently addressed as terminating your relationships with clients, and research on termination with clinical supervisors and counseling or counseling psychology staff is very sparse. However, like termination of counseling relationship with clients, terminating relationships with your clinical supervisors and other counseling or counseling psychology staff at your internship includes themes and tasks.

As an intern, you came to the internship site with numerous adjustment issues, and it was your supervisor and other staff members who assisted you in your adjustment process. At the initial stage of your internship, you gradually built a sense of self professionally with the feedback and help from your supervisor and other counseling or counseling psychology staff, because interns depend on the feedback of training staff to develop their personal and professional identities (Yogev, 1982).

In this process, you would have definitely gained positive experiences, and these positive experiences are something you expected. Something you may not have expected is the negative experiences. These negative experiences may have included the confusion about what you should do, and even apprehension about your ability to handle clinical responsibilities. Some clients might have been difficult, and you might have been uncertain if you were able to manage the cases. Some of you might also have had personality conflicts with your supervisors or other counseling or counseling psychology staff. The most stressful events for the majority of you might be that you were constantly evaluated, formally or informally. On top of all these, you might have your own personal issues and dissatisfaction with the internship program (Kaslow & Rice, 1985). To have all these experiences conceptualized, you want to have a formal closure with your supervisors and other counseling or counseling psychology staff.

Terminating Your Supervisory Relationship

As mentioned above, you may have had many challenging moments during your internship. It is your supervisors and other counseling or counseling psychology staff members who may have helped you jump over the hurdles and grow as a professional. As you close all your cases and terminate your relationships with all your clients, you also want to terminate your relationships with your supervisors and other counseling or counseling psychology staff, because the closure or termination will help both you and them develop and grow as competent professionals.

For some of you, this termination may be simple, but for others it may be emotional. Whichever the experience will be, we believe terminating your supervisory relationship and relationships with other counseling or counseling psychology staff whom you have worked with will achieve the following gains. First, a formal closure or termination with your supervisor and other counseling or counseling psychology staff will help you see where you were and where you are now in terms of both professional and personal growth. Second, a formal termination will assist you in seeing more clearly area(s) in which you can grow. Third, it will help the clinical supervisors and other counseling or counseling psychology staff see what they have done well and what they need to improve for their training of future interns. Fourth, the formal termination will help everyone—you the intern, the supervisor, and the counseling or counseling psychology staff—have an emotional conclusion for either the positive or the negative. Finally, through this formal termination, you will further develop your professional identity.

To conclude the training education, many internship sites have a farewell dinner or party, which provides a meaningful occasion for both interns and training staff. Some sites even have a group retreat to terminate the training experience. However, having a termination with your supervisor and other counseling or counseling psychology staff at an individual level may serve more for the purpose of learning. Exercise 11.5 will provide you an opportunity to prepare for the termination of your relationship with your supervisor and other counseling or counseling psychology staff individually. The exercise is based on the model of intern development by Kaslow and Rice (1985). This model describes counseling or counseling psychology interns' training from a developmental perspective. The model includes three phases: early phase, midphase, and individuation phase. During the early phase, the intern experiences all the initial adjustment to the internship site, which may consist of confusion, frustration, apprehension of difficult clients, self-doubt, feelings of vulnerability, dependence, etc. The midphase is the time that the intern begins to grow away from his or her dependence on the training staff, have a better sense of self as a semiautonomous professional, have a greater sense of professional identity, become aware of separateness from the training staff, and often wish to share new experiences with the training staff. During the individuation phase, the intern achieves his or her own individuality and attains a certain amount of object constancy. For example, the intern often takes more leading roles, intervenes more actively and directly with his or her clients, and challenges or disagrees with his or her supervisor, making plans for his or her following year.

EXERCISE 11.5

Time to Say Goodbye

Directions: In this exercise, you are asked to write a reflection of you as an intern at three phases of your internship training and then use it as a reference to have an individual termination meeting with your supervisor and the counseling or counseling psychology staff who have trained you during your internship. After completing this reflection, we also recommend you come out with a creative metaphor for your terminations (see Hundley and Casado-Kehoe's article in the Additional Resources).

Phases of My Internship	**My Experiences**	**My Thoughts and Emotions (Then and Now)**	**My Feedback for You**	**Your Feedback for Me**
Early or Initial Phase				
Midphase				
Individuation Phase				

KEYSTONES

- Termination is an integral part of counseling, and it is imbedded in the counseling process from the very beginning.
- Termination becomes mature when the client's goals for therapy are all achieved.
- Abandonment means a counselor fails to take the clinically indicated and ethically appropriate steps to terminate a counseling relationship.
- A counseling relationship begins when a client requests assistance and understanding; this is a precondition for an appropriate termination.
- The *ACA Code of Ethics* emphasizes four essential elements of termination: counselor competence, counselor values, appropriate termination, and transfer of services.
- Factors involved in termination include trust, power, caring, and agreement.
- From a developmental perspective, counseling termination is a positive transition rather than a loss for clients.

- Recognizing his or her own areas of competence and foreseeing potential unexpected life situations are key for the counselor to avoid inappropriate termination.
- Terminating supervisory relationships and relationships with other counseling or counseling psychology staff is also an essential step for the intern to become mature professionally.

ADDITIONAL RESOURCES

Web Based

APA (2002, 2010). *Ethical principles of psychologists and code of conduct.* Retrieved from http://www.apa.org/ethics/code/principles.pdf

ACA (2014). *ACA code of ethics: Termination and referral* (A.11). Retrieved from http://www.counseling.org/knowledge-center/ethics

Deardorff, W. W. (2012). *Difficult therapy termination issues: Ethics and risk management.* Retrieved from http://www.behavioralhealthce.com/index.php/component/courses/?task=view&cid=94

Terry, L. (2011). *Semi-structured termination exercises: A compilation from the groups in college counseling centers listserv.* Retrieved from http://www.apadivisions.org/division-49/publications/newsletter/group-psychologist/2011/04/termination-exercises.aspx

Print Based

Craige, H. (2009). Terminating without fatality. *Psychoanalytic Inquiry, 29,* 101–116.

Garcia-Lawson, K. A., & Lane, R. C. (1997). Thoughts on termination: Practical considerations. *Psychoanalytic Psychology, 14*(2), 239–257.

Hundley, G., & Casado-Kehoe, M. (2006/2007). The wisdom jar: A creative metaphor for terminating counseling supervision. *Journal of Creativity in Mental Health, 2*(2), 33–38.

Lenz, S., Zamarripa, M. X., & Fuentes, S. (2012). A narrative approach to terminating therapy. *Journal of Professional Counseling Practice, Theory, and Research, 39*(2), 2–13.

Parsons, R. D., & Zhang, N. (2014). *Becoming a skilled counselor.* Thousand Oaks, CA: Sage.

Seligman, L. (1984). In the field: Temporary termination. *Journal of Counseling and Development, 63,* 43–44.

Roe, D., Dekel, R., Harel, G., & Fennig, S. (2006). Clients' reasons for terminating psychotherapy: A quantitative and qualitative inquiry. *Psychology and Psychotherapy: Theory, Research and Practice, 79,* 529–538.

Westmacott, R., & Hunsley, J. (2010). Reasons for terminating psychotherapy: A general population study. *Journal of Clinical Psychology, 66*(9), 965–977.

REFERENCES

Baird, B. N. (2002). *The internship, practicum, and field placement handbook: A guide for the helping professions* (3rd ed.). Upper Saddle River, NJ: Pearson Education.

Barnett, J. E., MacGlashan, S. G., & Clarke, A. J. (2000). Risk management and ethical issues regarding termination and abandonment. In L. Vandecreek & T. L. Jackson (Eds.), *Innovations in clinical practice: A source book* (pp. 231–245). Sarasota, FL: Professional Resource Press/Professional Resource Exchange.

Bostic, J. Q., Shadid, L. G., & Blotcky, M. J. (1996). Our time is up: Forced terminations during psychotherapy training. *American Journal of Psychotherapy, 50,* 347–359.

Deardorff, W. W. (2012). *Difficult therapy termination issues: Ethics and risk management.* Retrieved from http://www.behavioralhealthce.com/index.php/component/courses/?task=view&cid=94

Hardy, J. A., & Woodhouse, S. S. (2008). *How we say goodbye: Research on psychotherapy termination.* Retrieved from http://www.divisionofpsychotherapy.org/hardy-and-woodhouse-2008/

Hodges, S. (2011). *The counseling practicum and internship manual: A resource for graduate counseling students.* New York, NY: Springer.

Kaplan, D. (2014). Ethical implications of a critical legal case for the counseling profession: Ward v. Wilbanks. *Journal of Counseling and Development, 92,* 142–146.

Kaslow, N. J., & Rice, D. G. (1985). Developmental stresses of psychology internship training: What training staff can do to help. *Professional Psychology: Research and Practice, 16*(2), 253–261.

Kramer, S. A. (1990). *Positive endings in psychotherapy: Bringing meaningful closure to therapeutic relationships.* San Francisco, CA: Jossey-Bass.

Manthei, R. J. (2007). Client-counsellor agreement on what happens in counseling. *British Journal of Guidance & Counselling, 35*(3), 261–281.

Marx, J. A., & Gelso, C. J. (1987). Termination of individual counseling in a university counseling center. *Journal of Counseling Psychology, 34,* 3–9.

Metcalf, L., Thomas, F. N., Duncan, B. L., Miller, S. D., & Hubble, M. A. (1996). What works in solution-focused brief therapy? In S. D. Miller, M. A. Hubble, & B. L. Duncan, *Handbook of solution-focused brief therapy.* San Francisco, CA: Jossey-Bass.

Pearson, Q. M. (1998). Terminating before counseling has ended: Counseling implications and strategies for counselor. *Journal of Mental Health Counseling, 20*(1), 55–63.

Pekarik, G. (1985). Coping with dropouts. *Professional Psychology: Research and Practice, 16,* 114–123.

Penn, L. S. (1990). When the therapist must leave: Forced termination of psychodynamic therapy. *Professional Psychology: Research and Practice, 21*(5), 379–384.

Pope, K. S., & Vasquez, M. J. T. (2007). *Ethics in psychotherapy and counseling: A practical guide* (3rd ed.). San Francisco, CA: Jossey-Bass.

Quintana, S. M. (1993). Toward an expanded and updated conceptualization of termination: Implications for short-term, individual psychotherapy. *Professional Psychology, 24,* 426–432.

Roe, D. (2007). The timing of psychodynamically oriented psychotherapy termination and its relation to reasons for termination, feelings about termination, and satisfaction with therapy. *Journal of the American Academy of Psychoanalysis and Dynamic Psychiatry, 35*(3), 443–453.

Vasquez, M. J. T., Bingham, R. P., & Barnett, J. E. (2008). Psychotherapy termination: Clinical and ethical responsibilities. *Journal of Clinical Psychology, 64*(5), 653–665.

Ward, D. (1984). Termination of individual counseling: Concepts and strategies. *Journal of Counseling and Development, 63,* 21–25.

Williams, L., & Winter, H. (2009). Guidelines for an effective transfer of cases: The needs of the transfer triad. *The American Journal of Family Therapy, 37,* 146–158.

Yogev, S. (1982). An electric model of supervision: A developmental sequence for beginning psychotherapy students. *Professional Psychology, 13,* 236–243.

Younggren, J. N., & Gottlieb, M. C. (2008). Termination and abandonment: History, risk, and risk management. *Professional Psychology: Research and Practice, 39*(5), 498–504.

12

Self-Care and Self-Protection—Necessary for All Counselors

What is to give light must endure burning.

Viktor Frankl (1963)

Viktor Frankl certainly knew of what he spoke. The Austrian neurologist and psychiatrist and founder of logotherapy was a survivor of the Holocaust, during which he experienced both the gift and the cost of caring for others. All who work in the service of others—giving care and shedding light—are at risk of getting burned.

Consider the following. It is 7:00 p.m., you have just finished your last session, and it is time to close the doors and go home. But before you head out, you decide to get just one more note done, and then send a quick e-mail and contemplate how you will handle your first client of the morning, as she has been particularly challenging over the past couple of sessions. Glancing at the clock, you realize another 45 minutes have past. As you begin to head out, you receive a notice from your answering service that you have an "emergency" message. The emergency thankfully turned out to be one that could be handled with a phone call, but it was a phone call that kept you in the office until 8:45 p.m. Upon arriving home, you are exhausted, throw a pizza in the oven, and promise to get to the gym tomorrow. Tomorrow . . .

Although the specifics of the scenario may be unfamiliar to you, the theme of physical and emotional drain is not. The very nature of our profession engages us in unpredictable schedules, unexpected demands, and interactions that are intense and emotionally draining. We spend each day listening to the challenges of others and have to be empathetic and attentive, and manage our client's emotions as well as our own. Repeat the above experience more than once a month and it is not hard to imagine the fatigue—physical, emotional, and psychological—that can result.

It is a sad reality that although counselors receive training that positions them to assist others who are mired in life's stress and conflict, they receive very little training on how to manage their own stress and that which accompanies the very career with which they are engaged (Emerson & Markos, 1996). In fact, it is a bit ironic that professional counselors not only assist those who are struggling with life demands but also engage in services that promote wellness and yet often find it difficult to maintain their own wellness and healthy lifestyle (Puig et al., 2012). Over 63.5% of those surveyed by the American Counseling Association (ACA, 2010) reported knowing a colleague whom they would consider impaired. The seriousness of the situation moved the American Counseling Association to organize a task force with the sole purpose of decreasing impairment and enhancing wellness among professional counselors (ACA, 2010). There is a proverb (Luke 4:23) that states, "Physician, heal thyself." It is a proverb that could be and should be directed to those aspiring to become counselors, as well as to those who are identified as professional counselors. Our failure to attend to self-care not only threatens our own personal health and well-being but can result in a significant depletion of our professional resources and competency and, as such, threaten the level of service we provide our clients. It is clear that care for self is not just a good idea—it is a professional concern and ethical mandate (see ACA, 2014, C.2.g, Impairment).

The current chapter reviews conditions of burnout and compassion fatigue. Specifically, upon completion of this chapter, readers will be able to

- describe the nature of burnout and compassion fatigue,
- explain the factors contributing to the development of burnout and compassion fatigue,
- describe steps to be taken to prevent and, when necessary, intervene with burnout and compassion fatigue, and
- develop a personal self-care plan.

Counseling: Challenging the Well-Being of the Counselor

What an awesome gift it is to be invited into others' journeys and invited to walk with them as they navigate the challenges they find. Being a counselor is an awesome gift—and an awesome responsibility. Our profession is not one that can be "called in." It is not the typical 9-to-5 job, regardless of the formal hours of employment. Ours, like other helping professions, requires us to not simply "do" *with,* or *for,* or *to* another. Rather, we are called to "be" with that other. It is in this process of being with the other that we increase our risk for burnout and compassion fatigue.

As poetically and poignantly described by Jeffrey Kottler in his book *On Being a Therapist* (1989), "The therapist enters the relationship with clarity, openness and serenity and comes fully prepared to encounter a soul in torment" (Kottler, 1989, p. 3). He continues:

> To take on a client, any client, is to make tremendous commitment to that person that could last years if not a lifetime. . . . It will have moments of special closeness and times of great hardship. The client will, at times, worship you, scorn you, abuse you, play with you and want to devour you. And through it all, regardless of what is going on in your own life—sickness, births, deaths, joys, disappointment—you must be there for the client, always waiting. (Kottler, 1989, p. 8)

Yes, it is a gift, yet one demanding an exhausting presence on the part of the counselor. Counselors engage in this emotionally demanding work in isolation, enveloped in confidentiality, and often carrying unrealistic expectations of their ability to make a difference (Schaufeli, 2003). The stress resulting from these conditions has been shown to contribute to counselor depression and anxiety (Tyssen, Vaglum, Gronvold, & Ekeberg, 2001), reduced self-esteem (Butler & Constantine, 2005), and an increased sense of loneliness (Lushington & Luscri, 2001). Further, beyond these personal costs, the negative consequence of the stress encountered as a helper has been shown to interfere with professional functioning by negatively affecting a counselor's ability to attend and concentrate (Skosnik, Chatterton, Swisher, & Park, 2000) and engage in effective decision making (Lehner, Seyed-Solorforough, O'Conner, Sak, & Mullin, 1997).

While you are just in the inaugural phase of your career and perhaps have only touched on the experience described by Kottler (1989), even you are not immune from the reality of needing to be available—physically, psychologically, emotionally—to those you serve and, as such, are not immune to that drain that such availability can create. In fact, there is evidence that younger and newer helping professionals are particularly susceptible to occupational stress (Skovholt & Ronnestad, 2003) and by extension the negative effects accompanying that stress.

As noted by Remen (1996), the expectation that one can be immersed in the suffering of his or her client and not be touched by it is as unrealistic as expecting to be able to walk through a rainstorm without getting wet. Surely, even with your initial field experience, you have sat with clients sharing stories of frustration, anxiety, confusion, and depression. Whether you were responsible for assisting these clients or merely positioned as an observer of the counseling dynamic, engaging, even tangentially, with the stories of client suffering can take its toll, directly or vicariously. If you have navigated through your field experience without experiencing this deeply personal impact of engaging with clients—without getting wet, as it were—it simply means you have not gone out in the rain or been open to a real/authentic encounter. If you have found yourself insulated from this experience—then you are doing something wrong!

Burnout

Pines and Maslach (1978) described *burnout* as a condition "of physical and emotional exhaustion, involving the development of negative self-concept, negative job attitude, and loss of concern and feeling for clients" (p. 234). Burnout is insidious, in that it is not announced by a sudden dramatic onset but rather develops gradually, having no clear beginning or ending point, but varying in degrees (Schaufeli, Maslach, & Marek, 1993). This was certainly the experience of one licensed counselor, Celeste, who found herself in free fall (Case Illustration 12.1). Although the details of the story and the uniqueness of pain and disruption are singular to this particular counselor, the elements that contribute to the downfall and the spiral exhibited are all too characteristic of one in burnout.

CASE ILLUSTRATION 12.1

A Counselor in Free Fall

Celeste M. was a well-respected licensed professional counselor. She had successfully worked in her private practice for over 20 years and had a reputation for being extremely effective in her specialty area, working with abused women and children. She had been an active member of her community, served on her Church's parish council, and participated as a "big sister" for more than 10 years. Her pattern of engagement and her record of effective practice belied the storm that was slowly unfolding. No one in her family, among her friends, and in her church community could have predicted the rapid decline and unraveling of both her personal and professional life.

The withdrawal and change in the mood started slowly but soon escalated to the point where Celeste's family and colleagues became concerned. Initially most felt it was simply that she was overworked. After all, she was carrying a caseload of 30 clients, and it appeared she was on the phone all hours of the day consulting and counseling. Her family had always shared their concern about her tendency to skip meals and "overcommit" at the expense of her ability to vacation, recreate, or even sleep.

The initial signs of burnout–her withdrawal from family gatherings, and even her resigning as secretary of the parish council–were excused as simply a result of her being too busy with her clients. But then it became apparent that she was not only withdrawing from her social contacts and her nonprofessional responsibilities but also beginning to miss appointments and, quite atypically, "complain" about her clients.

Though all of these should have been warning signs, they went either unnoticed or excused by those who cared about her. The wake-up call came as a result of a luncheon meeting with her former professor and mentor. Over the course of the 90-minute lunch meeting, Celeste ordered two martinis, while only picking at the salad she ordered. Her

(Continued)

(Continued)

lunch choice initially elicited little concern from Dr. G., but the announcement that she had to "run back to the office" in order to meet her 2 o'clock appointment made her decision to have a two-martini lunch a point of real concern for her mentor.

Through his caring—and skillful—confrontation, Dr. G. was able to convince Celeste to cancel the remainder of her appointments for the day. The afternoon was filled with more sharing between these two friends, and Dr. G. helped Celeste review the changes that she had been experiencing in both her personal and professional life.

A simple lunch meeting with an old professor, mentor, and friend proved lifesaving. With Dr. G.'s support, Celeste admitted to being burned out and depressed. She agreed with Dr. G. that it would be essential, as an ethical counselor, to take time away from the office, to give herself a sabbatical during which she would focus upon her own healing.

The experience of burnout is multidimensional, potentially affecting a counselor physically, cognitively, emotionally, and interpersonally, and even affecting his or her core values (Grosch & Olsen, 1994.) Physical symptoms include low energy, chronic fatigue and exhaustion, sleep difficulties, headaches, gastrointestinal disturbances, increased symptoms of premenstrual stress, and colds. The cognitive symptoms range from increased cynicism and negative attitudes to depersonalization (Maslach, Schaufeli, & Leiter, 2001). Emotional symptoms can range from boredom, moodiness, annoyance, and frustration to feelings of depression, anxiety, helplessness, and hopelessness (Lambie, 2002; Maslach et al., 2001). In addition, burnout can affect a counselor interpersonally, as evident by an increase in his or her social withdrawal and dehumanizing attitude toward clients, and behaviorally in the form of elevated aggression, defensiveness, substance abuse, and even absenteeism (Lambie, 2002). Finally, research suggests that burnout can affect the counselor's spiritual dimensions of life, as manifested in a counselor's loss of faith; loss of meaning and purpose; feelings of alienation and estrangement; despair; and changes in values, religious beliefs, and religious affiliation (Maslach et al., 2001).

While most certainly affecting all facets of a counselor's personal life (Feldstein, 2000), burnout can also result in the deterioration in the quality of care or service provided to clients (Maslach, 1993). Beyond draining the counselor's energy and cognitive clarity necessary to attend to his or her clients, burnout often manifests as "low morale, absenteeism, tardiness, a decrease in average length of stay on the job, high turnover, increased accidents on the job and poor performance" (Pines, 1993, p. 387).

Counselors at Risk

Burnout was initially described as a stress response syndrome experienced by people who provided services to other people (Maslach, 1982). More recent research has supported the notion that those within the mental health profession are at high risk of burnout (Bakker, Demerouti, Taris, Schaufeli, & Schreurs, 2003; Imai, Nakao, Tsuchiya, Kuroda, & Katon, 2004). In one study, up to two thirds of mental health workers sampled were experiencing some level of burnout (Morse, Salyers, Rollins, Monroe-DeVita, & Pfahler, 2012).

Although it may be intuitively appealing to believe that the longer one has toiled in the field the greater the risk of burnout, a belief that may provide those who are students in the field some comfort, such is not the case. Research such as that reported by Rupert & Morgan (2005) noted that those in their early phases of professional life are particularly sensitive to the possibility and signs of burnout. In fact, therapist age is one of the therapist characteristics most consistently linked with burnout. One explanation for these findings is that those new to the field and in the early phases of their career experience the greatest amount of stress as they attempt to become acclimated to the rhythm and demands encountered within professional practice while at the same time lacking the skills to balance the depth of professional caring with professional distancing.

Research investigating the factors contributing to burnout highlights the fact that counselors experience many of the same organizational factors contributing to the burnout rates for all health workers. However, in addition to long hours, heavy caseloads, being on call, interference from outside agencies, and isolation within the work setting, the very nature of the work and role expectations encountered by counselors have been found to contribute to their higher levels of burnout (Schaufeli, 2003; Evans & Villavisanis, 1997).

Counselors engage in work that is, by definition, emotionally draining (Bakker, Van der Zee, Lewig, & Dollard, 2006). Counselors are required by the very definition of their roles to provide care for others—even when it is at the expense of their own well-being (Lee et al., 2007). In addition, the counselor's ability to experience and convey empathy is not only a fundamental skill of effective counselors but may also place a counselor at high risk for burnout. As Larson (1993) summarized, "empathy is a double-edged sword; it is simultaneously your greatest asset and a point of real vulnerability" (p. 30).

The Unfolding of Burnout

As previously stated, burnout is particularly insidious in that it develops over time, without a grand announcement. Symptoms tend to be progressive, worsening over time, with individuals suffering from acute to chronic burnout with symptoms that range from mild to severe (Hamann & Gordon, 2000).

Typically, it starts with a counselor experiencing a loss of caring and commitment. As the process continues, the counselor develops negative feelings and attitudes toward clients. The counselor may "blame" the client for the lack of progress being experienced even though the source of the failure rests in the counselor's own limited energy and resources to facilitate the counseling. During this phase, the counselor becomes increasingly aware of his or her own sense of failure and feelings of incompetence and futility. It is not unusual for the counselor to become detached from his or her clients, labeling them as work tasks rather than individuals. This process of dehumanizing one's client often takes the form of a counselor referring to his or her client as "the borderline," "my repeat," "the whiner," or even "my 3 o'clock." Such labeling not only dehumanizes but provides the detachment from the counseling relationship the counselor in burnout seeks (Maslach et al., 2001).

This labeling and dehumanizing is clearly antithetical to the role and function of a counselor, and it is the counselor's attempt at self-protection. Disengagement is the counselor's attempt to reduce the drain due to empathic attachment (Skovholt, 2001). Sadly, while serving as an attempt at self-defense, the increased negative attitudes toward clients and the lack of empathy exhibited significantly affect the establishment of the therapeutic relationship and, as such, negatively affect the achievement of counseling outcomes. Because of the depletion of emotional energy and disconnection of the empathic attachment, it is not surprising to find the counselor's "failure to perform clinical tasks appropriately" (Lee et al., 2007, p. 143). As burnout continues to develop, the counselor may exhibit increased inflexibility, distancing from clients, and disbelief in effectiveness of treatment (Fothergill, Edwards, & Burnard, 2004). With this progression, the counselor can feel helpless and hopeless about the work he or she is doing and experience discouragement and apathy, all contributing to a failure in the performance of his or her clinical duties (Lee, Cho, Kissinger, & Ogle, 2010; Morse et al., 2012).

Preventing Burnout

As is evident from the above, taking care of oneself and learning ways to manage stress and avoid burnout is not only a good idea but one that is essential to ethical and effective practice. A number of factors contribute to the creation of a self-care protocol, including increasing one's awareness of early indications of burnout, developing and engaging in healthy life habits, and taking time to recharge.

Increase Self-Awareness

Because the effects of stress are accumulative and burnout will develop over time, the earlier one recognizes the effects of stress on personal and professional functioning, the easier intervention can be employed. It is important to monitor changes in your behavior, energy levels, social engagement, and physical health.

While it may seem a cliché, it is important to be sensitive to any reduction in your general loss of joy about life or enthusiasm about your profession. Exercise 12.1 invites you to reflect on your current state of well-being and the potential early indicators of burnout. The items listed in this self-reflection exercise have been gleaned from the research of Freudenberger (1974, 1975), Maslach and Jackson (1981), and Lee and colleagues (2007). The "self-assessment" is meant to serve as a stimulus for self-reflection and is not presented as an empirically validated measure. For those seeking a measure with good psychometric properties, you are referred to the Maslach Burnout Inventory (MBI), available at http://www.mindgarden.com/products/mbi.htm. The MBI is the most commonly used instrument measuring burnout. It has been configured to assess three dimensions of burnout: emotional exhaustion, depersonalization, and personal accomplishment (Maslach, Leiter, & Schaufeli, 2009).

EXERCISE 12.1

Burnout Self-Assessment

Directions: Place a check mark next to each of the following descriptors that reflect any changes you have noted over the past 3 months. It is suggested that you share your results with your site or university supervisor.

_______ 1. Tire more easily

_______ 2. Feel fatigued rather than energetic

_______ 3. Have trouble feeling happy

_______ 4. Work harder and harder and accomplish less and less

_______ 5. Increasingly cynical and disenchanted

_______ 6. Increasingly experience sadness

_______ 7. Forgetting–schedules, assignments, etc.

_______ 8. Increasingly irritable

_______ 9. Feel work and responsibilities are interfering with the opportunities to enjoy recreation and/or socializing

_______ 10. Experience physical complaints (e.g., aches, pains, headaches, or a lingering cold)

_______ 11. Have difficulty laughing at jokes about yourself

_______ 12. Joy is elusive

_______ 13. Feel less competent at school/work

_______ 14. Increasingly question my competency as a counselor

_______ 15. Increasingly question my effectiveness as a counselor

Engage in Healthy Life Habits

Thomas Skovholt (2001) has suggested that counseling is a form of one-way giving. In the absence of occasional emotional replenishment, counselors will sooner or later realize that their resources are drying up. If a counselor isn't committed to self-support and modeling healthy life habits, how is he or she expected to support his or her clients' progression toward health and well-being? As elusive as self-care may seem, it may ultimately be one of the most important ethical directives to be embraced by a counselor. Such health-care programming is multidimensional, addressing issues of nutrition, exercise, social engagement, interior life, play, and work management.

Nutrition

You know it. We all understand it. We probably assist our clients with it. The concept is simple. Good nutrition fuels the body and provides the building blocks that help a person handle the stresses of everyday life. Sadly, for many counselors, both those in the profession and those in training to become professional, the experience of too many clients scheduled within the day, paperwork that crowds out lunch times, and phone call consults or office meetings that invite an extra cup of coffee, a Danish, and a skipped meal is often the pattern that defines their nutritional intake.

Take a moment. Take a moment to reflect, not so much on what you know, or what you say, but what you do! Be honest. Do you find yourself, more times than not, eating at your desk? In your car? Or on the run? Do you find energy drinks and cups of coffee to be your primary resource for maintaining energy and focus? How often is a meal skipped or replaced with a power bar or power drink? Is fast food or microwavable dishes the mainstay of your diet?

It is easy to assume that this pattern of eating is a function of living on a graduate student's "income" or the temporary effect of balancing too many demands of school, work, field placement, and so forth. Sadly, the fact is that for many counselors on the edge of burnout, these patterns are not temporary but rather have become a way of life.

Eating at regular intervals, consuming balanced diets, and drinking water are essential for maintaining energy and providing the fuel necessary for the physical, mental, and emotional demands of counseling. It is not just a good idea, it is an ethical necessity if one is to be truly effective and of service to his or her clients.

Exercise

Granted, it may not be feasible for one to join a gym and commit to a three-day-a-week personal trainer and exercise regime, but it is essential to engage in some form of exercise. The research is abundant. Exercise, even moderate exercise such as walking, swimming, jogging, bike riding, shooting hoops, or dancing, improves not only one's physical well-being but also mental clarity.

Social Engagement

Another factor that can contribute to the maintenance of one's emotional and physical well-being and, as such, ward off the potential for burnout, is finding support and distraction in social engagement. Having a supportive social network, both personally and professionally, can serve as a resource supplying directions and suggestions when such is needed or simply emotional comfort and invitations to engagement in life when energy feels depleted. Engaged in a profession that is truly "one way," with the counselor attending to and caring for another, one may find similar support and care that can be life giving.

In addition to engaging in nonprofessional social contact, it is useful and valuable to avail oneself of professional support. One avenue for eliciting the support necessary to combat the sense of isolation that can accompany a counselor's professional life is seeking personal counseling and/or professional supervision. Availing oneself of the support, encouragement, and alternative perspectives found within counseling and supervision helps the counselor maintain a footing in reality, maintain objectivity and professional distance within his or her practice, and unearth personal issues and feelings that may be contributing to the sense of burnout.

Nurturing an Inner Life

Research (e.g., Firestone, Firestone, & Catlett, 2003) highlights the value of engaging in spiritual, philosophical, and religious activities as a means of fostering personal growth and well-being. Nurturing one's inner life can be done by engaging in inspirational reading, meditating, or simply finding time to commune with and in nature. It is suggested that these opportunities to step out of life's demands and step into our inner life allow one to reflect on the meaning derived from work and the priorities one assigns to life.

Whether it is through scheduled engagement in yoga, meditation, prayer, or spiritual readings, the need to quiet the demands of our professional life and seek renewal in the connection within our own sacred space is key to the avoidance of burnout and the maintenance of professional readiness.

Play and Be Playful

Counseling is serious business. The responsibilities embraced by counselors are not to be easily dismissed. The "heaviness" of our profession seeks counterbalance in the light side of life.

It is healthy to structure time for play and engagement with humor. It is important to structure time for hobbies, recreation, leisure reading, or game playing. It is healthy and helpful to experience entertainment that evokes a laugh. These experiences offer a counterbalance to the intensity, the stress, and the draining forces encountered in our professional lives (Skovholt, 2001).

Work Management

It is important to navigate through our work environment and work schedules in ways that nurture our well-being and reduce stress levels. Learning to prioritize our tasks, setting achievable goals, avoiding overtime, and learning to schedule short breaks throughout the day are all strategies that can encourage our healthy living, even at work. In addition, given the nature of our work—work that by nature tends to be isolating—it is important to seek out appropriate, supportive professional relationships. Engaging in supervision, peer consultation, professional support groups, and mentoring relationships can help diffuse the negative impact of such isolation (Skovholt, 2001).

Recharge

A third element to a program of burnout prevention is the inclusion of a time and process that facilitates one's ability to shut down and allow for personal and professional recharging. Shutting down and recharging are essential not only for cell phones, laptops, iPads, and other such devices but also for human beings, especially those who, like counselors, are intensely engaged in caring for others. The very nature of what we do requires counselors to be totally engaged with the oftentimes painful and difficult journey of another. To be effective for clients and caring of and for themselves, counselors must find time to recharge.

As graduate students with what we are sure are extensive "things to do" lists, the idea of taking time to recharge may seem like wishful thinking. There is simply too much that you need to do. There are demands to finish reports, complete assignments, develop thesis and research, and simply keep up with all the reading. These things often require more than the 24 hours typically found within a single day. But then you knew that! You also probably know that most graduate students find the time needed to complete their many tasks by depriving themselves of sleep.

The problem with this strategy is that sleep deprivation negatively impacts not only physical energy but mental ability and emotional stability. In the absence of adequate deep sleep, one restricts engagement in REM sleep, which plays a key role in learning and memory. Further, REM sleep replenishes the brain's supply of neurotransmitters, including the feel-good chemicals like serotonin and dopamine, which boost your mood during the day (Saisan, deBenedictis, Barston, & Segal, 2008).

To say that losing sleep as a strategy to address all the demands you encounter as a student-counselor is ineffective, is an understatement. Sleep deprivation is counterproductive to the goals and ideals you hold as both a student and future professional and consequently needs to be avoided. Structuring your schedule to allow for adequate sleep is a must.

Compassion Fatigue

Compassion fatigue has been described as a caregiver's reduced capacity or interest in being empathic or "bearing the suffering of clients" (Figley, 1995, p. 7). Initially, compassion fatigue was associated with counselors and caregivers who by the nature of their services or clientele are brought into contact with those who have experienced trauma and thus, by extension, are affected by that story of trauma shared by the client (Figley, 2002). But compassion fatigue is not restricted or limited to those who work in the area of trauma counseling.

By definition, all counselors in their role as caregivers are brought into close physical and emotional contact with their clients. The very nature of our work engages us in processes targeted to helping our clients find relief from their emotional suffering. The empathy we experience and convey invites our absorption of both the client's story and his or her suffering (Figley, 1995). In fact, the more empathic the counselor, the more at risk he or she is for internalizing the clients' stress, distress, and trauma. It is this empathic connection with clients and the resultant prolonged exposure to their stories of suffering that serve as the basis for the development of compassion fatigue (Weiss, 2004).

Symptoms

Similar to burnout, compassion fatigue often presents as physical and emotional exhaustion. However, in addition to exhaustion, those experiencing compassion fatigue often exhibit a wide variety of symptoms spread across multidimensions. Those with compassion fatigue often exhibit an impaired ability to concentrate (cognitive symptom); an increase in feelings of sadness, guilt, or anxiety (emotional impact); and changes in eating and sleeping patterns (behavioral effects). Further, those with compassion fatigue often report experiencing increased aches and pains (somatic symptoms), evidence of increasing mistrust and isolation (interpersonal aspects), reduction in work efficiency and effectiveness, and a change in their fundamental values and beliefs (spiritual impact). The extent of the potential symptoms accompanying compassion fatigue can be found in Table 12.1.

Table 12.1 Compassion Fatigue Symptoms

Physical Symptoms

_____ I have had increased absenteeism "sick days"

_____ I have been feeling physically ill

_____ I have been feeling fatigued

_____ I have been feeling keyed-up and nervous

_____ I am doing less rather than more exercise

_____ Normal sleep has been more difficult for me

_____ I have lost enjoyment in intimate and sexual activities

Psychological Symptoms

_____ I have noticed myself being more cynical and pessimistic

_____ I have noticed that I have been trying to avoid feelings by numbing or shutting down

_____ I have had work-related nightmares/bad dreams

_____ I have lost interest and enjoyment in activities

_____ I have difficulty in making decisions or make poor decisions

_____ I feel as though I have lost some of my self-esteem

Emotional Symptoms

_____ I have anger directed toward my supervisors or coworkers

_____ I have been feeling flat, depressed, and hopeless more than I used to

_____ I have been more angry and irritable than normal

(Continued)

Table 12.1 (Continued)

_____ I have moments of dread when thinking about going to work
_____ I am having trouble finding hope
_____ I am less connected to my spiritual and religious beliefs than I used to be
_____ I have felt overwhelmed more than three times in the past week

Spiritual Symptoms

_____ I have been avoiding spending time with my friends and family
_____ I fear for the safety of myself and my loved ones
_____ I have engaged in less rather than more activities that used to bring me pleasure
_____ I have had a lack of time for self
_____ I find it difficult to trust others
_____ I have feelings of despair and hopelessness

Professional Symptoms

_____ I have been unable to get work or something specific to work out of my head
_____ I have had unwanted memories pop up in my head of past events from work
_____ My productivity at work has been reduced
_____ I have felt like quitting my job more than once
_____ I find paperwork and menial tasks getting in the way of my enjoyment of work

Five or more checked could indicate that you are suffering from compassion fatigue symptoms

Source: Gentry, J. E. (2002). Compassion fatigue: A crucible of transformation. *Journal of Trauma Practice,* 1(3/4), 36–71.

It is not surprising, given the breadth and depth of impact experienced by one with compassion fatigue, that for some counselors, compassion fatigue results in their core beliefs, personal and professional identities, and worldview being shaken. This was certainly true for LJ, a student intern at children and youth services (see Case illustration 12.2).

CASE ILLUSTRATION 12.2

A Graduate Student Who Simply Cared

The placement at Children and Youth Services was demanding, both in the quantity and nature of the caseloads assigned. LJ, a graduate student engaged in his second clinical internship, was quite knowledgeable and skillful in working with children who were abused and displaced. Having previously worked in the field as a case worker, LJ was quite familiar with the various support services available in the county and showed a great efficiency connecting his clients with community resources.

His well-developed professional skills and high level of personal maturity belied the fact that he was still a counselor-in-training. As a result, over the course of the year-long internship, he was assigned a heavier than typical caseload and given more autonomy than typically assigned to student-interns. As the year progressed, LJ found himself working primarily with preschool-aged children who had been severely abused. Although he felt that his previous work as a case worker prepared him for working with this clientele, what he was unprepared for was the impact of moving from simply knowing about the abuse, to walking with the client through their telling of their stories of abuse in the hope of finding some form of healing. The seemingly endless flow of client stories graphically detailing and depicting experiences of abuse that included being burned, whipped, cut, and sexually abused began to take their toll.

Working and walking in this "darker side" of the human condition not only eroded LJ's ability to be objective, to maintain appropriate professional boundaries, and to effectively and professionally service his clients, but ate away at his personal worldview. His classmates began to notice the changes.

What was once an energetic, enthusiastic, and optimistic individual, happy to be engaged in a profession to which he felt "called," was now a sarcastic and cynical counselor who was very negative about his clients and his profession. The once creative and hope-filled class participant now openly posited the existence of evil and the belief that counseling and therapy were powerless against such evil. He disclosed that he doubted the value of this profession and was unsure if he even wanted to continue in his program of study.

The change in values and worldview were dramatic and did not go unnoticed by his professor and site supervisor. Thankfully, through their intervention and support, LJ was able make the adjustment needed to both his personal and professional life in order to return to his previous (yet now wiser) state of functioning.

Risk Factors

Research has identified a number of factors that have been associated with increased incidence of compassion fatigue. As noted above, those counselors who work with clients who report abuse and have experienced trauma appear to increase their susceptibility to compassion fatigue (Pearlman & Saakvitne, 1995). In addition to the nature of the population served, counselors who have heavy caseloads and work inordinately long hours also appear to have a greater risk for compassion fatigue (Creamer & Liddle, 2005). Beyond work-related factors, several personal characteristics or attributes appear to place a person at risk for developing compassion fatigue. Research identifies those who may be overly conscientious, who are somewhat perfectionistic, and who have low levels of social support as having an increased risk of experiencing compassion fatigue (Meadors & Lamson, 2008). Further, those counselors who are under high levels of stress within their personal lives and those who have a history of personal trauma also appear to be more susceptible to the experience of compassion fatigue (Meadors & Lamson, 2008). But, perhaps what might be most important to those just entering the field is the finding that "newer" therapists appear to experience the most difficulty (Adams, Matto, & Harrington, 2001).

Assessing the Risk

One of the often used and researched measures of both compassion satisfaction and fatigue was developed by B. Hudnall Stamm. The Professional Quality of Life (ProQOL) Compassion Satisfaction and Compassion Fatigue Version 5 (2009) is inserted below. The ProQOL can be directly accessed at http://www.proqol.org/uploads/ProQOL_5_English.pdf and can be used at regular intervals to track changes over time, especially when strategies for prevention or intervention are being tried.

PROFESSIONAL QUALITY OF LIFE SCALE (PROQOL)

COMPASSION SATISFACTION AND COMPASSION FATIGUE (PROQOL) VERSION 5 (2009)

When you *[help]* people you have direct contact with their lives. As you may have found, your compassion for those you *[help]* can affect you in positive and negative ways. Below are some questions about your experiences, both positive and negative, as a *[helper]*. Consider each of the following questions about you and your current work situation. Select the number that honestly reflects how frequently you experienced these things in the *last 30 days*.

1 = Never	2 = Rarely	3 = Sometimes	4 = Often	5 = Very Often

___ 1. I am happy.

___ 2. I am preoccupied with more than one person I *[help]*.

___ 3. I get satisfaction from being able to *[help]* people.

___ 4. I feel connected to others.

___ 5. I jump or am startled by unexpected sounds.

___ 6. I feel invigorated after working with those I *[help]*.

___ 7. I find it difficult to separate my personal life from my life as a *[helper]*.

___ 8. I am not as productive at work because I am losing sleep over traumatic experiences of a person I *[help]*.

___ 9. I think that I might have been affected by the traumatic stress of those I *[help]*.

___ 10. I feel trapped by my job as a *[helper]*.

___ 11. Because of my *[helping]*, I have felt "on edge" about various things.

___ 12. I like my work as a *[helper]*.

___ 13. I feel depressed because of the traumatic experiences of the people I *[help]*.

___ 14. I feel as though I am experiencing the trauma of someone I have *[helped]*.

___ 15. I have beliefs that sustain me.

___ 16. I am pleased with how I am able to keep up with *[helping]* techniques and protocols.

___ 17. I am the person I always wanted to be.

___ 18. My work makes me feel satisfied.

___ 19. I feel worn out because of my work as a *[helper]*.

___ 20. I have happy thoughts and feelings about those I *[help]* and how I could help them.

___ 21. I feel overwhelmed because my case [work] load seems endless.

___ 22. I believe I can make a difference through my work.

___ 23. I avoid certain activities or situations because they remind me of frightening experiences of the people I *[help]*.

___ 24. I am proud of what I can do to *[help]*.

___ 25. As a result of my *[helping]*, I have intrusive, frightening thoughts.

___ 26. I feel "bogged down" by the system.

___ 27. I have thoughts that I am a "success" as a *[helper]*.

___ 28. I can't recall important parts of my work with trauma victims.

___ 29. I am a very caring person.

___ 30. I am happy that I chose to do this work.

YOUR SCORES ON THE PROQOL: PROFESSIONAL QUALITY OF LIFE SCREENING

Based on your responses, place your personal scores on page 301. If you have any concerns, you should discuss them with a physical or mental health care professional.

Compassion Satisfaction

Compassion satisfaction is about the pleasure you derive from being able to do your work well. For example, you may feel like it is a pleasure to help others through your work. You may feel positively about your colleagues or your ability to contribute to the work setting or even the greater society. Higher scores on this scale represent a greater satisfaction related to your ability to be an effective caregiver in your job.

The average score is 50 (SD 10; alpha scale reliability .88). About 25% of people score higher than 57 and about 25% of people score below 43. If you are in the higher range, you probably derive a good deal of professional satisfaction from your position. If your scores are below 40, you may either find problems with your job, or there may be some other reason—for example, you might derive your satisfaction from activities other than your job.

Burnout

Most people have an intuitive idea of what burnout is. From the research perspective, burnout is one of the elements of Compassion Fatigue (CF). It is associated with feelings of hopelessness and difficulties in dealing with work or in doing your job effectively. These negative feelings usually have a gradual onset. They can reflect the feeling that your efforts make no difference, or they can be associated with a very high workload or a non-supportive work environment. Higher scores on this scale mean that you are at higher risk for burnout.

The average score on the burnout scale is 50 (SD 10; alpha scale reliability .75). About 25% of people score above 57 and about 25% of people score below 43. If your score is below 43, this probably reflects positive feelings about your ability to be effective in your work. If you score above 57 you may wish to think about what at work makes you feel like you are not effective in your position. Your score may reflect your mood; perhaps you were having a "bad day" or are in need of some time off. If the high score persists or if it is reflective of other worries, it may be a cause for concern.

Secondary Traumatic Stress

The second component of Compassion Fatigue (CF) is secondary traumatic stress (STS). It is about your work related, secondary exposure to extremely or traumatically stressful events. Developing problems due to exposure to other's trauma is somewhat rare but does happen to many people who care for those who have experienced extremely or traumatically stressful events. For example, you may repeatedly hear stories about the traumatic things that happen to other people, commonly called Vicarious Traumatization. If your work puts you directly in the path of danger, for example, field work in a war or area of civil violence, this is not secondary exposure; your exposure is primary. However, if you are exposed to others' traumatic events as a result of your work, for example, as a therapist or an emergency worker, this is secondary exposure. The symptoms of STS are usually rapid in onset and associated with a particular event. They may include being afraid, having difficulty sleeping, having images of the upsetting event pop into your mind, or avoiding things that remind you of the event.

The average score on this scale is 50 (SD 10; alpha scale reliability .81). About 25% of people score below 43 and about 25% of people score above 57. If your score is above 57, you may want to take some time to think about what at work may be frightening to you or if there is some other reason for the elevated score. While higher scores do not mean that you do have a problem, they are an indication that you may want to examine how you feel about your work and your work environment. You may wish to discuss this with your supervisor, a colleague, or a health care professional.

WHAT IS MY SCORE AND WHAT DOES IT MEAN?

In this section, you will score your test so you understand the interpretation for you. To find your score on **each section,** total the questions listed on the left and then find your score in the table on the right of the section.

Compassion Satisfaction Scale

Copy your rating on each of these questions on to this table and add them up. When you have added them up you can find your score on the table to the right.

3. _______
6. _______
12. _______
16. _______
18. _______
20. _______
22. _______
24. _______
27. _______
30. _______

Total: ___________________

The sum of my Compassion Satisfaction	*So my score equals*	*And my Compassion Satisfaction level is*
22 or less	43 or less	Low
Between 23 and 41	Around 50	Average
42 or more	57 or more	High

Burnout Scale

On the burnout scale you will need to take an extra step. Starred items are "reverse scored." If you scored the item 1, write a 5 beside it. The reason we ask you to reverse the scores is because scientifically the measure works better when these questions are asked in a positive way though they can tell us more about their negative form. For example, question

1. "I am happy" tells us more about the effects of helping when you are *not* happy so you reverse the score

*1. _____ = _____
4. _____ = _____
8. _____
10. _____
*15. _____ = _____
*17. _____ = _____
19. _____
21. _____

You	*Change*
1	5
2	4
3	3
4	2
5	1

26. _____
*29. _____ = _____
Total: ___________

The sum of my Compassion Satisfaction	*So My Score Equals*	*And my Compassion Satisfaction level is*
22 or less	43 or less	Low
Between 23 and 41	Around 50	Average
42 or more	57 or more	High

Secondary Traumatic Stress Scale

Just like you did on Compassion Satisfaction, copy your rating on each of these questions on to this table and add them up. When you have added them up you can find your score on the table to the right.

2. ______
5. ______
7. ______
9. ______
11. ______
13. ______
14. ______
23. ______
25. ______
28. ______
Total: ______

The sum of my Compassion Satisfaction	*So My Score Equals*	*And my Compassion Satisfaction level is*
22 or less	43 or less	Low
Between 23 and 41	Around 50	Average
42 or more	57 or more	High

B. Hudnall Stamm, 2009-2012. Professional Quality of Life: Compassion Satisfaction and Fatigue Version 5 (ProQOL). www.proqol.org. This test may be freely copied as long as (a) author is credited, (b) no changes are made, and (c) it is not sold. Those interested in using the test should visit www.proqol.org to verify that the copy they are using is the most current version of the test.

Source: B. Hudnall Stamm, 2009-2012. Professional Quality of Life: Compassion Satisfaction and Fatigue Version 5 (ProQOL).

Reducing the Risk

There are a number of effective strategies, targeting modification in work setting and practices along with adjustment to one's lifestyle, that help counselors reduce the risk of compassion fatigue. We can appreciate that for you, who are still in training and not yet fully engaged in your professional life, the thought of adjusting your lifestyle as a means of reducing your risk of compassion fatigue may be low on your list of priorities. However, it is important to reiterate the point previously made. Research (Adams et al., 2001) highlights the fact that those who are newer to the experience of the counseling dynamic are at greater risk. Therefore, it is never too early for you to begin to develop those patterns of professional practice and lifestyle that promote wellness.

Work Setting

In response to the immersion within the pain of one's client, it is important to create a supportive work environment that not only allows for breaks and modified caseloads (when working with particularly draining clients), but also encourages peer support and proper debriefings following particularly difficult sessions and clients. In addition, research suggests that counselors who experience a sense of autonomy and control while working in settings that offer supervision will have lower incidence of compassion fatigue (Boscarino, Figley, & Adams, 2004; Ortlepp & Friedman, 2002).

Although your field placement is but an introduction to the life and experience of the professional counselor, it does provide you with the material to review and consider as you contemplate ways in which that work setting could be modified or the demands adjusted in order to facilitate counselor well-being while reducing the potential for compassion fatigue. Exercise 12.2 invites you to assess your current placement regarding how it might facilitate counselor wellness or contribute to compassion fatigue.

EXERCISE 12.2

Modifying Work Setting

Directions: Below, you will find a listing of work setting characteristics that have been associated with either the facilitation of counselor well-being or the development of compassion fatigue. Your task is to review the list, identifying those elements that you have encountered within your field placement, and develop a recommendation for reducing the potential of compassion fatigue in those engaged as counselors.

Element	Facilitates Counselor Well-Being	Invites Compassion Fatigue	Recommendation
Frequency of trauma- and abuse-based referrals			

(Continued)

(Continued)

Element	Facilitates Counselor Well-Being	Invites Compassion Fatigue	Recommendation
Number of cases carried (caseloads)			
Expectations of counselor availability outside of work hours			
Schedules that allow for frequent breaks			
Schedules and resources supporting lunch breaks			
Realistic expectations and measures of counselor performance			
Supportive climate (peer/supervisory)			
Degree of non-client-related work assignments			

Lifestyle Adjustments

As with burnout, the prescription for reducing the risk of compassion fatigue is to engage in a lifestyle that is characterized by a healthy balance between those activities that are draining and those that are renewing. By achieving and maintaining a greater sense of wellness, counselors and counseling students may enhance their personal growth and development; experience more satisfaction; and, as a result, remain better able to meet the demands of their training and future work environments (Roach & Young, 2007).

As is true when reducing the risk for burnout, counselors who engage in exercise, maintain healthy diets, and structure their days to allow for adequate rest and renewal of their energy reduce their risk of compassion fatigue. But beyond these fundamentals, counselors must understand and value the need to establish and maintain professional boundaries as a significant way of reducing the risk of compassion fatigue. For too many counselors, especially those new to the profession, the desire to help seduces them to work beyond the hours of a contract, volunteer for extra duty, and border on obsessing about cases and treatment plans. Setting appropriate boundaries separating the world of work from that which is personal is essential for the health of a counselor.

Beyond these limits, counselors attempting to reduce the risk of compassion fatigue must be skilled at balancing empathy with professional distance and objectivity (Radey & Figley, 2007).

Intervening When Necessary

Even when the counselor is knowledgeable about the concept of compassion fatigue and research regarding risk factors, the possibility of falling prey to its grasp is still very present. Experiencing compassion fatigue is neither evidence of professional incompetence nor personal weakness. In fact, as suggested by Gentry (2002), the symptoms of compassion fatigue can be viewed as evidence of what is right and potentially effective within the counselor—the ability to be empathic and caring. The invitation for the counselor experiencing compassion fatigue is to continue doing what he or she is doing, but with a bit of fine-tuning (Gentry, 2002).

For those experiencing compassion fatigue, the good news is that the symptoms of compassion fatigue appear to be very responsive to being treated and rapidly ameliorated (Gentry & Baranowsky, 1998; Pearlman & Saakvitne, 1995). One model for assisting those with compassion fatigue is the Accelerated Recovery Program for Compassion Fatigue (Gentry & Baranowsky, 1998). The elements of this program are as follows.

Intentionality, Recognition, and Acceptance

As may be obvious, yet essential, any attempt to resolve compassion fatigue starts with the recognition and acceptance of the experience of compassion fatigue. Accepting the symptoms serves as a springboard for the identification of the possible cause and a commitment to resolving the issue. Recognition and acceptance may seem obvious, but for many counselors the tendency appears to be to deny or ignore symptoms until they reach a point of personal and professional disruption. The faster one can recognize the occurrence of compassion fatigue and resolve to address the issues underlying the symptoms, the faster one may return to both professional and personal wellness.

Connection

The second element necessary for recovery is for the counselor to take steps to establish or reestablish healthy, intimate relationships. One of the root causes for compassion fatigue is the sense of increasing isolation and the experience of losing one's connections, both within and outside of the professional arena. Reconnecting can be facilitated by the experience of supportive colleagues and a work setting that provides mentoring and supervision. Beyond this professional connection, it is important for the counselor to maintain, and if lost reestablish, intimate contacts and engagement with close friends. The opportunity to engage in genuine, healthy, caring interactions allows for counselor self-disclosure and invites empathic understanding and supportive responses.

Anxiety Management/Self-Soothing

A third element in the Accelerated Recovery Program for Compassion Fatigue is the promotion of the counselor's self-soothing and maintenance of non-anxious states. Developing the skills necessary for self-regulation and management of anxiety is believed to be core to buffering one from compassion fatigue. Further, it is believed that increasing the counselor's ability to self-soothe and manage anxiety will prove effective in reducing the chances that he or she will seek other, less healthy alternatives (e.g., drinking and drugs) for anxiety reduction.

Self-Care

The fourth element in the compassion fatigue treatment regimen is to engage counselors in healthy, wellness-oriented life decisions. Evidence suggests that counselors who engage in career-sustaining behavior and are committed to personal emotional wellness are better protected from burnout or compassion fatigue (Rupert & Kent, 2007). Developing a system supporting a healthy lifestyle is core to both prevention and intervention. Beyond the fundamentals previously outlined (e.g., healthy eating, exercise, etc.), it is important to establish boundaries around the demands of work and the opportunities of nonwork life. Setting limits to hours worked, size and types of caseloads, and even client expectations (such as constantly being on call) is difficult but essential if one is to move from a state of compassion fatigue to compassion satisfaction and wellness.

What Next?

Although the steps to buffering oneself from the possibility of burnout and compassion fatigue can be described and detailed, the information within this chapter is only useful if it is embraced and enacted. Exercise 12.3 invites you to engage in a self-assessment and commitment to the development of and engagement in a healthy life plan. It is hoped that committing to your own plan of health and well-being will start now, not someday, and that you fully appreciate the fact that caring for self is the best way for you to be positioned to care for others.

EXERCISE 12.3

Committing to Wellness

Directions: Below is a list of activities that can contribute to one's general state of health and wellness and could prove valuable in lowering the risk of experiencing compassion fatigue. Your task is to engage in an honest self-assessment and plan for a commitment to a healthier life style. Identify at least one of the items of self-care that you feel you have been lax in performing and commit to increasing your engagement in that form of self-care starting immediately. It is suggested that you repeat this process monthly as a way of promoting your own health and wellness.

Domain	Specific	I am committed to . . .
Physical Health	Eat 4–6 meals a day	
	Eat well-balanced meals, including fruits and vegetables	
	Reduce sugar intake	
	Monitor caffeine intake	
	Exercise–some form of exercise–30 min at least three times a week	
	Schedule dental care twice annually	
	Promote consistent and sufficient sleep	
	Engage in enjoyable physical activities–dance, swim, golf, bowling. etc.	
	Other (your ideas)	
Social Connection	Go out with friends	
	Talk with friends and family	
	Visit family member/friend	
	Smile and say 'Hi" to those you encounter in the course of your typical day	
	Disengage from thoughts of clients when in nonwork social settings	
	Attend a group educational or recreational experience (lecture, concert, sporting event)	
	Other (your choice)	
	Connect with colleagues about professional issues/questions and concerns	
	Connect with colleagues about nonprofessional issues/activities	
Psychological Domain	Engage in self-reflection	
	Read for recreation	

(Continued)

(Continued)

Domain	Specific	I am committed to . . .
	Contract for personal counseling, coaching, or spiritual direction	
	Increase your awareness of personal baggage and issues as well as ways of managing them	
	Engage in stress reduction activities	
	Employ anxiety reduction techniques	
	Seek out opportunities to learn and expand skill and knowledge outside the professional realm (e.g., learn foreign language or to play an instrument)	
	Give yourself permission and take the opportunity to "zone out" as a way of decompressing (e.g., watching television, playing a video game, etc.)	
Affective Domain	Engage in activities that make you laugh	
	Find opportunities to celebrate life with others (e.g., birthdays, holidays, and anniversaries)	
	Provide self with affirmation and praise	
	Freely express feelings of sadness or loneliness (freedom to cry)	
	Reconnect via review of old pictures or tapping memories of loved ones and loving experiences	
	Appropriately disclose feelings of anger and frustration (rather than repressing or displacing)	
	Find time to sing	
	Find opportunities to dance	
	Grant yourself permission to do or attempt to do those activities you always wished you could do	
	Other (your ideas)	

Domain	**Specific**	**I am committed to . . .**
Inner Life	Engage in meditational readings	
	Engage in personal reflection	
	Meditate	
	Commune with nature	
	Participate in structured spiritual activity (church service, prayer group, retreat, etc.)	
	Engage with spiritual director or mentor	
	Find opportunities for expression of gratitude	
	Celebrate your gifts of life	
	Read about another's spiritual journey	
	Seek a moment, or an opportunity, to be in awe	
	Other (your ideas)	
Professional Domain	Set realistic daily task demands	
	Identify those tasks/activities that are exciting and life giving and integrate those with those activities that tend to be more draining	
	Move away from the desk–by way of a simple break or a quick visit to a colleague or a short walk	
	Close your door to allow for quiet, uninterrupted time to complete a task	
	Say "no" to an invitation to do more when you already have enough	
	Leave work issues and concerns within the office	
	Engage in peer support regarding client and case issues as well as regarding personal questions and concerns	

(Continued)

(Continued)

Domain	Specific	I am committed to . . .
	Engage with a supervisor or mentor	
	Establish your work space so that it is both comfortable and comforting	
	Set boundaries with colleagues, especially when their interactions are intrusions on your limited time or when their requests are overburdening	
	Take a moment to review your day while identifying one aspect that was professionally satisfying	
	Other	

KEYSTONES

- Counselors engage in emotionally demanding work, which has been shown to contribute to counselor depression, anxiety, and reduced self-esteem and interfere with professional functioning by negatively affecting a counselor's ability to attend and concentrate and engage in effective decision making.
- Burnout is a condition "of physical and emotional exhaustion, involving the development of negative self-concept, negative job attitude, and loss of concern and feeling for clients" (Pines & Maslach, 1978). The experience of burnout is multidimensional, potentially affecting a counselor physically, cognitively, emotionally, and interpersonally, and even affecting his or her core values.
- In addition to long hours, heavy caseloads, being on call, interference from outside agencies, and isolation within the work setting, the very nature of the work and role expectations encountered by counselors have been found to contribute to their higher levels of burnout.
- Burnout evolves over time, starting with a counselor experiencing a loss of caring and commitment, and continues with the counselor exhibiting increased inflexibility, distancing from clients, and disbelief in effectiveness of treatment.
- It is important for counselors to engage in self-assessment, commit to healthy lifestyle choices, and take time to recharge as ways of preventing burnout.
- Compassion fatigue has been described as a caregiver's reduced capacity or interest in being empathic or "bearing the suffering of clients."
- The impact of compassion fatigue is multidimensional, but most significantly, it can shake a counselor's core beliefs, personal and professional identities, and worldview.
- Counselors who work with clients experiencing trauma and abuse are at high risk for compassion fatigue.

- In addition to engaging in healthy lifestyle decisions and creating a supportive work environment, counselors need to develop and maintain appropriate personal and professional boundaries as a way of reducing risk for compassion fatigue.

ADDITIONAL RESOURCES

Web Based

Florida State University Traumatology Institute: www.fsu.edu/traumatologyinstitute. Located in the School of Social Work, the Traumatology Institute develops cutting-edge research, assessment, and training and education programs focusing on the traumatized, which include individual children, adults, families, organizations, and nation states.

ProQOL.org. (n.d.). *ProQOL 5.* Retrieved from http://proqol.org/ProQol_Test.html

PTSD Support Services. (n.d.). *Compassion fatigue self-test.* Retrieved from http://www.ptsdsupport.net/compassion_fatugue-selftest.html

University of Buffalo School of Social Work. (n.d.). *Self-care exercises and activities.* Retrieved from http://socialwork.buffalo.edu/resources/self-care-starter-kit/self-care-exercises-and-activities.html

Print Based

Azar, S. T. (May, 2000). Preventing burnout in professionals and paraprofessionals who work with child abuse and neglect cases: A cognitive behavioral approach to supervision. *Journal of Clinical Psychology,* 643–663.

Brohl, K. (2004). The new miracle workers: Overcoming contemporary challenges in child welfare work. In *Understanding and preventing worker burnout,* pp. 141–157. Washington, DC: Child Welfare League of America.

Figley, C. R. (Ed.). (2002). *Treating compassion fatigue.* New York, NY: Brunner/Rutledge.

Harrison, R. L., & Westwood, M. J. (2009). Preventing vicarious traumatization of mental health therapists: Identifying protective practices. *Psychotherapy Theory: Research, Practice, Training, 46*(2), 203–219.

Racanelli, C. (2005). *Is it burnout and/or compassion fatigue? How to identify, differentiate, prevent and intervene.* New York: New York University School of Social Work.

Radey, M., & Figley, C. R. (2007). The social psychology of compassion. *Clinical Social Work, 35*(1), 207–214.

Rothschild, B. (2006). *Help for the helper: Self-care strategies for managing burnout and stress.* New York, NY: W. W. Norton.

Shallcross, L. (2011). Taking care of yourself as a counselor. *Counseling Today.* Retrieved from: http://ct.counseling.org/2011/01/taking-care-of-yourself-as-a-counselor/

Skovholt, T. M., & Trotter-Mathison, M. (2011). *The resilient practitioner: Burnout prevention and self-care strategies for therapists, counselors, teachers, and health professionals* (2nd ed.). New York, NY: Routledge.

Stebnicki, M. A. (2008). Empathy fatigue: Healing the mind, body, and spirit of professional counselors. New York, NY: Springer.

Trippany, R. L., White Kress, V. E., & Wilcoxon, S. A. (2004). Preventing vicarious trauma: What counselors should know when working with trauma survivors. *Journal of Counseling & Development, 82,* 31–37.

Volk, K. T., Guarino, K., Edson Grandin, M., & Clervil, R. (2008). *What about you? A work-book for those who work with others.* The National Center on Family Homelessness. Retrieved from http://508.center4si.com/SelfCareforCareGivers.pdf

REFERENCES

Adams, K. B., Matto, H. C., & Harrington, D. (2001). The traumatic stress institute belief scale as a measure of vicarious trauma in a national sample of clinical social workers. *Families in Society: The Journal of Contemporary Human Services, 82,* 363–371.

American Counseling Association. (2014). *ACA code of ethics.* Washington, DC: Author.

American Counseling Association's Task Force on Counseling Wellness and Impairment. (2010). *Assessment tools and wellness programs.* Retrieved from http://www.counseling.org/knowledge-center/counselor-wellness/assessment-tools-and-wellness-programs

Bakker, A. B., Demerouti, E., Taris, T. W., Schaufeli, W. B., & Schreurs, P. J. G. (2003). A multigroup analysis of the Job Demands-Resources Model in four home care organizations. *International Journal of Stress Management, 10,* 16–38.

Bakker, A. B., Van der Zee, K. I., Lewig, K. A., & Dollard, M. F. (2006). The relationship between the Big Five personality factors and burnout: A study among volunteer counselors. *Journal of Social Psychology, 126,* 31–50.

Boscarino, J. A., Figley, C. R., & Adams, R. E. (2004). Compassion fatigue following the September 11 terrorist attacks: A study of secondary trauma among New York City social workers. *International Journal of Emergency Mental Health, 6,* 57–66.

Butler, S. K., & Constantine, M. G. (2005). Collective self-esteem and burnout in professional school counselors. *Professional School Counseling, 9*(1), 55–62.

Creamer, T., & Liddle, B. (2005). Secondary traumatic stress among disaster mental health workers responding to the September 11 attacks. *Journal of Traumatic Stress 18*(1) 89–96.

Emerson, S., & Markos, P. A. (1996). Signs and symptoms of the impaired counselor. *Journal of Humanistic Education and Development, 34*(3), 108–117.

Evans, T. D., & Villavisanis, R. (1997). Encouragement exchange: Avoiding therapist burnout. *The Family Journal: Counseling and Therapy for Couples and Families, 5,* 342–345.

Feldstein, S. B. (2000). *The relationship between supervision and burnout in school counselors. Dissertation Abstracts International, 61*(2-A), 507 (UMI No. AAI9959913).

Figley, C. R. (Ed.). (1995). *Compassion fatigue: Coping with secondary traumatic stress disorder in those who treat the traumatized.* New York, NY: Brunner/Mazel.

Figley, C. R. (2002). Compassion fatigue: Psychotherapists' chronic lack of selfcare. *Psychotherapy in Practice, 58*(11), 1433–1411.

Firestone, R. W., Firestone, L. A., & Catlett, J. (2003). *Creating a life of meaning and compassion: The wisdom of psychotherapy.* Washington, DC: American Psychological Association.

Fothergill, A., Edwards, D., & Burnard, P. (2004). Stress, burnout, coping and stress management in psychiatrists: Findings from a systematic review. *International Journal of Social Psychiatry, 50,* 54–65.

Freudenberger. H. J. (1974). Staff burn-out. *Journal of Social Issues, 30*(1), 159–165.

Freudenberger. H. J. (1975). The staff burn-out syndrome in alternative institutions. *Psychotherapy: Theory, Research and Practice. 12*(1), 73–82.

Gentry, J. E. (2002). Compassion fatigue: The crucible of transformation. *The Journal of Traumatic Stress, 1*(3–4), 37–61.

Gentry, J., & Baranowsky, A. (1998). *Treatment manual for the Accelerated Recovery Program: Set II.* Toronto, Canada: Psych Ink.

Grosch, W. N., & Olsen, D. C. (1994). Therapist burnout: A self psychology and systems perspective. In W. N. Grosch & D. C. Olsen (Eds.), *When helping starts to hurt: A new look at burnout among psychotherapists* (pp. 439–454). New York, NY: W.W. Norton.

Hamann, D. L., & Gordon, D. G. (2000). Burnout: An occupational hazard. *Music Educators Journal, 87,* 34–39.

Imai, H., Nakao, H., Tsuchiya, M., Kuroda, Y., & Katon, T. (2004). Burnout and work environments of public health nurses involved in mental health care. *Occupational and Environmental Medicine, 61,* 764–768.

Kottler, J. (1989). *On being a therapist.* San Francisco, CA: Jossey-Bass.

Lambie, G. W. (2002). The contribution of ego development level to degree of burnout in school counselors. *Dissertation Abstracts International, 63,* 508.

Larson, D. G. (1993). *The helper's journey.* Champaign, IL: Research Press.

Lee, S. M., Baker, C. R., Cho, S. H., Heckathorn, D. E., Holland, M. W., Newgent, R. A., & Yu, K. (2007). Development and initial psychometrics of the Counselor Burnout Inventory. *Measurement and Evaluation in Counseling and Development, 40,* 142–154.

Lee, S. M., Cho, S. H., Kissinger, D., & Ogle, N. T. (2010). A typology of burnout in professional counselors. *Journal of Counseling & Development, 40,* 142–154.

Lehner, P., Seyed-Solorforough, M., O'Conner, M. F., Sak, S., & Mullin, T. (1997). Cognitive biases and time stress in team decision making. *IEEE Transactions on Systems, Man, & Cybernetics Part A: Systems & Humans27*(5), 698–703.

Lushington, K., & Luscri, G. (2001). Are counseling students stressed? A cross-cultural comparison of burnout in Australian, Singaporean and Hong Kong counseling students. *Asian Journal of Counselling, 8*(2), 209–232.

Maslach, C. (1982). Understanding burnout: Definitional Issues in analyzing a complex phenomenon. In W. S. Paine (Ed.), *Job stress and burnout.* Beverly Hills, CA: Sage.

Maslach, C. (1993). Burnout: A multidimensional perspective. In W. B. Schaufeli, C. Maslach, & T. Marek (Eds.), *Professional burnout: Recent developments in theory and research* (pp. 19–32). Philadelphia, PA: Taylor & Francis.

Maslach, C., & Jackson, S. E. (1981). The measurement of experienced burnout. *Journal of Occupational Behavior, 2,* 99–113.

Maslach, C., Leiter, M. P., & Schaufeli, W. B. (2009). Measuring burnout. In C. L. Cooper & S. Cartwright (Eds.), *The Oxford handbook of organizational well-being* (86–108). Oxford, UK: Oxford University Press.

Maslach, C., Schaufeli, W. B., & Leiter, M. P. (2001). Job burnout. *Annual Review of Psychology, 52,* 397–422.

Meadors, P., & Lamson, A. (2008). Compassion fatigue and secondary traumatization: Provider self care on intensive care units for children. *Journal of Pediatric Health, 22*(1), 24–34.

Morse, G., Salyers, M., Rollins, A., Monroe-DeVita, M., & Pfahler, C. (2012). Burnout in mental health services: A review of the problem and its remediation. *Administrative Policy in Mental Health and Mental Health Services Research, 39(5),* 341–352.

Ortlepp, K., & Friedman, M. (2002). Prevalence and correlates of secondary traumatic stress in workplace lay trauma counselors. *Journal of Trauma Stress, 15*(3), 213–222.

Pearlman, L. A., & Saakvitne, K. W. (1995). Treating therapists with vicarious traumatization and secondary traumatic stress disorders. In C. R. Figley (Ed.), *Compassion fatigue: Coping with secondary traumatic stress disorder in those who treat the traumatized* (pp. 150–177). New York, NY: Brunner/Mazel.

Pines, A. (1993). Burnout. In L. Goldberger & S. Breznitz (Eds.), *Handbook of stress: Theoretical and clinical aspects* (2nd ed., pp. 386–402). New York, NY: Free Press.

Pines, A., & Maslach, C. (1978). Characteristics of staff burnout in mental health settings. *Hospital & Community Psychiatry, 29*(4), 233–237.

Puig, A., Baggs, A., Mixon, K., Park, Y. M., Kim, B. Y., & Lee, S. M. (2012). Relationship between job burnout and personal wellness in mental health professionals. *Journal of Employment Counseling, 49*(3), 98–109.

Radey, M. & Figley, C. R. (2007). The social psychology of compassion. *Clinical Social Work Journal, 35,* 207–214.

Remen, R. N. (1996). *Kitchen table wisdom: Stories that heal.* New York, NY: Riverhead Books.

Roach, L. F., & Young, M. E. (2007). Do counselor education programs promote wellness in their students? *Journal of Counselor Education and Supervision, 47*(1).

Rupert, P., & Kent, J. (2007). Gender and work setting differences in career-sustaining behaviors and burnout among professional psychologists. *Professional Psychology: Research and Practice, 38*, 88–96.

Rupert, P. A., & Morgan, D. J. (2005). Work setting and burnout among professional psychologists. *Professional Psychology: Research and Practice, 36*(5), 544–550.

Saisan, J., deBenedictis, T., Barston, S., & Segal, R. (2008). *Understanding sleep: Deep sleep, REM sleep, cycles, stages, and needs.* Retrieved from http://www.helpguide.org/life/sleeping.htm

Schaufeli, W. B. (2003). Past performance and future perspectives of burnout research. *South African Journal of Industrial Psychology, 29,* 1–15.

Schaufeli, W. B., Maslach, C., & Marek, T. (Eds.). (1993). *Professional burnout: Recent developments in theory and research.* Philadelphia, PA: Taylor & Francis.

Skosnik, P. D., Chatterton, R. T., Swisher, T., & Park, S. (2000). Modulation of attentional inhibition by norepinephrine and cortisol after psychological stress. *International Journal of Psychophysiology, 36*(1), 59–68.

Skovholt, T. M. (2001). *The resilient practitioner: Burnout prevention and self-care strategies for counselors, therapists, teachers, and health professionals.* Boston, MA: Allyn & Bacon.

Skovholt, T. M., & Ronnestad, M. H. (2003). Struggles of the novice counselor and therapist. *Journal of Career Development, 30,* 45–58.

Tyssen, R., Vaglum, P., Grønvold, N. T., & Ekeberg, Ø. (2001). Suicidal ideation among medical students and young physicians: A nationwide and prospective study of prevalence and predictors. *Journal of Affective Disorders, 64*(1), 69–79.

Weiss, D. S. (2004). The Impact of Event Scale–Revised. In J. P. Wilson & T. M. Keane (Eds.), Assessing psychological trauma and PTSD (2nd ed., pp. 168–189). New York: Guilford Press.

13

Transition From Practice to Career

Know thyself and know your enemy, and you can fight a hundred battles with no danger of defeat.

Sun Tzu

Although this quote is speaking about war, the competition for employment and entry into your chosen career in today's job market is no less intense than fighting a battle in the field. For most of you as graduate students, the goal of practice at an internship site and of your efforts to get an advanced degree in the helping field is ultimately to find employment. To win the battle or to achieve the goal, you must begin to function as a professional. This should start day one when you begin your training program, setting high standards and expectations for your practice. With such high standards and expectations, you will be able to evolve as a competent professional counselor ready for employment in the counseling field.

We believe transitioning from internship to career and employment is a critical component in your professional development and an important step that you must take during your internship. In this chapter, we will familiarize you with some of the major steps to be taken as you transition from your role as student in practice to that of employed professional. After completing this chapter, readers will be able to

- understand the important connection between counseling internship and career,
- understand the meaning of doing,
- integrate what you have learned during your internship into your job search,
- understand the options that you may have after you complete your internship, and
- prepare yourself for employment by creating a job search package.

Connection Between Internship and Career

In Chapter 1, the process of transitioning from counseling intern to professional counselor was discussed in great detail. We noted that this transition meant a counseling intern emerges as a counseling professional through a series of qualitative changes, including (a) a psychological shift from student to professional, (b) a performance outcome shift from grades to effectiveness, (c) a mental and behavioral shift from dependence to independence, and (d) a responsibility shift from focusing on self to focusing on others (e.g., clients, employers, and the public).

This internship experience invites the intern to shift focus from classroom knowledge and skill to real-life application. Further, the experience in internship fosters the intern's value acknowledgement and declaration of professional identity. Truly, the successful field experience transports the intern from the perception of self as student to self as professional.

As one moves through his or her field experience toward the end of this phase of professional training, thoughts will most likely turn toward the next phase of professional life—entry into one's career as a counselor.

We have chosen to focus on the concept of *career* as opposed to "job" or even "employment" because, as a professional counselor, you are stepping into an experience that far exceeds the requirements and payoffs of a job. As a professional counselor, your choice of the what and where of your employment is in service of your professional ambition and, in general, provides one of the paths toward your lifelong goals. Because entry into the profession involves more than gaining a paycheck, it is important that you employ the time, energy, reflection, and focus necessary to find, select, and engage in that which will be truly life giving.

Apprenticeship: Stepping Into the World of the Professional

Clinical practicum/internships have been viewed as an essential component of professional training in almost all mental health disciplines (Freidheim, 1994). This apprentice nature of the field experience is significant.

"An internship is a job that gives students practical, supervised experience in the professional working world" (Paterson, 2001, p. 39). As with all apprenticeships, those in field work are able to observe, model, and grow through the corrective feedback of their mentors. But unlike many forms of apprenticeship, those in field work as counselors-in-training are also introduced to the responsibilities of those professionally caring for another. From this aspect, the role of the intern is similar to the role of a full-time counseling professional. Ethics and legal issues are not just topics in professors' lectures and classroom discussions. During internship, they are issues in reality and are faced by both the intern and the professional counselor. Similarly, as counselor-in-the-field, the demands experienced by those professionals serving as your mentors will be your reality as well. The demands of conducting individual and/or group sessions, maintaining appropriate paperwork, participating in professional activities, and presenting with a professional demeanor take on increased significance given the legal and ethical implications of each. While one who is in apprenticeship is called an intern or field placement student, the reality is that the overlap of what the intern does and what the professional counselor does is significant, so much so that those in the field truly transition from student to a role of counselor. This transition allows those in field placement to move from the concept of counseling and being a counselor to a lived experience as a counselor. Such a transition is essential for one to make the vocational decision to embrace this field, this practice as their career, and once they do—the search for employment begins.

Preparation for Employment

While many students, especially those who find themselves burdened with student loans and other forms of debt, are eager to find a job . . . any job . . . following graduation, it is important to realize that it is a career you are seeking and not merely a job. As a career, the role and function you serve will need to fit within your life vision and your life goals and serve as a life-giving experience, one that goes beyond the amount printed on a check.

Therefore, as you prepare for stepping into the arena of professional counseling, it is important that you take time to evaluate your needs, your aspirations, your strengths, and your areas for growth. Clearly, the process of searching for employment will bring you under the scrutiny of potential employers. But as an individual venturing into what will be your career, you need to be able to scrutinize the opportunity being presented to ensure that it does meet your goals and values and will serve as a path toward professional growth and development.

As you begin the journey into your career, it is important to take the time for reflection and self-evaluation of what you desire and what you offer. Following such an evaluation, you will need to take those steps necessary to "package" and "present" that which you bring to the table.

Self-Evaluation

Self-evaluation is a critical step to transition you from an intern to a part-time or full-time professional counselor. Self-evaluations or assessments are simply methodologies used to collect data in a structured process designed to elicit your perceptions about your quality as a person and counseling professional (Michaelson, 2001). Taking the time for honest self-reflection and evaluation will help you to (a) know what your interests are, (b) become aware of what your values are, (c) fully understand what skills you possess, and (d) understand what your strengths and areas of challenge are. The value of the profile that results from such an honest self-evaluation is that it will serve you in searching for that placement, that career opportunity for which you have the knowledge and skill and at which your needs can be met. To have a better self-evaluation, we invite you to do Exercises 13.1 to 13.4.

EXERCISE 13.1

What Are Your Areas of Strength?

1.
2.
3.
4.
5.
6.
7.
8.
9.
10.

EXERCISE 13.2

Values Concerning What You Will Do as a Professional

Directions: The following is a list of values that are related to your professional career. Use the numerical number to rank which one you value the first, second, third, and so on.

- Helping others
- Searching for meaning of life
- Moral fulfillment
- Establishing identity
- Independence
- Making decisions for myself and others
- Job stability and security
- Job flexibility
- Location
- Opportunities for advancement
- Status
- Supervising others
- Handling challenging issues
- Good salary and benefit

Note: You may add more items to the list.

EXERCISE 13.3

What Are Your Interests?

1. List all the classes you have taken and the training activities you have received that you enjoyed in your graduate program.
2. List all the accomplishments (e.g., projects, presentations, publications, workshops, group work, etc.) you have achieved in your graduate program.
3. List all the major tasks that you have done successfully and enjoyed as a counseling graduate student.
4. List all the professional relationships you have had and enjoyed as a counseling graduate student.

EXERCISE 13.4

What Are Your Skills? Do You Enjoy the Skills You Have Identified?

1. Counseling skills (individual, couple, family)
2. Group counseling skills
3. Administration or management skills
4. Communication skills (e.g., oral and written)
5. Interpersonal skills
6. Research skills
7. Creative skills
8. Supervision skills

Note: For each skill you have identified, give one or two examples.

Now, with the results of your self-evaluation as the reference point, you may start to search for the job that most closely meets your criteria. There is no doubt that it is highly unlikely that you will find the "perfect" job, but as you process the opportunities, it is helpful to identify those that provide the greatest advantages and the fewest disadvantages.

With the job possibilities identified, the process of marketing yourself begins. Your self-promotion will take form in the development of your résumé, your letter of interest, and your personal interview.

Résumé

The creation of your résumé is a critical element in your job search package, and it functions as an advertisement, a self-promotion, that will allow you to stand out among all applicants and provide you with a foot in the door and the opportunity to interview for the job. Self-promotion? Marketing of self? These are terms that most counselors-in-training find foreign. After all, many of you have spent the past couple of years at the direction of others—perhaps even fearing self-promotion. Sadly, many graduate training programs spend more time on telling students what their deficits are than what their strengths are, and consequently it would not be unusual for you to feel somewhat apprehensive about self-promotion. But now is not the time to be shy or humble. It is essential that you truly toot your own horn!

So, how does one create a résumé that can accurately reflect his or her knowledge, skills, and experiences as a professional and as a person? Before you write your résumé, request a couple of résumés from your supervisor, counselor staff, or peer interns who have gone through the job search process. Then you may write down all the information about your education, counseling experiences, research activities, computer skills, awards, and personal hobbies. It is okay to include more information than you need for your final product. Meanwhile, you may get résumé advice through the university career center or a local community career center. Many college and university career centers offer résumé workshops, and it may be a good idea to attend one of those workshops because this type of workshop is often effective in helping people get job interviews.

There is no one right or correct way to develop your résumé, but there are a few key elements to consider as you give form to your own résumé. Table 13.1 highlights elements to keep in mind as you craft your résumé. It is important to remember that you want to convey *more* than your knowledge, your skill, and/or your experience. As a counselor and a future employee, it is important that those reading your résumé develop a sense of who you are as a person (your values and goals) and your current professional identity.

Table 13.1 Crafting a Résumé

1. Purpose: Sell Yourself!

As a one- or two-page sales instrument, your résumé must be crafted in a way that places you in the best light possible. This marketing of self should be used as the lens through which you critically pass all information you are thinking about including. For example, is listing the names and contact information for references the best use of this "advertising" space? A statement, or quote from a reference highlighting your value and uniqueness, may be more effective as a lead-in to a line such as "References available upon request."

2. Tone: Visionary

Although there is a need to identify training and experience, it should be framed within your vision of your future—the direction for your life and your vocational goals. Use experience and training as a springboard to tell the reader what you will do for him or her. As such, your résumé cannot be massed produced—tailor it to the job and the reader!

3. Visual Impact: The Rule of First Impressions

Your résumé is most likely one of a multitude sitting on the employer's desk. What about it draws his or her eyes to it?

Take a quick look at your résumé, just a couple of seconds. Now look away. What do you remember? What sticks out in your mind's eye? Are these the things you want to highlight?

4. Choose Your Words: Craft a Picture

Although there are various forms a résumé can take—descriptive paragraphs, bullets, a combination—it is important, regardless of format, to choose words that provide the picture of your abilities. For example, one could state that he or she "'worked with children who had social difficulties" or, as an alternative, note "facilitated social adjustment for school-aged population." Both descriptions require seven words, but which offers a picture of professionalism and counseling competence?

5. Standing Above the Crowd

When you think of those about to embark on a career of counseling, what types of descriptors or characteristics come to mind? List them! Perhaps you imagined words such as caring, empathic, and sensitive, or fragments such as wanting to make a difference, hoping to assist others, and curious about the human condition. Regardless of the words you generated, if *you* feel that they can be globally applied to those seeking a counseling position, then, needless to say, their use will *not* help you stand above the crowd.

What did you do or experience that may separate you from others? Did you author or coauthor research? Participate in a specialized training experience? Receive some form of commendation or recognition?

6. Succinct yet Impactful

The résumé is not a full job application and, as such, will not provide all the details of your training or experience. While some suggest it should a single page, others note that two pages will also be acceptable. It is important to assess the value of the material provided while also assessing the visual appeal. It is suggested that for visual appeal you don't overstuff a single page, or needlessly stretch a two-page résumé.

Given the space limitations, you will need to be highly selective as to the material you wish include. Select those experiences that reflect those directly relevant to the qualifications you wish to highlight, along with your current knowledge, skill, and aspirations. You don't need to include all jobs or volunteer positions unless they speak directly to your current competency.

To build an attractive or effective résumé, you want to know what the essentials are to make you stand out as a superior candidate for the job you are applying for, because most employers may not take much time to go through a résumé. The major function of your résumé is no more than an advertisement, with the purpose to win you an interview. So, it must be clear, well organized, creatively designed, and well written. It contains all necessary facts that the employer wants to know, such as your counseling experience, requisite educational levels, research activities, reference contact information, computer skills, awards, professional affiliations, and hobbies that reflect part of your personality. The effect you want from these details is to make the people who read your résumé interested, excited, and believe you are the best candidate that should be invited for an interview. Table 13.2 is a sample résumé of someone who is looking for a job in the field of counseling.

Table 13.2 Sample Résumé

Sara Smith

1024 Whispering Street, Narberth, PA 19072 | E-mail: Sarasmith@gmail.com | Tel: xxx-xxx-xxxx

OBJECTIVE

To obtain the position of School Counselor at XYZ School

EDUCATION

Master of Education in School Counseling, Chester College, West Chester, PA — December 2013
CACREP Accredited; GPA: 3.98
University of Pittsburgh, Pittsburgh, PA — June 2010
Bachelor of Science in Psychology, Business Option

SUMMARY OF QUALIFICATIONS

- School counseling experience in an urban-setting charter school
- School counseling experience in both individual and group formats
- Classroom guidance experience in developing curriculum and lesson plans
- Teaching experience as a substitute in an elementary and secondary school
- National and university awards

INTERNSHIP EXPERIENCE

Intern, Collegium Charter School, West Chester, PA — August 2012 to December 2013

Individual Counseling

- Counseled students in grades 6 through 12 with issues of depression, anxiety, low self-esteem, poor academic performance, and retention.
- Counseled students on a weekly basis in accordance with IEPs to meet specific goals.
- Assisted students having achieved 60% to 90% of guidance goals in IEPs.
- Helped numerous students cope with short-term crisis such as bullying or grieving.

Group Counseling

- Led and co-led boys, girls, and mixed groups weekly.
- Facilitated the groups on topics on academic issues, relationship issues, behavioral problems, bullying, sexual harassment, assertiveness training, and issues about transitioning to high school and college.

- Met with co-leaders on a regular basis to discuss all issues related to group counseling.

Classroom Guidance

- Co-developed a Studying Skills curriculum for the 10th grade.
- Taught and co-taught classes on studying basics, time management, organization, importance of education in meeting life goals, and learning style.
- Co-developed and co-wrote the Comprehensive Middle School Guidance Bullying Program.
- Co-taught lesson plans on bullying prevention, school policy on reporting, strategies on how to handle bullies, and alternative behaviors for bullies.

TEACHING EXPERIENCE

***Teaching Assistant*, Friends School, Germantown, PA** August 2010 to June 2011

- Substitute taught in the middle school and high school.
- Supported a 6th-grade teacher during math, English, and social studies.

RESEARCH EXPERIENCE

***Graduate Assistant*, Counselor Education Department** August 2011 to May 2012

Chester College, West Chester, PA

- Performed research with professors in the Counselor Education Department to develop resources for counselor trainees.
- Acknowledged for research in the *Theory of Counseling, 2011 Edition*, by Dr. Jeff White.

***Research Assistant*, Pittsburgh, PA** June 2008 to June 2010

- Studied the nature of abusive husbands and their motives in a clinical psychology lab.
- Worked in a cognitive psychology lab, examining the causes of errors in routine skills.
- Performed own research study titled "Mathematical Errors in Routine Skills."

AWARDS AND HONORS

• Outstanding Graduate Student Scholarship	Chester College	February 2012
• The ACA Foundation Graduate Student Essay Award		March 2012
• Dean's list	University of Pittsburgh	2007–2010

PROFESSIONAL DEVELOPMENT

• Membership in American School Counselor Association (ASCA)	Oct. 2011 to present
• Membership in American Counseling Association (ACA)	Oct. 2011 to present
• Membership in Pennsylvania School Counselor Association (PSCA)	Oct. 2011 to present
• Membership in Pennsylvania Counseling Association (PCA)	Oct. 2011 to present

COMPUTER SKILLS

- Proficient in using Microsoft Office tools: Word, Excel, and PowerPoint
- Knowledgeable in computer software and hardware technology and PC desktop management

HOBBIES

- Swimming, tennis, singing, and chess

(Continued)

Table 13.2 Sample Résumé (Continued)

REFERENCES

William Brown, Ph.D. Professor Department of Counselor Education Chester College West Chester, PA 19382 (610) 285-3540 wbrown@cc.edu	Kathleen Harrison, M.A. Licensed Counselor Collegium Charter School West Chester, PA 19382 (610) 269-8430 kharrison@gmail.com

The actual résumé consists of four sections: (a) fact, which includes your contact information, education, and objective; (b) the confirmation, which consists of your abilities, qualities, achievements, and qualifications; (c) the evidence, which contains two parts, the specifics of what you have done concerning your skills and expertise and the related experiences; and (d) the support, which includes the awards, publications, and the references that can prove and support what you said in the previous sections. Actually, one element in the first section, the objective, and all the elements in the second and third sections are the most important and powerful information that will make the people on the hiring committee who read your résumé feel interested and excited about you as a potential candidate who possesses the qualities and expertise they want.

A résumé objective is a statement in which you succinctly identify what position or job you are looking for. By including an objective statement in your résumé, you convince the hiring committee that you know what you want to do and are clear about your career direction. It also shows that you are experienced and familiar with the counseling field. The more clearly your objective statement is tied to the job description, the better chance you may have to get an interview. One thing you need to keep in mind when you include a résumé objective is that you want to tailor your résumé to fit the job you are applying for.

The second section confirms your abilities, qualities, and achievements with a summary of qualifications (see Table 13.2). This summary of three to four sentences must be concise and very specific, succinctly describing your most important abilities and qualities related to the job you are applying for. It also provides you with an opportunity to attract the hiring committee's attention and make them have a desire to read the rest of your résumé. Some key elements in the summary of qualifications may include your expertise, the depth of your skills, the environments in which you have gained experiences, your awards and accomplishments, and personal characteristics as a counselor.

In the third section of your résumé, you will present the evidence in two parts about your abilities, expertise/skills, awards, and accomplishments. The first part is your experiences and expertise closely related to the area you are interested in; the second part is about other related experiences. The order of listing your experiences, awards, and accomplishments depends on the type of job you are applying for. We suggest you arrange the order based on the job you are applying for. For example, if you apply for a counseling clinical job, you may want to list your counseling clinical experiences first in reverse chronological order, experiences gained at the present time first. If you apply for a teaching position, you may want to list your teaching experiences first in reverse chronological order, with the most recent teaching experience at the beginning. More specifically, use action verbs highlighting your best experiences that are most useful to the position you are applying for and valuable to the employer, including your accomplishments and the contributions you have made in each position. Then, you want to have the outcomes of your accomplishments and contributions measured in very specific terms. For example, your résumé might read "provided psychotherapy sessions for about 20 to 25 adults with a variety of clinical issues such as schizophrenia, schizoaffective disorder, substance abuse, anxiety, major depression, OCD, ADHD, and more on a weekly basis; co-led three substance abuse groups of women in the past year" (see Table 13.2 as well). Also, when you describe your past experience, use past tense, and use present tense to illustrate your current experience, a job or task you are still doing or working on at the present. The information about your related experiences is also useful because these experiences may show the people who read your résumé you have more knowledge and experiences in the fields that are related to the area you are interested in. These experiences may include the paid or unpaid jobs you had before, the community services you participated in, or a leadership position you held in an organization.

The last section of your résumé is pretty straightforward. You may simply list your awards and publications in reverse chronological order and then provide information about your professional organization affiliations and the references. Concerning your references' contact information, check with your supervisors and professors regarding the best way and time to get touch with them in case they take vacation or travel out of the country. Once you finish your résumé, you may share it with your supervisor, a couple of counseling staff members, and peers who have already interviewed for jobs. If it is possible, you may schedule an appointment with one of the career counselors in the career center at your college or university to help you polish your résumé. Another source to gain feedback and get advice is to send your résumé for free online counselor critique at www.resume-check.com.

Cover Letter

You have three opportunities to convince the employer to hire you as the best candidate for the job before you get it. The cover letter is one of the opportunities for you to describe what you cannot say in your resume. Particularly, you want to use the cover letter to articulate how what you have will benefit the employer and why you are the best fit for the position you're applying for, emphasizing your skills and qualifications. This last point is important to remember. Your cover letter should not be a composition of clichés, or generalized platitudes and empty promises. It is important to take time to research the job for which you are applying. Know what the expectations are, know a little about those working there, and attempt to discern the values of the culture. These are elements that will allow you to make a personal connection. These are the elements to which you can match your unique characteristics and qualifications.

A typical cover letter includes three main parts: the introduction, the main body, and the closure. In the introduction paragraph, you tell the hiring committee where you heard about the job, your education, your interest, and your qualifications for the position in a couple of sentences. The main body may include (a) your interest or passion about the job you are looking for; (b) your knowledge, skills, and experiences as well as administrative skills; and (c) your personality.

To describe your interest, discuss why you are interested in the job and what has been appealed to you about the position. To discuss your professional knowledge, skills, and experiences, articulate how your knowledge, skills, and experiences will be useful to and benefit the institution or the organization you want to work for. Your personality is as important as all other things because the employer looks for not only a skillful and experienced worker but also a conscientious individual who can fit into the organization's culture. You should always keep in mind that there are many people out there who have the same or similar education, skills, and experience as you. In many situations, it is the job applicants' unique characteristics that make them stand out. The last part of the letter is the conclusion, in which you may summarize what you have talked about in the main body of the letter and express your excitement and a possible interview.

The length of the cover letter should be kept within one or, at the maximum, one and a half page, and the font size can be either 12 or 11 point. Table 13.3 is a sample cover letter, which can be used as your reference.

Letters of Recommendation

Many employers only ask you for a list of references, and they do not really need letters. But some may request the inclusion of actual letters. When seeking references, it is important to identify those who truly can speak, in specific terms, to your work ethic, your academic training and acumen, and your clinical experience and skills. Someone who knows your work and you as a person would be ideal. It would be the best to have one of your clinical supervisors, your academic advisor, and one of your professors who have taught you or with whom you have done research as your references. But regardless of whom you ask, be sure that they are "excited" about the possibility of supporting you with their reference. Getting a lukewarm or generic reference can be as costly as a bad one!

Once you have identified individuals you hope will serve as a reference, contact them and provide them with the specific information about the type of job to which you are applying *and* the type of experience, skills, or professional qualities you would

Table 13.3 Sample Cover Letter

Jennifer Johnson

8 Jefferson Circle, Philadelphia, PA 19103 | E-mail: jjohnson@gmail.com | Tel: xxx-xxx-xxxx
Delaware County Community College

Dear Hiring Committee Members,

Please accept my application for the Enrollment Services Specialist position within the Enrollment Services Center at Delaware County Community College. I am currently completing my graduate studies within a CACREP-accredited College Counseling program at Chester College and expect to graduate with a Master of Science degree in December 2015.

Since August 2014, I have interned in three higher education environments: the Career Development Office at University of Delaware, the Career Services Center at the University of Sciences, and the Achieve Center for Student-Athletes at Saint Joseph University. In the career centers, I performed individual counseling and classroom presentations for undergraduate and graduate students. I also provided résumé/cover letter review, internship/job search assistance, mock interviews, and workshop presentations.

In my higher education counseling field experiences, I performed a Values' Workshop at University of Delaware and a Career Management Portfolio Project at the University of Sciences. The Values' Workshop was created for undecided students to discover how their major could correspond with their core values. The Career Management Portfolio Project was an 8-week program that provided students with insight regarding their career path, interview skills, cover letter, résumé, and the job search process. At the Achieve Center at Saint Joseph University, I had the opportunity to conduct one-on-one meetings with student-athletes to discuss their academic progress throughout the semester. Through these higher education field experiences, I strive to become a higher education professional that demonstrates empathy and optimum customer service.

During my higher education counseling field experiences, I was an assistant teacher at Spring Hill School in Philadelphia, Psychology Instructor at Temple University for pre-college students, and a graduate assistant in the Counselor Education Department at Chester College. As an assistant teacher, I had the opportunity to substitute teach in the middle school and high school. At Temple University, I developed the course curriculum for high school students to learn about psychology during the summer. As a graduate assistant, I assisted walk-ins for prospective and current graduate students. I also promoted upcoming events in the graduate business center and conducted research for professors within the department.

I am excited about the opportunity to be considered as part the staff team within the Enrollment Services Center at Delaware County Community College. I am confident my counseling and teaching experiences as well as my strong desire to work at a college setting make me an asset to your center and the college. I look forward to hearing from you and appreciate your consideration.

Sincerely,
Jennifer Johnson

like them to address. If they agree and are enthusiastic, then obtain their contact information, e-mail address, and work phone number. (Also see Letters of Recommendation in the Advanced Education section in this chapter).

Job Interviews

Once you have all the needed application materials ready, follow the instructions in the job description to submit them. After you send your application materials to the employer, you are waiting for a response. Generally, soon after the employer receives your application, the person who is in charge of collecting application materials will send you a notice informing you that your application has been received and will be processed within a certain number of days and that you will hear from them thereafter. If, after a week or so, you do not hear back from the employer, you may want to write the employer an e-mail message asking if additional information may be required. Although you don't want to appear pushy or needy, you do want to convey a continued interest in the position.

Once all application materials have been reviewed, employers will generally contact applicants, and schedule interviews with those whom they have a continued interest in. If you don't get an invitation, although it is certainly disappointing, it is important that you respond professionally and productively. It is not a bad idea to send a letter or e-mail to the employer thanking him or her for the opportunity to apply and wishing him or her well on the continued search. Such a note demonstrates maturity and professionalism and may be the "tickler" the employer needs to keep your file on hand. Further, if you fail to get invited to the next phase of the process, it would be helpful if you could find out what more you could have done, or what specifically they were looking for that you failed to present. Gaining this information is not easy because most employers are reluctant to provide such specific feedback, but it does not hurt to reach out and invite them to provide you with the feedback that may help you present yourself better in the next situation.

If you do receive an invitation for an interview, congratulations, you have made a step further to be employed. It is important to feel good—pat yourself on the back—but remember, there is still much to accomplish. The next major challenge is still ahead . . . the interview!

The job interview is a special situation and one of the highlights in the job searching process because of its dynamic characteristics and complexity. In this special situation, you as the applicant are expected to actively present yourself and repeatedly call attention to the best of your credentials. It is an opportunity to use active ingratiation tactics while remaining genuine and professional. Failure of self-presentation will put you in a disadvantaged position (Paulhus, Westlake, Calvez, & Harms, 2013).

To be successful will require quite a bit of preparation. Galassi and Galassi (1978) reviewed more than 60 years of research on employment interviews and then created a four-phase model to help individuals interview more effectively. Although this model was constructed 30 years ago, we think it still has much relevance and usefulness to individuals who look for job placement today. We have adapted the model a little bit to fit students in the field of counseling.

Phase 1 is developing realistic expectations. These include the interviewing process—the format, content, and length of the interview. Interviews can be structured or unstructured, and no matter which kind, the interviewers' styles can vary; for example, some may be very warm and supportive whereas others may be typical or conventional. Other factors include realistic expectations about the content of the questions and the length of the interview, which can be from a couple of hours to an entire day. Interviewees should not be surprised with some silence during the interview produced by the interviewers.

Phase 2 is developing interviewing skills. At this phase, you as the interviewee want to develop interview skills that can maintain the interviewers' attention on your objective and job-related characteristics during the interview. Here, the objective means your image management. You want to present yourself honestly but in a way that would not let the interviewers develop a negative impression of you due to subjective factors that are unrelated to job performance, because a variety of subjective factors influence interviewers. There are four sets of factors that are concerned with making a favorable impression during interviews: (a) interviewers' initial impression, (b) your communication and interpersonal skills, (c) your attitude or traits, and (d) your way of handling difficult or problem questions.

Factors related to interviewers' initial impression include your attire, physical attractiveness, and punctuality. Regarding attire, you may want to dress in a conservative manner. For women, short skirts and low necklines should be avoided because they create an unfavorable impression. Pantsuits, in some instances, do not help with a good impression either. For men, excessive facial hair, beards, and long hair often create a negative impression. Another important factor is punctuality, which is considered as important or more important than your appearance. The rule of thumb is to arrive about 10 minutes early for the interview. Extremes in attire, appearance, and punctuality often divert the interviewer's attention.

Factors related to your attitude and traits that help form a favorable impression are in your statements that reflect your maturity, cooperation, dependability, dedication, sincerity, trustworthiness, and motivation. Other traits that you want to convey to the interviewers include your interest in the organization, being socially aware and pleasant, and your enthusiasm about work and career and your willingness to take extra responsibilities by going above and beyond. During the interview, you may want to emphasize your specialty several times or whenever possible if you have any (e.g., alcohol and substance addiction, working with an older population, career, etc.).

You want to show that you are prepared for the interview by displaying knowledge of and asking relevant questions about the job and the organization. One thing to keep in mind is that your grades may not be as important as you might think in the decision-making process.

Communication and interpersonal skills are as critical in interviews as they are in the counseling process. As a counseling professional, using standard English and fluent speech are important for creating a favorable impression. Your nonverbal behaviors, such as eye contact, attentive posture, smiling, and interpersonal distance, are also crucial in winning a favorable impression.

The last factor of Phase 2 is answering difficult questions. Table 13.4 contains a list of frequently asked question in interviews for a counseling position. Whenever there are questions that you think are prejudicial or unfair, keep the answers short but end with a positive tone.

Phase 3 is using effective training procedures and is about how training programs may help applicants looking for jobs and prepare them for interviews. Suggestions of interview training techniques include behavior rehearsal, coaching, and feedback, which have been used to teach interviewees verbal and nonverbal job-interview behaviors and have proved to be helpful. Taping a mock interview would be a very useful way to improve interviewing behavior and reduce job interview anxiety. In the process of practicing your interview, you may also want to focus on your belief and attitude. Some students have difficulty with interviews because of their counterproductive attitudes and irrational beliefs. Neither believing that you must be perfect nor taking an attitude of "no big deal" will help you with your job interview.

Phase 4, preparing for "rejection shock," is straightforward. No matter how good you are or how well you are prepared, most of you will experience rejection at some point. To avoid rejection shock, which is characterized by emotional and physical symptoms, lack of motivation, low esteem, alienation, or even depression, you need to learn some strategies. There are two points to keep in mind regarding rejection: (a) rejection is not uncommon due to a tight job market; and (b) persistence pays, so keep trying! In addition, "understanding the economic forces influencing employment and unemployment is crucial along with tools to encourage personal resourcefulness and resiliency" (Duys, Ward, Maxwell, & Eaton-Comerford, 2008, p. 240).

Table 13.4 Common Interview Questions

- Tell us about yourself.
- Why are you interested in us?
- What are your strengths and weaknesses?
- How would your peers describe you?
- How would you describe your interpersonal skills?
- How would you see yourself 5 years from now?
- Can you tell us about a project or group work that you initiated?
- What type of situations put you under pressure, and how do you handle the pressure?
- Can you tell us a difficult client situation you had before and how you handled it?
- Can you tell us a time you handled a conflict?
- In what type of environment do you thrive?
- What challenges are you looking for in a position?
- How would you describe your leadership style?
- Why should we hire you or why are you the best person for this position?
- What questions do you have for us?

Phone/Online Video Interview

When you are invited for an interview, it can be a phone interview or site interview. Nowadays employers often conduct phone or online interviews first, before they invite candidates to their sites. If you get a phone or online interview, treat it as seriously as when you are invited to have an on-site interview. The employer may give you a few days and times to choose from. At this point, it is advisable to be as flexible as you can. It is helpful to select one of the options the employer provides. If there is a conflict that prevents you from engaging at the suggested times, it is important to reiterate your interest in the job, and your disappointment at the conflict, sharing honestly about your situation and providing them your available times.

Both phone and online video interviews have advantages and disadvantages. The advantages include *convenience.* For example, you don't need to travel but can stay at home or in your office. Some may stay in their beds while talking. However, we suggest that those who have phone interviews choose a place they're familiar with, where they feel the most comfortable, and that is quiet in order to prevent any unexpected interruptions. In addition, if you use a wireless phone or cell phone, you want to choose the place where you know your phone can receive the best signals and perform well. The second advantage is *saving time.* Because it is a phone interview, you have no need to travel and spend time on the road. As a result, the third advantage becomes *cost efficiency*—saving you money or the travel expense, because nowadays many institutions and organizations do not cover their candidates' travel expenses. Finally, phone interviews save you not only time and money, but also *unnecessary hassle.* This means you don't need to worry about getting up early in the morning to catch a flight, airplane delays due to weather or other circumstances, or the possibility of getting lost due to unclear travel instruction or road construction. All these can become potential stressors that can affect your job interview performance.

One disadvantage of the phone interview is that you and the interviewers cannot see each other, and the nonverbal communication for both parties is almost useless except for the tone of voice. This can be a challenge for many, particularly those who use a significant amount of body language while they communicate with others. To overcome this disadvantage, we suggest that you use a speaker phone (assuming vocal clarity) and engage in your usual communication style, making no restriction on any part of your nonverbal behaviors while you are talking with the interviewers on the phone.

Using online video for the interview brings with it numerous technological challenges and possible personal discomfort. Online video interviews may be negatively affected by connection difficulties, delayed data transfer and lag time, and even twisted or distorted imaging. On a more personal note, some find the performance on camera to be somewhat unnerving. We suggest that you do online video mock interviews with a friend or a peer before your actual interview.

Like most social skills, presenting on camera is something that can improve with practice. If you have little or no experience with performance on camera or with use of technical tools such as Skype or FaceTime, we suggest that you practice. Becoming aware of all these advantages and disadvantages about phone and online video interviews, particularly the disadvantages and challenges, is the first step to fully preparing yourself for a successful phone or online video interview.

On-Site Interview

The on-site interview is the last chance for you to show the employer that you are the right person for the job. There are three stages for a job interview: the preparation stage, the interview stage, and the follow-up stage. To prepare for the "stress" of the interview, we have provided a checklist in Table 13.5 for your reference. These are some of tasks at the preparation stage that you need to complete in order to equip yourself well for the interview. Of course, practicing your interview is critical because your actual presentation of the interview (e.g., your answers to all the questions, the verbal message you convey, and your speech and presentation style) will make a significant impact on your chance of being hired.

Table 13.5 On-Site Interview Checklist

Before the interview, study the interview schedule and check all the following:

- Make sure you remember the name or names of the person or people you have interacted with.
- Obtain a cell phone number for the contacting person in case something happens, if possible.
- Find out the length of the interview day.
- Find out what events will be included.
- Find out how many people will interview you, who they are, and the length of each meeting.
- Are you expected to do a role-play of a counseling session? What does it look like? Who would be the client? How long? Who would observe?
- Are you expected to do a presentation or teach class? Who would be the audience? What is the topic, or your choice of the topic? How should it be delivered?

Travel

- Make sure your alarm clock works so you can get up early enough if you have an early morning flight.
- Leave plenty of time for traffic jams or potential detours.
- If you encounter delays due to any circumstances, call the contact person as soon as possible.
- Find out where you stay or meet with someone after you arrive.
- Save all the receipts if your travel expense is not prearranged by the employer.
- Bring with you extra interview items such as socks, shoes, and clothing. Bring with you exercise clothes and shoes if you stay overnight.
- Make sure your cell phone is fully charged.
- Bring with you extra copies of your résumé, articles or papers, handouts, and sample syllabi (if you are expected to teach).
- Make sure your files are safely saved on your USB or that you have saved copies online (e.g., in your Dropbox or e-mail account).
- Put all important materials in your carry-on luggage.

Following their research on job interview outcomes, Parton, Siltanen, Lawrence, Hosman, and Langenderfer (2002) concluded that those interviewees who use a powerful speech style were evaluated more favorably than those who use a powerless speech style, and that a powerful speech style results in attributions of competence and employability. Specifically, they found the following factors to impact the outcome of an interview: (a) the quantity of verbal messages contributes more positively to interview outcomes than nonverbal cues; (b) verbal messages are more effective than paper credentials; (c) standard dialects are more desirable than nonstandard dialects; and (d) a powerful speech style is clearer and more persuasive and has more positive impact on interview outcomes than a powerless speech style, particularly a powerful speech style conveying an impression of the interviewee's self-control and control over others. In general, their findings suggest that interviewers often form a positive impression of and favor those who use a powerful speech style that reveals characteristics such as social attractiveness, superiority, dynamism, control over self, and control over others.

While there will be a formal beginning and ending to one's interview, it is important to realize that the informal and yet still important process of evaluation begins with the initial "hello" and truly doesn't end until you exit the building. It is important to behave naturally while at the same time realize that you are on stage and being assessed. Be alert to both your verbal and nonverbal messages. When the interview lasts an entire day, you may meet many people throughout and discuss the same subjects over and over. In this situation, you want to be enthusiastic with each person who interviews you. If you are invited to share a meal, remember your goal. That is, you are *not* there to be fed or to party or to simply socialize. You are there to demonstrate your professionalism and the degree to which you will fit in and contribute to the culture. Therefore, select food items that will allow you to eat and yet converse comfortably. If invited to have an alcoholic beverage, and if that fits your own personal style, be aware of the norm at the table. But you must remember, you can't let the drinking affect your behavior. Remember the names of those who interview you and ask for a business card of each person, if possible. At the end of the interview, ask the person whom you have had communication with about the approximate time you may hear from him or her about the decision. With this information, you may negotiate with other places that you have interviewed with or received an offer from.

The best way to follow up after your interview is to send a thank-you e-mail or thank-you note. If you write a thank-you e-mail, you may include everyone who participated in the interview process. If you write a thank-you note to mail, you need only send it to the person who was in charge or who directed the interview process; however, you do want to convey your appreciation for the kindness of all involved, identifying each person by name. After the interview, if you have any new information (e.g., an award, a grant, or a publication) that you think may help you to win the job, call the chair of the hiring committee and ask if you can send it to him or her. Finally, if you don't hear anything after the period of time that was stated as that making a decision, it is appropriate to contact them expressing your continued interest and desire to know about their decision.

Job Interview Questions

Job interview questions are not as broad as people usually think, and there are usually no more than 20 questions. Typically, the interview targets two specific aspects: (a) your competency (i.e., knowledge, skill, and experience) to do the job; and (b) the "fit" of your style, personality, and nature to the work culture.

The first aspect, job competency, is pretty straightforward. The questions will target your ability to function in the role being offered. The second target may be assessed based less on the content of your response and more on the style with which you answer the questions, interact with those doing the interviews, and even handle unexpected or stressful events.

In Table 13.4, you will find a list of questions frequently asked during counseling-related job interviews. Although it is not suggested that you memorize your answers, it would be helpful to allow the questions to serve as a guide to your reflections about your current strengths, areas of growth, professional identity, and outlook on our profession.

Let's take a few frequently asked questions and see how you can answer them skillfully during your interviews. A typical interview starter may be "Tell us about yourself." In responding, you want to highlight the keys points about your education, your experience, and what made you get where you are now. Some people may go in depth talking about their skills, experiences, and personality. Actually, the detailed questions about those areas will follow the first question, and there will be other chances for you to provide detailed information about your skills, experiences, and the other aspects of you. As with all of your responses, it is important to speak clearly and comfortably, looking at the interviewer or scanning all interviewers if there are more than one. Further, it is important to be aware of the nonverbal messages sent by those in attendance. Check for their understanding. Check for the completeness of your response. Check to see if and when you may be going beyond that which was requested or desired.

A second type of question attempts to get at your motivation for seeking this employment. "Why do you want to work for us?" or "Why are you interested in us?" This is a question the interviewers use to see if you have a thorough understanding of yourself and the employer for whom you are hoping to work. This is where your preparation and homework come into play. You need to incorporate your understanding of the values and mission, as well as the client population served by this organization and incorporate that knowledge into your response. You want to bridge your own values, professional or career goals, and personal dreams with the employer's values, mission statement, and goals or plans. To prepare to answer this question well, you will want to fully explore the institution or organization before the interview. Of course, you also need to know well what your values, goals, and personal dreams are.

"What are your strengths?" To answer this question, you need to fully understand the job requirements and then articulate your answers from the areas of your counseling skills, people skills, teamwork spirit, conscientiousness, work ethics, and administrative expertise that apply to the position. In other words, the interviewers have just given you the opportunity to sell yourself for the position. You want to relate your strengths to the job at hand and show the interviewers how your strengths can be assets and problem solvers for the institution. Describing your strengths in a measurable manner and providing concrete examples to support your assertion will make your answers more convincing. For example, if you say that one of your strengths is being creative, then you need to give at least one example of a time you created something for the employer during your internship or at your previous job. Using many positive adjectives to describe yourself without concrete evidence for support would make your answer weak.

"What are your weaknesses or areas that you may improve?" or "In what area do you see you can improve?" To answer this question, include three key elements: strength, weakness, and correction. As we all know, a weakness can be the downside of a given strength. You want to recognize this trait while you answer the question. When you say you have a weakness, then you must clearly indicate how you have taken steps to correct it. For example, "I consider myself to be someone who is efficient and always enjoys getting tasks completed ahead of time, but I've noticed that sometimes the quality of my work is not as high as I expect if I fail to balance my need to be efficient with my desire to be effective. So, in order to achieve both efficiency and effectiveness, I have put more effort in emphasizing details and quality in all the work I do by triple checking everything to ensure complete accuracy."

"How do you deal with a conflict or conflicts?" Before you answer this question, you must understand what the interviewer is looking for in your answer. It is always appropriate to ask for clarification. Using your active listening skills, you might state, "I understand the question is about conflict; I'm not sure if it refers to conflicts with clients, coworkers, or all the above?" Once clarified, it is important to craft your answer in a way that highlights your interpersonal and conflict management skills. You want to include a description of how you react to conflict, your general approach, and evidence of its successfulness. "Why should we hire you?" This question offers you the opportunity to highlight your strengths, experiences, and personality attributes, particularly the ones that others do not possess. To answer this question, you must explore what you offer internally, for most candidates have what you have externally, such as advanced degree, and clinical and research experiences. So your answer may include your motivation, efficiency, effectiveness, conscientiousness, flexibility, generosity of your time to do extra work, or multicultural expertise. These aspects reflect your character, personality traits, and unique qualities that other candidates may not have. By articulating your uniqueness and relating it to the nature of the job you are interviewed for, you have distinguished yourself from others.

To answer the questions naturally, you must make your answers personal and authentic and you must feel comfortable saying them. To best be able to truly articulate why you are the perfect fit for the job, you need to believe it.

None of us are perfect nor a perfect fit (initially) to any job. But you do have valuable experience, useful knowledge and skills, and the personal disposition that will allow you to be a real contributor to your place of employment. But these facets needed to be grounded in your reality and not simply reflect platitudes. As such, an accurate self-assessment is crucial before your interview. To do an accurate self-assessment, you must include some outside perspectives. A good resource to use for an outside perspective is your university's career center or career counseling center.

The goals of such a self-assessment process would be (a) to deep-down believe and understand you are the perfect candidate; (b) to know what makes you the perfect match, you have to look inside yourself at your unique profile of motivations, strengths, values, and personality traits, which means you do an accurate self-assessment; and (c) to apply your entire understanding of self to all the interviews. If you can do this, your interview will be natural and your answers will be convincing and persuasive.

Employment for International Students: Special Opportunity/Special Challenge

Employment for interns who are not American citizens or permanent residents is different than for interns who are domestic students. International students who come to the United States to study are generally issued an F-1 visa and their spouse and dependents are issued an F-2 visa. If you hold an F-1 student visa, you may be eligible for the 12-month Optional Practical Training (OPT), which means you are legally allowed to work for a year after you graduate. The eligibility criteria to apply for OPT include being a lawful full-time F-1 student for a full academic year, being in good academic standing with your university, having a valid passport, having not had more than 12 months of full-time Curriculum Practical Training, and being physically present in the United States and in F-1 status at the time of application. You may want to check with your university's office of international studies or Office of International Program Center about the most current policies, regulations, and procedures concerning employment for international students who are about to graduate.

Job Offers and Your Decision

A job offer is often made on the phone. An on-site offer is rare but it does happen. When receiving an offer via phone, it is important to shift from your "oh boy!" response to a professional stance in considering what is being offered. This starts with taking a deep breath and then thanking the person who makes the offer to you. Upon hearing the news, inform him or her that you are both honored and somewhat humbled by the offer. Further, inform the person making the offer that you know that he or she can appreciate how important a decision this is for you as well as the organization and that you would like to know about how much time you have to consider the offer and give them your decision. Once you get a job offer, you will have to decide whether you want to take the offer. Your decision must be based on your criteria that you have used to search for the job. Some criteria may include salary, career advancement opportunities, nature and responsibilities of the position, cultural environment (e.g., staff, supervisor, and administrative structure), and geographic location. In reviewing the offer, you may want to inquire about any flexibility or points that could be negotiated, for example, salary, start date, benefits, and so forth. This is more likely if the position offered was advertised as "competitive" or "based on experience." Under these conditions, you may have some negotiation room.

As with most decisions you will make, accepting or rejecting the job offer deserves your time, energy, reflection, and research. Gather research depicting the salary range of the position you have been offered or that of similar positions. Discuss with your supervisor and/or career counselor their opinion about the limits to negotiating—for example, beyond salary can you negotiate fringe benefits, work load, or relocation package? Talking with others will help you gain a realistic view of what you may be able to ask for and achieve.

Placement Resources

There are a variety of placement resources that you can use in your job search process. The most easily accessed ones that people often use are networking, career centers, professional organizations, direct employer contact, and online sources.

Networking

Networking is a powerful strategy in your job search process. According to Carolyn Thomas (2012), director of career services at Xavier University, "Despite the use of technology and the on-line application process most jobs (80%) are still filled through networking. Some positions may not even be posted if a referral has already been made from the inside" (p. 2). The author further suggests that networking is relationship building and everyone is included. We think that as a counseling graduate student, your most important network should include your internship supervisors, faculty advisors, professors, classmates, previous interns, alumni, and counseling professionals whom you have met at conferences or workshops. Of course, your parents, relatives, and friends are also important. Let all these people know that you are looking for a job and pass your contact information to them when appropriate.

Advanced Education

When thinking about your future, some of you may consider advanced education as an option. As a master's-level student, you may see that a terminal degree or gaining advanced credentials such as a special certificate or license or advanced degree may open more opportunities in the near future.

Doctoral Programs

To apply for a related doctoral program, you want to prepare yourself for a year before you enroll into the program. The enrollment of most doctoral programs begins in the fall of each academic year. The application deadlines are usually between December 1 and February 15, although some programs may set their deadlines a little bit earlier or later. Application deadlines for programs at schools with a quarter system may be around the end of January or early February. The materials you want to prepare for application include (a) GRE, (b) résumé or vita, (c) letters of recommendation, (d) both undergraduate and graduate official transcripts, (e) personal statement or statement of purpose, (f) a research paper, and (g) financial support.

Your official GRE score is effective for 5 years. If you have taken the GRE exam at the time you applied for your current graduate program and you're satisfied with the score, you may not need to take it again, because your score is not more than 1 or 2 years old. If you are not satisfied with the score and you got it a year or two ago, you might want to prepare yourself to retake it and make sure your score arrives at the graduate admissions office(s) in time. Some schools may want all application materials to be in their hands on the date of the deadline, whereas others may be willing to wait for a few days or a couple of weeks after the date of the deadline. The bottom line is that you want to check and make sure of the requirements with the schools or programs that you apply for.

We have already discussed your résumé or vita earlier in the chapter. There may be some differences between applying for a doctoral program and a job. Many doctoral programs have a focus on research, and they look for applicants who have potential to do research during their tenure in the doctoral program. To apply for these programs, place an emphasis on research in your résumé or vita and list your research activities at the beginning of your résumé. To apply for those programs that emphasize practice, for example, PsyD programs, you may want to list your clinical experiences at the beginning of your résumé. It is important to prepare your résumé and application to fit with the characteristics of the doctoral programs you are applying for.

Letters of Recommendation

Letters of recommendation for a doctoral program are another important component of your application. Most doctoral programs require three letters, whereas others require five. Unlike many employers, who only require references, not actual letters, almost all doctoral programs want to see the actual letters of recommendation. Although you don't need to write the letters, you still want to prepare your letters ahead of time. It may not be hard to get three or five professors to write letters of recommendation for you, but it may not be easy to get three or five high-quality letters. To get high-quality letters of recommendation, it's important to collaborate or interact with the professors in addition to taking classes with them. You want them to know you as a person, not just as a student. Many students provide their professors a résumé right before they need the letters. As you already know, a résumé is only an outline of what a person has done and it won't say much about who you are as a person. Therefore, it is necessary to have some interactions with the professors you think can write a good letter of recommendation for you to let them know who you are, what you are doing, and what you want to be in the future. Also, write or tell your professors ahead of time or at least before you submit your online application that you want them to write a letter. You need to give them sufficient time because they have millions of things in their life more important than your letters. You don't want to surprise them by submitting your applications without telling them you have used their e-mail addresses. So, a few things you may want to do before your actual application submission: (a) discuss with your professors about your decision and what types of programs you are going to apply for; (b) inform your professors which programs you are going to apply for; (c) ask them if they are willing to write a good letter of recommendation for you; (d) ask them for permission to use their e-mail addresses in your application; (e) tell them that they will receive online links in their e-mail from the schools you are applying for; and (f) let them know the deadlines and time range for when the letter needs to be submitted. Of course, the last but not the least is that after your professors have submitted the letters, send them a card or at least an e-mail message to thank them for the letters they have written for you.

Official Transcript

The next task for you is to request your official transcript. Most programs require you to have your official transcript for both undergraduate and graduate schools directly sent by the universities you attended to their graduate admissions offices. To get your official transcript sent to each admissions office, you need to start early to make the request. Your alma mater may charge a fee for each transcript you request; be sure to make the appropriate payment ahead of time so it is not delayed.

Personal Statement

Almost all doctoral programs require applicants to write a personal statement. The personal statement gives you, the applicant, an opportunity to tell the admissions committee how your background and life experiences, including opportunities and challenges, have motivated your decision to pursue a doctoral degree. This could be a journey that has led you to your decision to seek a doctoral degree. The personal statement is also an opportunity for you to tell the admissions committee your reasons for wishing to pursue a doctoral degree in that specific area at their college or university. In the statement, you also want to tell the application reviewers about the motivating influences that aroused your interest in the subject, and your career goals and objectives, both long- and short-term. These are some general ideas about a personal statement, and you want to find out what specific requirements the admissions committee from the programs you apply for expect to see. It is very common for programs to require you to answer additional questions besides the personal statement.

Many doctoral programs require applicants to include a research paper in the application. A research paper can be a published article, a paper presented at a professional conference, or a paper you used to satisfy a course requirement. There are two major things that the admissions committee is looking for: your research interest and your writing skills. So, select a paper that represents your interest and your writing skills. Unless you have a published article, have your faculty advisor or someone read your paper before you submit it.

Financial Support

Concerning financial support, it can be good news for you. Most doctoral programs provide some type of financial support, for example, fellowship, teaching assistantship, research assistantship, or assistantship in on-campus offices or off-campus community clinics. These graduate assistantships are a win-win situation for both you and the university. You get professional experiences, which will be a great help at the time you look for a permanent job after you graduate; the university trains doctoral students with work experiences and gains the financial advantage of hiring a doctoral student who costs less than a full-time employee. Most graduate assistantships include tuition waiver and a stipend, the amount of which is various from school to school. You want to find out exactly how much the school will provide, because the stipend may not be sufficient to cover your total expense. The cost of living in the area where the school locates is a crucial factor for you to consider while you calculate the amount you need to live for 3 to 5 years, or even longer due to special circumstances that may occur in your life.

Postscript

Looking at life beyond your field experience can be both exhilarating and anxiety provoking. Whether your chosen path will take you to the world of work or to continuing education, stepping into new challenges is by its very nature a bit unnerving. As you begin to consider your future direction, take time to celebrate that which you have already accomplished.

The new challenges will remain. The tasks and steps to take as you progress in your profession will be waiting. But in the meantime, find time to celebrate you. Find time to reflect on your growth. Find time to feel the pride of entering a profession that you will find both meaningful and valuable. Find time to . . . celebrate your transition from student to professional!

KEYSTONES

- Going from internship to employment is a challenging transition that needs thorough preparation.
- The counseling internship is a step of value acknowledgement and declaration of professional identity.
- From the client's perspective, what an intern does and what a professional counselor does is the same: he or she helps the client accomplish his or her mental health, wellness, education, or career goals in counseling. Self-evaluation is a critical step in the process of transitioning from a practicum student/intern to a professional counselor.
- The résumé and cover letter function as advertisement of your skills, knowledge, and experiences, the purpose of which is to win you a job interview.
- A job interview is a special situation in which you must present yourself well and constantly call attention to your credentials.
- Verbal messages produce more positive impact on interview outcome than nonverbal messages and paper credentials.

- Standard dialects and powerful speech style more positively affect interview outcomes than nonstandard dialects and less powerful speech.
- Networking is a powerful strategy for job search.
- Advanced education may be an option for more opportunities in the future.

ADDITIONAL RESOURCES

Web Based

DrKitVideos. (2011, June 20). *Mental health counselor (university setting) career video from drkit.org* [video file]. Retrieved from http://www.youtube.com/watch?v=18vLjdgsuq4

Hansen, R. S. (n.d.). *Frequently asked questions about salary negotiation: The complete job offer and salary negotiation FAQ for job seekers.* Retrieved from http://www.quintcareers.com/salary_negotiation_FAQ.html

JobTestPrep. (2005, December 5). *Interview questions and answers* [video file]. Retrieved from http://www.youtube.com/watch?v=VFTNOF77bMs

sokario bichukle. (2014, January 3). *Therapist interview questions and answers* [video file]. Retrieved from http://www.youtube.com/watch?v=zsiGUEXy6gU

Successful interviewing: http://www.career.ucla.edu/Portals/14/Documents/PDF/CareerGuide/2014/CG_2014_2015_Chapter7_082814.pdf

Virginia Western Community College. (2009, September 25). *Mock job interview questions and tips for a successful interview* [video file]. Retrieved from http://www.youtube.com/watch?v=BkL98JHAO_w

Print Based

Beshara, T. (2012). *The job search solution: The ultimate system for finding a great job now.* New York, NY: American Management Association.

Feller, R. W. (2003). Aligning school counseling, the changing workplace, and career development assumptions. *Professional School Counseling, 6*(4), 262–271.

Formo, D. M., & Reed, C. (2011). *Job search in academe: How to get the position you deserve.* Sterling, VA: Stylus.

Yate, M. (2013). *Knock 'em dead 2014: The ultimate job search guide.* Avon, MA: Adams Media.

REFERENCES

Duys, D. K., Ward, J. E., Maxwell, J. A., & Eaton-Comerford, L. (2008). Career counseling in a volatile job market: Tiedeman's perspective revisited. *Career Development Quarterly, 56*(3), 232–241.

Freidheim, E. (1994). *History of psychotherapy: A century of change.* Washington, DC: American Psychological Association.

Galassi, J. P., & Galassi, M. D. (1978). Preparing individuals for job interviews: Suggestions from more than 60 years of research. *Personnel & Guidance Journal, 57*(4), 188–192.

Michaelson, G. A. (2001). *Sun Tzu: The art of war for managers.* Avon, MA: Adams Media.

Parton, S. R., Siltanen, S. A., Lawrence, A., Hosman, L. A., & Langenderfer, J. (2002). Employment interview outcomes and speech style effects. *Journal of Language and Social Psychology, 21,* 144. doi:10.1177/02627X02021002003

Paterson, J. (2001). Career connections. *Careers & Colleges, 21*(3), 38–40.

Paulhus, D. L., Westlake, B. G., Calvez, S. S., & Harms, P. D. (2013). Self-presentation style in job interviews: The role of personality and culture. *Journal of Applied Social Psychology, 43,* 2042–2059.

Thomas, C. (2012). The power of networking. *Diversity Employers,* 2–3.

14

Transitions: Self as Counselor

You have your identity when you find out, not what you can keep your mind on, but what you can't keep your mind off.

A. R. Ammons

For the past year, perhaps two, and maybe even longer, the requirements and demands of graduate education have called your attention and your energy to the acquisition of the knowledge, skills, roles, and responsibilities that define counseling. It is quite possible that your focus on completing assignments, passing tests, and moving through the various program requirements has taken your mind and energy away from other life interests. This experience of "putting your life on hold" as you complete your education may be a defining characteristic of being a graduate student. But you are in transition. It is a transition that will move you from placing your life on hold as you study counseling to living a life that incorporates and reflects you as counselor.

Through your field work, you have been introduced to and engaged in the world, the experience, and the life of a counselor. The experience is most likely limited and clearly only a beginning, but a valuable beginning. It is hoped your experience in the field has not only contributed to your professional knowledge and skill but expanded your sense of what it means to be a professional counselor. Engaging in those tasks that distinguish a counselor's role as unique from that of other mental health professionals has, we hope, contributed to your understanding and valuing of your uniqueness and the increasing sense of "you" as a professional counselor.

As your identity as a professional counselor comes into focus, you will notice that the theories, research, knowledge, and skills that you have called upon as student now seem to have been assimilated into your very being. With an increasing assimilation of a professional identity into one's concept of self, the previous sense of having to step into a prescribed role and put on the hat of a counselor as if it were an add-on or "have to" is replaced by a natural sense of simply "what is." No longer is one consciously acting as a counselor or doing counseling, one is simply being one's self, a self which has many facets, one of which is the facet of *being* a professional counselor.

As your professional identity develops, there comes the realization that you *are* a counselor and no longer need to *try to act like* a counselor. You are a counselor—and yes, the acquisition of knowledge and skills continues, but the realization and valuing of both the profession you have embraced and the role you have assimilated will be firmly implanted.

The current chapter invites you to reflect on and engage in the process of crafting your professional identity. Specifically, after completing this chapter readers will be able to

- describe what is meant by professional identity,
- identify the elements that contribute to the uniqueness of the counseling profession and those called counselors, and
- provide a preliminary articulation of your own professional identity.

Identity

The concept of *identity* is not new to you. As applied to an individual, identity formation entails the development of an awareness and an expression of one's uniqueness. It is a process that defines each of us as both similar to and different from others.

One's self-identity takes shape as a result of unfolding maturation, assimilation of life experiences, and personal meaning making. As such, one's self-identity continues to evolve in response to these changing conditions. Consider the evolving "you." How might your view of self as well as your worldview and your place within that world have changed since your preschool years, or your middle school and high school experience? Did moving from home to a more inclusive experience of school challenge your beliefs about yourself and your world? Did your early educational experience not only provide new knowledge, insights, and skills but expand your assumptions about your own strengths and limitations as well as the profile and characteristics of the world outside of your own neighborhood? These are the types of stimuli that spur the unfolding of our identities.

The effect of our social engagements and educational experience on our evolving sense of self is clear. Consequently, it is not a stretch to assume that your current experience as a graduate counseling student has both challenged your existing identity and invited you to refine this identity to incorporate your vocational calling. Before proceeding in our discussion on the development of your *professional identity,* it may be useful to take a moment to reflect on the changes that have already occurred as a result of your experience in your graduate program. Exercise 14.1 is provided to guide this reflection.

EXERCISE 14.1

Self-Identity: The Impact of Graduate Education

Directions: As noted in the text, one's identity is a work in progress. Our identities take shape and are reshaped in response to our unfolding maturity, the changing nature of our lives, the experiences we encounter, and the meaning we make of all of this. You are invited to take a moment to reflect on the following questions. It is suggested that you share your response with a colleague or classmate. It is hoped that such sharing will help you understand the impact of graduate studies as well as those experiences that are truly unique to yourself.

Questions for Reflection

1. Has there been specific information about the human condition, perhaps presented in a class on multicultural counseling, development across the life span, or theories of counseling, or even in your field work, that has significantly challenged your previous beliefs, expectations, or assumptions about yourself or the world in which you live? What was the information and how has it affected you?
2. As part of your graduate education, you may have received feedback from a professor or classmate regarding your interpersonal style or your ability to demonstrate specific counseling skills. Has any of this feedback challenged your view of yourself? Again, what specifically was this feedback and how has it affected you and your view of self?
3. Although your experience in the field has been limited, what, if anything, has surprised you about the role of counselor, as enacted at the site, and what impact has that experience had on your own motivation for becoming a counselor?
4. How has your understanding of the role of counselor changed as a result of your graduate studies? How has your evolving sense of counseling as a profession and the role of counselors reshaped your view of self as a future counselor?

Perhaps in reflecting on the questions provided in Exercise 14.1, you discovered that you have experienced changes in your view of self and/or your worldview. The one question not asked in the exercise but one that serves as a foundation for this chapter is the following: "Have the experiences within your graduate education increased your understanding and assimilation of what it means to be a counselor?" As will be seen, the increasing clarity of what it means to be a professional counselor (i.e., professional identity) does not stand alone or outside of one's personal identity but rather continues to be integrated and assimilated into the very substance of one's self and worldviews.

For those engaged as counselors, their profession both reflects and gives shape to their personal identity. Just as their personal identity has developed as a reflection of their emerging gender, ethnic, and racial identities, those called to counseling as a profession now experience the reshaping of their personal identities to include a facet of professional identity. As is true for the unfolding and evolving nature of our personal identities, your professional identity as a counselor will continue to evolve and emerge as you learn and experience more about yourself and the profession to which you have been called. The very fact that you are doing field work suggests that your sense of what it is to be a counselor and, more specifically, what it means for *you* to be a counselor has started to take shape.

Although the responsibility and the gift of developing a professional identity falls on your shoulders, it is a process of crafting that is not done alone, nor in isolation from counselors who have gone before or those giving form to our profession today. Your professional identity will find its roots in a rich history and the context of a professional community, but, as you will see, it is the very personal nature of this identity that, while reflecting the profession as a whole, does so with your unique stamp.

To Be a Counselor

At a basic level, professional identity reflects one's understanding and embracing of who counselors are, what counselors do, and how counselors are different from other mental health professionals. There have been numerous attempts to define professional identity (e.g., Gray, 2001; Puglia, 2008; Weinrach, Thomas, & Chan, 2001), and though there is no one generally agreed-upon definition, the essence of professional identity is well depicted in the following definition: "the possession of a core set of values, beliefs, and assumptions about the unique characteristics of one's selected profession that differentiates it from other professions" (Weinrach et al., 2001, p. 168). A somewhat more detailed and comprehensive presentation of the concept of professional identity was offered by Remley and Herlihy (2007) and includes six components: (a) knowledge and understanding of the profession's history, (b) knowledge and understanding of the philosophical foundations of the profession, (c) knowledge of the roles and functions of counselors and how they are similar to and different from those of other mental health professionals, (d) a sense of pride in the profession, (e) involvement in professional organizations and advocacy (i.e., professional engagement), and (f) knowledge and understanding of professional counselor ethics.

The articulation of our professional identity as counselors is relatively recent. In the early 1980s, the term *counseling* was often embraced by many professions and generally meant the provision of ideas, advice, or information. With the early work of Carl Rogers (1959) and the emergence of the humanistic perspective on counseling, focus shifted from counseling as advice giving to counseling as a unique relationship and helping dynamic. The focus during this period shifted from counselor as a source of expert information to counselor as one trained and skilled in the development of a therapeutic relationship. This view of counseling as a unique process—and the counselor as one possessing special knowledge and skills—provided the foundation for reclaiming the overgeneralized use of the term *counseling* and redefining it as a distinct profession and professional process.

In 2007, the American Counseling Association highlighted that which made counseling and counselors unique. The definition of counseling offered by the ACA was "a relatively short-term, interpersonal, theory-based process of helping persons who are basically psychologically healthy, resolve developmental and situational problems" (Maples, 2008). This definition and the ACA's emphasis on the relational element, the value of theory-based service, and the service provided to those who were basically psychologically healthy, provided the essence of the counselor's professional identity. The inclusion of value-laden terms, such as "short term," "theory-based" for "psychologically healthy" individuals targeting developmental and situation problems, set the boundaries for defining counseling and counselors as different from others serving the mental health needs of others.

This meaningful beginning of the articulation of our professional identity as counselors has continued to be reshaped, refined, and reformulated. In 2010, additional characteristics, which were articulated in words such as "professional," "empowering," and "wellness," were crafted into the definition. The result of this continued evolution is our current definition of counseling: "A professional relationship that empowers diverse individuals, families, and groups to accomplish mental health, wellness, education, and career goals" (ACA, 2010).

We are sure that you have seen and perhaps discussed this definition of counseling sometime during your graduate studies. But it is valuable to take a moment to truly reflect on the implications of the words incorporated. As core to our professional identity, understanding the definition is insufficient. It is essential that all who call self "counselor" not only understand but value and personally own all that is implied in that definition. Exercise 14.2 is offered as a guide to this reflection.

EXERCISE 14.2

More Than Terms—Values

Directions: Before moving on to our discussion on the uniqueness of counseling and counselors, we suggest you take a moment to consider your own current understanding and valuing of the elements that compose the definition of counseling as offered by the ACA (2010). It may be useful to compare and contrast your response to those of your classmates or colleagues.

The definition: *A professional relationship that empowers diverse individuals, families, and groups to accomplish mental health, wellness, education, and career goals.*

1. What does the element or value of *professionalism* mean in terms of what you will do? How you will be? And what you can't do or be? How does this element of professionalism distinguish you from "lay" helpers?

2. The inclusion of the word *empower* is substantive. How do you envision this descriptor, this value, as it directs your approach and orientation, as a counselor, to the services you will provide?

3. How does the inclusion of *wellness* as a goal direct you, as a counselor, to perform or provide services that differ from other mental health service providers?
4. In reviewing the description of the ACA's definition of counseling, what courses or training experiences would you assume are unique to those going through formation as a counselor versus those engaged in other professional mental health training programs?

A Closer Look at Defining Characteristics

As is true of our personal identity, which serves as a reference point for identifying that which is unique to oneself, a counselor's professional identity reflects that which distinguishes and uniquely defines the counselor, as contrasted to others within the helping professions. Defining this uniqueness—the elements and characteristics that distinguish a counselor from others within the helping professions—is not as easy as it first appears.

The very nature of what we do and how we do it often blurs the boundaries that separate counseling as a profession from that, for example, of social work or psychology (Mellin, Hunt, & Nichols, 2011). Quite a few of those serving in each of these professions draw from the same theory and research base, employ many of the same strategies of change, and often work within the same work setting. And although one's title or job role may serve as the reference for identifying differences, the real uniqueness to our professional identity lies within the values and perspective we bring to our role of counselor.

Counselors approach all that we do from four unique perspectives: developmental, wellness, prevention, and empowerment. It is the collective embodiment of these values, these perspectives, that provides the uniqueness to our professional identities more than job titles or role definitions.

Because of their central role to the definition of counseling as a unique profession among those serving the mental health needs of our clients, these perspectives need to be both understood and embraced as lenses through which you view all that you do as a professional counselor.

A Developmental Perspective

Counselors approach their work with clients believing that many of the challenges confronting individuals are transitory, most often reflecting normative glitches that serve as part of the regular progression of the human experience (Cook-Greuter & Soulen, 2007).

This is not to suggest that counselors do not accept the reality of the existence of serious, long-standing psychological problems, but rather that they do not approach each professional engagement assuming and looking for pathology. Consider the following case illustration (Case Illustration 14.1).

CASE ILLUSTRATION 14.1

Thomas

As a high school freshman, Thomas flew under the radar. His grades were generally in the B range, and his teachers described him as a little quiet and socially withdrawn but not a problem. Because of this rather benign profile, it was a bit of shock to Mrs. H., the school counselor, to learn that a number of his classmates had to escort him out of the freshman dance for fear that he would be discovered to have been drinking. Even though there was no official notification of his behavior and Mrs. H. had only heard through the "grapevine," the rumors regarding "did you hear?" were gaining momentum, and she felt it was wise to call Thomas down to her office.

As a school counselor for over 21 years, Mrs. H. had worked with students who presented with drug and alcohol dependency issues, and she had consulted with and referred to a number of service providers in her community who specialized in D & A issues. And although she "respected" the power of addictions and the reality that for some, drugs and alcohol were vehicles for self-soothing, she also knew that for many this was a time of social experimentation. She knew that as a normative process in defining adolescents' sense of self as unique and in response to their growing drive toward independence, many often engage in behaviors which are "out of character" and, while potentially dangerous, reflect immature social choices rather than pathology or dysfunction.

As she waited for Thomas to arrive at her office, Mrs. H. checked his cumulative folder, looking for evidence of changes in grades, teacher comments, or family dynamics that might suggest that this was more than a normative crisis. The absence of any change in these data, along with the suggestion that Thomas's new peer group came to his rescue directed her attention to the normative issues that may be involved and the steps she might take that would prevent future bad decision making and facilitate his journey toward self-identity and wellness. Although this was her initial operating hypothesis, she waited for Thomas and the data he would provide to support or redirect this initial position.

The counselor in our case illustration was not naïve, nor was she in denial of the real possibility that her client's behavior could have been indicative of a serious disorder. However, her initial hypothesizing about the situation included her understanding and valuing of the typical challenges often experienced by those within this developmental period.

A Wellness Perspective

A second unique element characterizing counseling and a counselor's perspective is the focus on wellness. In contrast to other mental health providers, who target client pathology, disease, and/or deficits, counselors generally approach their work from a strength-based orientation. "The goal of counseling is to help the person accomplish wellness rather than cure an illness" (Remley & Herlihy, 2007, p. 24).

Counselors operating from a wellness perspective place mental health along a continuum (Remley & Herlihy, 2007). They attempt to build upon a client's strengths and resources as they support and facilitate movement toward some level of optimal well-being. Case Illustration 14.2 highlights this wellness perspective.

CASE ILLUSTRATION 14.2

Finding Exception

The series of rejections seemed unending and certainly overwhelming. The client, Alicia, a 42-year-old, recent divorcee, presented as feeling depressed with a sense of hopelessness and helplessness. As she shared her story, she was quick to report "evidence" that supported her beliefs that she was a "failure as a wife," ill-prepared and "unable to be self-sufficient," and, given recent events, "destined to spend her life alone."

Alicia presented a compelling case in support of her negative self-concept and projections of a dire, unhappy future. But as she spoke, focusing on the negative, to the exclusion and minimization of the positives, she provided the counselor with ample evidence of her positives, her resources. It became very clear that she was a woman who possessed achieving, resilient, and self-determining qualities.

While acknowledging the experience of helplessness and sense of hopelessness she currently experienced, the counselor invited Alicia to identify a time—an experience—in her past when she made some personal decisions that, while difficult, proved successful. While initially resisting, Alicia eventually, with the encouragement of the counselor, was able to label her decision to go away to college as one of those difficult yet successful decisions that she made and enacted on her own.

In reviewing that experience, Alicia and the counselor began to identify the steps she took to research and evaluate possible colleges, the efforts she employed to secure funding (including gaining college-provided grants and aid), and even the specific actions she took to physically move from her home and relocate 1200 miles away to her new college setting. The process of revisiting this "success" highlighted the strengths Alicia brought to this challenge of getting to a college of her choosing, strengths which had utility and applicability to her current concerns about finding employment, and even reconnecting in social relationships.

Together, Alicia and the counselor decided to employ a goal scale, which identified where she currently saw herself in relationship to gainful employment and what might be the next small step she could take to advance toward that goal. Encouraged by the resources identified and using the steps and processes employed in acquiring her college goals, Alicia began to formulate a plan for engaging in a process of search for a job and gaining employment.

The counselor depicted in Case Illustration 14.2, while respectful of the challenges the client was facing, chose to invite the client to reclaim her strengths and to employ those resources to facilitate her movement toward wellness.

A Prevention Perspective

Similarly to others working in the area of mental health services, counselors engage clients directly and provide assistance in the form of interventions and remediation. What may be less clear to the lay observer is that counselors approach all that they do, even direct services, from a preventive perspective.

Counselors are trained in theories of and research in psychotherapy and strategies of change. They are skilled in providing empirically supported and theoretically sound interventions. However, as a reflection of a counselor's professional identity, even when engaged in direct service, targeting intervention or remediation, counselors do so in a way that reflects their valuing of prevention.

Counselors providing intervention services not only assist the clients in navigating out of their current situation but also attempt to leave clients better prepared for resolving similar problems in the future and navigating the life challenges they may encounter on their own (Remley & Herlihy, 2007). This focus on reducing the possibility of a reoccurrence of a problem is known as tertiary prevention. An example could be seen in the counselor who not only employs a solution-focused approach to assist a client with a current concern, but assists the client in understanding the processes of goal setting and goal scaling and the analysis of exception as a basis for developing action strategies, strategies that could be used to avoid and/or reduce the potential for future problems.

In addition to providing such tertiary prevention and direct intervention services, counselors often engage in programs that help identify those populations that are at risk for stress and distress but who have yet to develop full-blown disorders. Engaging those who are at risk is considered a secondary preventive activity. An example of secondary prevention would be when a college counselor responds to data showing that those engaged in Greek life are more at risk for alcohol abuse than those students not engaged in Greek sororities/fraternities by instituting an educational program specifically targeting those in Greek life with the goal of reducing this potential of abuse.

Finally, as a reflection of a counselor's valuing of prevention, many counselors engage in primary prevention programming. Primary prevention includes efforts directed toward an entire population (e.g., all parents of a community, all sixth-grade students, all transfer students, or all "new" parents) with the goal of increasing adaptive skills, improving resilience, and optimizing healthy functioning, and, as a result, reducing the risk for dysfunction. School counselors who provide classroom guidance curriculum targeting resiliency, or marriage and family counselors who offer newly engaged couples training in communication skills, are reflecting this valuing of primary prevention.

The evidence of engagement in prevention programming, whether it be at the tertiary, secondary, or primary levels, is certainly one of the perspectives that marks the uniqueness of a counselor's professional identity. As such, it is important for you to begin to view your own practice through this lens and opportunity for providing prevention service. Exercise 14.3 invites you to reflect on the services currently provided at your field placement site as they may reflect this prevention focus.

EXERCISE 14.3

More Than Intervention–Prevention

Directions: Your task is to reflect on the type of services provided at your current field placement site and identify elements of prevention, where they exist, and consider modification of current practices to include prevention.

a. What theories or models of direct client service (counseling) are typically employed by the counselors at your location? Is there an inclusion of an educational component fostering the development of the client's knowledge and skills to facilitate his or her ability to handle similar situations in the future (tertiary prevention)?

b. Considering the population typically served at your field placement site, what unique conditions, characteristics, or situational factors place them at risk? Do the counselors at your field placement site provide programs and services targeted to those at risk in the hope of reducing that risk and increasing their abilities to cope with these factors (secondary prevention)?

c. Do the counselors at your field placement site provide outreach and primary prevention programs targeting whole populations (e.g., all high school seniors, all parents of newborns, all college freshmen, all home visitors, etc.) in the hope of fostering the development of optimal functioning?

d. Upon reflection of the actual services provided by those at your field placement site, how might you adapt the "what is" in order to expand the impact to include

- tertiary prevention,
- secondary prevention, and
- primary prevention?

An Empowerment Perspective

As may be apparent in the discussion of the previous elements of a counselor's perspective, counselors respect and value clients' abilities to be self-sufficient and self-reliant in addressing their concerns. In working with clients who are experiencing some difficulty in navigating through life's challenges, counselors attempt to support and facilitate clients' abilities to solve their problems by themselves (Lewis, 2011).

This is truly a paradigmatic shift from a disease or illness perspective, in which the client is viewed as damaged and the helper as one with the knowledge, skill, and expertise to heal. Counselors, with an empowerment perspective, approach all that they do with the intent of helping clients identify and expand upon their strengths and resources as the means for assisting them in achieving their goals. The goal is to assist the client in moving away from dependency or reliance on this "other" to resolve or even facilitate the resolution to their current difficulties. This is not to suggest that counselors deny or reject the realities of their abilities to be of assistance but rather that they value the fundamental strength, resiliency, and resourcefulness that each client brings to the situation.

This empowerment perspective not only positions the counselor to encourage client independence but also gives shape to counselors' interest and engagement in advocacy efforts. Counselors value and engage in activities that are geared toward helping those individuals and groups who feel powerless and marginalized to gain not only awareness of those external influences on their lives that are creating a sense of powerlessness, but also control over their lives (Puglia, 2008). As a profession that values empowerment, we have employed our collective voice to push for a number of social-political programs that address client and community needs (ACA, 2010; Chang, Hays, & Milliken, 2009). Some of these efforts have targeted the special needs of diverse client populations (Chang et al., 2009), veteran services (Barstow & Terrazas, 2012), and those who are educationally disadvantaged by way of K–12 programming (ASCA, 2010). The form that a counselor's valuing of empowerment and engagement in advocacy takes is reflective of the uniqueness of the counselor, the profile of the clients served, and the culture and mission of the setting in which he or she works. The following exercise (Exercise 14.4) directs you to reflect on the issues and needs of those clients served at your field placement. Specifically, the goal of the exercise is to identify opportunities for facilitating and advocating for your clients' empowerment.

EXERCISE 14.4

Empowerment and Advocacy Efforts

Directions: As you have done with the previous exercises, you are asked to review the services and programs provided at your field placement site and respond to each of the following.

Questions for Reflection

1. In what ways are clients assisted in identifying their current strengths and resources as a way of addressing the challenges they are confronting?
2. In what ways are clients assisted in developing new resources that may be needed for addressing the challenges they are confronting?
3. What, if any, actions have been taken by counselors at your site (individually or collectively) that advocate for the needs of specific marginalized populations or populations needing services and resources?

Professional Identity: Both Common and Unique

At our core, counselors share a professional identity that has incorporated each of the previously described perspectives. At our broadest level, counselors share that which makes us unique among helping professionals as well as embody a common mission and vision.

But counselors, while embracing a common professional identity, do so in a way that reflects their diversity in both interests and practice. There is not one form or focus of counseling; there are many, and each specialization of service provided and population served further contributes to the evolving professional identities and uniqueness of the counselor so engaged.

The identification of counselor specialization has given form to the creation of 19 divisions in the American Counseling Association (see Table 14.1). The existence of these divisions not only supports the developing professional identities of those with defined interest and practice but also focuses the service and advocacy for diverse needs and populations.

You are invited to complete Exercise 14.5 as a way of appreciating the connectedness and uniqueness of counselors specializing in different areas of service, as well as beginning to consider the impact of your own choice of specialization on your developing professional identity.

Table 14.1 American Counseling Association Divisions

- Association for Assessment in Counseling and Education (www.theaaceonline.com)
- Association for Adult Development and Aging (www.aadaweb.org)
- Association for Creativity in Counseling (www.creativecounselor.org)
- American College Counseling Association (www.collegecounseling.org)
- Association for Counselors and Educators in Government (no website currently available)
- Association for Counselor Education and Supervision (www.acesonline.net)
- Association for Humanistic Counseling (afhc.camp9.org)
- Association for Lesbian, Gay, Bisexual and Transgender Issues in Counseling (www.algbtic.org)
- Association for Multicultural Counseling and Development (www.multiculturalcounseling.org)
- American Mental Health Counselors Association (www.amhca.org)
- American Rehabilitation Counseling Association (www.arcaweb.org)
- American School Counselor Association (www.schoolcounselor.org)
- Association for Spiritual, Ethical, and Religious Values in Counseling (www.aservic.org)
- Association for Specialists in Group Work (www.asgw.org)
- Counselors for Social Justice (counselorsforsocialjustice.net)
- International Association of Addictions and Offender Counselors (www.iaaoc.org)
- International Association of Marriage and Family Counselors (www.iamfconline.com)
- National Career Development Association (www.ncda.org)
- National Employment Counseling Association (www.employmentcounseling.org)

EXERCISE 14.5

Same Yet Different

Directions: Counselors share a singular identity in that we all adhere to a common code of practice, embrace a rich history, and embody those perspectives unique to counseling. However, counseling is a large umbrella covering numerous specialties and interests (see Table 14.1). Your task is the following:

Part 1. Review the various divisions and specialty areas found in Table 14.1 and select any two as your target. Research the mission, vision, goals, and methods employed by those affiliating with that specialty. Compare and contrast, looking for points of similarity and points of clear distinction.

Part 2. Using the same two specialty areas identified for Part 1, review their websites and current literature to identify one major issue (e.g., political, economic, social, or scientific) or controversy currently stimulating discussion among their members. Is this the same issue across divisions, or does it reflect something unique about the specialty area?

Part 3. Identify special training and/or credentialing required or suggested for members of each of these divisions.

Responding to the Calling

Although you are new to our profession and thus may find the task of crafting a professional identity a bit challenging, you are in good company. As may be apparent from the previous discussion, counseling is a young profession (Remley & Herlihy, 2007), and we continue to struggle to identify that which not only binds us but distinguishes us from other helping professions. But as you continue to identify your place within this profession, one element is clear. Counseling ***is*** a *profession.*

Those who align themselves with this profession view what they do as much more than a job; it is a vocation. This distinction is important. As a vocation, those called to counseling see personal value and worth in what they do. They experience a congruency among the mission of this profession; the roles they play; and their own personal values, beliefs, and interests. Thus, crafting your professional identity is more than an academic project. It requires personal reflection and the identification of those points of confluence between your personal values and perspective and that which characterizes counseling as profession.

Through the Lens of a Counselor

As noted in the previous discussion, counselors share, value, and employ a wellness, development, prevention, and empowerment perspective in all that they do. Although your experience in the field has been somewhat limited, it should have provided you the opportunity to approach your work through each of these valued perspectives. Exercise 14.6 invites you to reflect on your field experience in light of these perspectives and to challenge yourself to identify the value you place on each of these perspectives.

EXERCISE 14.6

Valuing Perspective

Directions: As noted in the text, counselors, as a foundational element to their professional identities, embrace and value a developmental, wellness, prevention, and empowerment perspective in what they do. In the previous section, each of the perspectives was described and illustrated. Your task is to engage in personal reflection to identify the degree to which *you personally value* each of these perspectives and have incorporated each into your own practice decisions.

Specifically, the focus of this exercise is for you to identify one experience that you have had that has highlighted the value of each of these perspectives. Perhaps it was an experience of the powerful impact achieved by advocating for a client or the joy of working with a client who gained awareness of his or her personal strengths; the goal is to highlight the value of these perspectives. It may be useful to discuss your reflections with a colleague, classmate, or professor as a way of gaining further clarity about the value of each.

An experience reflecting the value of . . .

- a developmental perspective
- a wellness perspective
- a prevention perspective
- an empowerment perspective

It is possible that at this point in your professional development you may understand each perspective and even see the value in them, while failing to take complete ownership of each perspective as a personal value and a guide to your own practice decisions. That would not be unusual. The hope is that with continued reflection and ongoing search to find value in each of these perspectives, you will assimilate each into your personal values and evolving professional identity.

Professional Ethics: From Knowing to Valuing

Our professional ethics are fundamentally the articulation of values and beliefs that not only guide our practice decisions but also serve as a vehicle for communicating to the public the specific responsibilities and expectations to be associated with the role of counselor. As a student, you need to understand the general principles of conduct and code of ethics that guide counseling practice. As you transition from student to professional, however, you will need not only to know and understand these principles, but to embrace them as your own and incorporate them among your personal values.

Although the specific codes will continue to evolve and change in response to increasing public awareness, emerging needs and services provided by those within our profession, and even legal decisions, the codes that exist as well as those that may be developed will find a foundation in five general moral principles (see Table 14.2).

Table 14.2 Moral Principles Underlying Counselors' Code of Conduct

Principle	*Description*	*Illustration*
Autonomy	Respecting and promoting individual freedom of choice and action	All actions that reduce client dependency and support client empowerment and decision making, including the acquisition of informed consent throughout the relationship. For example, a counselor who is able to help a client understand the consequences of disengaging from mandated counseling in order to help the client make an informed decision.
Nonmaleficence	Doing no harm intentionally nor engaging in actions that have the potential of harming others	Taking steps to understand the possible risks of employing particular interventions as well as taking steps to maintain professional boundaries and prevent the imposition of counselor values and personal needs into the relationship. For example, a counselor, who is self-aware of his own deviation from normal practice routines and policies with a particular client, seeks supervision as a way of monitoring for loss of objectivity and possible boundary violation.
Beneficence	Being proactive not only to do good but to prevent harm	Going beyond the provision of not harming to engaging in activities that promote health, well-being, and good for the client, including serving as an advocate. For example, a counselor who actively supports and pursues as advocate for the client insurance benefits that will allow for continuation of needed counseling.
Justice	Providing equal treatment to all—and when modifying treatment, being able to demonstrate value and justification for differential treatment	Not only not knowingly participating or condoning unfair discriminatory practice but serving as a voice for those who are disenfranchised and marginalized. For example, a counselor who is willing to challenge institutional policies as applied to providing support for a client with special needs. Not only advocating for the client but doing so in ways that make current policies more just.
Fidelity	Honoring one's commitments so that others can develop a sense of trust	Being clear about the expectation of a client as well as explication of the role and function of the counselor. For example, the counselor, when challenged to disclose information, maintains the promise of confidentiality.

It is essential that you remain knowledgeable about the specifics of our *Code of Ethics* (ACA, 2014), but it is also important that you continue to craft your professional identity in ways that reflect your valuing of these foundational moral principles. Exercise 14.7 is offered as a tool for guiding your inclusion of these principles into your unfolding professional identity.

EXERCISE 14.7

Valuing Values

Directions: Similarly to what you were asked to do in Exercise 14.6, your task here is to engage in personal reflection to identify the degree to which *you personally own and value* each of the following moral principles. It is important to note whether you value these principles at an intellectual level or have also moved to valuing these principles personally and consequently have assimilated each in such a way that they serve as actual guides to your practice decisions.

When the principle is either one you do not understand or cannot or do not fully and personally embrace, consider steps that you can take to assist you in assimilating these principles as the foundation to living out your code of ethics.

Moral Principle	Understand and value at least at the conceptual/ intellectual level	Have assimilated as a personal/professional value that guides my decisions and actions	Steps I can take to further embrace this principle
Autonomy			
Nonmaleficence			
Beneficence			
Justice			
Fidelity			

Contributing to the Professional Community

Although it may be obvious, the very concept of possessing a professional identity implies that one recognizes that he or she is part of a larger community of professionals. The development of one's professional identity is enhanced by engaging in strong relationships with mentors and colleagues who aspire to teach and learn from one another. As such, counselors with a strong professional identity become involved in professional organizations and participate in activities, including attendance and presentations at conferences, workshops, and seminars; advocacy for clients and the profession; and participation in research (Puglia, 2008). It is connecting to the professional community and serving as an active and committed contributor to the professional dialogue that strengthens both the identity of the professional and his or her place within it.

Perhaps at this stage of your professional development, you feel as if your ability to contribute to the professional community is somewhat limited. This need not be the case. Even as a student-member, your voice is important. For example, the American

Counseling Association provides the means for students to have a strong voice in the future of our profession. But whether you engage at a national level with the ACA or by attending your local, state, or regional conferences or engage in the activities of student groups, such as Chi Sigma Iota, the international honor society for counseling graduate students and professionals, your presence, your voice, and your perspective will not only contribute to the collective wisdom and identity of the profession but also afford you the opportunity to have your own professional identity enhanced by this community of professionals.

With Pride

When a profession is conceptualized as unique, a collective identity of shared values, beliefs, and assumptions develops, all of which contribute to pride and security (Daniels, 2002). In addition to knowing the history of our profession, the uniqueness of the values and perspectives that guide what we do, it is also essential to manifest a professional pride in being a counselor.

Having a sense of pride in choosing counseling as a profession is a significant part of having a strong professional identity. Gray (2001), for example, defined the counselor professional identity as "understanding and having a sense of pride in one's profession . . . [that] is essential both for one's own internal satisfaction with one's chosen career and for the continued societal recognition of the profession" (p. 12). Your pride in becoming a counselor and working as a member of the counseling profession will not only contribute to your vocational satisfaction but also position you to stand as an advocate for the profession and those we serve (Myers, Sweeney, & White, 2002).

Although the stress and demands of graduate education can place you in survival mode, it is important to find the time and the opportunity to step back or even out of the demands of academia to reflect on the "why" of your decision to become a counselor. It is important to renew your excitement and your pride in your career choice and the profession to which you seek admission. As such, we end this chapter with a final exercise (Exercise 14.8).

EXERCISE 14.8

A Sense of Pride

Directions: This final exercise invites you to (a) reflect on the stories shared by a sampling of professional counselors, (b) investigate the points of pride held by those with whom you work, and (c) identify that which elicits your pride as a counselor.

Part A: As you review each of the following, consider how you would feel if you were in the role of the counselor.

1. Mary C. (secondary school counselor): "It was, or is, a little thing, but I received a handwritten letter that reminded me (after 21 years in the field) why I entered this

profession. The letter was from a student that I had three years ago. A nice boy—but one for whom high school was not meeting his needs. He had turned 18 the summer of his senior year and entered school that fall in full protest. The year was not going well—he was not engaged. He was not completing assignments and, beyond failing, he was starting to get into real disciplinary issues. He was very clear that he simply hated school, wanted to work as an apprentice (with a family member who owned his own custom home building company), and wanted to find an alternative route to completing his high school requirements. We met and while I know it was somewhat countercultural, I advocated for his withdrawing from school and attending night school, leading to his GED. Well the note was simple. It read,

'Ms. C., I wanted to just say hi and give you a little update. I hope you remember me [he gave his name]. Well, thanks to you I did drop out. I know that probably sounds funny to thank you, but I did get my GED, and I worked with my uncle for the past three years. I love working with my hands—but he has encouraged me to consider getting into architecture since, according to him, I have a lot of creative ideas and natural abilities. So I wanted to let you know that I took classes at community college (all A's) and am now applying for a four-year degree. It has been quite a trip, but I have been happy and if I can brag, "productive," and truly wanted to say thanks. I believe I would not be where I am if it were not for you. It seemed like another lifetime but the guy you helped move on, has moved on . . . and intends to pay it forward. God Bless [signed]'

2. Raul R. (a licensed professional counselor): "A moment of pride? I am sure there are many over the 10 years I have been practicing, but the one that came to mind immediately occurred this past November. It started with a phone call, and while my practice is not one that takes walk-ins or provides crisis telephone counseling, the young woman on the phone had simply picked my name out of the phone book in a moment of desperation. She explained that her husband of 12 years had simply walked out, that she was without a job, living away from her family and friends, and simply felt that "life wasn't worth living." In the discussion that followed, it became clear that she was at risk and that at the moment I was the only lifeline or connection she had. We spent quite a bit of time—well, over an hour and a half—on the phone. She cried, I listened, she identified concerns, and I listened. It appeared that her ability to simply vent and to feel heard and cared for, while clearly not the solution to all the challenges she faced, helped soothe the immediate pain. As our relationship strengthened and it became evident to her that I did care and that I did understand, I was able to ask her if we could find her some support in this moment—support beyond me. She would not allow me to contact emergency services but said that she would like to meet with her minister. I was able to get the name and number and, remaining on the phone with her, I contacted the minister, who responded immediately and went to her house.

(Continued)

(Continued)

As I was informed later, the minister was able to take her to the emergency room and she did follow up with community services. I have not heard from her directly, but the minister, with whom I have developed a friendship and professional relationship, informed me that she was doing well, was employed full-time, and was volunteering in the church's community outreach programs. Because of the nature of my practice, I don't typically encounter such crisis situations, but I am happy that I was available and proud that I was able to use my knowledge and skill to maybe save a life.

Part B: Although both of the examples presented above are somewhat dramatic and perhaps atypical of day-to-day experience, they highlight the value of counseling and the reasons for feeling pride in one's vocational choice and functioning. But there are a multitude of small victories that make what a counselor does so valuable. Your task is to "interview" your site supervisor(s) or other counseling professionals at your field location. The task is to identify experiences that help them know that "today was a good day" or that "today was worthwhile." Share your findings with a colleague or a classmate so that you can expand your database for feeling proud of your profession.

Part C: Your professional experience may have been limited to this point, but there were probably moments, experiences, or things you observed that highlighted the value of counseling to those with whom you work. Take time to reflect on those experiences, those moments when you felt that you or perhaps your supervisor was making a difference. It may have been a time of simply being available to someone who needed a connection, or the provision of information that eased another's anxiety, or a specific service that you were able to provide or observe another providing that pointed to the contribution that counseling made in the life of another. List these reflections and share them with your classmates or colleagues.

It is hoped that as you revisited your field placement experience and reflected on that which makes counseling a unique profession, you have experienced both an affirmation of your vocational choice and a real sense pride in becoming a counselor. The exercises and illustrations provided in this chapter were meant to stimulate development of your professional identity—a development that will continue throughout your professional life.

KEYSTONES

- Although there is no one generally agreed-upon definition, the essence of professional identity is well depicted in the following definition: "the possession of a core set of values, beliefs, and assumptions about the unique characteristics of one's selected profession that differentiates it from other professions" (Weinrach et al., p. 168).
- Remley and Herlihy (2007) provided a definition that includes six components: (a) knowledge and understanding of the profession's history, (b) knowledge and understanding of the philosophical foundations of

the profession, (c) knowledge of the roles and functions of counselors and how they are similar to and different from other mental health professions, (d) a sense of pride in the profession, (e) involvement in professional organizations and advocacy (i.e., professional engagement), and (f) knowledge and understanding of professional counselor ethics.

- The uniqueness of counseling as a profession is evident in the definition of counseling offered by the American Counseling Association: "A professional relationship that empowers diverse individuals, families, and groups to accomplish mental health, wellness, education, and career goals" (ACA, 2010).
- One of the significant defining elements of the uniqueness of counseling as a profession is that counselors approach all that we do from four unique perspectives: developmental, wellness, prevention, and empowerment.
- As a profession, those who align themselves with counseling view what they do as much more than a job; it is a vocation.
- Integrated in one's professional identity is both the knowledge of and valuing of our professional code of ethics and the moral principles underlying their foundation.
- The development of one's professional identity is enhanced by engaging in strong relationships with mentors and colleagues who aspire to teach and learn from one another.
- Your pride in becoming a counselor and working as a member of the counseling profession will not only contribute to developing professional identity and your vocational satisfaction but also position you to stand as an advocate for the profession and those we serve.

ADDITIONAL RESOURCES

Web Based

American Counseling Association: www.counseling.org
American Mental Health Counselors Association: www.amhca.org
American School Counselor Association: www.schoolcounselor.org
Chi Sigma Iota: www.csi-net.org

Print Based

Calley, N. G., & Hawley, L. D. (2008). The professional identify of counselor educators. *The Clinical Supervisor, 27,* 3–16.

Granello, D., & Young, M. E. (2012). *Counseling today: Foundations of professional identity* (MyHelpingLab Series). Columbus, OH: Merrill.

Hazler, R. J., & Kottler, J. A. (2005). *The emerging professional counselor.* Alexandria, VA: American Counseling Association.

Nassar-McMillan, S., & Niles, S. C. (2010). *Developing your identity as a professional counselor: Standards, settings and specialties.* Belmont, CA: Brooks/Cole.

Sangganjanavanich, V. F., & Reynolds, C. A. (Eds.). (2015). *Introduction to professional counseling.* Thousand Oaks, CA: Sage.

REFERENCES

American Counseling Association. (2010). *20/20: Consensus definition of counseling.* Retrieved from http://www.counseling.org/knowledge-center/20-20-a-vision-for-the-future-of-counseling/consensus-definition-of-counseling

American Counseling Association. (2014). *ACA code of ethics.* Alexandria, VA: Author.

American School Counselor Association. (2010). Ethical principles for school counselors. Retrieved from http://www.schoolcounselor.org/asca/media/asca/Resource%20Center/Legal%20and%20Ethical%20Issues/Sample%20Documents/EthicalStandards2010.pdf

Barstow, S., & Terrazas, A. (2012). Pressure increases on VA to improve mental health treatment. *Counseling Today.* Retrieved from http://ct.counseling.org/2012/06/pressure-increases-on-va-to-improve-mental-health-treatment/

Chang, C. Y., Hays, D. G., & Milliken, T. F. (2009). Addressing social justice issues in supervision: A call for client and professional advocacy. *The Clinical Supervisor, 28,* 20–35. doi:10.1080/07325220902855144

Cook-Greuter, S. R., & Soulen, J. (2007). The developmental perspective in integral counseling. *Counseling & Values, 51,* 180–192. doi:10.1002/j.2161-007X.2007.tb00077.x

Daniels, L. G. (2002). The relationship between counselor licensure and aspects of empowerment. *Journal of Mental Health Counseling, 24*(3), 213.

Gray, N. D. (2001). *The relationship of supervisor traits to the professional development and satisfaction with the supervisor of post-master's degree counselors seeking state licensure* (Unpublished doctoral dissertation). University of New Orleans, LA.

Lewis, J. A. (2011). Operationalizing social justice counseling: Paradigm to practice. *Journal of Humanistic Counseling, 50,* 183–191. doi:10.1002/j.2161-1939.2011.tb00117

Maples, M. F. (2008). Counseling & life coaching: Complementary or competitive? (ACAPCD-21). Alexandria, VA: American Counseling Association. Retrieved from http://counselingoutfitters.com/vistas/ACAPCD/ACAPCD-21.pdf

Mellin, E. A., Hunt, B., & Nichols, L. M. (2011). Counselor professional identity: Findings and implications for counseling and interprofessional collaboration. *Journal of Counseling & Development, 89,* 140–147. doi:10.1002/j.1556-6678.2011.tb00071.x

Myers, J. E., Sweeney, T. J., & White, V. E. (2002). Advocacy for counseling and counselors: A professional imperative. *Journal of Counseling and Development, 80,* 394–402.

Puglia, B. (2008). *The professional identity of counseling students in master's level CACREP-accredited programs* (Unpublished doctoral dissertation). Old Dominion University, Norfolk, VA.

Remley, T., & Herlihy, B. (2007). *Ethical, legal, and professional issues in counseling* (2nd ed.). Upper Saddle River, NJ: Prentice Hall.

Rogers, C. (1959). A theory of therapy, personality and interpersonal relationships as developed in the client-centered framework. In S. Koch (Ed.), *Psychology: The study of a science: Vol. III. Formulations of the person in the social context* (pp. 184–256). New York, NY: McGraw-Hill.

Weinrach, S. G., Thomas, K. R., & Chan, F. (2001). The professional identity of contributors to the *Journal of Counseling & Development:* Does it matter? *Journal of Counseling and Development, 79,* 166–170.

Index

Abandonment of clients
defined, 264
fidelity principle and, 102–103
termination vs., 259, 264
See also Termination of counseling
ACA Code of Ethics. *See* Ethics of practice and *ACA Code of Ethics*
Accelerated Recovery Program for Compassion Fatigue, 305–306
Accountability, 85–89, 123
Accreditation, 46–47
Acute phase of crisis, 193
Addams, Jane, 82
Addiction and substance abuse counseling
accreditation and, 46–47
Breaking Free (gambling addiction), 66
role and function of counselors in, 61, 62–63 (table)
self-appraisal on, 37–38
Advanced education, 337–340
Advocacy
beneficence and, 97, 98 (table), 99
professional identity and, 16–19, 352
Aggression from clients, 215–219
AIDS virus and exposure, 208–210, 209 (table)
Altekruse, Michael K., 143
American Association for Marriage and Family Therapy (AAMFT), 237
American Association of Multicultural Counseling Development (AAMCD), 174
American Association of Pastoral Counselors, 18–19 (table)
American College Counseling Association, 18 (table)
American Counseling Association (ACA)
on confidentiality, 202
cross-cultural approach and, 167, 174
definition of counseling, 10, 346–347
divisions in, 353 (table)
engaging with, 17
information on, 18 (table)
specialties defined by, 36
student engagement in, 357–358
See also Ethics of practice and *ACA Code of Ethics*
American Mental Health Counselors Association, 18 (table), 19
American Psychological Association (APA), 168, 236–237, 240
American Rehabilitation Counseling Association, 19 (table)
American School Counseling Association (ASCA)
on confidentiality, 202
engaging with, 17
on ethnic and cultural diversity, 167
information on, 18 (table)
model of appropriate and inappropriate activities, 60–61, 154
record-keeping requirements, 236
Ammons, A. R., 342
Anxiety
compassion fatigue treatment and, 306
evaluation and, 6
over job interviews, 330
performance anxiety, 6, 7
self criticism and, 7
videotaping and, 145–146
Appraisal, core knowledge on, 28, 34–35
Arredondo, P., 174
ASCA model, 46
Assessment
"Assessment (Analysis)" in DAP format, 252
"Assessment" in DART system, 254
"Assessment" in SOAP notes, 245, 246 (table)
core knowledge on, 28
Environmental Assessment and Prevention Measures, 216–217
of suicide risk, 199–205, 200 (table), 201 (table)
See also Evaluation and performance assessment; Self-assessment
Association of Suicidology, 196

At-risk populations and secondary prevention, 14
Audiotaping and supervision, 145–147
Autonomy, levels of, 52
Autonomy of clients
boundaries defining, 94 (table)
as ethical principle, 91–93, 92 (table), 356 (table)
respecting, 223–224

Baird, Brian N., 155, 157–158, 253, 254
Barton, Bruce, 134
Baum, L. Frank, 258
Beginning of counseling relationships, 259–260, 260 (table)
Beneficence principle, 97–100, 98 (table), 356 (table)
Betz, R. L., 152
Borders, L. D., 148
Boundaries
client autonomy and, 94 (table)
compassion fatigue and, 304
defined, 224
loss of objectivity and violations of, 226–227
multiple relationships and crossing of, 225–226
supervision vs. therapy and, 156, 157
Brown, K., 124
Brown, L. L., 148
Burkard, A. W., 153
Burnout
counseling profession and, 286–287
defined, 285
prevention of, 288–292
Professional Quality of Life Scale (ProQOL), 296–302
symptoms of, 286
unfolding of, 287–288

Caplan, Gerald, 192
Career, transition to
advanced education, 337–340
competition for employment, 315
cover letters, 325–326, 327 (table)
international students and employment, 336
internship–career connection, 316–317
job interview questions, 330, 330 (table), 334–336
job interviews, 328–332, 332 (table)
job offers and decisions, 336–337
letters of recommendation, 326–328
placement resources and networking, 337
résumés, 320–325, 320–321 (table), 322–324 (table)
self-evaluation, 317–319
Career counseling, 39, 63, 64t
Career development, core knowledge self-appraisal on, 27, 33–34
Carroll, M., 145
Case conceptualization, 108–118, 147
Case illustrations
Alda (multiculturalism), 180–181
Beyond Remediation to Prevention, 15
Breaking Free (gambling addiction), 66
Case Conferencing (confidentiality), 220–221
A Case of Child Abuse (multiculturalism), 182–183
A Changing Picture (case conceptualization), 109–111
Cocreating Meaning (multiculturalism), 184–185
Confronting My Own Ethnocentrism and Racism, 174–175
A Counselor in Free Fall (burnout), 285–286
Debt Collection (termination), 264
Dr. Zach's Time Study, 70–73
Finding Exception (wellness perspective), 349
Gaining Permission to Engage the Parents, 77–78
A Graduate Student Who Simply Cared (compassion fatigue), 294–295
I'm Happy With the Therapy (termination), 263
Is It Really a Distraction? (single subject design), 123–124
Is She Really Helping? (multiculturalism), 178–180
It's Difficult for Me to Go On (suicide assessment), 203–204
Jeff Gates (DART notes), 255
Kabira (empowerment), 16–17
Lack of Progress, 268
Losing Perspective (supervision), 157
Midconversation Adjustment, 119–121
More Than One Person (wellness), 13–14
Needing a Sitter (supervisory conflicts), 154
No Longer Objective (termination), 271
Not Comforting (ethics), 86–87
Out of Area of Competence, 269
A Real Surprise (documentation), 240
Sarah (role play in supervision), 149–150
Sensitivity to Client Culture, 101–102
Sliding-Scale Fees, 270
Something Not Quite Right? (case conceptualization), 114–115
Thank God for Dr. L. (supervision), 136–137
Thomas (development perspective), 348
The Use of Role-Play in Supervision: Mary, 148–149
Ward versus Wilbanks (termination and values), 262

Where Is the Way Out? (HIV), 210
Why Does He Want to Know That? (multiculturalism), 167–168
Case notes, 241–243, 242 (table). *See also* Documentation and record keeping
Chi Sigma Iota, 358
Classroom vs. on-site supervision, 144
Client, identifying, 222–223
Clinical mental health counseling self-appraisal, 40–41
Closure in internship relationships, 277–279. *See also* Termination of counseling
Codes of ethics. *See* Ethics of practice and *ACA Code of Ethics*
Coercive power, 75
Collective identity, 10
College and university counseling, 43–44, 47
Commission on Rehabilitation Certification (CRCC), 36
Commission on the Accreditation of Rehabilitation Facilities, 47
Communication
documentation and, 234
informational power, 76–79
job interviews and, 329, 331
professional self-reflection and, 129
simulated client contacts, 7–8
speech style, powerful vs. powerless, 333
Community, professional, 357–358
Compassion fatigue
Accelerated Recovery Program for Compassion Fatigue, 305–306
defined, 292
effects pf, 294–295
Professional Quality of Life Scale (ProQOL), 296–302
risk factors for, 295–296
risk reduction, 303–306
symptoms of, 293, 293–294 (table)
Compassion satisfaction, 299
Competence
boundaries of, 95–96, 98 (table), 227, 234
multicultural competence vs. counseling competence, 172–173
Ridley, Mollen, and Kelly model of, 172
termination, referral, and, 261
termination and being out of area of, 268–269
See also Multicultural competence
Confidentiality and disclosure
AIDS virus and, 208–210, 209 (table)
duty to warn and protect, 207–208
ethics of, 93
legal risks, 220–222
need-to-know basis for disclosure, 221
suicide assessment and, 202
Conflicts and conflict resolution, 152–156, 335
Continuing education, 98 (table), 128
Core knowledge and skills. *See* Self-appraisal of core knowledge and skills
Council for Accreditation of Counseling and Related Educational Programs (CACREP)
core and specialty standards of, 25, 28, 36, 37
on internship, 74
on multiculturalism, 168, 170–171
on supervision, 138
supervisor training and experience and, 53
Council on Rehabilitation Education (CORE), 36
Counseling, concept and definitions of, 345–347
Counseling plans, 98 (table)
Counselor roles and functions in potential field site
formal vs. informal systems and, 69–74
the ideal vs. the real and, 58–59
intern influences on, 74–80
job description vs. performance assessment criteria and, 64–65
mission and, 65–69
similarities and uniqueness of settings, 58
standards of professional organizations, 59–64, 60–61 (table), 62–63 (table), 64 (table)
Counselors, definition of, 9–10
Countertransference, 156–158, 226, 274–275
Cover letters, 325–326, 327 (table)
Credentialing bodies, 36–37, 36 (table)
Crisis prevention and intervention
definition of crisis, 192
HIV/AIDS exposure, 208–210, 209 (table)
homicide and violent behavior, 205–208
loss of control, experience of, 193
mission statements and, 47
phases of, 193–195
quick resolution, need for, 192
site policy on, 210–211
suicide, 195–205
See also Risk management
Cross, W. E., 180
Cultural awareness. *See* Multicultural competence
Cultural encapsulation, 166–167

DAP (Data, Assessment, Plan) format, 251–253
DART (Description, Assessment, Response, and Treatment Plan) system, 253–255

Data gathering and integration, in case conceptualization, 108–114
"Data (Description)," in DAP format, 252
Debriefing of military personnel, 15
De-escalation, 218–219
Dehumanizing, 288
Delworth, U., 135
Dept. of Health and Human Services, Office of Applied Studies, 61
"Description," in DART system, 253–254
Developmental perspective, 11–12, 258, 347–348, 354–355. *See also* Human growth and development
Developmental supervision models, 152
Disclosure. *See* Confidentiality and disclosure
Discrimination and justice, 100
Diversity
  minority identity development models, 180–181
  population served and, 49
  social and cultural foundations core knowledge, 26–27, 30–31
  suicide and, 196
  See also Multicultural competence
Doctoral programs, 337–340
Documentation and record keeping
  case notes, 241–243, 242 (table)
  DAP format, 251–253
  DART system, 253–255
  ethical and legal aspects of, 228–229, 234, 235–237, 236 (table)
  importance of, 233
  IPSN format, 248–251, 249–250 (table)
  progress (session) notes, 239–241, 243
  purpose of, 234–235
  SOAP notes format, 243, 244–248, 246–247 (table)
  suicide and, 205
  treatment plans, 238
Doing vs. knowing, 2–3
Duranti, Luciana, 233
Duty to warn and protect, 207–208

Eastern Michigan University (EMU), 262
Education, continuing, 98 (table), 128
Effectiveness, 98 (table), 122–124
Employment transition. *See* Career, transition to
Empowerment perspective, 16–19, 351–352, 354–355
Environmental assessment of a site, 216–217
Equitable treatment, 101
Ethics of practice and *ACA Code of Ethics*
  accountability and, 85–89
  autonomy, 91–93, 92 (table), 94, 356 (table)
  beneficence, 97–100, 98 (table), 356 (table)
  competence, boundaries of, 95–96, 98 (table), 227, 234
  confidentiality, 93
  documentation and, 234, 235–237, 236 (table)
  fidelity, 102–103, 356 (table)
  idea vs. real and, 104
  interpersonal behaviors and, 84–85
  justice, 100–102, 356 (table)
  legal risks and, 219–220
  malpractice claims and, 85
  multiculturalism and, 167–171
  multiple relationships and, 225–226
  need and value of professional ethics, 83–91
  nonmaleficence, 95–97, 356 (table)
  personal values and moral principles, 355–357, 356 (table)
  professional development and, 124
  right to terminate counseling, 93–94
  self-monitoring and "time-outs" from practice, 89–90
  termination and, 260–264, 268–269
  values and ethical codes, 82–83
  See also Legal risks
Ethnicity. *See* Diversity; Multicultural competence
Evaluation and performance assessment
  job descriptions vs. criteria of, 64–65
  outcomes vs. grades focus, 5–6
  seeking evaluation and soliciting corrective feedback, 6–7
  site supervisor evaluations and faculty supervisor grades, 151
  See also Supervision
Exercise, 290
Exercises
  Adapting the Ideal to the Real, 8
  Analyzing a Mission Statement, 47–48
  An Evolving Professional Identity, 21
  Boundaries Defining Client Autonomy, 94
  Burnout Self-Assessment, 289
  A Call for Professional-to-Professional Intervention, 88–89
  Case Conceptualization: An Emerging Picture, 111–113
  Clarifying Expectations (supervision), 138
  Committing to Wellness, 306
  Considering Salient Elements of the Client Story, 116–117
  The Counseling Relationship Demanding Ethical Behavior, 84–85
  Cultural Encapsulation, 166–167

DAP Session Notes, 252
Developing Informational Power, 78–79
Developmental Challenge or Pathology, 11–12
Directed Self-Assessment, 125–127
Documentation, 229
Embodying Beneficence, 99–100
Empowerment and Advocacy Efforts, 352
Engaging the Four Perspectives of Counseling, 20
Ensuring Fidelity, 103
Environmental Assessment and Prevention Measures (violence), 216–217
Exploring My Ethnic Roots, 176–177
How Is Case Conceptualization Actualized in My Supervision?, 147
Impaired?, 90
Interviews (suicide risk), 198–199
The Lived Experience (ethics), 104
Looking for an Alternative Hypothesis (case conceptualization), 117–118
A Matter of Values (multiculturalism), 164–165
Modifying Work Setting, 303–304
More Than Intervention—Prevention, 351
More Than Terms—Values (definition of counseling), 346–347
Moving Forward (multiculturalism), 186–187
Multicultural Dimensions in Supervision, 158
My Action on Termination in Counseling, 265
My Caseload Review, 276–277
My Habit of Clinical Documentation, 239
My Professional Development Plan, 131
My Style of Resolving Conflicts, 156
Needs of the Transfer, 275
A Personal Plan for Risk Management, 230
The Possibility of Doing Harm, 96–97
Practice Reflecting Sensitivity (multiculturalism), 169–170
A Preliminary Search (documentation), 238
Resources in My Reach, 261
Respecting Client Autonomy, 224
Role-Play (suicide assessment), 205
Same Yet Different (specialization), 354
Securing a Site, 54–55
Seeking Growth, 4–5
Self-Assessment, core areas, 28–35
Self-Assessment, specialty areas, 37–44
Self-Awareness Assessment (multiculturalism), 177
Self-Identity: The Impact of Graduate Education, 344
A Sense of Pride, 358–360
In Service of the Mission (role and function), 68
Session Notes (IPSN notes), 251
Session Notes (SOAP Notes), 247
Site Policy and Procedures (crisis), 210–211
Site Profile, 51
A Snapshot of Crisis Prevention, 194–195
The Tale of Two Counselors (role and function), 66–67
Time to Say Goodbye, 279
Values Concerning What You Will Do as a Professional, 318
Valuing Perspective, 355
Valuing Values, 357
What Are Our Expectations?, 143
What Are Your Areas of Strength?, 318
What Are Your Interests?, 319
What Are Your Skills? Do You Enjoy the Skills You Have Identified?, 319
What Does the *Code of Ethics* Say About MCC?, 171
When to Break Confidentiality, 222
Which Questionnaire Should I Use? (suicide assessment), 201
Why Did I Do That? (reflection in practice), 122
Expert power, 75–76

F-1 student visas, 336
Fairness, 100–101
Farewell rituals, 278
Faughey, Kathryn, 215
Federal Health Insurance Portability and Accountability Act of 1996 (HIPAA), 237
Feedback, 6–7, 146–147, 150–151, 157
Fees, 101, 269–271
Fidelity principle, 102–103, 356 (table)
Field experience
ideal-to-real shift, 7–8
knowing-to-doing shift, 2–3
other-taught vs self-taught and, 3–7
self-as-student vs. self-as-emerging professional, 9
as unique learning experience, 2
See also Counselor roles and functions in potential field site; Matching self to site
50-minute hour, 239–240
Forced termination, 271–272, 272–274 (table)
Formal vs. informal systems, 69–74
Frankl, Victor, 282
Freud, Sigmund, 157
Freudenberger, H. J., 288
Functions and roles. *See* Counselor roles and functions in potential field site

Gentry, J. E., 305
Gilliland, B. E., 192

Giordano, Maria A., 143
Goals, 128–129, 130 (figure)
Grades vs. outcomes, 5–6
Graduate assistantships, 340
Gray, N. D., 358
GRE exam, 338
Groups, 27, 32–33
Group supervision, 144–145

Hart, G. M., 152
Head-Start programs, 14–15
Health care settings and accreditation, 46
Healthy life habits, 289–291
Helping relationship, core knowledge self-appraisal on, 27, 31–32
Herdman, J. W., 61
Herlihy, B., 345
Hiding, tendency toward, 6
HIPAA (Federal Health Insurance Portability and Accountability Act of 1996), 237
HIV/AIDS exposure, 208–210, 209 (table)
Homicide, 205–208
Hosman, L. A., 333
Human growth and development, 26, 29–30

Ideal vs. real
- counselor roles and functions and, 58–59
- ethics and, 104
- field experience and, 7–8
- reflection in practice and, 118

Identity, professional
- collective, 10
- common professional identity and specialization, 353–354, 353 (table)
- counseling, concept and definition of, 345–347
- developmental perspective and, 11–12, 347–348, 354–355
- empowerment and advocacy perspective and, 16–19, 351–352, 354–355
- ethical principles and, 355–357, 356 (table)
- evolution of, 21
- multicultural competence and, 185–187
- nurturing, 19–20
- personal identity and assimilation of, 342–343, 344–345
- prevention perspective and, 14–16, 350–351, 354–355
- pride, sense of, 358–360
- professional community and, 357–358
- self-as-student vs. self-as-emerging professional, 9
- self-identity, 343–344
- self-perception as counselor, 9–10
- shared values and perspectives, 10–11
- wellness perspective and, 12–14, 348–349, 354–355

Identity development models, 180–181
Independence in clients, 16
Independent, self-directed learning, 3–5
Individual Psychotherapy Session Note (IPSN) format, 248–251, 249–250 (table)
Individual supervision, 144–145. *See also* Supervision
Informal vs. formal systems, 69–74
Informational power, 76–79
Informed consent, 92 (table), 96, 228
Inner life, nurturing of, 291
Insurance, 219, 269–270
Integration phase of crisis, 194–195
Integrative supervision models, 152
Intentionality, 122
International Association of Counseling Services, 47
International students and employment, 336
Intern development, phases of, 278–279
Internship–career transition. *See* Career, transition to
Internship closure, 277–279
Interpersonal behavior and ethics, 84–85
Interviews for jobs. *See* Job interviews
IPSN (Individual Psychotherapy Session Note) format, 248–251, 249–250 (table)
IS PATH WARM rubric, 199, 201 (table), 202
Issues addressed at a field site, 50

Jackson, S. E., 288
James, K. J., 192
Job descriptions vs. performance assessment criteria, 64–65
Job interviews
- applications, 334
- four phases of, 328–330
- getting an interview, 334
- on-site interview, 332–333, 332 (table)
- phone and online video interview, 331–332
- questions, 330, 330 (table), 334–336
- *See also* Career, transition to

Joint Commission, 46
Justice principle, 100–102, 356 (table)

Kaslow, N. J., 278
Kelly, S. M., 172
Kern, Carolyn W., 143
Kim, J., 180
Kiselica, M. S., 176

Knowing vs. doing, 2–3
Knowledge and skills appraisal. *See* Self-appraisal of core knowledge and skills; Self-appraisal of specialty knowledge and skills
Knowledge base of counselors, 10, 75–76
Kottler, Jeffrey, 284

Labeling, 288
Langenderfer, J., 333
Larson, D. G., 287
Lawrence, A., 333
Legal risks
  client autonomy, 223–224
  competence, practicing within, 227
  confidentiality, 220–222
  documentation and, 228–229, 235
  ethical and efficient practice and, 219–220
  identifying the client, 222–223
  liability insurance and, 219
  professional boundaries, 224–227
Letters of recommendation, 326–328, 338–339
Lewis, C. S., 24
Liability insurance, 219
Life circumstances, changes in, 271–272, 272–274 (table)
Lifestyle and counselors, 289–291, 304–305
Lifestyle development counseling, 27, 33–34
Litigation and documentation, 235. *See also* Legal risks
Lowell, James Russell, 58, 59, 74

Malpractice claims, 85
Marriage, couple, and family counseling self-appraisal, 41–42
Maslach, C., 285, 288
Maslach Burnout Inventory (MBI), 288–289
Matching self to site
  accreditation, 46–47
  checklist for securing a site, 54–55
  core knowledge and skills self-assessment, 25–35
  educational and formative experiences, importance of, 45–46
  issues addressed, 50
  mission statements, 47–48
  models and theories, preferred, 50
  population served, 49–50
  professional development and, 54
  responsibility and autonomy, expectations for, 51–52
  services provided, 50
  site profile chart, 51
  site supervisor, assessing, 52–53
  specialty credentialing and, 36–37, 36 (table)
  specialty knowledge and skills self-assessment, 37–44
McNamara, K., 180
Microaggressions, 178, 180
Minorities. *See* Diversity; Multicultural competence
Mission statements, 47–48, 65–69
Mitchell, Margaret, 191
Models and theories preferred at a field site, 50
Mollen, D., 172
Monitoring
  beneficence and effectiveness monitoring, 98 (table)
  professional development planning and, 130
  reflection in practice and, 121
  self-monitoring, 89–90, 125
Moore, Lawrence, 207
Morales, Eduardo, 163
Morgan, D. J., 287
Morris, J. R., 152
Moskowitz, S. A., 155
Multicultural competence
  classroom vs. field work and, 171–172
  client worldview, awareness of, 178–182
  counseling competence vs., 172–173
  counseling profession and, 166–167
  cultural encapsulation, 166–167
  cultural values, sensitivity to, 101–102
  ethical standards and, 167–171
  experience with diverse populations and, 49
  intervention strategies, culturally appropriate, 182–185
  necessity and urgency of, 163
  professional development and, 174
  professional identity and, 185–187
  self-awareness of cultural values and biases, 174–177
  supervision and, 158–159
  tripartite model (awareness, knowledge, skills), 173–174, 182
  valuing of need for, 164–166
  See also Diversity
Multiple relationships, 225–226

National Association of Social Workers (NASW), 237
National Board for Certified Counselors (NBCC), 36
National Career Development Guidelines (NCDA), 63
"The National Substance Abuse Treatment System" (Dept. of Health and Human Services, Office of Applied Studies), 61

Negi, N. J., 176
Network for Innovation in Career Guidance and Counseling (NICE), 63, 64t
Networking, 337
Nonmaleficence principle, 95–97, 356 (table)
Norcoss, John C., 163
Normative challenges vs. psychopathology, 11–12
Novalis, 1
Nutrition, 290

"Objective," in SOAP notes, 244–245, 246 (table)
Objectivity, loss of, 226–227
Online video interviews for jobs, 331–332
On-site interviews for jobs, 332–333, 332 (table)
On-site vs. classroom supervision, 144
Optional Practical Training (OPT), 336
Outcomes vs. grades, 5–6
Outward adjustment phase of crisis, 193–194

Paperwork. *See* Documentation and record keeping
Parsons, Richard D., 124, 363
Parton, S. R., 333
Performance assessment. *See* Evaluation and performance assessment
Personal statements in doctoral program applications, 339
Perspectives
- developmental perspective, 11–12, 258, 347–348
- empowerment perspective, 16–19, 351–352
- prevention perspective, 14–16, 350–351
- professional identity and, 347
- shared values and, 10–11
- valuing, 354–355
- wellness perspective, 12–14, 47, 348–349

Pfost, Karen S., 248
Phone interviews for jobs, 331–332
Pines, A., 285
Placement resources for job search, 337
Placement site choice. *See* Counselor roles and functions in potential field site; Matching self to site
"Plan," in DAP format, 252
"Plan," in SOAP notes, 245, 246 (table)
Play, 291
Poddar, Prosenjit, 207
Population served, as site characteristic, 49–50
Posttraumatic stress disorder, 15. *See also* Secondary traumatic stress (STS)
Powelson, Harvey, 207
Power, social, 75–77
Practice, reflective. *See* Reflection
Presser, Nan R., 248
Prevention perspective, 14–16, 350–351, 354–355
Pride, sense of, 358–359
Prieto, L. R., 152
Primary prevention, 14, 350
Primary responsibility, 92 (table)
Privacy, respect for, 92 (table)
Processing models of supervision, 152
Professional community, 357–358
Professional development, 4–5, 54, 124–132, 174
Professional development planning, 128–131
Professional identity. *See* Identity, professional
Professional organizations
- advocacy and, 17–19
- information on, 18–19 (table)
- roles and functions as defined by, 59–64
- *See also specific organizations*

Professional orientation self-appraisal, 25–26, 29
Professional Quality of Life Scale (ProQOL), Compassion Satisfaction and Compassion Fatigue, Version 5, 296–302
Progress, lack of, 268
Progress (session) notes, 239–241, 243. *See also* Documentation and record keeping
Psychometric theories, 28
Psychopathology vs. normative challenges, 11–12
Psychotherapy-based supervision models, 152

Race. *See* Diversity; Multicultural competence
Real vs. ideal. *See* Ideal vs. real
Recharging, 291–292
Recognized ASCA Model Program (RAMP), 46
Recommendation letters, 326–328, 338–339
Records. *See* Documentation and record keeping
Referrals, 261–264. *See also* Termination of counseling
Reflection
- case conceptualization (reflection *on* practice), 108–118
- for efficacy and accountability, 122–124
- moment-to-moment decisions (reflection *in* practice), 118–122
- professional development planning, 128–131
- self-assessment, 124–128, 129 (table)

Rejection shock, 330
Remen, R. N., 284
Remley, T., 345
Research
- case conceptualization and, 109–111
- core knowledge self-appraisal on, 28, 35
- on multicultural counseling, 166

systematic data collection and single subject design, 123–124
on violence, 215
Research papers, 339
Resources, identification of, 129
"Response," in DART system, 254
Responsibility, 51–52, 87, 92 (table)
Résumés, 320–325, 320–321 (table), 322–324 (table)
Rice, D. G., 278
Rickard, K. M., 180
Ridley, C. R., 172
Right to terminate counseling, 93–94
Risk management
client aggression and physical harm, 215–219
legal and ethical risks, 219–229
personal planning for, 229–230
See also Crisis prevention and intervention
Roberts-Wilbur, J., 151–152
Rogers, Carl, 345
Role-play, 147–150, 205
Roles and functions. *See* Counselor roles and functions in potential field site
Roosevelt, Theodore, 214, 229
Ruiz, A. S., 180
Rupert, P. A., 155, 287

SAD PERSONS Scale (SPS), 199, 200 (table)
School counseling
accreditation and, 46
ASCA model of appropriate and inappropriate activities in, 60–61, 60–61 (table), 154
self-appraisal on, 42–43
SD card recording, 146
Secondary prevention, 14–15, 350
Secondary traumatic stress (STS), 299–300
Self-appraisal of core knowledge and skills
appraisal and assessment, 28, 34–35
CACREP Standards and, 25
directed self-assessment as reflection, 125–127
groups, 27, 32–33
helping relationship, 27, 31–32
human growth and development, 26, 29–30
lifestyle and career development, 27, 33–34
professional development planning and, 131
professional orientation, 25–26, 29
research and evaluation, 28, 35
social and cultural foundations, 26–27, 30–31, 170–171
Self-appraisal of specialty knowledge and skills
addictions, 37–38
career counseling, 39
clinical mental health counseling, 40–41
credentialing bodies and, 36–37, 36 (table)
marriage, couple, and family counseling, 41–42
school counseling, 42–43
student affairs and college counseling, 43–44
Self-assessment
on burnout, 288–289
for professional development, 124–128, 129 (table)
for self-care and self-protection, 306–310
Self-as-student vs. self-as-emerging professional, 9
Self as teacher, 3
Self-awareness, 174–177, 288–289
Self-care and self-protection
burnout, 285–292
compassion fatigue, 292–296, 293–294 (table), 303–306
need for, 282–284
Professional Quality of Life Scale (ProQOL), 296–302
professional self-reflection and, 129
self-assessment and commitment to, 306–310
See also Well-being of counselors
Self criticism, 7
Self-direction, 3–5, 16
Self-evaluation for employment preparation, 317–319
Self-identity, 343–344. *See also* Identity, professional
Self-monitoring or self-supervision, 89–90, 125
Self-soothing, 306, 348
Services provided, as site characteristic, 50
Session (progress) notes, 239–241, 243. *See also* Documentation and record keeping
Sexual misconduct, 95
Sexual partner disclosure and HIV, 208–210, 209 (table)
Siltanen, S. A., 333
Single subject design (A-B-A), 123–124
Site choice. *See* Counselor roles and functions in potential field site; Matching self to site
Skovholt, Thomas, 289
Sleep deprivation, 292
Sliding-scale fees, 270
SMART goals, 129, 130 (figure)
Smith, Allison L., 148
SOAP notes (Subjective, Objective, Assessment, Plan), 243, 244–248, 246–247 (table)
Social and cultural foundations
self-appraisal, 26–27, 30–31
Social engagement, counselors and, 290–291, 305
Social power, principles of, 75–77
Socrates, 107

Specialties and specialization, 36–37, 36 (table), 353–354, 353 (table)
Specialty knowledge and skills. *See* Self-appraisal of specialty knowledge and skills
Speech style, powerful vs. powerless, 333
Standard of care, documentation and, 234
Stoltenberg, C., 135
Stress. *See* Self-care and self-protection
Stringer, E. T., 124
Structured group supervision (SGS), 151–152
Student affairs counseling, 43–44
"Subjective," in SOAP notes, 244, 246 (table)
Substance abuse counseling. *See* Addiction and substance abuse counseling
Sue, D., 177, 180–181
Sue, D. W., 177, 180–181
Suicide
  assessment, 199–205, 200 (table), 201 (table)
  documentation and, 205
  myths about, 195–196
  risk factors and common characteristics, 196–199, 197–198 (table)
  statistics on, 195
Sun Tzu, 315
Supervisee Bill of Rights, 139
Supervision
  audio- and videotape and case presentation, 145–147
  boundaries of competence and, 96
  case conceptualization, 147
  classroom vs. on-site, 144
  conflicts in supervisory relationships, 152–156
  defined, 135–136
  documentation and, 228
  expectations for, 138–143
  feedback and evaluation, 150–151
  generic tasks and professional competencies, 145
  importance and purpose of, 134–135, 159
  individual, triadic, and group, 144–145
  levels of responsibility, expectations for, 51–52
  models of, 151–152
  multicultural dimensions of, 158–159
  need for, 136–137
  role-play method, 147–150
  student-to-professional transition and, 159
  Supervisee Bill of Rights, 139
  Supervision Agreement, 140–142
  therapy vs., 156
  transference and countertransference and, 156–158
  valuing evaluation and growing through, 6–7
  when and how often, 137–138
Supervisors
  assessing potential supervisors, 52–53
  closure with, 277–279
  qualifications for, 137–138
  shadowing a potential supervisor, 70
  training and experience of, 53
Systematic data collection, 123–124

Tarasoff, Tatiana, 207–208
Termination of counseling
  area of competence and, 268–269
  beginnings and, 259–260, 260 (table)
  decision-making issues, 267
  defined, 259
  developmental perspective on, 258
  ethics of, 260–264, 268–269
  factors in appropriate termination, 264–266, 266–267 (table)
  fee issues, 269–271
  lack of progress and, 268
  life circumstances and forced termination, 271–272, 272–274 (table)
  negative effects of premature termination, 267
  right of, 93–94
  steps and strategies, 275–277
  transferring clients, 274–275
Termination of internship relationships, 277–279
Tertiary prevention, 15–16, 350
Theoretical orientation of a supervisor, 52–53
Theory and the ideal vs. the real, 7–8
Therapy vs. supervision, 156, 157
Thomas, Carolyn, 337
Transcripts, official, 339
Transference, 156–158. *See also* Countertransference
Transferring clients, 274–275. *See also* Abandonment of clients; Termination of counseling
"Treatment Plan," in DART system, 254
Treatment plans, documentation of, 238
Triadic supervision, 144–145
Troiden, R. R., 180
Trust, 102

Values
  collective identity and, 10
  definition of counseling and, 346–347
  ethics and, 82–83
  imposition of, 96
  professional career and, 318
  sensitivity and respect for, 101–102
  shared values and perspectives, 10–11

termination and, 262
valuing, 357
Vasquez, M. J. T., 266
Vicarious Traumatization, 300
Videotaping and supervision, 145–147
Violent behavior, 205–208, 215–219
Vulnerability, 6

Ward, Donald, 276
Ward, Julia, 262
Weed, Lawrence L., 244
Welfare of clients, promotion of, 103
Well-being of counselors
counseling as challenge to, 283–284
exercise, 290
inner life, 291
life decisions oriented toward, 306
nutrition, 290
play, 291
recharging, 291–292
self-assessment and commitment to, 306–310
social engagement, 290–291
work management, 291
work setting and, 303–304
See also Self-care and self-protection
Wellness, defined, 12
Wellness perspective, 12–14, 47, 348–349, 354–355
Wilbur, M. P., 151–152
Williams, L., 274–275
Winter, H., 274–275
Work management, 291
Work setting and compassion fatigue, 303–304
Worldviews, 96, 178–182, 344

Zhang, Naijian, 363

About the Authors

Naijian Zhang, PhD, is a Full Professor in the Department of Counseling and Educational Psychology at West Chester University of Pennsylvania. Dr. Zhang has over 20 years' experience of teaching in counseling, higher education/student affairs, and language programs at college and university. Dr. Zhang was also a university administrator in student affairs for 4 years. Dr. Zhang authored and coauthored over 20 articles, book chapters, and books.

His most recent books include *Becoming a Skilled Counselor* in 2013, *Rentz's Student Affairs Practice in Higher Education*, and *Psychology* in 2009. He is a recipient of the Travel Award from the American Psychological Association (APA), Outstanding Research Award, and Outstanding Service Award from the American College Personnel Association (ACPA). He has served on the editorial board of the Journal of College Counseling and as Ad Hoc Reviewer for The Counseling Psychologist. In addition, Dr. Zhang has practiced over 15 years and is currently a licensed psychologist in Pennsylvania. He frequently gives presentations and conducts counseling training workshops internationally.

Richard D. Parsons, PhD, is a full professor in the Department of Counselor Education at West Chester University. Parsons has over thirty-two years of university teaching in counselor preparation programs. Prior to his university teaching, he spent nine years as a school counselor in an inner-city high school. Parsons has been the recipient of many awards and honors, including the Pennsylvania Counselor of the Year award. Parsons has authored or coauthored over 80 professional articles and books. His most recent books include the series of four training texts for school counselors, *Transforming Theory into Practice* (Corwin Press) and individual titles, *Counseling Strategies that Work! Evidenced-based Interventions for School Counselors* (Allyn & Bacon), *The School Counselor as Consultant* (Brooks/Cole), and *Teacher as Reflective Practitioner and Action Researcher* (Wadsworth). Parsons has a private practice and serves as a consultant to educational institutions and mental health service organizations throughout the tri-state area of Pennsylvania, New Jersey, and Delaware.